UNFINISHED BUSINESS

STUDIES IN SECURITY AND INTERNATIONAL AFFAIRS

UNFINISHED BUSINESS

Why International Negotiations Fail

edited by

GUY OLIVIER FAURE

with the assistance of

FRANZ CEDE

THE UNIVERSITY OF GEORGIA PRESS

Athens & London

© 2012 by the University of Georgia Press

Athens, Georgia 30602

www.ugapress.org

Designed by Walton Harris

Set in 10/14 Minion Pro

Printed digitally in the United States of America

Library of Congress Cataloging-in-Publication Data

Unfinished business : why international negotiations fail /
edited by Guy Olivier Faure, with the assistance of Franz Cede.

      p.   cm. — (Studies in security and international affairs)
Includes bibliographical references and index.

ISBN 978-0-8203-4314-3 (hardcover : alk. paper) —

ISBN 978-0-8203-4315-0 (pbk. : alk. paper)

1. Diplomatic negotiations in international disputes.

I. Faure, Guy Olivier. II. Cede, Franz.

JZ6045.U54 2012

327.1'7—dc23   2012014022

British Library Cataloging-in-Publication Data available

CONTENTS

ABOUT THE PROCESSES OF INTERNATIONAL NEGOTIATION (PIN) PROGRAM

Since 1988, the PIN Program, conducted by an international steering committee of scholars and practitioners, has met three times a year to develop and propagate new knowledge about the processes of negotiation. The committee, for twenty-two years based at IIASA (the International Institute for Applied System Analysis) in Laxenburg, Austria, but now located at Clingendael, Netherlands, conducts a book workshop every year devoted to the current collective publication project, which involves analysts and diplomats from a wide spectrum of countries, in order to tap a broad range of international expertise and to improve the understanding and the practice of negotiation. It also offers miniconferences (roadshows) on international negotiation in order to disseminate and encourage research on the subject. Such roadshows have been held at the Argentine Council for International Relations, Buenos Aires; Beijing University; the Center for Conflict Resolution, Haifa; the Center for the Study of Contemporary Japanese Culture, Kyoto; Geneva Center for Strategy and Policy; the Swedish Institute of International Affairs, Stockholm; the University of Cairo; University Hassan II, Casablanca; the University of Helsinki; School of International Relations, Tehran; Nanjing–Hopkins Center; Harvard University, Cambridge, Massachusetts; Carleton University, Ottawa; University of Warsaw; and the UN University for Peace, San Jose, Costa Rica. The PIN Program publishes a semiannual newsletter, PIN Points, and sponsors a network of over four thousand researchers and practitioners in negotiation. The program has been supported by the William and Flora Hewlett Foundation, the Smith-Richardson Foundation, and the U.S. Institute of Peace.

Members of the PIN Steering Committee are Rudolf Avenhaus, the German Armed Forces University at Munich; Mark Anstey, Michigan State University in Dubai; Franz Cede, University of Budapest/Austrian Foreign Ministry; Guy Olivier Faure, University of Paris V–Sorbonne; Fen Osler Hampson, Carleton University; Paul Meerts, the Netherlands Institute of International Affairs–Clingendael; Valerie Rosoux, Catholic University at Louvain; Rudolf Schüssler,

University of Beyreuth; Gunnar Sjöstedt, the Swedish Institute of International Affairs; Mikhail Troitskiy, MGIMO in Moscow; I. William Zartman, the Johns Hopkins University; and Ariel Macaspac Penetrante, University of Vienna, administrator.

Selected Publications of the PIN Program

Engaging Extremists: States and Terrorists Negotiating Ends and Means. I. W. Zartman and G. O. Faure, editors. Washington, D.C.: United States Institute of Peace, 2011.

Negotiating with Terrorists. G. O. Faure and I. W. Zartman, editors. London: Routledge, 2010.

Negotiated Risks: International Talks on Hazardous Issues. R. Avenhaus and G. Sjöstedt, editors. Berlin: Springer, 2009.

Escalation and Negotiation. I. W. Zartman and G. O. Faure, editors. Cambridge: Cambridge University Press, 2005.

Peace versus Justice: Negotiating Backward- and Forward-Looking Outcomes. I. W. Zartman and V. Kremenyuk, editors. Lanham, Md.: Rowman and Littlefield, 2005.

Negotiating European Union. P. W. Meerts and F. Cede, editors. Basingstoke: Palgrave Macmillan, 2004.

Getting It Done: Post-Agreement Negotiations and International Regimes. B. I. Spector and I. W. Zartman, editors. Washington, D.C.: United States Institute of Peace Press, 2003.

How People Negotiate: Resolving Disputes in Different Cultures. G. O. Faure, editor. Dordrecht: Kluwer Academic Publishers, 2003.

Professional Cultures in International Negotiation: Bridge or Rift? G. Sjöstedt, editor. Lanham, Md.: Lexington Books, 2003.

Containing the Atom: International Negotiations on Nuclear Security and Safety. R. Avenhaus, V. A. Kremenyuk, and G. Sjöstedt, editors. Lanham, Md.: Lexington Books, 2002.

International Negotiation: Analysis, Approaches, Issues. V. A. Kremenyuk, editor. 2nd ed. San Francisco: Jossey-Bass, 2002.

Preventive Negotiation: Avoiding Conflict Escalation. I. W. Zartman, editor. Lanham, Md.: Rowman and Littlefield, 2001.

International Economic Negotiation: Models versus Reality. V. A. Kremenyuk and G. Sjöstedt, editors. Cheltenham: Edward Elgar, 2000.

Power and Negotiation. I. W. Zartman and J. Z. Rubin, editors. Ann Arbor: University of Michigan Press, 2000.

International Multilateral Negotiation: Approaches to the Management of Complexity. I. W. Zartman, editor. San Francisco: Jossey-Bass, 1994.

Negotiating International Regimes: Lessons Learned from the United Nations Conference on Environment and Development (UNCED). B. I. Spector, G. Sjöstedt, and I. W. Zartman, editors. London: Graham and Trotman, 1994.

Culture and Negotiation: The Resolution of Water Disputes. G. O. Faure and J. Z. Rubin, editors. Newbury Park, Calif.: Sage, 1993.

International Environmental Negotiation. G. Sjöstedt, editor. Newbury Park, Calif.: Sage, 1993.

Processes of International Negotiations. F. Mautner-Markhof, editor. Boulder, Colo.: Westview Press, 1989.

ACKNOWLEDGMENTS

We are grateful to the United States Institute of Peace and the Smith Richardson Foundation for their support of this project of the Processes of International Negotiation (PIN) Program. We are also grateful to Isabelle Talpain-Long and Ariel Macaspac Penetrante for taking part in monitoring the manuscript, to Michael J. Carr for his meticulous and diplomatic editing, and to Cihan Ak for his careful last-minute editing.

PART ONE

What Is to Be Learned from "Failed" Negotiations?

Introduction

GUY OLIVIER FAURE AND I. WILLIAM ZARTMAN

Most studies of negotiation take completed negotiations as their subject and explain how the outcome was obtained. For historians, an accurate account (or accounts) of the proceedings is a reward in itself. For social scientists, the process as a causal path becomes the focal point, whether political science, economics, sociology, psychology, or another discipline is used to provide the terms of analysis for explaining the outcome. For the practitioner, these analyses need to be translated into practical insights and advice if they are to be useful.

Some negotiations, however, do not end in a signed agreement but rather break up as they started, in disagreement. Analysts have paid little attention to these negotiations (with Camp David as a notable rule-proving exception), although historians have done much better. How can their "outcomes" be explained since the parties started with disagreement and ended with disagreement? Failure is overdetermined, and because it is overdetermined, what can one learn from it? These questions frame the inquiry of this book.

Although some observers simply regret what they consider failures, it is more useful to draw lessons from them. Most case studies on negotiation concern successes. In so doing, they reflect the ideology of a society that valorizes success and models. One might even contend that there is no failure but only lessons that are the down payment for later success. Social science invites a more reasonable attitude and instead considers that as much, if not more, can be learned from a failed negotiation as from a negotiation that produces a mediocre outcome.

THE ARGUMENT

This volume is a collective effort that begins with a few assumptions. Its working hypothesis is that failure can be explained, and in many ways, so that, just as with success, a single unsuccessful instance of negotiation can be subject to many explanations, each using a different term of analysis or analytical approach. It is quite possible and even desirable to give several equally conclusive explanations for a failed negotiation. As in any theory, conclusiveness comes with the logical use of particular concepts and their realistic application to the case, termed internal and external validation, respectively.

Another assumption is that explanations can be produced either inductively or deductively. Cases can be examined intensively and their details allowed to speak for themselves. The resulting inquiries can then be distilled to provide focused explanations that can serve as hypotheses to be tested on other cases. Or conceptual explanations can be devised as logical exercises using given terms of analysis and then tested on cases to provide external validation. This book will use both approaches in an effort to build a comprehensive explanatory web with which to capture the phenomenon of negotiation failure.

The third assumption is that it is the process that explains the outcome; this is the hallmark of the Processes of International Negotiation (PIN) Program that sponsors this study. Thus, processes — whether inappropriate by nature or poorly conducted — factor largely in failures.

Finally, it is important to identify the sense in which this study uses the term "failure." There are as many ways of defining it as there are analytical approaches to explain it, and it will be worthwhile to examine some of the leading approaches and the problems of identification that they pose. But first, to avoid any ambiguity, "failure" in this study refers to a discrete negotiation round convened for achieving an agreement but instead breaking up in continued disagreement. The term "incomplete" — or, better, "uncompleted" — may raise fewer eyebrows, but it too has its own ambiguities (as the words "incomplete" and "uncompleted" suggest). The negotiation may be resumed later, with the parties in that new round reaching an agreement that eluded them in the first encounter; in such an instance, the first encounter is here considered incomplete, or a failure. The status quo ante may involve working cooperation that continues after the breakup, but the inability to produce the changes for which the negotiation was convened makes it incomplete, a failure. The terms "failed negotiations" or "unsuccessful negotiations" here refer to a discrete set of sessions that come up empty. However, we recognize that there may be other ways of looking at the problem for another study.

THE CONCEPT OF FAILURE

While many experts focus on conceptualizing "successful" negotiations (Buttery and Leung, 1998; Ertel, 1999; Kremenyuk, 2002; Spector, 1996; Zartman, 1978), their terms of analysis and findings have not been carried over to help us understand the cases of failure. Following the distinction made by Easton (1965) and Sharkansky (1970) between "output" (understood as agreement) of negotiation as a decision-making process and the set of consequences resulting from the decision made, outcome is equated to an agreement reached. An agreement is frequently referred to as an "exchange of conditional promises" (Iklé, 1964:7), that is, "a formal contract . . . or at least a mutually recognized exchange of tacit commitments" (Underdal, 2002:112).

Failure is both a fact and a judgment. A negotiator fails if she or he is unable to reach some kind of agreement, even if he or she has satisfied some of the goals. The widely accepted "success-failure" dichotomy in evaluating negotiations may not capture the complete reality of a negotiation, but it does correspond to a common and public evaluation of the event. The outcome of a negotiation can be judged as successful when the agreement reached is acceptable to all parties involved, and therefore a failure when it is not. This will be the case when each side sees an overall benefit in the arrangement agreed upon. Although there is a lack of any verification mechanisms for these subjective judgments, parties perceive that not making or adhering to the agreement will mean an unacceptable net loss. In an ideal world, fully successful negotiations meet the general interests of all the parties. The "win–win" formula, providing that it includes a sense of fairness in gains, best describes this result. This should be a guarantee that the agreement will be not just signed but durable and sustainable.

The use of the notion of failure raises two problems: its polymorphous nature and its subjective character. Should, for instance, failure address just the goals of each party at the negotiation table? Should it include its implementation? Should an agreement that is not implemented be considered as the outcome of a successful negotiation? The Vance-Owen peace plan (1993) over the three warring factions in Bosnia led to a number of cease-fires but not to the end of the war, in other words a co-signed failure, until it was finally replaced by an agreement at Dayton (Daalder, 2000; Touval, 2002; Zartman, 2005). Should a judgment of failure include short- and long-term consequences, as in the case of the Versailles Treaty following World War I, or should one just consider that the winners struck a satisfying deal? Should a stalled negotiation be considered as a failure or simply as a protracted deadlock? If negotiators have not overcome a deadlock, one may even think that they have not gone far enough, explored to the limits and thus, not performed a good job (Axelrod, 1970). Thus, the point is not to avoid deadlocks but to avoid being stuck in a deadlock.

Now come the subjective evaluations: when should one consider protracted deadlock as a failure (Crocker, Hampson, and Aall, 2004 and 2005)? The never-ending Doha Trade Negotiations Round of the WTO that started in 2000 and whose closure had been planned for December 2005 is a similar case, for until now there is not even a hint that an agreement is under way. To provide a meaningful answer, one should relate the joint costs incurred because of the deadlock to the joint gains if an agreement had been reached. Is the failure/success dichotomy helpful in evaluating a negotiation process? In other words, can one consider that all parties having signed an agreement means that the negotiation has been "successful"? The negotiation of Munich (1938) between the four powers over the annexation of Czechoslovakia's Sudetenland ended with a general agreement among the parties involved in the agreement but did not include the very subject of their accord and can hardly be regarded as a success for the parties outside (Zartman et al., 1996). Another variation of this basic category is the Copenhagen Conference on Climate Change, COP15 (2009). The final accord "recognizes" the scientific case for keeping temperature rises to no more than 2° Celsius but does not contain commitments to emissions reduction to achieve such a goal. This type of "success" is like an agreement on disarmament without any measure of control.

A negotiation may fulfill more than one function and thus serve other purposes than reaching an agreement. Negotiation may be used as a channel for communicating, collecting information, maintaining contact, pursuing a longer-time activity, engaging a permanent activity, or acting as the surrogate of a regime (Spector and Zartman, 2003). Negotiation may also be used as a tactical tool within a much broader strategy. This was typically the case of the U.S.-Soviet relations during the Cold War. Partial agreements may be concluded while preparing for an all-out nuclear confrontation. In the same vein, some observers tend to consider that negotiation is used as a tactical tool within the Israeli strategy when a fait accompli cannot be used or does not do the job. Negotiation can also be "failed" voluntarily in order to allow a different type of action such as a military intervention. Some observers explain the Rambouillet negotiations failure (1998–99) on the Yugoslav issue as a calculated strategy on the U.S. side to either obtain a capitulation of Milosevic or to trigger a war, and posit that the United States used a take-it-or-leave-it strategy to provoke a Serb refusal (Daalder and O'Hanlon, 2000; Zartman, 2005). Negotiation has been instrumentalized toward other ends, such as gaining time, giving the other side or external observers the impression of a willingness to come to terms, testing the commitment of the other side, or gaining some recognition as a legitimate counterpart, among other tactics. These types of strategic choices move the negotiations in a broader context, and the final outcome cannot be just explained by the negotiation process.

In a negotiation for each party, how much of the objectives should be met to consider the negotiation successful and the agreement signable? Subjective evaluation takes an essential role. The level of expectation and the needs for an agreement for each party are explanatory variables for signing or deadlocking. They are not tangible in reality but are produced by the brain. Probably one of the longest negotiations that has not yet reached any agreement over the termination of belligerence is the Korean War. Since 1953, meetings have been organized in Panmunjom between U.S. and North Korean forces, still with no result. Can we consider this as a failure? Certainly, but at least it creates a channel of communication between the two sides. Within the former and current context both sides may be still satisfied with the status quo, and the negotiations might go on for a long time.

Considering the situation prevailing at the time of the negotiation, two types can be defined: win–lose and lose–lose. In the first case, an added value by the negotiation could be to turn the win–lose situation into either a win–win or a win–lose case in which both sides improve at least their situation. This is, for instance, the usual case with cease-fires. In the second case, lose–lose, one party may consider that keeping the battle going makes the other suffer more losses than the first party, thus justifying the continuation of the lose–lose course. That was typically the case with the German strategy concerning the Verdun battle during World War I. One could speak of an absolute winner in the win–lose case and of a relative winner in the lose–lose case if one party is losing less than the other.

The analytical dichotomy of failure/success is viewed as sometimes more adequate to business than to diplomacy, since the scope of negotiation is narrower and more limited in time range. If there is no agreement, there is no business. But the question remains of the degree of success. How far from the Pareto optimal is the final agreement? Has each side maximized its own utilities? Did they both achieve a positive-sum outcome? Kesner and Shapiro (1991) argue that, in experimental studies, equating agreement with success is a product of negotiation reward structures. Usually, experimental studies offer more incentive to the participants to reach an agreement than to not reach agreement. These studies focus on the quality of agreements, and results of nonagreement are disregarded as data and as meaningful outcome.

Failure can also be classified according to the degree of immobility of the process.

- A tactical deadlock orchestrated by one party to increase its leverage under the assumption that the context will some time turn more favorable. This was the case in 1916 with the first attempts to put an end to World War I.

- A partial failure, in which some issues have been agreed upon while for the others there is no possible accord as they are considered as vital. This is the case with the never-ending Doha Round of the WTO negotiations or the Arab-Israeli negotiations at Oslo and ever since.

- A tactical nonimplementation of an agreement with either the intention to renegotiate some issues or because of second thoughts. This is the case with North Korea and with nuclear issues. This is also the case with the United States and the Biological Weapons Convention in Geneva.

- A strategic defection by one party for not getting the minimum acceptable with regard to fairness. The Camp David 2 negotiations belong to this category.

- A decision — unilateral or common — to agree to disagree at a certain point for no expectation of a positive outcome in the foreseeable future. This has been the case with most of the Israeli–Palestinian negotiations since the Oslo accords. The Cyprus case is another illustration of such type of situation.

- A breakoff of negotiations as one party tries to impose its views by resorting to force. The Munich case belongs to this category; the London Conference on Belgium is another illustration, and the Sri Lanka-LTTE negotiations a third.

- A use of negotiation as a smoke screen. The EU negotiations with Iran on nuclear issues could belong to this category.

While all these considerations are relevant to a full discussion of the enormous grey area between golden success and abject failure, this book focuses on one relatively clear type of failure: the failure to reach agreement in a discrete set of negotiations. Other shades of failure (and success) can be debated elsewhere.

THE LITERATURE

The literature on international negotiations focuses clearly on negotiations that have reached some kind of agreement. This leads to an impressive collection of "success stories" in business and diplomacy. Such an approach falls short of telling us all what we ought to know about causation. Very few publications focus on the issue of failed negotiations in a systematic and comparative fashion. Among them can be mentioned Arrow, Mnookin, Ross, Tversky, and Wilson (1995), whose text provides a number of very valuable insights but is limited to the domain of alternative disputes resolution; in particular, they address situations of mediation, litigation, arbitration, and resolution of legal disputes in America. From a psycho-sociological perspective, the various authors explore diverse obstacles, such as those pertaining to strategies, to the principal/agent relation, to cognitive biases, and to the phenomenon of reactive devaluation. Context, identity, information available, emotions, uncertainty, and risk are investigated as major causes standing in the way of reaching an agreement. However, the study is more concerned with family disputes, business conflicts, or workers' strikes than with international relations. Underdal (1983) discusses four major obstacles to negotiation success: uncertainty, inaccurate information, process-generated stakes, and politically inadequate models for the design of substantive solutions. A growing literature deals with intractable conflicts and deadlocked negotiations (Crocker, Hampson, and Aall, 2004 and 2005; Lewicki, Gray, and Elliott, 2002; Narlikar, 2010), but it focuses on the nature of the problem, not the failure of the process. However, apart from these publications there is a conspicuous paucity of comparative and analytical literature on the subject of failed negotiations, beyond publications dealing with individual case histories.

A number of negotiation components have been studied regarding their impact on the absence of agreement, such as the practice of secrecy, deceptive misrepresentation of preferences (Ross and Stillinger, 1991), the absence of a win–win option (Metcalfe and Metcalfe, 2002), the absence of a middle ground for each issue (Downie, 1991), the presence of possibilities to segment concessions (Geary, 1990), the asymmetry in availability of information (Moravcsik, 1999), and the dominant distributive dynamics on the process (Lax and Sebenius, 1986). Other dimensions that have been investigated include the lack of risk-taking spirit, lack of a sense of a historical moment, and the inability to set limited short-term goals or to make use of a mediator (Spector, 1998). If hard liners take a leading role, it makes any agreement much more unlikely (Koh, 1990).

Negotiation processes may not work, because parties have incompatible goals, which leaves no ZOPA (zone of potential agreement), so that whatever they do, they cannot reach any mutually acceptable outcome. There can also be a ZOPA but they may adopt irreconcilable strategies, turning what could be a win–win outcome into a lose–lose game. Cultural misunderstandings concerning the nature of the game, the strategy of the counterpart, or the tactics used, or negative interpretations of moves that were not meant to be competitive, may lead to conflicting attitudes and failures. Cognitive misrepresentations of the other or of the situation may entail doubts, defensive strategies, and no agreement. A cognitive process such as demonization of others tends to disqualify them and lead to their rejection as legitimate counterparts (Faure, 2009).

Other investigated causes of failure lie in the perception of the problem, of the other parties, trust, overconfidence, and loss aversion. Comparative gains, cognitive biases, and dissonance about the past could also be added to this list (Ross and Stillinger, 1991). The use of terms with high emotional content such as "genocide" can also explain failures to agree (Koh, 1990). Public opinion may play its part, as well as high transaction costs (Moravcsik, 1999). Although less important in international conferences, cultural differences may play their role with the misunderstandings they introduce in the process and also because of the gap between the values of each proponent (Faure and Rubin, 1993). Lack of preparation, ineffectiveness of chair or co-chairs, and inadequate timing are also explanatory factors analyzed by practitioners such as Koh (1990). Studies of reasons for failures have also shown that the absence of an international control mechanism, rather than being an incentive to sign because of the absence of real consequences, deters parties from reaching an agreement (Koh, 1986).

THE ANALYSIS

In most of the studies carried out on negotiations, the result validates the method and the criteria for evaluation that can be put forth. Turning to failed negotiations has the methodological advantage of avoiding such a bias while offering several different angles for apprehending the data. In this book, two analytical approaches can be distinguished. Stories of failures provide inductive material to be used to extract dominant causes for the particular cases. These causes can then be used deductively. The nature of the subject suggests a double approach. In proceeding this way, empirical findings can be put to use in the analytical part of the study. With regard to the conceptual framework that is used in parts III, IV, V, and VI of the volume, the editors used as categories of analysis the following four elements: actors, structure, strategy, and process. This conceptual framework has been drawn from the bulk of research on international negotiation, theory, and practice, done among others by the PIN Program on international negotiation seen as processes (Kremenyuk, 2002; Mautner-Markhof, 1989; Zartman, 1994a).

The method is first based on case studies presented by experts in each domain. Each of the eight cases is followed by an analysis offering explanations for the absence of outcome. The diversity of the selected cases is meant to reflect not a proportional representation of what is happening in this world as a sort of homothetic projection of all the failed negotiations in a limited period of history. Rather, our choice serves another, typological purpose. We selected negotiation cases that illustrate the main types of failure or at least protracted deadlocks that can be observed. We have bilateral failures with such cases as the Munich and Iran-EU negotiations. We have plurilateral cases with Security Council negotiations and multilateral failures with international conferences such as the Geneva Biological Weapons Convention.

We have also taken issues architecture and content into account with a care to have examples where "negotiation arithmetic" can be practiced by adding or subtracting issues (Lax and Sebenius 1991). The purpose served is to show that even using these sophisticated approaches does not necessarily lead to agreement. This is typically the case with an international conference such as Camp David 2 or the Biological Weapons Convention. Issue linkage or decomposition of issues as important techniques to develop positive-sum approaches are shown in these cases with their limits for not being guaranteed successful outcome (agreement).

Finally, we considered it essential to introduce mediation as a structural condition to reflect a most common practice when parties are stuck because of seemingly intractable differences. This is illustrated with the Cyprus case and Camp David 2. Again, it demonstrates that structural answers to a complex problem may not be a much adapted response to achieve a satisfying agreement.

Whereas the final chapters offer an "across the board" analysis, providing conclusions beyond each of the cases broadening the validity of the observations, parts III and IV of the book are based on the opposite approach. They go from concepts to cases or illustrations. Four analytical domains are distinguished and divided into ten subsections altogether. The relevance of each of the theories is illustrated by applying them to concrete situations.

The deductive part of the book, part II, involves authors who are not only analysts but who also have participated in the negotiations that they analyze. Axel Marschik and Jez Littlewood have participated in the mutltilateral negotiations of which they write, and Moty Cristal and Deborah Goodwin have been involved in Israeli-Palestinian and in hostage negotiations, respectively; Raymond Saner has been negotiating with the involved parties in Cyprus. Daniela Fridl was not involved in the 1830 negotiations over Belgium, of course, but she has been in charge of simulations of these and others for the University of Maryland. The lessons that each of these analyses draws from their cases of failure fit into the more general deductive explanations offered in the rest of the book.

The inductive part of the book offers typical cases of incomplete or failed negotiations from which interpretations are drawn about the reasons for the absence of outcome. They were chosen from among many to illustrate different types of failed negotiations — bilateral, multilateral, and mediated (trilateral), mainly in the present but also historical, and including terrorism. This part starts with "The UN Security Council and Iraq" by Axel Marschik. The author was closely involved as deputy chief of Austrian mission to the UN and had extensive knowledge as a close witness to these negotiations. One of the most interesting aspects of his analysis is the way some actors manipulated the information variable. Moty Cristal in the next chapter, on the Palestinian-Israeli Camp David summit of 2000, illustrates another failure while raising the issue of identity and the question of the biased mediator, here the United States.

Anthony Wanis-St. John presents the Iran-EU negotiations of 2003–5, with the role of public opinion on the Iranian side as a factor in the deadlock. The very high suspicion the EU nourishes over hidden motives on the part of the Iranian government made any dialogue almost impossible and in any case unfruitful. The Cyprus conflict, discussed by Raymond Saner, led to an amazing amount of effort to reunite the two sides of the small island with absolutely no result since the Greek coup and Turkish invasion in 1974. Saner identifies a number of reasons for the continuing stalemate, such as the lack of identification of the bargaining space, the absence of creative options, and the lack of clear incentives to end the current situation, as the status quo seems still bearable. Overall, external stakeholders' interferences were a major cause of protracted deadlock.

The Biological Weapons Convention was the first multilateral disarmament treaty banning the production of an entire category of weapons. However, the 5th Review Conference on the BWC in Geneva in 2001 was still a total failure. As analyzed by Jez Littlewood, the causes were to be found in the change in the international environment and a strong split between the United States and its Western allies. Furthermore, the U.S. administration decided that the proposed protocol did not suit the national interests of the country. The Negotiations on the Status of Belgium at the London Conference of 1830–33, presented by Daniella Fridl, show that power prevails when social unrest coincides with the interests of the most important nations of that time in Europe. Deborah Goodwin studies two hostage negotiations (the Waco siege and Munich Olympics) and their dramatic outcomes, analyzing the difficulties linked to this type of situation, in which life and death may be at stake. Two most divergent mindsets, on one side the representatives of a government and on the other side either religious people receiving their instructions from God or political terrorists ready to die for their cause, give very little room for an agreement that would not involve surrender from one side.

The deductive part of the book, beginning with part III, is structured around the PIN analytical framework: actors, structures, process, and strategies. From the point of view of actors as causes of failure this part begins with the psychological causes. Christer Jönsson emphasizes the importance of perception, examining biases such as selective perception and stereotypes. Negotiating means making decisions and judgments can be subjected to bounded rationality and group processes such as groupthink. Attribution theory may also play an essential role in understanding failure situations, as dispositional factors tend to be used to explain the behavior of others while situational factors will be used to explain one's own negative attitude. The cultural dimension is introduced by the actors themselves and could become a reason for failure. Negotiators bring divergent values and norms to the negotiation table, and their behaviors may also be quite misunderstood. Catherine Tinsley, Masako Taylor, and Wendi Adair contend that cultural differences may sometimes be a convenient way to justify a failure without having to show any proof of it. They propose a way to avoid dire consequences of cultural gaps by anchoring on the stereotypes of the other party. Thus, cognitive flexibility and active information searching would help to avoid intercultural failures.

Part IV considers "structures" as a cause for failure. In their chapter "Structural Dimensions of Failure in Negotiation," Anthony Wanis-St. John and the late Christophe Dupont shed some light on the role of structural elements as explanatory variables in cases of failure. Negotiation structure includes parties, issues, and power relations. The term "structure" is simultaneously a noun and a verb, which means that it is not just conditions that negotiators have to accept and cope with, but also contextual variables amenable to skilful manipulation by the actors of the process. Institutions as such may also be at the origin of negotiation failures. Brook Boyer points out three levels of analysis: international regimes, domestic levels, and micro-organizational levels. The ambiguous nature of some organizations generates a latch-on effect regarding their norms and principles of action to attractive precedents through anchoring, reference points, or framing. The absence of effective micro-level institutions such as secretariats and chairpersons to support the functioning of international conferences can also hinder negotiation processes. The content of the issues themselves may lead negotiations to continue on at great length with little progress, or simply to break off. P. Terrence Hopmann identifies classes of issues that seem most likely to lead to a dead end, such as parties negotiating not to reach an agreement but for side issues. Another reason can be when conflicts keep going even when their causes have disappeared. A most challenging obstacle is when issues cannot be aggregated or disaggregated in various sorts of ways, thus preventing any agreement. Identity conflicts are among the most representative of this category of intractable issues. In all cases one has to consider not just issue content as objective data but perceptions of it; in other words, how each party frames the problem. If a positive-sum game is framed as zero sum, it is going to be played zero sum, and as a possible consequence it is going to turn intractable.

Negotiation is first of all a process in which parties develop strategic actions aiming to reach an objective. Thus, part V examines "strategies" as an analytical category to explain failures. Cecilia Albin argues that most negotiation strategies contain both claiming and creative behaviors. Both types of strategies need to be balanced because they carry inherent contradictions and elicit tensions. Failures are often the product of these contradictions when they result in excessive claiming. Uncertainty is another important cause of failures that has been explored extensively in bargaining models. Uncertainty is the consequence of insufficient information, and the degree to which the negotiation process produces new information is a key determinant of a successful outcome. Andrew Kydd distinguishes three types of uncertainty: on private information about each party's bargaining leverage, mistrust between parties, and uncertainty about the state of the world. As a general rule, negotiation defined as the resolution of a conflict of interests under uncertainty is prone to failure. Because it is impossible to eliminate uncertainty and to only have credible information, the main action of negotiators is at least to minimize the potential costs. Third parties and objective scientific knowledge may help bring the parties back on the road to an agreement.

The "process" itself may be an important cause of failure, as shown in the essays in part VI. Negotiation dynamics have something to do with orchestration, and the combination of its various components may lead to the best or to the worst. After having elaborated the concept of ripeness to analyze the pre-process leading to the negotiation table, I. William Zartman develops the concept of "mutually enticing opportunity" (MEO) to directly address the core of the process between initiation and implementation. A MEO is a resolving formula that addresses the post-agreement interests of the parties. This distinction provides an explanation for the reasons why resolving formulas do not lead to agreement. Peace negotiations offer ample opportunities for spoilers to divert the process from its initial purpose or make it totally ineffective. Karin

Aggestam brings the focus on how spoiling affects the dynamics of negotiations in various stages according to three broad questions. Under what circumstances is spoiling behavior developed and able to block a peace process? To what extent may spoiling undermine good faith negotiations? How may spoiling prevent or hamper negotiations on implementation of peace accords? Last but not least, of the topics dealt with in part VI comes complexity as an intrinsic dimension of international and especially multilateral negotiation. Laurent Mermet raises the following question: are some situations or some issues just too complex to be negotiated? Then he shows that complexity has somehow shifted the role of the social scientist from observer to participant. He has to turn into a "cognitive" negotiator. His task becomes to avoid losing Ariadne's thread in the labyrinth of the process and reroute attention to better translate a given situation into agreeable language. Reframing as a cognitive exercise is part of the explanation.

The final part of the book aims to draw conclusions from what has been previously done in descriptive, analytical, and prescriptive terms. Guy-Olivier Faure shows from an analytical viewpoint what can be learned from the cases that could be useful for preventing negotiations from failing or remaining incomplete. Thus, he isolates thirty-nine explanatory factors of nonachievement of negotiations and shows their relevance in explaining protracted stalemates and failures. Franz Cede takes his part as a practitioner and draws lessons for future action. He provides eight recommendations for saving negotiations otherwise doomed to fail. In the end, the study of failures is designed to help explicate how they happened and draw lessons for still addressing the causes of the protracted deadlocks and avoiding such a situation in the future.

PART TWO

Selected Cases

The UN Security Council and Iraq

AXEL MARSCHIK

Rarely have negotiations in the Security Council been so unanimously re-garded as a failure as the debates on the disarmament of Iraq in early 2003. Considering the months of increasingly bitter discord before the talks finally fell apart, the fact that the UN members were united again, if only in frustra-tion with the system, almost came as a relief. The gravity of the criticism, fu-eled by the oil-for-food scandal, led to a reform process that culminated in the UN Reform Summit in September 2005 and to an ambitious agenda to improve the work of the organization throughout the UN system.

The deliberations in the Security Council in early 2003 are a good example of "failed" negotiations at the UN: complex diplomatic and technical discus-sions, draft texts, amendments and compromise proposals, and, after intense consultations, public debates and lobbying efforts, a breakdown of negotia-tions, an acrimonious blame game and recourse to force outside the system of the UN Charter. This was a decidedly different outcome compared to the nego-tiations a few months earlier, when the Security Council unanimously adopted SC Res. 1441. The fact that the council failed to find agreement mere months after such an accord was reached on the same issue, however, indicates that, already in 2002, something was amiss. Contrary to appearances, the negotia-tions resulting in SC Res. 1441 were in fact "incomplete" and only managed to postpone but not to avoid conflict. This becomes all the more evident if they are examined in the light of the consultations on Iraq a decade earlier. The first time the Security Council dealt with the issue after the Iraqi invasion of

Kuwait in 1990, the council's consultations produced unambiguous results and brought peace and security to Kuwait. The work in the council in 1990 is often heralded as exemplary; the negotiations can be characterized as "complete."

This chapter will examine the three phases of negotiations on Iraq in the Security Council and seek to determine why they merit such different classification. Any qualification of the negotiations requires a yardstick against which the process of deliberation is examined. Considering the wide scope of consultations in the council, that cannot simply be the existence of a formal agreement at the end of a negotiation process. Sometimes the fact that the negotiations did not result in a decision could be the best result. The central criteria for qualifying UN negotiations must be the way they contribute, within reasonable time, to the essential purpose of the United Nations to maintain international peace and security.

Before analyzing the negotiations, it is worthwhile to recall that the deliberations in the council are heavily influenced by its unique structure. The council members essentially belong to two classes: the five permanent members, China, France, Russia, United Kingdom, and United States (the "P5"); and the ten states elected for two-year terms (the "E10"). The P5 not only benefit from the permanence of their membership, which gives them unrivaled knowledge of process, practice, and precedents and a close relationship with the UN Secretariat staff. They also have the advantage of the veto right, with which each permanent member can prevent a decision on substance in the council. The formal use of the veto is not the only problem — the potential use of the veto already assures that the P5 will, in essence, dominate the negotiations.[1] The need to ensure that no P5 state opposes a proposal has, over time, resulted in a negotiation-process that, on important issues, largely excludes the E10. The role of the E10 is largely reduced to contributing to the required nine votes a resolution needs to pass. This is hardly relevant unless the E10 are united and/or the P5 are divided.

Due to the domination of the council by the P5, much of this article will be devoted to the tactics of the permanent members and their sometimes difficult relations. During the Cold War the United States, the UK, and France usually sided together in ideological opposition to the Soviet Union, while China played a reserved role as sole developing state among the P5 and placed particular emphasis on state sovereignty (Huntington, 1999:42). Since the mid-1990s Russia and China have moved closer together in order to create a power counterbalance to the United States (most often supported by the UK), while

France has sometimes sought an individualist position to assert itself as an independent global player. The UK and France are the most active of the P5, which is not least due to the mounting pressure to justify their individual permanent seats in the council in light of increasing political integration in the European Union and of the ongoing efforts to reform the Security Council and change its composition. All permanent members, however, recognize that their role is uniquely advantageous. Jeopardizing the system by acting outside it (such as by the NATO operation in the Kosovo-crisis in 1999) is rare and a sign of problematic intra-P5 relations (Voeten, 2001:855). If the UN system is bypassed, the P5 — including those involved in the action — are the first to emphasize the continued validity and legitimacy of the system. They know too well that to undermine the Security Council is to undermine their domination of the world's premier political body.

NEGOTIATING A RESPONSE TO IRAQ'S MILITARY INTERVENTION IN KUWAIT IN 1990

Resolutions

In 1990 the Security Council demonstrated resolve in dealing with the Iraqi invasion of Kuwait.[2] Hours after the military incursion on August 2, the council unanimously agreed on SC Res. 660 (S/RES/660 [1990] of August 2), condemning the action, demanding Iraq's withdrawal, and announcing further steps to ensure compliance. Though some states later abstained on the resolutions imposing sanctions (SC Res. 661 [S/RES/661 (1990) of August 6]), a naval blockade (SC Res. 665 [S/RES/665 (1990) of 25 August 25]), and flight restrictions (SC Res. 670 [S/RES/670 (1990) of September 25]), the council showed continued determination by adopting, three months after the incident, SC Res. 678 (S/RES/678 [1990] of November 29) authorizing states to use all "necessary means" to enforce the sanctions. This resolution served as a basis for the military campaign by the large coalition of states that liberated Kuwait.

Negotiation Process

The discussions in the council benefited from the existence of an undisputed crisis and a need for urgency. The negotiations showed general agreement on the facts and the legal consequences of the invasion. Problems arose once the debate turned to sanctions and the question of authorizing enforcement, which neither the Soviet Union nor China were initially prepared to support. Bilateral negotiations between the United States and the Soviet Union produced language that China could finally also accept. To achieve this, the United States not only employed the tactical threat of outside action (with support of the UK) but was also prepared to pay the costs of compromise (including through debt concessions, support for World Bank loans, and financial aid) (Voeten, 2001:845–55). SC Res. 678, which passed with two votes against (Cuba, Yemen) and one abstention (China), was clear in scope and content and set the stage for the ensuing military operation.

Analysis

Many reasons are seen as factors for the success of the council negotiations, in particular:

- *Political crisis.* The Iraqi invasion into Kuwait was uniformly recognized as an international crisis that demanded an immediate response.

- *The global political climate.* The end of the Cold War proved an ideal moment for the major powers to demonstrate their commitment to cooperate and make best use of the UN's system of collective security. The UN Charter contains a clear mandate for the council if one state attacks another. The wider membership wanted the council to respond unambiguously and make use of its newfound operationality and relevance.

- *A determined driving force.* As former Ambassador to the UN, U.S. president George H. W. Bush knew the organization well and had confidence that the United States could achieve its goals through the UN. The United States was the driving force behind the negotiations in the council and was prepared to make a substantial investment to win over the Soviet Union and China.

- *Interest in P5 cooperation.* China and the Soviet Union were skeptical about the need to use force, but they were prepared to accommodate the Western council members, since their interest in protecting Iraq was less than the interest in the potential benefits of a functioning council.

- *Agreement on the facts and legal consequences.* There was no factual dispute or doubt as to the illegality of the incursion into Kuwait. The council's authority and the legality of its actions were, in general, not disputed (Marschik, 2005:457–65).

- *A limited objective.* The Security Council gave permission to free Kuwait with all necessary means. This excluded, in the view of many, other measures, such as regime change in Baghdad.

Conclusion

In responding to the invasion of Kuwait, the Security Council acted swiftly, unambiguously, and determinedly. The goals of the consultations — the condemnation of Iraq and the liberation of Kuwait — were clear and shared by all. Though opinions differed on the methods of liberation, the potential consequences of the resolutions were clear not only to the members of the council but also to the addressee, Iraq, and to the rest of the UN membership.

One resolution, the long-term consequences of which were not clear at the time of adoption, was SC Res. 661. The severity of the Iraqi sanctions regime, the consequences for the general population, and the gradual disregard and usurpation of the sanctions to the benefit of the regime in Baghdad were not foreseen at the time of negotiations. The attempts to salvage the sanctions regime and alleviate the effects on the general population by means of the oil-for-food program demonstrate the inadequacies of SC Res. 661 (Joyner, 2003:329) but have no impact on the qualification of the negotiations of the resolutions on Iraq in 1990 as "complete": They adequately and appropriately addressed the central issues. The need to free Kuwait, the legitimacy of the military operation, and the responsibility of Iraq were satisfactorily established and accepted. Politically, the Security Council had achieved its purpose of reestablishing international order.

AGREEING TO AMBIGUITY IN 2002

SC Res. 1441

After a decade of deteriorating relations among the major powers in the council, the terrorist attacks of September 11, 2001, revived the spirit of cooperation.[3] The main issues of contention in the Iraqi dossier had been

Baghdad's compliance with the disarmament obligations and the effect of the sanctions. The United States and UK maintained that the Iraqi regime was disregarding the resolutions, especially its obligations to cooperate with the UN and IAEA inspectors, and profiting from the oil-for-food program.[4] Both states flew combat missions in the Iraqi no-fly zone and used military force in December 1998 to destroy structures allegedly linked to weapons of mass destruction (WMDs). France and Russia stressed the positive aspects of the inspections, which, in their eyes, had worked relatively well until 1997. They argued that the sanctions brought too much misery to the general population, and they worked, together with other states and some NGOs, to reduce them.

For the Iraqi dossier the new cooperation after 2001 resulted in two main developments: In late spring of 2002, SC Res. 1409 (May 14, 2002) reduced the negative impact of the sanctions on the Iraqi population by simplifying the oil-for-food program; and, in view of increasing pressure from Washington, Iraq signaled that it was prepared to discuss the return of UN and IAEA inspectors. After weeks of negotiations, the council unanimously adopted SC Res. 1441 (November 8, 2002), which gave Iraq a last chance to prove disarmament. The resolution demanded full documentation about Iraq's weapons programs (within thirty days) and immediate unrestricted access to all sites that the UN and the IAEA wished to inspect. The head of the UN's monitoring mission in Iraq (UNMOVIC), Hans Blix, and of the IAEA, Mohammed El Baradei, were requested to report sixty days after the start of inspections. Any lack of cooperation on the part of the Iraqi authorities should immediately be reported. The resolution reminded Iraq that it had been repeatedly warned about serious consequences of noncompliance with its obligations and that the resolution constituted a final warning.

Negotiation Process

The negotiations were conducted almost exclusively by the five permanent members. The United States, supported by the UK, declared its determination to achieve disarmament. Though President George W. Bush made clear that the United States would act unilaterally if the UN did not enforce its resolutions, the United States decided to seek a mandate from the Security Council to gain support from allies and a reluctant public (Byers, 2004:174).[5] The goal was a resolution that would legitimize military action. The draft presented by the United States to the P5 on October 1, 2002, included the following main points:

- Determination that Iraq had been in material breach of the resolutions;

- Resumption of inspections with military components and preferential treatment of the P5;

- Mandate to use force in case of further noncompliance.

For various economic and political reasons, France and Russia opposed military action in Iraq and were only prepared to accept increasing the political pressure on the regime in Baghdad. Supported by China, they sought to prevent any "automaticity" in the resolution, that is, provisions that could be interpreted to legitimize the use of force without further recourse to the council. Any mandate for military action would, in their view, have to be negotiated in an additional resolution. A public debate on October 17 demonstrated that a large majority of states preferred such a two-step approach.[6]

On October 18 the United States presented a "compromise" draft resolution, elements of which had been negotiated directly with France. Any uncooperative act on the part of Iraq would be reported to the council and lead to an immediate meeting. The provisions for military accompaniment of the inspectors and the special status for the P5 were dropped. France interpreted the agreement as an acceptance of the two-step approach by the United States, but the United States, at the same time, recalled their view that the existing breaches by Iraq already legitimized enforcement. The compromise was part of the UK/U.S. draft resolution presented to the whole council on October 23. The draft raised many questions, but several council members, worried that the United States could lose patience with the UN process, seemed prepared to accept a degree of ambiguity. The French delegation, however, countered with a new set of proposals to make very clear that a second resolution was required before enforcement action could be undertaken. Russia presented elements for a complete package with incentives for compliance and a road map leading to the eventual lifting of sanctions.

At this point of the negotiations Hans Blix and Mohammed El Baradei played an important role. It would be their responsibility to ensure that the inspections worked on the ground, and they shifted the focus of the discussions to more technical questions.[7] Both tried to avoid taking sides, but they refused to be put in the position that their actions would determine peace or war. Blix insisted that he and El Baradei could only be asked to inspect and report. Any consequences of their reports would be the sole responsibility of the council. Blix thereby indirectly supported the two-step approach.

The brief impasse was overcome at the end of October when U.S. and UK negotiators secured an agreement with Russia and China to include a reference to the existence of a "material breach."[8] The United States also incorporated a provision to the effect that any erroneous statement or uncooperative behavior by Iraq would constitute a further material breach of the new resolution that would have to be reported by the inspectors, whereupon the council would convene (see OP 4 of SC Res. 1441). France, together with Russia and China, succeeded in obtaining an explicit mention of a "last chance" for Iraq and to refine a reference to SC Res. 678 in such a way that it could not be later misinterpreted as an immediate justification for recourse to force (see OP 2 of SC Res. 1441).

Sensing that the negotiations among the permanent members had reached the final stage, some of the ten elected members of the council requested amendments, such as a reference to a possible lifting of sanctions if Iraq complied with all obligations, the recognition of the territorial integrity and sovereignty of Iraq, or the establishment of a WMD-free zone in the Middle East. On November 6, the United States and UK presented a final draft resolution that incorporated many of these proposals. Almost all council members indicated that they would vote in favor of the resolution. Only Syria requested more time to receive instructions from Damascus.[9] The unanimous adoption of the resolution on November 8, 2002, was initially hailed as a UN success and a sign that the United States was prepared to adopt a multilateral approach in disarming Iraq.

The explanations of votes by the council members at the adoption of the resolution, however, indicated the extent of the remaining disagreement. France showed satisfaction that the resolution contained no triggers and reflected a two-step approach. Only UNMOVIC and IAEA had the right to report violations, and the council would then consult on possible consequences. China and Russia made similar points, and all three states later issued a joint declaration on SC Res. 1441 to this effect.[10] The United States, on the other hand, welcomed the agreement in the council to give Iraq a final warning. Though U.S.

ambassador Negroponte conceded that the resolution did not contain hidden triggers, he stressed the right of every state to enforce existing resolutions and to protect itself from threats.

For the wider UN membership the disagreement on the way forward was worrisome. While some gained solace from the fact that, at least, the debate was still at the UN, others doubted whether the negotiations had achieved any result apart from sending UN inspectors into a "mission impossible." The primary goal — to send an unambiguous signal as to how the UN and its members would proceed with the Iraqi issue — was clearly not met.

Analysis

The negotiations on SC Res. 1441 demonstrate the complexity of the process of elaborating a resolution at the UN. The positions of the leading antagonists, the United States and France, were almost contradictory. Yet agreement was achieved on various vital points: the existence of a material breach of the previous resolutions, a final warning, and the deployment of inspectors to monitor and report on Iraq's compliance with the disarmament obligations. Several factors facilitated finding agreement on these points:

- *Related interests.* All sides sought to maintain the good cooperation in the council since 2001. The United States in particular did not want to jeopardize the alliance against terrorism. The other council members had an interest in preserving the Security Council as the forum of action in international security issues.

- *Focus on technical issues.* Renewing the role of the UN inspectors for technical functions shifted the focus of negotiations from larger political consequences to more technical questions regarding the implementation of the inspections.

- *Varied coalitions among the P5.* Varying constellations of negotiating parties enabled progress in different fields. The United States secured an important compromise with Russia and China on the question of a breach. France consulted closely with Russia on its position, negotiated directly with the United States on some questions, and relied on its EU channels with the UK.

- *A short-term solution.* The resolution was an intermediary step establishing further inspections and follow-up procedures. The fact that the the resolution did not bring "closure" to the issue facilitated its adoption.

- *Ambiguity.* An important factor that permitted agreement was precisely the uncertainty about the future course of action. As Byers (2004) points out, the members of the council agreed to the ambiguities of the resolution with their eyes open, as it were; they were, in fact, agreeing to disagree. For France and Russia the resolution postponed any military action and kept the UN involved. For the United States and UK it provided the legitimacy of a multilateral final warning. The different interpretations of the resolution enabled both sides to claim that the council was united behind their position.

At the same time, the resolution did not achieve the goal of laying out a clear course for the future. Some reasons for this are:

- *Dispute about facts.* In stark contrast to 1990, the central question — whether Iraq implemented its disarmament obligations — was perceived differently by the two factions. While the United States and UK claimed the continued existence of Iraqi weapons or weapons programs and the lack of cooperation by Iraq, France and Russia doubted the existence of a real and imminent threat and saw indications of a readiness to cooperate on the part of Iraq.

- *Irreconcilable goals.* The United States and UK sought a resolution that could serve as a threat of future force. France and Russia, supported by China, wanted to prevent military action.

- *Exclusive process.* The E10 have a substantial interest in unambiguous agreements in the council. They can act as mediators in situations of discord among the P5 and subsequently contribute to a "correct" interpretation of the final outcome, but they were excluded from meaningful participation in elaborating the resolution.

- *Urgency.* Political pressure prevented a thorough discussion about the follow-up. The United States wanted a resolution soon; the other states wanted to involve the United States as quickly as possible in the UN setting.

Conclusion

Though the council agreed on a resolution, it was unable to agree on the main objective of the exercise: to define the future course of action. The outcome of the negotiations merely hid the continued disagreement over how to proceed. The concern that the United States would act outside the system created enough pressure to achieve consensus on a text but not on a consensual understanding on the way forward. The negotiations in the council were unable to create firm parameters and procedures that would contribute to growing trust, cooperation, stability, and security, in other words, toward establishing peace and security. At the same time, the negotiations cannot be qualified as "failed": all members of the council agreed on several important elements that would be decisive in the future debate. It is therefore argued that the negotiations — even though they resulted in a unanimous resolution — were "incomplete."

FAILURE TO AGREE IN 2003

The Resolution That Never Was

According to sc Res. 1441, Iraq had to submit all relevant information on its wmd programs to the inspectors by December 8, 2002. At this date Iraq submitted twelve thousand pages of documents, which contained hardly any new information.[11] The United States gradually amassed its necessary troop strength in the region. Negotiations on the further course of action were held under the increasing conviction that war was unavoidable.

On February 24, 2003, the uk circulated a draft resolution in the name of the uk, the United States, and Spain that contained as its single operative element the decision that Iraq had not used the final opportunity to comply with its disarmament obligations. France countered with a joint French, German, and Russian memorandum that proposed strengthening the inspections foreseen under sc Res. 1441. A revision of the U.S./uk/Spanish draft resolution of March 12 introduced a final ultimatum with six benchmarks that Iraq had to comply with by certain dates:

- A declaration on television by Saddam Hussein

- Thirty interviews with Iraqi scientists outside Iraq

- Handing over of all anthrax stock

- Destruction of all remaining Al Samoud II rockets

- Declaration on all unmanned flight programs

- Handing over of all mobile chemical and biological production centers.

This text, however, failed to find adequate support in the council, and the draft was never put to a vote.

Negotiation Process

Considering the precarious state of affairs at the beginning of 2003, the Security Council remained ominously inactive in the first half of January. Negotiations, mainly with the five newly elected members in the council (among them Germany and Spain), were conducted between capitals directly. In New York, diplomats waited for the first formal reports from Blix and El Baradei to the council scheduled for the end of the month. But at a ministerial-level council meeting devoted to terrorism on January 20, German foreign minister Joschka Fischer formally declared Germany's opposition to military action against Iraq and urged the council to give the inspectors time to do their job. Immediately following the meeting, a press statement by Foreign Minister Dominique de Villepin of France made clear that France and Germany, two traditionally close EU partners, had collaborated to use the meeting on terrorism to signal their principled opposition against military measures in Iraq.

The presentation of the reports by UNMOVIC and the IAEA on January 27 made the widening political trench between the two sides apparent. The United States and UK seized on the sober reports that no new evidence on WMDs had been provided by Iraq as proof for further noncompliance. They were supported in this view by Spain and Bulgaria. France, Germany, and Russia, on the other hand, saw the reports as proof of the success of the inspections. Most other council members seemed prepared to give the inspectors time to complete their job.

On February 5, the Security Council met at the foreign minister level. The United States had suggested the meeting to enable Secretary of State Colin Powell, in a two-hour presentation and assisted by satellite pictures and telephone transcripts, to present the case against Iraq.[12] Powell concluded that Iraq was continuously violating SC Res. 1441 and had failed to use its last chance to avoid enforcement. The council members should not shirk from their responsibility to ensure compliance with the relevant resolutions. UK, Spain, Bulgaria, and, to some extent, Chile supported this argument. The other states urged Iraq to comply with its obligations but reiterated their request for more time for inspections.

In the United States, Powell's presentation in the council increased public support for a military intervention. At the same time, many diplomats and UN experts were surprised that the United States were not able to build a stronger case and produce a "smoking gun" (Blix, 2004:152–56). The presentation also gave the other side an opening to rely on U.S. information to substantiate their call for more UN inspections, and France later circulated a proposal to this effect.

On February 14, Blix and El Baradei presented a second report to the council.[13] After Blix's rather harsh assessment in January, many expected another negative report. However, in his presentation Blix rejected some of the allegations supplied by the United States at the February 5 meeting and gave a cautiously positive evaluation of the cooperation by the Iraqi regime. He pointed out that the inspection team established by SC Res. 1441 was still not fully assembled and would receive additional technical support in the immediate future. In the debate de Villepin presented France's position — war can still be avoided with better inspections — with made-for-media eloquence. Germany and China supported the plea for more time. Expecting to reap the rewards for having played the multilateral game, the United States was clearly disappointed with Blix's evaluation. Secretary of State Powell reiterated his view that Iraq was not cooperating and that the council should now address the consequences of Iraq's material breach of the resolution. Disarmament, not inspection, was the goal of the resolutions. This was supported by the UK, Spain, and Bulgaria, but Chile's reaction seemed to indicate a shift in its position.

By mid-February, with troop buildup nearly complete, it seemed almost certain that the United States would resort to force. The question was whether Washington would continue to seek authorization from the Security Council through a new resolution. Apparently, France even privately urged the United States at this stage to abandon the goal of a second resolution and act, if it must, outside the UN system. The ambiguity in SC Res. 1441 could serve the

United States as a vague legal justification. This would be challenged by others, including France, but it would be a disagreement on interpretation. If a text were put to a vote and failed, however, the illegality of any subsequent act would be clear (Byers, 2004:165–73). Though many in Washington had, at this point, reached a similar conclusion, the United States did not want to lose its European allies. By mid-February, UK prime minister Tony Blair had come under significant domestic pressure, including from within his own party, to only participate in a military operation if it was legitimized by the UN. The UK delegation thus intensified its efforts to produce a text acceptable to both sides and, after consultations with Blix, internally started working on a text with objective benchmarks.[14]

When the United States, the UK and Spain presented their first short draft resolution on February 24, it was generally expected that the political influence of these countries would suffice to sway the remaining uncommitted council members. A French/German/Russian memorandum to prolong and intensify inspections was immediately rejected by the United States; it was made clear that the U.S. delegation would veto any draft that continued inspections. Concerned, however, that the diplomatic clout of the United States would be hard to match in persuading the undecided council members, France, Germany, and Russia issued a joint declaration on March 5 in Paris that contained an indirect threat of a veto from the two permanent members. This move, dismissed as political grandstanding by the other side, proved to be an essential instrument for the six uncommitted elected members to continue to decline taking sides, arguing that a French or Russian veto made their positions irrelevant.[15]

At the final presentation of the inspectors in the council on March 7, El Baradei reported that the IAEA inspections were going well and that no indication of any resumption of nuclear programs had been detected. Blix still found fault in the level of Iraqi cooperation but acknowledged Baghdad's efforts to improve this. He announced that UNMOVIC would need a few more months to finalize its mandate. In the debate, UK foreign minister Jack Straw introduced a new proposal to give Iraq a further last chance: the coalition draft resolution would include an ultimatum of March 17.[16] France and Germany retorted that they would not accept an ultimatum while Iraq was cooperating. They argued that giving inspectors only two and a half months in total to complete their work was insufficient, and a deadline of only a few days was a pretext for war.

The United States showed decreasing interest in the UN process and demanded a "strategic decision" by Iraq to avert a military confrontation. At the margins of the council, delegations from both sides claimed to possess an adequate number of votes to adopt or block the resolution, but the prevailing rumor among the wider UN membership was that the U.S./UK side had difficulties in securing the necessary support.

On March 12 the UK individually proposed an amendment to the U.S./UK/ Spanish draft with six specific benchmarks and a slightly later deadline as a last chance for peace. Since the resolution still contained the authorization of enforcement without prior determination by an independent arbiter, France, Germany, and Russia rejected the proposal. China saw an inadequate role for UNMOVIC. The six undecided council members welcomed the proposal, recognizing some of the requests they had made, but they stressed the need for a larger role for UNMOVIC. Many delegations hoped that the proposal would reactivate negotiations in the council. The following day, however, informal consultations on the new package showed that France, Russia, China, and Germany had difficulties in entering meaningful negotiations. Politicians had, by then, created such strong domestic public opinions against a resolution that they had lost their flexibility to compromise. At the same time, the United States seemed to gradually withdraw from the negotiations. Perhaps Washington had begun evaluating the possible consequences of a vote (the disadvantage of a negative vote would outweigh by far the advantages of a complex resolution that receives just the minimum of support). A Chilean attempt to rally the "undecided six" behind a nonpaper that incorporated five of the six conditions proposed by the UK and that gave an ultimatum of three weeks failed.[17]

When news of the convening of a U.S./UK/Spain summit in the Azores on March 16 reached New York, the prospects for a new resolution were dead and the efforts to achieve agreement in the council ended. The day after the summit, the UK informed the council that the U.S./UK/Spanish draft resolution would not be put to a vote. In the evening of the same day, President Bush issued an ultimatum to Saddam Hussein to leave Iraq within forty-eight hours. Secretary-General Annan ordered the evacuation of all inspectors. After a final council meeting on March 19, the army of TV transmission cars disappeared from First Avenue, and media attention turned from the council chamber in New York to the battlefield in Iraq.

Analysis

The practical reason why the council failed to adopt a resolution is, of course, the lack of support for the UK/U.S./Spanish draft resolution in the council. Considering the clout of the cosponsors, it is surprising that the small states in the council were able to withstand the political pressure and the economic incentives offered (McWhinney, 2004:70). It is certainly true that the Paris declaration — the threat of a veto by France or Russia — had a significant impact, but there are several reasons for the failure of the negotiations:

- *General political climate.* After the terror attacks in 2001 the outpouring of sympathy for the United States and the support for its retaliation against the Taliban in Afghanistan gradually gave way to concern over an increasingly hard-line U.S. foreign policy.[18] It has been argued that the lingering shock of 9/11 and the relatively brief campaign in Afghanistan (and the failure to capture Osama Bin Laden) hardened Washington's determination to send an unequivocal message of strength and power. This did not go down well with France, Russia, and China, who strive for a multipolar world — and that means reining in the superpowers (Glennon, 2003:25).[19] Safeguarding the UN system, its principles, and its charter was important for these states, as was the opportunity to demonstrate international relevance.[20] Increasingly, the objective of the two factions was less to find common ground on a resolution than to enable politicians to explain their position and lobby for public support of their policies (Sebenius, 2002:234–35).[21]

- *Disagreement on the facts.* The United States and UK argued that Iraq possessed and wanted to produce WMDs, was an immediate threat to world security, and refused to cooperate with inspections. France and Russia believed Iraq could be or had been trying to build WMDs but did not see any imminent threat that could not be contained long-term by UN inspections and cooperation by Iraq (Blix, 2004:127).[22] This dispute on facts took up substantial time and was unbridgeable even with reports from independent UN inspectors on the ground.

- *Irreconcilable goals.* The United States and UK wanted a mandate to use force. France and Russia, supported by China, wanted to prevent such a mandate.

- *Lack of a decisive precipitating event.* While Iraq's invasion of Kuwait in 1990 was a dramatic action that required an international response, the situation in Iraq in early 2003 was not much different from the years before. Many states were not convinced that absent an individual incident or an additional provocation from Iraq the international community should drastically alter the course of action it had followed (albeit not very successfully) over the last years.

- *Lack of trust.* A central theme of the negotiations was the mistrust among the parties. This was prevalent in the arguments and evidence presented by other delegations, even among allies, as well as in attitudes toward the reports submitted by Blix and El Baradei. The most negative impact on the negotiations came from the lingering mistrust as to the "real" motivation and goal of the whole exercise: While the United States and the UK officially stuck to the theory of Iraq being an immediate WMD threat and that disarmament was the sole purpose of their initiative, many believed that "regime change" was the real goal and that personal or economic interests (revenge, oil) were the motive (Teixeira da Silva, 2004:214).[23]

- *Splits among the ten elected Council members.* In the elaboration of SC Res. 1441 the role of the E10 had been minimal. In view of the disagreement among the P5 it was expected that they would become much more relevant. The three cosponsors of the resolution required at least six votes from the E-10 to achieve the necessary nine votes for adoption of the resolution. If they had acted together or at least in a large group, the E10 could have become influential. From the outset, however, the E10 were split, and at the end of negotiations they were unable to unite even for single issues.[24] Without coordination and cooperation the E10 could not exercise any influence (Blix, 2004:106–9).[25]

- *Rigid coalitions.* The emergence of two distinct opposing camps prevented ad-hoc coalitions on individual issues. Though fora for trans-camp dialogue did exist (the EU members France and the UK had many opportunities to consult), the firm entrenchment in opposing factions made the search for compromises or alternatives difficult.

- *Public opinion.* The two camps made extensive use of the media to convey their message. After having ignited their respective domestic

publics, the governments had to show consistency and backbone.
These are important character traits, no doubt, but they provide less
room to maneuver in negotiations. In the end, both sides were unable
to make last-minute concessions in order to keep negotiations alive.

- *Time pressure.* Though often a quintessential factor in decision making at the UN, the immense pressure in this case (due to climate conditions in Iraq that would affect a military operation) worked against
  the search for alternatives, especially in the final days of negotiations.

- *Closure.* The draft resolution was designed to decide the issue of
  whether force would be used, the question that SC Res. 1441 had
  managed to avoid answering. This should be the final resolution on
  the issue without further recourse to the council. States that did not
  want enforcement at this stage had to prevent the adoption of the
  resolution to keep the council involved.

After the discontinuance of negotiations many commentators offered
opinions on how a compromise could still have been reached. Possibly, if the
United States had been prepared to accept the continuance of inspections for
a few more months, France, Germany, and Russia would have been more inclined to accept a trigger with objective benchmarks. But these speculations
fail to take into consideration that the discussions in the council in March 2003
were no longer devoted merely to the technical issue of how to proceed with
the disarmament of Iraq. The negotiations had evolved into a debate on the
parameters of the international order. While the United States and the UK were
trying to convince the council members that it would be in their interest not
to weaken the multilateral system of the UN by a large unilateral enforcement
action, the other states were increasingly doubtful that a system that reduces
their role to rubber-stamping the policies of the superpower merits strengthening. Faced with a unipolar world, Russia, China, and France instead chose to
retain a minimum of independence and influence, even if it merely sufficed to
raise the cost — political and financial — of unilateral action by the superpower.

CONCLUSIONS AND OUTLOOK

A comparison of the three instances of negotiations on Iraq permits an identification of some factors that contribute to the success or failure of negotiations

in the Security Council. The analysis indicates substantial influence from out-side forces: the global political climate; the existence of a decisive precipitating event or a political crisis; public pressure and public opinion; the relevance of other interests (such as maintaining good cooperation among the parties involved for other issues); the possibility of unrelated trade-offs; and the sig-nificance of ulterior motives or wider objectives. Other factors were more re-lated to the issue or the process: technical questions were easier to solve than larger political ones; it was easier to implement limited or short-term goals than to achieve closure; constructive ambiguity facilitated agreement but did not contribute to the success of the negotiations; lack of a common under-standing of the facts, rejection of existing monitoring and verification systems, and the provision of conflicting intelligence reports undermined the positions of all parties; and issue-related urgency (a real or alleged threat) created nega-tive time pressure. Finally, some factors originating in the unique forum and in the relationship among the parties involved influenced the outcome: the existence of an atmosphere of trust among the P5; a major driving force will-ing to make compromises (a determined permanent member with adequate resources to achieve a result and carry the burden of trade-offs); flexibility in coalition building during the consultations (no rigid coalitions); and an effec-tive mediating role of the elected members when the P5 are divided (though the examples discussed indicate that this requires that the E10 are united).

The negotiations in 1990 benefited not only from the undisputed existence of an international crisis, an agreement on the facts, and a determined driving force, but also from the general political climate that saw a role for an effective UN Security Council. Though the resolutions adopted in 1990 are not without fault, the negotiation process was complete in achieving its main goal: reestab-lishing peace, security, and independence for Kuwait. The process preceding the adoption of SC Res. 1441 in 2002 suffered from the emerging disagreement on the extent of the danger that the regime in Baghdad represented and on the hardening of national positions. An agreement was possible mainly because the resolution focused on technical questions (renewed inspections), was ac-cepted as an intermediary step, and remained ambiguous as regards the de-cisive political questions. However, though the resolution was unanimously adopted, the negotiations were incomplete as they fell short of their goal of settling the issue for a reasonable time.

The negotiations on the draft resolution in 2003 failed essentially because of irreconcilable national positions built up gradually and publicly by the central players, which, together with a lack of trust and time, increasingly eliminated room for compromise. The final debates were less about disarming Iraq than about the future of the international system; the discussions were not so much diplomatic negotiations as declarations of policy. As such, they did not seek to achieve consensus on a text but rather to maximize publicity. In this respect, perhaps, the UN debates were thoroughly complete. However, in the eyes of the international community and the aspirations of the drafters of the charter, the UN is more than a stage for political rhetoric. As clearly emerged in the course of the Iraqi crisis in 2003, the international public sees the UN as the highest authority on peace and war and expects it to address and solve international security threats. In this respect as well as measured against the criterion of contributing to international peace and security, the Security Council negotiations on Iraq in 2003 clearly failed.

The fact that the negotiations in the Security Council failed does not mean, however, that the council itself or the UN system failed. Disappointment with a decision (or lack of decision) by an executive organ should not necessarily put the institution itself into question. It is true that disagreement in the UN Security Council is often interpreted as failure of the organ.[26] Agreement has particular importance in an organ that has a mandate to ensure peace.[27] Even a weak or unsubstantial agreement is often preferable to conflict.[28] But the UN is no pacifist organization, and the Security Council was never designed to decide by consensus. The council specifically foresees voting — which embodies the potential for disagreement. The drafters of the charter even gave five states the right to block an agreement by veto, and these states have not had qualms about using this right in the past. The failure to reach agreement in negotiations is thus part of council procedure and practice. Irrespective of the disappointing outcome, these deliberations and their inconclusive end were no failure of the UN system.

This is corroborated by the fact that even after the harsh criticism in 2003, the UN and the Security Council have maintained their relevance: since 2003, the council meets more often and has established more missions than ever before.[29] The reform of the composition and working methods of the council has received new attention. Many states have declared their interest in becoming permanent or elected council members. The major powers continue to use the Security Council as the central international instrument for questions of peace and security and even expand its traditional role to novel fields.[30] They will continue to do so as long as the council serves its purpose and the wider membership considers the organization the definite source of legality and legitimacy for international action.

It is interesting to note that the UN Reform Summit 2005, which was a direct result of the broad disappointment with the failure of the Security Council to deal with the disarmament of Iraq, contains no meaningful measures to improve the council's ability to address similar situations. The Summit Outcome Document devotes commendable attention to development, management, human rights, the rule of law, and peace building. It foresees specific measures of institutional reform of ECOSOC and the Secretariat. The two (of 178) paragraphs devoted to Security Council reform, however, reiterate the calls for more efficiency, transparency, inclusiveness, and accountability that have been raised faithfully in the organization for decades.[31] Once again, the Security Council has proved itself immune to meaningful reform. This will give ample opportunities in the future to continue to examine complete, incomplete, and failed negotiations of the council.

NOTES

The manuscript for this article was finalized in 2005 when the author was the deputy permanent representative of Austria to the United Nations in New York. The views expressed in this article cannot be attributed to the Austrian Foreign Ministry.

1. On the relationship between the P5 and the E10 in practice, see Mahbubani (2004:253).

2. Tactically, though, the threat of outside action is sometimes employed in the negotiations to achieve concessions. The Security Council measures regarding Iraq in 1990 have been extensively discussed in literature. It suffices to briefly recall the main developments. See, with further references, the special volume of the *European Journal of International Law* devoted to the Symposium on the Impact on International Law of a Decade of Measures against Iraq, EJIL 13 (1) (February 2002); see also Berman, 2004:153.

3. The crisis in the Balkans had strained relations between the West and Russia. However, in the same period every P5 member had endured acts of terrorism. Creating an effective counterterrorism regime under auspices of the Security Council was a uniting project.

4. SC Res. 1284 established UNMOVIC in 1999 and replaced UNSCOM, the predecessor mission that had been sent to Iraq in 1991 but had been expelled by the Iraqi regime after Operation Desert Fox in 1998.

5. On September 12, 2002, in his speech at the general debate at the UN, President

George W. Bush recalled the victims of the terror attacks the previous year and condemned the regime in Iraq, assuring the international community that the United States would take action with or without the UN. At the UN, many delegations were at first encouraged that President Bush had chosen the UN to deliver his speech, which was interpreted as willingness to use the institutional UN structures in the dispute with Iraq.

6. The debate also demonstrated that almost all states considered a formal Security Council decision on the consequences of noncompliance of SC resolutions an absolute necessity for the enforcement of resolutions.

7. Blix and El Baradei had enabled the start of the negotiations with their talks with Iraqi foreign minister Sabri in Vienna (September 30–October 1, 2002), which secured Iraqi acceptance of the resumptions of inspections. Blix's general affirmation of the operationality of the draft resolution enabled France to accept the inspection provisions. France often stated that it would be up to Blix to decide on their practicality.

8. This became OP 1 of SC Res. 1441. The United States regarded this point merely declaratory. As was stressed in several formal statements, the United States already considered themselves legally authorized to enforce the previous resolutions, since, according to the United States, Iraq had been in breach of several key requirements.

9. The consultation the following day brought some minor changes, which France and Russia had requested. They sought to make clear that only the inspectors would have the authority to determine the existence of noncompliance with Iraq's obligation to cooperate.

10. Russian foreign minister Ivanov also made a formal statement to that effect on November 9, 2002, that went even further: the resolution contained no trigger, left any authorization of enforcement to future council decision, averted the imminent threat of war, acknowledged all states' obligation to respect Iraq's sovereignty, and enabled the pursuit of a political solution of the whole issue.

11. Today, after years of unsuccessful searches for WMDs in Iraq, this is hardly surprising. In late 2002 and early 2003, however, the threat of WMDs and the apparent Iraqi unwillingness to cooperate became the formal casus belli of the proponents for military action.

12. The main points were: Iraq was conducting an elaborate operation to hide its WMD programs (such as mobile labs), which prevented the inspectors from finding evidence; there was a connection between the Iraqi regime and the Al Qaeda terrorist network; and the regime was responsible for well-documented human rights violations.

13. This report was not delivered under SC Res. 1441 but under SC Res. 1284: the resumption of inspections in Iraq had warranted a report under that regime.

14. UNMOVIC had prepared a document in this respect and Blix had offered it — together with the text for a draft resolution — to the UK; Blix, 2004:186–90.

15. At this stage Secretary-General Annan appealed almost daily to the P5 to find a

common way forward. He even went so far as to publicly declare that unilateral military action would not be legitimate. Increasingly, however, he also had to address concerns regarding the consequences of unilateral action outside the system for the future of the UN.

16. Straw thereby managed successfully to draw international attention away from the possibility of a new spirit of cooperation by the Iraqi authorities. The meeting had a significant impact on the undecided council members. In the subsequent days, Angola emphasized that the council had an obligation to enforce its resolution against uncooperative states.

17. When the United States indicated that they would not accept it, the three African states no longer wished to cosponsor the paper. Chile saw no point in presenting a paper that did not even have the support of all the "U6."

18. Cf. the National Security Strategy of the United States issued in September 2002, which stressed that the United States had the right to use its power to ensure that no other nation rivals its military strength and to use force preemptively.

19. See also Luck, 2004:135.

20. Many had initially believed that the French interest in a strong and relevant UN would, finally, result in their not blocking a resolution. The French and German cooperation in the council together with the apparent interest of President Jacques Chirac to position France as the power capable of restraining the "hyper-power" across the Atlantic, however, seemed to make the French delegation more likely to use its veto as a general political statement.

21. Underlying larger issues sometimes decisively determine the positions taken in negotiations (Sebenius, 2002:234–35).

22. As to the relevance of information in negotiations see Dupont and Faure, 2002:53–54.

23. Other motives are offered by Fraser, 2005:178. Hans Blix (2004) identified several complementary reasons for the positions of the council members. For the United States and UK he underlines the impact of the terror attacks in September 2001, the need to set an example, and an "almost religious fervor to fight evil."

24. Spain and Bulgaria supported the U.S./UK draft. Germany had coauthored the memorandum with France and Russia. Pakistan wanted a peaceful solution. Syria was opposed to making the sanctions tougher. Chile and Mexico argued in favor of prolonging inspections. Cameroon and Angola also expressed this view but still seemed undecided. Guinea managed to avoid classification altogether.

25. Their practical irrelevance can be illustrated as follows: while the P5 received the whole text of the Iraqi declaration of December 8, the E10 only received a "sanitized version" of the text — some 8,500 pages less than the P5. Even so, the document encompassed 3,500 pages and the E10 had only a single day to study the text before it was discussed in the council. See Blix, 2004:106–9.

26. For Glennon (2003:16) the reasons for the failure to agree on a resolution in early 2003 do not lie so much in the issue and factors surrounding the negotiations as in the organ involved. Not reflecting the distribution of power today, the Security Council is unable to function properly. It is certainly true that the distribution of rights in the council does not reflect the current distribution of political and military power. It is questionable, however, whether that would make the council, as an institution, incapable of "complete negotiations." This would either nullify all decisions or make only those valid that are supported by the dominant power or powers. Even in 1945, however, this philosophy was not the basis for the council decision-making procedures. Rather, the distribution of equal power in the council among five states irrespective of their actual politico-military might in 1945 was intended as a system of peer control.

27. As a consequence, UN resolutions often reflect the lowest common denominator of the positions of the member states. See Cede, 2002:151. Progress on difficult issues, if at all, is often only apparent over a longer period of time. From one year to the next the General Assembly's resolutions sometimes hardly change. But comparing texts — for instance the resolutions on women's or children's rights — with the thinking of ten or twenty years ago reveals the sometimes remarkable progress.

28. Especially if the conflict can be carried out with weapons of mass destruction. The search for agreement and the desire to avoid confrontations has strongly influenced the negotiating culture at the organization. Its impact differs from one UN body to the next. Over time, some committees have become more confrontational (such as the Third Committee, dealing with Human Rights where voting is now the norm). Others, such as the Fifth Committee (Budget) and the Sixth Committee (Legal) rely almost exclusively on decisions by consensus. Important issues such as UN reform, which was debated in summer of 2005 in the General Assembly plenary as well as in various informal smaller groups, are often adopted without a vote. (A prominent exception is the adoption of the Human Rights Council in March 2006.) This is often criticized as giving every member state the right to veto.

29. In 2004 Secretary-General Annan had to warn council members that so many peacekeeping missions were being established that, by the end of the year, the UN's capacities would be seriously overextended; see United Nations, 2004:4.

30. Compare the recent decision to investigate the Hariri assassination in Lebanon by sending a criminal investigator, or the broad and abstract legislation by the council on counterterrorism and nonproliferation. See Marschik, 2005:257.

31. See World Summit Outcome, 2005, paras 153 and 154. Two further provisions try to persuade the Security Council to improve its working methods on sanctions (paras 108 and 109).

Camp David, 2000

MOTY CRISTAL

Many perceive the 2000 Israeli-Palestinian Camp David summit as a failed negotiation because it failed to reach an agreement and was followed by the deadliest cycle of violence between Israelis and Palestinians. However, the following analysis, presented from a practitioner's perspective, suggests that these negotiations should be better defined as "incomplete" rather than "failed" as they did frame several conceptual breakthroughs on almost all contested issues, formulated the principles of the two-nation-states solution, and still await future detailed negotiations that ought to be conducted through a better designed process.[1]

This chapter will present the fourteen days of negotiations at Camp David in 2000 within their wider context, as the peak of a conflict-resolution process that commenced with the election of Ehud Barak as Israel's prime minister in May 1999 and ended with the conclusion of the Taba summit in January 2001, four months after the outbreak of the second Intifada.

In 1947 the UN offered a division of the mandated Palestine between a Jewish state and an Arab (Palestinian) one. Arab rejection of this proposal led to war, which is considered the symbolic root of the current conflict. The State of Israel was created, absorbing thousands of Jews who had survived the Holocaust while thousands of Arabs left the area. In 1967 Israel occupied the Palestinian-populated areas of the West Bank and Gaza Strip. The subsequent UN Security Council resolution 242 set the governing principle for the Middle East peace process: "land for peace." This distinction between "the 1947" and "the 1967" would emerge as the most intractable process challenges, where the two sides talk the land for peace "1967 talk" while walking the "1947 walk" of reconciling justice for Palestinians and recognition of the right of Israel to exist as a Jewish state. For some, Camp David reflected, at the highest level of intensity, the clashes between these two narratives (Bar-Siman-Tov et al., 2005).

The 1978 Camp David accord signed between Israel and Egypt set the basic principle of an interim period toward Palestinian statehood. This gradualism, through the 1987 first Palestinian uprising (Intifada) and the 1988 PLO acceptance of the two-state solution led to the procedural breakthrough of the 1993 Declaration of Principles (DOP) between the PLO and Israel (Oslo I), the subsequent "Oslo Process" of 1993–99, and the 1995 interim agreement (Oslo II).

The Oslo process soon derailed as a result of a series of events: Rabin's assassination (1995), the first wave of suicide bombings in Israel (1996), and the election of the hardliner Prime Minister Netanyahu.[2] Both sides have continued to negotiate and sign "implementation accords" (the 1996 Hebron Agreement and the 1998 Wye-River Agreement) but pursued their strategic alternatives in tandem. Israel continued to construct settlements in the West Bank, while the Palestinians continued to build up their paramilitary capabilities.

It is inevitable to argue today that Oslo—despite being presented as "breakthrough negotiations" (Watkins and Rosegrant, 2001) or a "notably significant chapter in the evolution of Arab-Israeli relations" (Rabinovitch, 2004)—was merely a procedural interim measure that aimed—and failed—to set a nonviolent stage for a genuine conflict resolution process (see also Korobkin and Zasloff, 2005). That long-waited setting arrived in May 1999 with the election of Ehud Barak as Israel's prime minister. Hopes skyrocketed in the Middle East.

AUGUST 1999–MARCH 2000: SETTING THE STAGE AND DESTROYING TRUST

Palestinian expectations were high. They wanted to see an implementation of the Interim Agreement while negotiating the contested issues of permanent status: Palestinian statehood, removal of settlements, the future of Jerusalem, and resolving the refugee problem. Barak, however, had different plans.

Barak, as IDF chief of staff and as a member of Rabin's cabinet, opposed the logic of Oslo. He saw it as a process during which Israel would give up tangible assets while receiving in return a false sense of security, and he was determined to reframe it. His "peace strategy" was clear to him, but he hardly shared it with the Palestinians: instead of gradualism, he favored an accelerated process of negotiating what matters most: end of conflict. But, and this Barak shared only with Clinton, "my first priority is Syria, not the Palestinians" (Dennis Ross, 2005).

The Palestinians, Yasir Arafat and his team of experienced negotiators, sensed these vibes, and expressed their dissatisfaction with Barak's comments about fifteen months of intense negotiations on permanent status. They, unlike Barak, knew the meaning of ripeness and process design. Gilead Sher, Barak's chief negotiator, admitted that "if things were coordinated with Arafat, rather than being imposed from a position of an occupier to the oppressed, Prime Minister Barak could have gained much more. This was a repetitive pattern, which harmed the already fragile thin layer of trust between the two sides" (Sher, 2001:25).

Egyptian and American pressure, as well as the established practice of implementation agreements, led to the signature of the Sharem el-Sheikh Memorandum in September 1999. These negotiations addressed the tensions between the Palestinian demand to comply with Israel's commitments according to the Interim Agreement (mainly, transfer of more territory to Palestinian control, release of prisoners, and favorable economic measures) on one hand, and on the other, Israel's interest to change the practice of Oslo and set a framework for negotiating the permanent status issues.

The five weeks of negotiating the Sharem Memorandum were indicative of our future negotiations. The Israelis realized that it would be a challenge to follow who reports what to Arafat as each Palestinian negotiator had his own different way, style, and agenda in reporting back. The Palestinians faced Israel's strategy of negotiating details rather than principles. Moreover, high-level and detailed interventions of U.S. secretary of state Madeline Albright and her team, as well as senior Egyptian mediators, indicated that negotiations would focus on an arbitrary "scoring points" logic, rather than on trust and mutual respect.

Barak perceived the September 1999 Sharem Memorandum as a procedural victory, as he managed to impose his framework on the Palestinians (Swisher, 2004:57). For the Palestinians it was an irreversible collapse of their hopes for a respectful and evenly balanced process.[3] The following months strengthened this perceived gap as Barak — rejecting professional criticism — practically abandoned the Palestinian track and focused all his energy, between September 1999 and March 2000, on the Syrian track.

An active U.S. mediation, a failed Israeli-Syrian high-level summit, and an embarrassing meeting in Geneva between President Clinton and Syrian president Hafiz el-Assad, failed to bring an Israeli-Syrian peace into being. The Palestinians observed these developments with frustration and cynicism (Malley and Agha, 2001), calling the winter of 2000 the "pursuit of the other woman." This failure jeopardized Barak's "peace strategy" of "Syria first," and he turned to his alternative and ordered the IDF to unilaterally pull out from Lebanon.

APRIL 2000–JUNE 2000: THE STOCKHOLM TRACK; FORMULATING THE ISSUES

But Barak did not waste time. While official delegations were meeting, Barak explored back channels and sent, separately and in tandem, his confidants Ben Ami and Sher to meet discreetly with Abu Alla and with Abu Mazen's people. These tracks served as the genuine "pre-negotiation" phase, in which authorized representatives of both sides shared their visions and determined the boundaries of the conversation, but did not frame solutions, exchange concessions, or bargain over the details. In late April 2000 these efforts were combined into the Stockholm track. Two meetings, held in Jerusalem and Tel Aviv, indicated the potential of this direction, and the good services of the Scandinavian facilitators were used again. This time, it was Swedish prime minister Göran Persson who offered his country house, two hours south of Stockholm.

Before departing their teams to Sweden, Barak and Arafat met in Ramallah. Ben Ami recalls that "in this meeting, I realized not only the conceptual abyss between the two leaders regarding their concepts of peace, but also the tragic absence of any personal chemistry between the two" (Ben Ami, 2004). This observation reflected Arafat's frustration. Barak had neither the strategic will nor the political ability to transfer more lands to Palestinian control. This point was where their bargaining strategies collided: Arafat nurtured gradualism while Barak endorsed the "once and for all" strategy.

The discrete Stockholm track lasted only two rounds before it was called off. However, this track formulated some of the most important issues in dispute. The teams reached a conceptual breakthrough on the territorial issue during the first round. Both sides accepted the formula of 100 percent minus Israel's needs. Israel acknowledged the 1967 line as a reference for the territorial bargaining, and the Palestinians agreed to take into consideration Israel's security needs and the settlements constructed in the last three decades.

However, during the second round, already known to the public, the teams resorted to the "bazaar mindset" and became entrenched in a classic positional bargaining, where "Israel sought to annex as much territory as she can, not directly attached to her vital national interests while the Palestinians wanted to gain as much as they can while ignoring previously recognized Israeli needs" (personal observation).

On the issue of refugees the conceptual formula of differentiating between "the narrative" and practical arrangements was reached, but it was still far from addressing the nontangible and contested issues of acknowledgment, recognition, and responsibility. Security issues were discussed as well, but without any solid understandings. Jerusalem, however, was hardly discussed.

The Stockholm track was the first time where Israeli and Palestinian officials were engaged in a formulating attempt, and three fundamental process considerations surfaced, reflecting even deeper gaps between the two sides: the different process design each side had in mind, the different bargaining strategies, and the role of the internal political dynamics on both sides.

Regarding different process design, the Palestinians pushed for "concessions hunting" in each of the issues, while Israel adopted the "package" design where concessions are exchanged across issues (Sher, 2001:154, 156), and "nothing is agreed until everything is agreed."[4] These different designs originated from different experiences during the Oslo period. In past negotiations, Palestinians gained concessions through their alternative source of power, the "power of weak" (see below), while the Israelis feared an ongoing bargaining process that would reduce their "tangible bargain chips" (i.e., territories). The deep root of this difference was the belief on both sides that adopting these strategies would benefit them *more* than the other side, assisting them in gaining greater public support. A classic zero-sum mindset.

Different bargaining strategies were reflected in the tensions between a "top-down" approach and "bottom up." Backed with favorable interpretations of international law, the Palestinians preferred to adopt the top-down strategy, sought to agree on principles first, usually with a strong declaratory echo. For example, "Israel acknowledges the Right of Palestinian refugees to return to their original villages," and only then to follow with flexible applications "and the numbers to be allowed to enter Israel will be agreed upon."[5] Israel adopted the opposite, bottom-up strategy: agreeing on the implementable practices of issues first and only then negotiating their framing in a manner sellable to the public. For example, Israel would agree on Israeli early deterrence stations in Palestine in consideration of Palestinian bonded areas in Israeli seaports and only then frame this concessions exchange as "mutual sovereignty arrangements."

Adopting these opposing strategies was a result of the deep mistrust between the two sides, fertilized with experiences throughout the Oslo years. Israel feared that once they agreed on the principle, the Palestinians would not comply with its arrangements. The Palestinians, however, needed to get historic recognition for wrongdoings done by Israel and an acknowledgement of their equal standing before bargaining over what this recognition or acknowledgment entailed.

One episode during Camp David reflected these fundamental differences. When criticized by his own people for ignoring Arafat during the summit, Barak replied: "If I'll sit with him, he'll write in his little notebook whatever I say, and then he will turn it as Israeli in-principle agreement"; he later said: "Arafat had no appetite either for small talk or for serious discussion about matters of substance."[6]

During the second round of Stockholm talks the parties withdrew back to positional bargaining due to the publicity of the "secret" talks. On the Palestinian side, an exchange of accusations between Abu Mazen, who initiated the track, and Abu Alla, who was the senior negotiator in Stockholm, caused a setback. On the Israeli side Gilead Sher recalls that "the leak changed the rules of the game . . . but we decided to continue" (Sher, 2001). Nevertheless, the eruption of a round of violence on the ground and the political pressure brought an end to the Stockholm track.

The next month witnessed dramatic changes that would affect the Israeli-Palestinian process. Israel unilaterally and rapidly withdrew from Lebanon. The scenes of Hizbulla militants plundering IDF posts encouraged — in retrospect — the Palestinian strategic alternative of resorting to armed conflict. Sheikh Hassan Nasarallah, not Arafat, was now the modern Saladin. President Assad died in early June, and Barak became more determined to achieve something. He ordered his team to start moving toward a summit.

JUNE-JULY 2000: LEADING TO CAMP DAVID;
LACK OF "TACTICAL RIPENESS"

Backed by the U.S. president, Barak started to gear toward a summit. Intensive shuttles of the American peace team, including Secretary of State Albright, two rounds of negotiations at U.S. Air Force bases outside Washington, D.C., and intensive meetings in the region aimed at convincing the Americans, and the Palestinians, to accept the "summit strategy" Barak had in mind months earlier.

However, the Palestinians insisted on having more progress before convening. Akram Hanieh, the editor of the leading Palestinian daily and a close aide to Arafat, who participated in the summit, writes: "The Palestinian position was clear and candid. During his two meetings with the American officials, President Yaser Arafat said in effect, 'Conditions are not yet ripe for holding a summit. Nothing was achieved in the earlier Eilat talks, and no progress was made in the Stockholm channel either.' He added that several more weeks of intensive negotiations would be needed before being able to move toward convening a trilateral summit" (Hanieh, 2001).

In the process of preparing for the summit, and based on these negotiation rounds, a basic formula emerged: in consideration of a Palestinian agreement to a declaration of ending the conflict and an agreed-upon mechanism to bring finality to the refugees' claims, Israel would agree to the establishment of a Palestinian state in the West Bank and Gaza (based on the Stockholm formula), to divide Jerusalem into two capitals (Israeli and Palestinian), and to a settlement regarding the refugees that would not threaten its Jewish nature.

However, despite being internally framed by the Israeli team during this period, this formula was neither presented nor communicated as such to either the Palestinians or the favorable U.S. mediators. Instead, as Hanieh states: "President Clinton called again to say that Barak had 'new offers' but did not agree to holding any preparatory talks . . . the American code word for promoting the summit became the 'rabbits' that 'Barak the magician' was expected to pull out of his hat" (Hanieh, 2001).

Furthermore, this formula did not even serve to set the agenda and to frame the negotiations in Camp David. Instead, the summit left the most contested issue — the refugees — hardly negotiated in a constructive way during all the fourteen days, and focused mainly on Jerusalem. Agreeing to divide Jerusalem and to share control over the Temple Mount was the dramatic conceptual breakthrough Barak would offer. With his collapsing government, diminishing political support, and "all or nothing" mindset — he shared it with hardly anyone, believing that this concession would be the "magic word" to end this protractible conflict. Barak did not come to Camp David in order to entrench, but he underestimated the need to further prepare, and more importantly the Palestinian need to acknowledge their national narrative. Arafat came to Camp David as if it was his bunker in Beirut, convinced that the Palestinians already compromised their interests.

Was there a "tactical ripeness" to convene the summit? In retrospect, it is evident that the U.S. mediators failed to address the different needs of the parties at this point. Before going to a summit, Arafat needed legitimacy gained through additional and substantial Israeli concessions. Barak — for political reasons as well — had to keep all the "goodies" in his pocket. In an environment of little or no trust only a creative and manipulative mediation could have pulled both parties toward a constructive summit. Aaron Miller, an experienced member of the U.S. peace team since the mid-1980s, admits that "on the eve of the summit no atmosphere or environment was worse for a high-level meeting between Israelis and Palestinians" (Aaron Miller, 2005).

CAMP DAVID SUMMIT: THE JERUSALEM SUMMIT

On July 11, 2000, President Clinton opened the Camp David summit,[7] and from there, accounts compete in dramatizing the moment: "Outside the confines of the President's official retreat in the deep woods of Maryland's Catoctin Mountains, the world below held its breath" (Swisher, 2004:251); "the curtain was about to rise on a new act in the Palestinian-Israeli conflict" (Hanieh, 2001:76); "and we were standing in front of an historic event" (Sher, 2001:152).

Structuring a summit such as Camp David requires a combination of art and political wisdom. In an attempt to establish a relaxed atmosphere, the U.S. peace team laid down the rules of the game. Some of these were dictated by the nature of the place: there were to be no suits and ties, but casual clothing. It seems that the Americans assumed that the absence of formalities would break down barriers between the two sides, Hanieh (2001:77) noted. Moreover, two additional rules, imposed by the Americans, challenged the attempt to construct the necessary structure for this sensitive process.

First, the Americans limited the number of Israelis and Palestinians allowed on the mountain, which forced both Barak and Arafat to choose between professional staff and political figures who could have been instrumental in explaining whatever outcome was reached. It is true that a successful summit should have a certain number of individuals, but the deliberations regarding the identity of the participants and the actual guest list must be conducted in consultation with the negotiating parties and not by coercion.

Second, the media was shut out: "There was only one telephone for each delegation, and external calls were rarely transferred to delegation members. The only official source of information was an American spokesman, who held daily press conferences (at which nothing of importance was said) at a press center thirty minutes from Camp David. Most of what appeared in the Arab, Israeli, and international press had nothing at all to do with what was actually happening at the Camp" (Hanieh, 2001:78). Taking into consideration the complexity and sensitivity of issues discussed, the results might have been different, though not necessarily an agreement, if more professional support and daily direct media briefings had been offered to the leaders. From a Palestinian perspective, "the Americans did not seem to realize that the reality of the conflict was stronger than the unreal world they had created at Camp David" (Hanieh, 2001:78).

The second process challenge, beyond the rules of the game, was setting the agenda and the negotiating structures. The U.S. peace team followed the known pattern of working groups on each of the contested issues, hoping to bridge the gap on each topic. During the fourteen days of the summit, the U.S. peace team, including President Clinton, showed an impressive acquaintance with the negotiated details and factual background.[8] However, this negotiation strategy, in the unripe environment, encouraged — structurally — a positional bargaining within each of the groups.

Realizing this dynamic, the U.S. mediators changed and reshuffled working teams, meeting settings, and draft exchanges throughout the summit, in a manner that created an even greater sense of chaos. Sher noted that "the early stages of the process, where the parties presented their positions, mapped their interests . . . had no continuity which could have led to resolution. Structured, concrete and constructive beginnings faded away" (2001:168), and Dennis Ross admits that "when I write about it in my book, I describe my own unease . . . that every day we changed our posture. We went in with one strategy, and everyday when we faced opposition, we changed" (2005).

Moreover, despite the great respect the Palestinians had for President Clinton, as they saw him as a person "who could listen and understand" (Hanieh, 2001:78), the common perception among the participants was that "too often the Americans functioned in this process as Israel's lawyer" (Aaron Miller, 2005). This American attitude could be explained, in retrospect, by their belief that "leadership is important, because that essentially makes all the difference" (Indyk, 2005), and that "we had a leader [Barak] who was prepared to contemplate unprecedented concessions," and that "we felt the process had a promise, we never wanted to break it" (Dennis Ross, 2005). These fundamental process failures — rigid procedural rules, an unproductive working process, and a strong perception of bias, prevented the U.S. peace team from presenting, as early as the first days, a draft proposal that could have set a different direction to the negotiation process.

On the issues of substance there was little progress, except for the issue of Jerusalem. In the territorial negotiations, instead of exploring the ZOPA framed in Stockholm, Israel used transparent bargaining tactics. Barak was convinced that playing tough is the name of the game. "The Palestinians will compromise," he used to say (personal observation). The first week was spent in useless bargaining while Israel tried to persuade the Americans to squeeze territorial concessions from the Palestinians.

The refugee issue suffered a formulating deadlock caused by the conflicting negotiating strategies as described above. The Palestinians demanded a solution that would implement UN resolution 194, meaning an Israeli acknowledgment of the right of return, while Israel pursued the opposite approach of first agreeing on practical arrangements, without recognizing the right itself. At a certain moment, when Nabil Sha'ath, a Palestinian negotiator, indicated a number of refugees to be allowed to return to Israel, a remark which could have broken the deadlock, he was interrupted by Abu Mazen, who "didn't want to discuss figures" (Sher, 2001:216).

Indeed, the most significant breakthrough was on the issue of Jerusalem. Compared to the other issues, the preparatory work on Jerusalem was minimal,[9] as Barak feared leaks. Backed by his chief negotiators, Sher and Ben Ami, he believed that Jerusalem was the most difficult issue that would be "traded" for territory and security measures.

At Camp David, both Israelis and Americans believed that refugees and the end of conflict could come second to Jerusalem. This made Barak and Clinton push for a deal on Jerusalem, while Arafat was left in his passive role. "'They are not ready for peace. Didn't I tell you?' This is what President Yaser Arafat told his delegation . . . it was immediately clear that the Israeli delegation was not prepared to take the risks needed for a historic reconciliation that would end the conflict," recalls Hanieh (2001:79).

But even the significant breakthrough on Jerusalem was achieved through bargaining mode. Starting with the offer to transfer the outer Arab neighborhoods to Palestinian sovereignty and ending with Clinton's proposal to divide the Old City, the heart, between Israel and Palestine.

It was only during the night of July 16 that Israelis and Palestinians started to outline an initial package, which still lacked an overall breakthrough. During the next four days the initial package was further developed, but President Clinton's scheduled trip to the G8 meeting in Japan imposed a tactical deadline.

The Americans, including the president, shuttled between the two sides, losing patience and signaling a slight despair. Contacts made with Arab and Muslim leaders, too little and too late, yielded no result. In a decisive meeting with Clinton, Arafat said, "The Palestinian leader who will give up Jerusalem has not yet been born" (Hanieh, 2001:92). Albright replied, "This is the saddest day. Go and speak with the Israelis" (Sher, 2001:196). Clinton departed for Japan on July 20, while the secretary of state held the fort, but nothing happened during that time: the Palestinian and Israeli negotiators were virtually off duty (Hanieh, 2001:91).

Upon his return, Clinton was briefed by his senior staff and initiated intensive rounds of joint presentations by Israelis and Palestinians. On Monday, July 24, Clinton presented to Arafat three formulating options for Jerusalem: postponing an agreement for five years, Palestinian custodianship over the Temple Mount and special legal regime in the Old City, and division of the Old City between Israel and Palestine.

Hanieh recounts: "Clinton continued to pressure Arafat . . . and at one point he repeated that Arafat had not presented anything and that the Israelis had taken the initiative regarding Jerusalem. Arafat looked at the American president and asked, 'Do you want to attend my funeral? I will not relinquish Jerusalem and the holy places.' A long moment of silence followed, and the exchange resumed more quietly" (2001:97). On the Israeli side there was already a sense of conclusion (Sher, 2001:230). At 1:00 a.m. on July 25, 2000, Saeb Erikat, the chief Palestinian negotiator — while thanking the U.S. president for his efforts — reiterated the Palestinian reply: "President Arafat instructed me not to accept anything less than Palestinian sovereignty on all areas of Jerusalem occupied in 1967, and first and foremost the Haram al-Sharif" (Hanieh, 2001:98).

The Camp David summit reached its end, and the blame game resumed. In political terms, however, this was the first time ever that Israel officially engaged in bargaining over the sovereignty of Jerusalem with the Palestinians (Albin, 2005). The Israeli taboo of negotiating Jerusalem had been broken, and the Israeli-Palestinian peace process noted another conceptual breakthrough.

AUGUST 2000–JANUARY 2001: NEGOTIATING IN THE SHADOW OF BLOOD

The aftermath of Camp David posed a strategic question for the negotiators. While the political leadership was engaged with the public, Israeli and Palestinian negotiators had to decide whether to rely on the Americans to present a comprehensive draft or to continue direct negotiations (Sher, 2001:237). We chose the latter, while starting to develop strategic alternatives such as interim arrangements and unilateral steps.

Building on the design of the Stockholm track and the ideas, drafts, and maps exchanged in Camp David, Israeli and Palestinian negotiators held dozens of quiet meetings in Jerusalem during August 2000, trying to formulate a "yesable" package. Throughout September 2000 joint teams and American representatives were meeting regularly in Jerusalem. When winds of violence started to blow on the ground, Arafat and Barak met at Barak's residence, in the last attempt to mandate the negotiators to finalize a framework agreement. The last round of peaceful negotiations in the United States was blown away with the eruption of violence in the region. On September 30, 2000, with the outbreak of the second Intifada, the most exciting and productive chapter in Israeli-Palestinian peacemaking came to an end.

Strongly believing in the need to present a formulating draft, and juggling between the front stage of violence and the back stage of negotiations, both sides were engaged in finding a comprehensive deal. It was only in the shadow of blood when the parties inevitably turned away from positional bargaining to interest-based negotiations: "Let us talk about our and your needs. . . . [L]et us be 'solution driven' and not 'justice driven,'" argued Sher, while Ben Ami said, "You can not talk about homeland in percentages. . . . [W]e have to accommodate needs. Both ours and yours, in order to allow each side to face its constituencies" (Sher, 2001:350).

Finally, on December 23, President Clinton presented his peace proposal.[10] Two weeks later, while the ground was burning from violence, the two delegations met — without any U.S. mediators — in Taba, Egypt. Clinton's parameters were on the table, and genuine conversations about the last remaining issue of refugees were held. But at that point, Barak and his government had no public mandate to negotiate.

A month later, Ariel Sharon came to power, and conflict management, rather than conflict resolution, became the official policy of Israel.

ANALYSIS IN BRIEF

This book aims to go beyond intuitive or conventional explanations such as the insufficient will or inability of a party to build up a positive-sum game, or the cultural misunderstanding prevailing between the parties. Such conventional explanations are still offered by practitioners and scholars who adopt either an Israeli-sided perspective, such as "Arafat's leadership failure" (Morris and Barak, 2002); a Palestinian-sided perspective that "Barak's generous offer was neither an offer nor generous" (Malley and Agha, 2001); or limited observations of insufficient preparation; poor mediation (Aaron Miller, 2005); lack of ripeness; or psychological barriers.

The Israeli-Palestinian permanent status negotiations serve as a classic case study for introduction of the notion of negosystem.[11] The complexity of Israeli-Palestinian negotiations is apparent. It involves various stakeholders, it is rooted in religious and national ethos, and it failed to be resolved despite the unprecedented volume of human, political, and financial investments. "The Palestinians and Israelis, against all theory and common sense, rushed into a mad cycle of imposing losses on themselves, and incidentally on each other, oblivious to the gains they could produce together" (Zartman, 2004). Therefore, a wider perspective might be helpful: a "negosystem" perspective that captures the systemic nature of the negotiations and goes beyond the systematic ones.

Capturing the nature of the Israeli-Palestinian negosystem requires four distinct theoretical and operational levels of analysis: defining the boundaries of the negosystem, determining its right structure, articulating its preferred outcome, and designing a process that would lead the system toward it.

What are the boundaries of the negosystem? The boundaries are the level of detail at which the negosystem's elements are defined. For example, the U.S. team, including President Clinton, failed to recognize the importance of such external factors as Muslim backing on the Jerusalem issue. It was not until the sixth day of the summit when Clinton approached Egyptian president Mubarak and Moroccan king Hassan. The parties and the mediators failed to identify and address other elements such as the different negotiation patterns as mentioned above, or the importance of confronting the instruments used by the parties to derail the system: the Israeli settlement activities or the continued Palestinian armament. The fourth element of the negosystem, which was neither acknowledged nor addressed during the negotiations, was concepts, such as sense of fairness, equability, or justice. These elements inevitably determined the boundaries and the nature of the negosystem.

What is the basic structure of the negosystem? Structural analysis in international negotiation is a well-defined concept, and it argues that the parties do the best they can under the circumstances, but once the structure is determined it provides the ingredients for making or explaining the outcome (Zartman, 2002).

The notion of power is predominant in structural analysis, and recently it has been expanded to alternative sources of power (Zartman, 2002). The common perception of this conflict is that the power asymmetry favors Israel (Albin, 2005). It is our belief that while Israel benefits from the traditional sources of political, military, and economic power, the Palestinians have an equal power across the negotiation table. The power of the Palestinians originated from alternative sources such as the veto power, the power of the weak (Zartman and Rubin, 2000), and — more overtly — the power of the demographic alternative. Barak was determined to bring an end to the conflict due to the demographic trends indicating that if occupation did not end, in less than a decade Israel would be either non-Jewish or nondemocratic. Israel had no BATNA (Better Alternative To Negotiated Agreement), other than to reach an agreement.[12] Zartman and Rubin (2000) conclude that perceived asymmetry is the more productive condition for negotiation, whereas a perception of equality actually interferes with efficient processes, and, more importantly, could convince scholars to define the basic structure of the Israeli-Palestinian negosystem as equal and unstable.

What is the preferred outcome of this negosystem? Unlike other social systems, a negosystem must have a preferred outcome or a peaceful equilibrium. Determining the preferred outcome is an ongoing assessment, based on intractability analysis and ripeness theory and its derivatives. Bar-Siman-Tov et al. (2005) argue that it is hard to draw a clear distinction between absence of a solution and absence of ripeness, and suggests that an irresolvable conflict, by definition, cannot ever reach ripeness.

Defining whether a conflict is resolvable or not requires answering two questions: What are the root causes of the conflict, and do the relevant stakeholders (primary parties or third party) want to and are they able to address them? Answering these questions in the context of the Israeli-Palestinian conflict indicates that it would be resolved only if the following four challenges would be met: an agreement would constitute a viable, independent and stable Palestinian state; it would grant the internationally recognized rights of the Palestinian people; it would assure the Palestinian people that justice has been done; and it would secure the existence of a Jewish and democratic State of Israel.

While Barak embarked on this process he believed that it was a resolvable conflict, therefore he had only one preferred outcome: a framework agreement. The Palestinian leadership, on the other hand, came to regard permanent status negotiations as an opportunity to be survived rather than seized.[13] Both sides had different outcomes in mind. Both leaders were ripe, but for different outcomes of this negosystem. Despite the fact that a comprehensive ripeness analysis goes beyond the scope of this chapter, we would mention that ripeness analysis served not only as a reflection tool but also as a policy-planning instrument in the weeks leading to Camp David.[14]

How can one plan, design, and execute a successful negotiation process? When the negosystem is clearly defined, its structure is understood by stakeholders, and its preferred outcome is shared by the parties, the challenge becomes how to plan and design a process that will lead the negosystem to its preferred, agreed, outcome. While Dupont and Faure (2002) articulate elements of the negotiation process and argue that theoreticians and practitioners are still trying to determine the common elements of negotiation process, the Camp David episode provides four clear lessons for process design, which cross all six types of processes mentioned by Dupont and Faure (2002): strategic approach, learning, decision-making, psychological, adjustment, and reactive processes.

Leadership Support

The Israeli-Palestinian process did not provide sufficient support for the leaders to make the necessary decisions. Arafat's and Barak's leadership styles were known within their environment, as well as the challenges embodied in the two-level game (Putnam 1988) they had to play. The isolation of Arafat in Camp David, the freedom given to Barak not to comply with the Interim Agreement commitment, the dynamic of Israeli propositions and Palestinian rejections, and the lack of international support built during the negotiations are some examples of actions that could have been taken by local (Israelis and Palestinians) and international actors in order to provide this support.

Blocking Strategic Alternatives

The Oslo process, as well as Camp David, provided incentives for both sides to develop, and actually resort to, their strategic alternatives. For both sides there were worse ways to inflict pain on the other side. Israel through settlement expansion, roadblocks, and closure, and the Palestinians through suicide terror. A well-designed process recognizes these strategic alternatives and replaces them — in a timely fashion — with tactical alternatives such as coordinated unilateralism, chain of interim agreements, and so forth.

Empowered and Manipulative Mediation

Some of the process flaws, such as trying to present a bipartisan stand while having rooted biases, losing the capability to influence and manipulate the sides, and not having a coherent mediation strategy, can be attributed to the American mediation. This lesson is much too important to be left as an off-hand remark, and it should serve for in-depth academic research. Members of the U.S. peace team, perhaps the most knowledgeable and committed mediators in the recent history of international mediation, are using the Camp David situation as an example of lessons learned as they comment on, write about, and teach others how to better mediate conflicts.

Summits Strategy

As summits are a common tool in conflict-resolution processes, the Camp David episode, as briefly described above, ought to be comprehensively taught from various process approaches in order to develop a manual for strategizing a summit. Reference will be made to issues such as tactical ripeness, preferred outcome, rules of the game, media policy, personal dynamics, professional support, international backing, tactical fallbacks, mediation modes, division of labor, managing failures, and so forth.

These four levels — detailed understanding of the system's elements, accurate definition of the system's structure, realistic agreed outcome, and a well-designed process — constitute an operational systemic view. The Camp David process did not fail due to one actor, leader, or mediator. It failed to reach an agreement, while achieving significant breakthrough, because it lacked a systemic view from those involved and leading it.

CONCLUDING REMARK

It is a challenge to share professional observations from an intensive and dramatic process you were personally part of. The aim of this chapter was to tell, in brief, the story of the Israeli-Palestinian permanent status negotiations conducted between May 1999 and January 2001 and to shed some light on negotiation elements that are less acknowledged in the "what went wrong" literature written since.

The Israeli-Palestinian permanent status negotiations are incomplete negotiations, rather than failed. The Stockholm track (May–June 2000) formulated the territorial conflict, the Camp David summit (July 2000) formulated Jerusalem, and the Clinton parameters (December 2000) drew the framework for a two-state solution. Still open are the issues of refugees and answers for the deep concepts of justice and mutual recognition. It is my hope that this chapter and the points raised, as well as this whole book, would encourage academics, scholars, negotiators, mediators, and policy professionals to systemically and systematically study and research these negotiations and assist in successfully applying the lessons in future negotiations. The Israeli and the Palestinian people deserve it.

NOTES

Moty Cristal was the deputy head of the Negotiation Management Center at the Israeli Prime Minister Office between 1999 and 2001.

The list of resources, beyond the writer's personal involvement in these negotiations, includes Israeli-Palestinian peace memoirs of Gilead Sher; Shlomo Ben Ami;
Yossi Beilin; Dennis Ross; Bill Clinton; Akram Hanieh; the *New York Review of Books*
articles exchange between Hussein Agha and Robb Malley on one hand, and Benni
Morris and Ehud Barak on the other; Ron Pundik; Clayton Swisher; the comprehensive
Charles Enderlin "shattered dreams" account; and personal notes on what went wrong
in Camp David 2000 compiled by the author at Tel Aviv University since June 2004;
as well as more than forty interviews conducted with Israeli negotiators since 2001. A
comprehensive compilation of articles presenting the Palestinian argument could be
found at http://www.palestinemonitor.org/.

1. See Zartman and Berman's (1982) integrative model of diagnostic phase (pre-
negotiation), formulating phase, and detailed negotiations.

2. For a detailed analysis of the Oslo negotiations, see the special volume of
International Negotiation Journal 2 (2) (1997).

3. For more on process and justice, see Albin, 2001.

4. However, an Israeli scholar suggests that Arafat was willing to exchange sover-
eignty over Temple Mount with giving up the actual implementation of the Right of
Return (Rubinstein, 2003). Support for this school of thought can be found in Akram
Hanieh (2001) as well.

5. Dennis Ross (2005) generalized it as Arab strategy: "They would all say: 'Accept
my principle and we'll see what we can negotiate.'"

6. Malley and Agha (2001); conversation with Barak, February 2003.

7. For a detailed day-by-day account of developments, see Gilead Sher's (2001) and
Dennis Ross's (2005) memoirs.

8. Sher (2001), Ben Ami (2004), as well as Hanieh (2001) describe with appreciation
the president's level of detailed information about Jerusalem.

9. When professional support was needed at Camp David, two Israeli experts were
allowed to join the negotiation teams.

10. For the complete document see http://www.fmep.org/documents/clinton
_parameters12-23-00.html.

11. The Negosystem model has been developed by the author for his PhD thesis at
the Department of International Relations at the London School of Economics and
Political Science. A "negosystem" comprises five elements whose changed interrelations
over time define and create the negosystem: actors/agents/stakeholders, negotiation
patterns (positional bargaining, from principles to details, etc.), instruments (siege, belligerent activities, international law, etc.), concepts (power, justice, fairness, sociopsy-
chological process, etc.), and the linkages among these four groups.

12. As indicated above, upon returning from Camp David, Israel started to explore unilateral alternatives.

13. As indicated by one of the Palestinian lawyers who took part in the negotiations (Dajani, 2005).

14. A memo prepared within Barak's office in June 2000 analyzed the absence of ripeness and indicated that the forthcoming summit would yield no agreement unless a short period of violence would create a perception of a mutually detrimental stalemate.

Nuclear Negotiations

Iran, the EU (and the United States)

ANTHONY WANIS-ST. JOHN

The international deadlock over Iran's nuclear program was not always characterized by coercion, threats, and unilateral action. During one period, there were direct negotiations for the purpose of achieving international oversight of the nuclear program and strengthening safeguards against nuclear weapons proliferation. Ambitious negotiations between Iran and the European Union (first led by France, Germany, and the United Kingdom and later joined by the high commissioner of the European Union for the Common Foreign and Security Policy [the E3/EU]) beginning in 2003 ultimately failed to persuade Iran to cancel plans to develop its own nuclear fuel cycle in exchange for European economic incentives and other cooperation.[1] The negotiations did, however, succeed in obtaining unprecedented Iranian cooperation with the International Atomic Energy Agency (IAEA), and even a temporary suspension of Iran's early work on enriching uranium for use as nuclear reactor fuel. The initial negotiations were supposed to pave the way to a coveted long-term comprehensive agreement between the EU and Iran. A long-term solution to the confrontation between Iran and the West on its nuclear program continues to elude the international community as of this writing.

The E3/EU-Iran negotiations have to date failed for what I argue are three principal and interrelated reasons. The first reason derives from social-psychological perspectives on negotiation: specifically, challenges in the perceptual domains regarding how negotiators confront uncertainty and ambiguity in the construal of offers and choices at the negotiation table. Put simply, as the case study will demonstrate, in these negotiations very *ambiguous* EU offers were made in anticipation of very *unambiguous* Iranian concessions. In the best of circumstances for international negotiation, this would have been problematic. However, in the context of decades of mutual international hostility, these difficulties posed more serious challenges to negotiated success. The problem manifests with each party believing its offers and positions to be clear, reasonable, and potentially acceptable by the other parties. (See Christer Jönsson's chapter in this volume, "Psychological Causes of Incomplete Negotiations," for a full discussion of such obstacles.)

The second and third principal reasons come from the field of negotiation analysis and concern the substance and process of the negotiation. In my co-authored chapter with the late Christophe Dupont elsewhere in this volume ("Structural Dimensions of Failure in Negotiation"), we look in depth at how the dynamics of parties, issues, and power distribution contribute to negotiation failure and interact with one another. In this chapter, the "issue" dimension is particularly salient in the failure to date to achieve any kind of permanent, negotiated resolution of the conflict. As the discussion of the case will demonstrate in detail, the zone of possible agreement (ZOPA), described by Sebenius as "the set of possible agreements that are better for each potential party than the noncooperative alternatives to agreement" (1992:333), was always so narrow as to make agreement impossible.

With regard to the process dimension, the EU negotiations with Iran can be described as incrementalist in nature. This means in both theory and practice that the negotiation process relies on a series of ever-more specific agreements leading to a final agreement. Early agreements are reached precisely because they do not address the issues in conflict. Rather, they begin with agreement on a "formula," or declarations of principles and gradually proceed to steps requiring positive implementation. Incrementalism is recommended as a negotiation process when parties can successfully build on early agreements, build confidence in each other and in the process, and arrive finally at the implementation of an agreement on the core issues that brought them into conflict.

With the combined difficulties of offer construal and the incrementalist approach, it can be argued that the ZOPA disappeared altogether.

At the heart of the conflict is Iran's strategy of attaining self-sufficiency regarding the production of nuclear fuel used to generate electricity from nuclear power plants. The United States and its allies argue that Iran's civil nuclear program can facilitate the initiation of a covert nuclear weapons program and thus oppose Iran's enrichment of uranium. In this chapter we look at the negotiations between the parties from an analytical standpoint, rather than a polemic one. The negotiations held early promise and proceeded from confidence-building measures to discussion of more comprehensive proposals. Despite early optimism, however, as of this writing, the process has decayed from problem-solving negotiation into confrontation and coercion through the progressive imposition of four UN Security Council–imposed sanctions on Iran.

Data on the negotiations comes from primary source documents and selected secondary sources. A more detailed analysis must await the emergence of a robust record of these negotiations, which — it may be hoped — will at least have laid the painful groundwork for an eventual agreement.

Deterrence and nonproliferation theories are not adequate to the task of explaining either the behavior of Iran in its pursuit of nuclear self-sufficiency, nor of the West in wavering between cooperation and confrontation, sometimes simultaneously. Evolutions of international relations (IR) theory, including the epistemic community focus (Adler and Haas, 1992), still leave us posing such fundamental questions as why Iran and the West are unable to move on from confrontation and stalemate, and sometimes give the impression that policy simply emerges without interactivity — such as negotiation — among the players. To begin with, Iran is not a clear case of proliferation; as of the publication of this article, there is no evidence of an active Iranian nuclear weapons program. A U.S. National Intelligence Council assessment concluded that Iran abandoned its weapons program in 2003 (NIC, 2007).[2] The multifaceted approach to Iran has, in recent years, encompassed blunt coercion, cooperative bargaining, and no small amount of incoherence from Western states and their allies. Contrasted with U.S. engagement with North Korea, the U.S. diplomatic *disengagement* from Iran is remarkable, since Iran does not yet have a nuclear weapon and has been disclaiming intentions to pursue weaponization. Multilateral diplomatic engagement with Iran on the nuclear issue has progressively given way to coercive diplomacy. As the parties abandoned the negotiations, each has resorted to self-help; the Iranian regime continues to pursue enrichment — ostensibly for civil power only — while the West seeks to hasten the Iranian regime's demise while attempting to delay Iran's acquisition of the technical capability to weaponize its nuclear program.

Certainly, a nuclear technological imperative helps explain part of the Iranian motivation to achieve nuclear self-sufficiency. But the Iranian regime also has deep internal divisions, including a popular political opposition that claimed to have been cheated out of an electoral victory in June 2009, all supplemented by Iran's geopolitical interests in Lebanon, Iraq, Afghanistan, and Palestine/Israel. Deterrence theorists often point to regime survival as a motive for the proliferation of nuclear weapons. In Iran, regime survival may be enhanced by a *civil* nuclear program, but the pursuit of a nuclear weapons program is far more problematic, and its impact on national security and foreign policy objectives is by no means straightforward. On the one hand, the mere suspicion that a nuclear weapons program is intended — in the absence of hard intelligence of a program — regularly invites implicit and overt threats of attack. The cases of South Africa, Ukraine, and most recently, Libya (see below), seem to offer hope that nuclear weapons are not always a desirable strategic asset and that decision makers can and do choose nonproliferation under certain circumstances (see Jentleson and Whytock, 2005/6, for a discussion of the Libya case). On the other hand, Iran's geopolitical situation makes the possession of nuclear weapons potentially attractive, especially to regime hardliners, who hope it would serve as a strategic deterrent against Israel and the United States, as well as Arab states opposed to the Shiite orientation of the regime. Additionally, the cases of Pakistan, India, and North Korea may be interpreted by some political factions in Iran as evidence that if a state can decisively and quickly attain nuclear weapons, then deterrence is deemed to have failed and gives way to containment strategies at worst (Pakistan), accommodation (India), or an ineffective and incoherent diplomatic dance that mixes cooptation and coercion (North Korea). In the theoretical domain, both neoliberal and neorealist lenses on the deterrence and nonproliferation question overlook almost entirely the fluid dynamics of bargaining, relying instead on broad-stroke analyses of cooperation versus defection and positing competing motivations for "acquiring the bomb." Classic and newer IR theories have focused, in turn, on systems, state, domestic politics, bureaucracies, international institutions, and the psyche of individual decision makers and how these determine the actions and outcomes of international politics (see Ogilvie-White, 1996, for a robust critique of the limitations of IR theory regarding nuclear proliferation).

In this article, negotiation theory is presented as a more accurate lens through which to see both the possibilities and limitations of bargaining over nonproliferation issues (see Sebenius, 1992, for an early comparison of negotiation analysis and IR theory as explanations for international coopera-tion). The analyst and the practitioner are on more solid ground when they understand the complex layers of motivations, multiple factions, contradic-tory and changing motivations, and priorities of the parties and understand that the game of international engagement can be changed by the parties themselves and the actions they take, in particular their negotiations with each other — outcomes are not predetermined by either unit-level or systemic dynamics.

THE CONTEXT OF THE E3/EU-IRAN NEGOTIATIONS: THE NPT AND IAEA REGIME

Iran, like nearly all other states, is a party to the nuclear Nonproliferation Treaty (NPT) that explicitly guarantees the "inalienable right" to peaceful nu-clear energy (Art. IV). This "right," for "non-nuclear weapons states," is con-tingent upon the renunciation of any possible quest to obtain nuclear weapons and become one of the "nuclear weapons states" (Art. II). The NPT is, at least on paper, a two-edged sword: it also commits the nuclear weapons states to pursue nuclear disarmament (Art. VI) and to refrain from transferring nuclear weapons or weapons technology to the "non-nuclear weapons states" (Art. I).[3] NPT signatories also enter into separate agreements with the IAEA, known as "safeguard agreements" and voluntary "additional protocols" under which they commit to put their nuclear facilities and materials under IAEA supervision to prevent the "diversion of nuclear energy from peaceful uses to nuclear weap-ons or other nuclear explosive devices" (IAEA, 1974).

In the post–Cold War period, the challenges to the NPT regime have grown: ostensible nuclear weapons states such as Israel have not signed the treaty, and others such as North Korea have withdrawn after developing their own nuclear arsenal. Pakistan and India have recently declared themselves to be nuclear weapons states. Libya has renounced its quest for such weapons, while South Africa and Ukraine have given up the ones they had developed or inherited, respectively. Nuclear weapons states have succeeded at keeping WMD-related discourse focused on the nonproliferation side of the equation while avoiding the disarmament side.

IRAN, THE EU, AND THE UNITED STATES: CONFLICT LEGACY
OVERSHADOWS SHARED INTERESTS

The United States has had no diplomatic relations with Iran since April 1980, as a result of the Iranian Revolution and the U.S. Embassy hostage crisis of 1979. The United States wants Iran to abandon its quest for a self-sufficient nuclear energy program because of concerns that Iran would either enrich uranium to weapons-grade levels or divert for weapons use the plutonium that civilian reactors yield as a by-product of nuclear fission. But without any formal channels of communication, the United States is constrained in its ability to influence Iran. Clear policy direction from Washington regarding Iran has been elusive, with hard-liners of various tendencies and pragmatists vying for influence. Iran, for its part, has sent out mixed signals to the international community, defending its right to civil nuclear power and energy self-sufficiency, while pursuing clandestine nuclear research programs over previous decades and taking actions that arouse suspicion of military nuclear intentions and programs.

Iran conveys a sense of historic grievance that contextualizes the current conflict, yet it is often overlooked by pundits, journalists, and analysts. Iranian communications to the IAEA, when noting Iran's support for nonproliferation, cite the brutal eight-year war with Iraq in the 1980s, and note that Saddam Hussein's regime used chemical weapons against Iran with tacit or overt U.S. approval. The Iranians constantly remind the international community too of having suffered a U.S.-backed coup in 1953 that brought the twenty-six-year regime of the shah to power. They also mention additional grievances: Iran's pre-Revolution investments in U.S. and European nuclear fuel contracts and consortia, from which they have to date allegedly received neither refunds nor fuel, and the July 1988 fatal shooting down of an Iranian civilian airliner by the USS missile cruiser *Vincennes*, and other events (Government of Iran, 2006b, 2006d).

In the wake of the U.S.-led war in Afghanistan to defeat the Taliban regime there, Iraq, Iran, and North Korea were described as the "Axis of Evil" by President George W. Bush in his January 2002 State of the Union Address, despite Iranian support for the post-9/11 war on terror. The language used mirrors the rhetoric used by Iranian elites who call the United States the "Great Satan." The Bush speech heralded the eventual U.S.-led war against Iraq, based — at least in part — on the alleged Iraqi quest to acquire weapons of mass destruction (WMD), including nuclear weapons. The lack of evidence

for any Iraqi WMD program has not prevented the United States from looking at Iran through a similar lens. Sandwiched between two volatile countries,
Iraq and Afghanistan, both of which have experienced violent internal conflict, Iran found itself contemplating U.S.-led coalition forces on its eastern
and western borders. It is no secret that Iran seeks an active role in sectarian politics within Iraq, supporting Shiite political and religious figures and
movements.

Shared interests between the United States, its allies, and Iran include the
necessity of countering Sunni-based al-Qaeda and related jihadist movements,
stability in war-torn Iraq and Afghanistan, and, not to be overlooked, access
to Iran's oil market. There have been brief attempts at informal consultation
between the United States and Iran in various forums, including an informal
group of countries that convened to discuss Afghanistan issues: the Group of
"6+2" — the six countries surrounding Afghanistan, plus the United States and
Russia (Muir, 2003). Such informal consultations have not grown into stronger
bilateral engagement.

Not all the world's players see Iran in the same light. Iranian policy makers
consider the "acquiring, development and use of nuclear weapons inhuman,
immoral, illegal and against its very basic principles. They have no place in
Iran's defence doctrine. They do not add to Iran's security nor do they help rid
the Middle East of weapons of mass destruction" (Government of Iran 2003,
also see the Tehran Declaration, IAEA, 2003e). The EU, as a multilateral entity
and as member states within it, has been listening to such Iranian declarations,
which have not been persuasive to the United States.

EU DIPLOMACY AND THE TEHRAN DECLARATION

In marked contrast with U.S. foreign policy, EU diplomacy recognized that "it
is very much in the EU's interest, as part of a foreign policy strategy for conflict prevention, that Iran should become a factor for stability in the region"
(EU, 2001). The EU is Iran's top commercial trading partner (with much of
that trade in the form of Iranian exports of oil to the EU), and the EU desires
positive public diplomacy with Arab and Islamic countries. The EU has also
transparently expressed its concern for the human rights situation in Iran and
expressed concern for the use of Iranian territory as a trans-shipment point in
the Afghanistan drug trade to the EU, and openly sought a constructive role
for Iran in resolving the Palestinian-Israeli conflict and the Israel-Hizbulla/

Lebanon conflict (EU, 2001). In pursuit of their complementary interests, the EU and Iran had launched negotiations over several issues of mutual concern, all under the banner of improving EU-Iran ties, by the end of 2001 (EU and EC, 2002).

By March 2003, a U.S./UK-led coalition had invaded Iraq and overthrown the government of Saddam Hussein, beginning a long military occupation and counterinsurgency campaign. The Iraq war brought the United States into an increasingly intimate hostility with Iran, and from early 2007, forces from the United States and its allies were targeting Iranian interests, diplomats, and agents in Iraq, while openly accusing Iran of arming Iraqi Shiite militias with armor-piercing shells. The drawdown of U.S. combat troops in Iraq in the summer of 2010 did not yet herald the onset of political stability or sectarian peace there, which invites an ongoing Iranian influence on Iraq's internal affairs.

At the beginning of the U.S. occupation of Iraq, Iran is reported to have sent out a feeler to the United States using the Swiss government as a "back channel," offering to accommodate U.S. concerns on proliferation and to coordinate with the United States on Middle East peace and Iraq, in exchange for security assurances and reestablishment of diplomatic relations. Washington appears to have been unable to craft a coherent policy response. (On the Iranian offer, see Samore, 2004; on back-channel negotiations generally, see Wanis-St. John, 2006 and 2011.) In the absence of U.S. leadership, European leaders began to assert themselves as Iranian uranium enrichment plans became operational.

In mid-2003, the Europeans explicitly requested of Iran that it not introduce nuclear material into its pilot uranium enrichment plant and went before the IAEA with this demand when it appeared that Iran would not comply.[4] The director general of the IAEA, Dr. Mohammed el-Baradei, in his June 2003 report to the IAEA Board of Governors, noted that Iran had "failed to meet its obligations under its Safeguards Agreement under the NPT" with particular regard to its acquisition of uranium and information on the enrichment, processing, and storage of its nuclear materials (IAEA, 2003a). In his August 26, 2003, report to the IAEA Board of Governors, the director general revealed that Iran had just disclosed the existence of an undeclared uranium enrichment program dating back to 1985 (IAEA, 2003b). This disclosure was to cast its shadow on the entire record of multilateral engagement with Iran, diminishing rather than building trust in subsequent Iranian disclosures. The United States meanwhile sought to use the IAEA as a forum to pressure Iran. At its September 2003 meeting, the IAEA Board of Governors issued a resolution that affirmed NPT member states' rights to develop peaceful atomic energy, but also issued stern warnings to Iran to provide more cooperation and transparency about its past and ongoing nuclear activities (IAEA, 2003d). The resolution stopped short of referring the matter to the UN Security Council, as the United States wished. Nor did the IAEA issue an "immediate finding of non-compliance by Iran with its safeguards violations," as the United States believed was justified (Government of the U.S. 2003).

Quiet European diplomacy proceeded in parallel with the IAEA process, however. Jack Straw, Domenique Villepin, and Joschka Fischer, the foreign ministers of the UK, France, and Germany respectively, were "engaged in a secretive effort to convince Iran to sign" the Additional Protocol to the NPT, and thus de-escalate the brewing crisis over the onset of enrichment (BBC, 2003b). They went public with their negotiations and held a summit with Iranian President Mohammad Khatami in late October 2003 in Tehran. Thus the "E3," the UK, France, and Germany — the three European powers taking the lead in negotiations with Iran — had emerged as a diplomatic coalition that could act in a quasi-unified way regarding negotiations with Iran.

On October 21, 2003, their negotiations began yielding positive results. The E3 issued what became known as the "Tehran Declaration." It was not a signed agreement between the E3 and Iran, but rather a joint statement by the E3 Foreign Ministers at the end of their mission to Iran, summarizing the understandings reached. Most critically at that moment, the E3 had persuaded Iran "voluntarily to suspend all uranium enrichment and reprocessing activities as defined by the IAEA" (IAEA, 2003e) by persistent, secret as well as open negotiations. Curiously, the IAEA, already deeply involved in its own negotiations with Iran to gain more information about Iran's nuclear research program, and attempting to negotiate access for its inspectors, barely mentioned the Tehran Declaration in a footnote on the fourth page of the Director General's Report to the Board of Governors of November 26, 2003 (IAEA, 2003c). This momentous negotiated de-escalation of the crisis needed to be transformed into a formal permanent agreement.

In exchange for Iran's substantive concession to voluntarily suspend enrichment and reprocessing of uranium, the European negotiators made ambiguous commitments to help Iran obtain "easier access to modern technology and supplies in a range of areas" (IAEA, 2003d). The Tehran Declaration also paved the way for further, more intense negotiations between the parties. The

FIGURE 1. Ambassador Ali Salehi of Iran and IAEA Director General Dr. Mohammed El-Baradei sign an additional protocol to Iran's NPT safeguards agreement (IAEA Vienna, December 18, 2003). Dean Calma/IAEA.

political purpose of such moves was to build the confidence in the international community that Iran was serious about its intention to develop nuclear energy for civilian uses only. Iran also committed itself to sign an "Additional Protocol" to its existing IAEA Safeguards Agreement, which could facilitate the discovery and monitoring of any "undeclared" nuclear activities that could be weapons-related. In this case, the Additional Protocol permitted the IAEA to begin more intrusive inspections of Iran's nuclear facilities, which became more salient after allegations of a longstanding clandestine nuclear program in Iran began coming to light in 2002. Despite the Tehran Declaration, Iran continued to work on its gas centrifuge program, one of the methods used to "enrich" uranium so that it can be used as a nuclear reactor fuel.

On December 18, 2003, Iran signed the Additional Protocol (figure 1). During early 2004, Iran affirmed that it was extending the scope of its suspensions of nuclear enrichment activities and applying them to all of its facilities. Iran was becoming more transparent about its capabilities and intentions through negotiation and inspections. Iran acknowledged to the IAEA that it had previously failed to declare that it had obtained designs for more advanced uranium enrichment equipment (known as "P-2" centrifuges). IAEA inspectors had, in September 2003, discovered that Iran had experimented with irradiating the metal bismuth (which itself is not a proliferation concern, but which can be used to produce polonium-210, a radioactive isotope used in civilian applications as well as some nuclear weapon designs, according to the IAEA (2004a). Allegations surfaced that Iran had obtained unsolicited information on the assembly of a nuclear weapon from Pakistan's notorious "A. Q." (Abdul Qadeer) Khan, who had spearheaded his country's nuclear weapons program.

Iran steadily maintained that Khan's information was unsolicited and that nuclear weapons had no place in Iran's national security doctrine. Iran was actively cooperating with the IAEA in its intensified inspections, verification, and sealing activities, but new questions about the past and present of Iran's nuclear program continued to arise, through 2004, eroding some of the good will the E3 and Iran had built up with the Tehran Declaration.

THE PARIS AGREEMENT

Negotiations between the Europeans and Iran continued the year after the Tehran Declaration, and the negotiators met for at least seven negotiation sessions in September and November 2003, and in February, March, June, September, and November 2004. Perhaps to allay EU member states' fears that the E3 were monopolizing European foreign policy and sidestepping formal European policy-making procedures, and perhaps also to gain more credibility and multilateral clout as official representatives of the entire EU community, the E3 were joined in 2004 by the High Representative of the European Union, Javier Solana. Thus the troika became a quartet of sorts and came to be known as the E3/EU. While the added diplomatic muscle did not ensure that negotiations with Iran would be any easier, it would, in theory, permit the European negotiators to make credible commitments and bind the EU when the time came to provide technical assistance, trade agreements, humanitarian assistance, or other quid pro quo.

According to the reports of the director general of the IAEA, the E3/EU negotiators sought to commit Iran to a more comprehensive voluntary suspension of enrichment activities, including a cessation of work on the construction of uranium-enrichment centrifuges (IAEA, 2004b). According to Iranian perspectives on the negotiations, the European negotiators' demands escalated from the simple voluntary suspension of enrichment activities to encompass a whole range of further concessions, including the "testing, assembling of the machines, manufacturing of centrifuge components, production of UF6 [uranium hexafluoride gas, which is fed into centrifuges for enrichment], and finally to suspend complete uranium conversion at UCF [Iran's Uranium Conversion Facility], and not to conduct R&D" (Government of Iran 2005b). Iran threatened to unilaterally reverse its voluntary additional measures of suspension in June 2004. Despite tensions, these negotiations indeed resulted in a more formal framework agreement between the E3/EU and Iran: the "Paris Agreement" of November 15, 2004 (IAEA, 2004a).

NEGOTIATIONS TOWARD A LONG-TERM AGREEMENT

In the Paris Agreement, Iran conceded to yet more vigorous IAEA verification of its suspended research and development activities. But the suspension and the Paris Agreement itself were but the framework within which Iran and the E3/EU were supposed to negotiate *another separate agreement* on long-term arrangements regarding Iran's nuclear program:

> Iran has decided, on a voluntary basis, to continue and extend its *suspension to include all enrichment related and reprocessing activities*, and specifically: . . . the assembly, installation, testing or operation of gas centrifuges. . . plutonium separation . . . and . . . uranium conversion. The IAEA will be notified of this suspension and invited to verify and monitor it. . . . The *suspension will be sustained while negotiations proceed* on a mutually acceptable agreement on long-term arrangements. (IAEA, 2004a, emphasis added)

An EU-Iran negotiation steering committee was set up to oversee the negotiations, as well as subsidiary working groups that were to actually attempt to resolve the interrelated nuclear, economic, and security issues. And the suspensions, once they were verified by the IAEA, were to trigger renewed negotiations on a separate EU-Iran Trade and Cooperation Agreement. The E3/EU specifically committed itself to actively "support the opening of Iranian accession negotiations at the WTO." The Paris Agreement received very mixed reviews in the Iranian press, which strongly asserted the Iranian national right to a peaceful energy program under the NPT, even if it resulted in referral to the UN Security Council (BBC, 2004). The U.S. secretary of state expressed support for the Paris Agreement and aligned the United States with the EU in its negotiation stance with her statement of March 11, 2005, noting that the

United States would drop its standing objection to Iran's bid for WTO membership and support the licensing of spare parts for civilian aircraft by the EU to Iran (U.S. Department of State, 2005). This tactical alignment should have strengthened the clarity of EU negotiation positions, had it been properly leveraged.

Despite numerous crisis moments, the incremental negotiation process appeared to be working as it should: early agreement on principles yielding to operational implementation on the core issues of the dispute. Additionally, the EU was achieving some alignment of its negotiation position with the most important "absent" party — the United States.

The next phase of E3/EU-Iran negotiations appears to have started with an Iranian framework proposal, followed up by an E3/EU counterproposal. The Iranian proposal was made at the end of March 2005, and it included technical limitations on its enrichment program in order to eliminate nuclear proliferation possibilities; legislative and regulatory measures to meet the E3/EU and IAEA interests; and enhanced monitoring (Government of Iran 2005a). The proposal itself, incorporated in a document entitled "General Framework for Objective Guarantees, Firm Guarantees, and Firm Commitments," is brief but structured in two columns that propose simultaneous actions by both the E3/EU in the right column and Iran on the left, with milestones including the establishment of a joint counterterrorism task force, guarantees that uranium would only be enriched at the non–weapons grade "low" level and immediately converted to fuel rods for civilian reactors, and that the E3/EU countries would themselves bid, contract for, and ultimately construct a series of new nuclear reactors in Iran. Iran would supplement its own domestically produced supply of nuclear fuel with guaranteed supplies purchased from the EU (Government of Iran, 2005a).

Despite the improving context, negotiations under the Paris Agreement were described as "in trouble" because both sides' positions on the possible resumption of uranium enrichment activities appeared to harden in the run-up to Iran's June 17, 2005, presidential election (Beehner, 2005). Unable to widen their zone of possible agreement, each side reminded the other of what would happen if they walked away from the negotiations. The Iranian negotiators insisted that Iran would accelerate enrichment efforts, and the EU negotiators threatened to refer the matter to the UN Security Council for possible enforcement action in that forum.

A "last ditch" negotiation session was set for May 25, 2005, in Geneva. That meeting resulted in an E3/EU commitment for the late July to early August delivery of a detailed European counterproposal for the long-term framework agreement. According to the Iranian disclosures on the negotiations, "Iran made it clear in Geneva that any proposal by the E3/EU must incorporate "E3/EU's perception of objective guarantees for the gradual resumption of the Iranian enrichment program, and that any attempt to turn objective guarantees into cessation or long-term suspension were . . . unacceptable to Iran" (Government of Iran, 2005c). On June 24, 2005, Mahmood Ahmedinejad was elected President of Iran and lost no time casting doubt on the eventuality of a successful conclusion to the negotiations with the E3/EU. President Ahmedinejad's election no doubt contributed to a hardening of Iranian views on a comprehensive settlement, but it should be recalled that the Iranian presumption against a permanent renunciation of uranium enrichment was a position they took early, and took care to repeat often. It appears to have been interpreted by the EU negotiators as an extreme starting position, rather than a reservation point beyond which Iran would not go.

In the days before the final E3/EU proposal was submitted to Iran, some of its content was communicated in a letter from the E3 Foreign Ministers to Iran dated July 25. Iran's response was entirely negative. Iran described the E3/EU "offers and incentives as demeaning and totally incommensurate with Iran and its vast capabilities, potentials and requirements" (Government of Iran 2005d). Before the European proposal was even conveyed formally, Iran stated that the E3/EU had tried to prolong negotiations in order to turn the voluntary and temporary suspension into a permanent abandonment of the Iranian fuel cycle. Communication from Iran underlined its sense of historical grievance that had in part driven the Iranian quest for dominance of the full fuel cycle. Past Iranian experience in relying on other countries for nuclear fuel had led, according to Iran, to Iran making investments in nuclear fuel consortia without ever getting access to the fuel, and to Iran making contractual payments for nuclear fuel that was never delivered. (See the Iranian recitations of these events [Government of Iran, 2005c].) The European proposal was finally delivered to Iran's representatives on August 5, 2005, but Iran, on August 1, had already indicated to the IAEA that it was going to resume uranium conversion activities, while continuing to suspend other enrichment-related activities (Government of Iran, 2005c). This move was condemned by the IAEA

Board of Governors in its statement of August 9, 2005 (Government of the UK, 2005), and marked a severe setback in the pursuit of a negotiated settlement with Iran.

While an available version of the proposed framework agreement reads like a very tentative draft, it contains the key issue trade-offs a final agreement would entail (EU, 2005). Eight of the most important aspects of the E3/EU proposal are included here:

1. "an assured supply of fuel over the coming years" in exchange for "a binding commitment not to pursue fuel cycle activities other than the construction and operation of light water power and research reactors" (III.34)

2. "E3/EU recognize Iran's right to develop a civil nuclear power generation programme" (III.15)

3. Iran would give up its desire to develop an independent fuel cycle in exchange for "sustained access to nuclear fuel for the Light Water Reactors forming Iran's civil nuclear industry" (III.22)

4. "any fuel provided would be under normal market conditions . . . and . . . subject to proliferation-proof arrangements . . . including the return of all spent fuel" (III.25)

5. E3/EU commit themselves to "the establishment of a buffer store of fuel, sufficient to maintain supplies . . . for a period of 5 years . . . located in a mutually acceptable third country" (III.25)

6. Stop construction of Iran's "Heavy Water Research Reactor at Arak" in exchange for an E3/EU expert mission to help identify "research requirements and the most suitable type of equipment to meet those requirements" (III.37)

7. E3/EU would provide "continued political support for Iranian accession to the WTO" (World Trade Organization) and "technical support to assist Iran in making the necessary adjustments to its economy" (IV.46)

8. "E3/EU would continue to promote the sale of aircraft parts to Iran and be willing to enter into discussion about open procurement of the sale of civil passenger aircraft to Iran" (IV.49)

These elements of the proposed framework outline a series of tentative and conditional EU undertakings in exchange for definitive Iranian concessions. They also fail to recognize the real contours of the zone of possible agreement.

NEGOTIATIONS TO SAVE THE NEGOTIATIONS AND THE DRIFT TOWARD COERCIVE DIPLOMACY

After Iran rejected the EU proposal, crisis negotiations took place but could not alter the fundamental defects in the negotiation structure itself. The official response from Iran characterized the proposal as "extremely long on demands from Iran and absurdly short on offers to Iran," and claimed that the proposal did not amount to anything different from a previous proposal the E3 had floated prior to the Paris Agreement, and which Iran rejected at that time. Iran demanded an apology (Government of Iran, 2005d). The Iranian Parliament in November 2005 took measures to reduce the negotiation scope of the government, passing a law requiring the government to stop Iran's voluntary inspections by the IAEA and resume its pursuit of a nuclear fuel cycle under the NPT, in case the IAEA referred the Iran portfolio to the UN Security Council. The IAEA director general el-Baradei seemed to sound a note of calm optimism in affirming "that Iran continues to fulfill its obligations under the safeguards agreement and additional protocol by providing timely access to nuclear material, facilities and other locations. This is, however, a special verification case that requires . . . the Agency's investigation to go beyond the confines of the safeguards agreement and the additional protocol." He ended his statement by noting, almost in passing, that Iran had resumed enrichment of uranium at its Isfahan Uranium Conversion Facility, but that "other aspects of Iran's suspension remain intact" (IAEA, 2005b). IAEA optimism notwithstanding, Iran drifted further from negotiations and back toward unilateral action, while the EU retreated to the U.S.-preferred avenue of coercion through UN sanctions.

By the end of 2005 it appeared that all further E3/EU-Iran negotiations would be futile. There seemed little left to discuss unless flexibility and creativity could help the parties find more optimal outcomes. One such possibility lay in a Russian proposal to sell Iran most of the enriched fuel it would need for civilian nuclear energy while letting Iran retain the capacity for small amounts of enrichment for research purposes. In late November 2005 the E3/EU agreed to renew negotiations with Iran if the latter would consider the Russian proposal. But the United States was continuing to push for UN

Security Council action unless Iran renounced all enrichment possibilities, and by early 2006, with Iran continuing to reinitiate its enrichment activities at numerous facilities (albeit under continued IAEA supervision), the E3/EU began openly supporting the United States in its bid to refer the matter to the UN Security Council (Center for Nonproliferation Studies, 2006) and called off negotiations.

The introduction of the Russian proposal would, if technologically feasible, have been the last, best opportunity for a negotiated agreement. But its acceptance would have required EU acceptance of Iran's ongoing enrichment activities, a position that was outside the rigidly constrained ZOPA. The U.S. push for additional sanctions most likely had the effect of stiffening intransigence on all sides and, I argue, resembled classic spoiler behavior by a major external stakeholder. Even the most cursory review of the press statements from the White House or the State Department or international speeches and conferences by the U.S. president and secretary of state reveals the record to be replete with transparent as well as opaque references to economic sanctions and military action.

The year 2006 contained few diplomatic surprises regarding Iran. Instead of substantive negotiations, the year marked a return to coercive diplomacy: the use of diplomatic instruments to force Iran to modify its policies and actions. These were remarkable mostly for their futility. The IAEA Board of Governors in an emergency meeting indeed voted to refer the Iran matter to the UN Security Council (IAEA, 2006a). Predictably, this only hardened Iran's resolve to pursue an enrichment capability, and Iran responded by threatening to roll back the additional IAEA monitoring and fully resume enrichment activities (Government of Iran, 2006a). In February, President Ahmedinejad suspended Iran's voluntary implementation of the Additional Protocol it had signed as a result of the Paris Agreement. The IAEA continued to find no evidence of nuclear weapons programs but remained concerned about a number of issues that had not been clarified, including contamination caused by weapons-grade highly enriched uranium found on imported hardware: "Although the Agency has not seen any diversion of nuclear material to nuclear weapons or other nuclear explosive devices, the Agency is not at this point in time in a position to conclude that there are no undeclared nuclear materials or activities in Iran" (IAEA, 2006a:¶53). The UN Security Council, as perhaps the Iranians foresaw, immediately revealed its structural weaknesses as an enforcement forum. In late March, a feeble UNSC Presidential Statement was issued calling on Iran to reestablish "full and sustained suspension of all enrichment-related and reprocessing activities" (UNSC, 2006a).

In April 2006, Condoleezza Rice, in response to a press inquiry about possible U.S. military action against Iran, said: "the President isn't going to take any of his options off the table. We are on a diplomatic course . . . But the President doesn't take any of his options off the table" (Government of the U.S., 2006a). Investigative reporter Seymour Hersh, in allegations that were widely repeated, wrote in the April 17, 2006, *New Yorker* that civilian appointees in the U.S. administration had been promoting plans for far-reaching military campaigns against Iran, including the possible use of tactical nuclear weapons that could penetrate underground facilities (Hersh, 2006).[5]

The Security Council's internal negotiations on what to do about Iran proceeded throughout the first part of the year, supplemented by "P5+Germany" talks aimed at creating a unified posture against Iran and a unified negotiation proposal that could build on the additional credibility of the new, larger coalition. In May 2006 Iran once again reached out to the United States in the form of a lengthy letter from President Ahmedinejad to President Bush (Government of Iran, 2006b), conveyed through their Swiss back channel and in which the Iranians hoped to ignite interest in direct bilateral contact. Little or no response appears to have been made by the United States. In early May an Anglo-French draft UN Security Council resolution calling upon Iran to halt enrichment and construction of a heavy water nuclear plant was rejected by China and Russia, ostensibly because of disagreement among the P5 over the specification of a deadline for Iranian compliance (Governments of UK and France, 2006).

In what appeared on the surface to be an innovative return to negotiation in a year of strategies of coercion, on May 31, Condoleezza Rice declared that "as soon as Iran fully and verifiably suspends its enrichment and reprocessing activities, the United States will come to the table with our EU-3 colleagues [Britain, France, and Germany] and meet with Iran's representatives" (Government of the U.S., 2006b). But Rice's move was either a classic case of "too little, too late," or the United States was making a high profile bargaining offer that it hoped might earn international goodwill but never be accepted by Iran.

In June 2006, EU High Representative Javier Solana also presented an incentive package to Tehran on behalf of the "E3+3" (the E3 plus Russia, United States, and China, or, if one is attached to classic terminology, the "P5+1") meant to induce Iran into resuming its suspension of enrichment in exchange for the suspension of UN Security Council discussions of the Iran issue (Government of France, 2006). The E3+3 proposal was designed to exchange one suspension (uranium enrichment) for another (UN Security Council sanctions against Iran) only as the backdrop to a resumption of negotiations toward comprehensive agreement. By including Russia, China, and the United States, the new proposal bore more weight than the E3/EU's mid-2005 proposal and also put less emphasis on Iran's implied permanent renunciation of enrichment in exchange for a wide range of political and economic concessions, including access to U.S. and European civilian aircraft manufacturers. The proposal also made explicit recognition of Iran's right to civilian nuclear power, and it incorporated a concrete offer for Russia to enrich all of Iran's UF6 and for the E3+3 to help Iran build new light water nuclear reactors.

But Iran sought "termination" (not mere "suspension") of the UNSC's consideration of the Iran dossier and an end to the intimidation of Iran, and also linked Iran's cooperation to a commitment from the E3+3 to make progress on nuclear disarmament regarding Israel in the pursuit of a Middle East Nuclear Free Zone. Among other things, the Iranian response described the trade sanctions imposed by the United States against Iran and enforced against third party states as a problem the United States and its allies had brought upon themselves, not something Iran should have to bargain over (Government of Iran, 2006a). Nevertheless U.S. officials, rather flexibly, told media outlets that, in the long run, a deal along the lines of the E3+3 proposal could result in the international community "allowing" Iran to eventually conduct its own enrichment (BBC, 2006a).

Javier Solana held several follow-up sessions with Iran's top nuclear negotiator, Ali Larijani, to clarify the E3+3 proposal, and the United States asked for a formal Iranian reply by the June 29 start of the impending G8 meetings. Iran declined to give an answer before August 22. Iran sent Dr. Larijani back to Europe to continue negotiations with Solana and the EU member state governments, and then declared that Iran would give a response before the G8 Summit of July 15. This is the point at which the E3+3 proposal's real contours needed to be framed and reframed by the negotiators as a mutually acceptable path toward principled compromise.

Instead, Iran continued to see the proposal as one in which they were being asked to give up something concrete in exchange for new negotiations, rather than for a reciprocal concession. This, I argue, has been one of the key defects of this renewed attempt at negotiation. Social-psychological factors regarding divergent construal of the problem being negotiated, and of what each side was putting on the table helped maintain a negative frame on negotiations, with unilateral actions being preferred to a negotiated agreement.

The start of the Hizbulla-Israel war in mid-July 2006 helped dampen Iranian enthusiasm for the E3+3 proposal, and negotiations over it began to founder. Iran's longtime role as an ally and supplier of weapons to Hizbulla helped to complicate the regional context of Iran's nuclear diplomacy and cast compromise in increasingly negative terms. Even Iranian moderates began to say openly that further nuclear negotiations would be "humiliating." By the end of July, Iran definitively took suspension of enrichment off the table as a negotiation issue and simply refused to restart comprehensive negotiations as long as they were contingent on prior suspension of enrichment (BBC, 2006b). The European/U.S. bargaining move to obtain renewed suspension as a precondition for comprehensive negotiations had not only failed, it had utterly backfired, *entrenching the very Iranian action it was meant to dissuade.*

Cynical observers might be tempted to interpret the U.S. overture as having been easy to make since it was almost certainly guaranteed to fail. Indeed one could, from a negotiation perspective, look at the entire UN Security Council dimension as part of a series of nested U.S. attempts to gain bargaining leverage by worsening the no-agreement outcome of the E3/EU-led negotiations, essentially to get Iran on the agenda of the IAEA as a proliferation concern, threaten to escalate matters from the IAEA to the UNSC in case of noncompliance, and to demand Iranian concessions in exchange for the end of UN sanctions (which is precisely what the E3+3 proposal suggested) — all attempts to influence the negotiation without actually being at the table.

It took the UNSC until July 31, 2006, to issue binding Resolution 1696 (UNSC, 2006b), under the UN charter's muscular Ch. VII provisions, threatening "appropriate measures" against Iran if it did not suspend enrichment by August 31. This was followed up only at the end of 2006 by UNSC Resolution 1737 (UNSC, 2006c), which actually imposed the sanctions on Iran in December 2006. The sanctions specifically called on all member states to prohibit the sale or provision of nuclear-related technology to Iran and to block related Iranian exports. The resolution also named Iranian officials and agencies involved in Iran's nuclear research and construction efforts and requires UN member states to freeze the assets of and report on any travel to or through their territories by such persons. Sanctions would be suspended if enrichment were suspended, but further enforcement measures are also envisioned in case of noncompliance by Iran.

Neither the enforcement mechanisms nor the crisis negotiations that began in late 2005 and continued into 2006 yielded any positive change in the confrontation. IAEA director general Mohammed el-Baradei expressed his consternation with all parties: "Iran should take a timeout from its enrichment activities, the international community a timeout from its application of sanctions and the parties should go immediately to the negotiating table" (IAEA, 2007b). He was in essence trying to make a plea for rough asymmetry between the preconditions of each side, and to prioritize negotiations coupled with IAEA inspections and oversight.

SANCTIONS AND ENRICHMENT

During 2007, Iran and the United States intensified their rivalry in Iraq, with U.S. raids and arrests of Iranian officials there, and accusations of lethal arms transfers to Iraqi militia groups fighting the coalition forces. The U.S. Department of State and the Department of the Treasury also embarked on international diplomatic efforts to get other countries to cut their banking and military technology ties with Iran (Cooper and Weisman, 2007). As is now well known, additional UN Security Council sanctions followed in March 2007, March 2008, and June 2009, supplemented by unilaterally imposed U.S. and EU sanctions. The UN Security Council sanctions resolution 1747 of March 24, 2007 (UNSC, 2007), repeated the prior UN demand for an immediate suspension of enrichment and reprocessing, and the demand for a return to and ratification of the NPT's Additional Protocol, which had been demanded in the IAEA Board of Governors' Resolution 14 of February 4, 2006 (IAEA, 2006b).

Interestingly, the March 2007 UN resolution incorporated the text of the general principles of the June 2006 E3+3 offer to Iran (see Annex II, UNSC, 2007) and reiterated that these principles were still valid as the basis for negotiation. The annex begins by attempting to make an eventual agreement more binding on the Western powers by offering to endorse such an agreement with a UN Security Council resolution and to "deposit" the agreement with the IAEA. Additionally, it declares that China, Russia, the United States, and Europe would participate in an "international facility in Russia to provide enrichment services for a reliable supply of fuel to Iran's nuclear reactors. Subject to negotiations, such a facility could enrich all uranium hexafluoride

[UF6] produced in Iran" (Annex II, UNSC, 2007). This language could perhaps be interpreted as leaving open the possibility of a small amount of enrichment remaining in Iran. The annex's provisions on trade and economic cooperation remained somewhat vague and tentative, speaking of "possible removal" of U.S. export restrictions on aviation technology and offering only "practical support for" WTO membership, no doubt intended as incentives but viewed by Iran as hollow offers.

In response to the March 2007 sanctions, Iran began planning to reduce its cooperation with IAEA inspectors, and Javier Solana and Ali Larijani met in mid-April 2007 for two days of inconclusive talks. A direct bilateral meeting of U.S. and Iranian officials was held at the end of May in Baghdad, but it did not produce any breakthroughs on Iraq and did not refer to the nuclear issue at all. Perhaps attempting to forestall further sanctions, Iran and the IAEA announced an agreed timetable and work plan for Iran to clarify several aspects of its nuclear activities in mid-2007, holding off consideration of a new round of UN sanctions until further IAEA reporting later in the year (IAEA, 2007a).

As Russia-U.S. tensions mounted over U.S. and NATO plans to extend a missile defense shield in Europe, Russia made unilateral overtures to the Iranian clerical leadership on Russian proposals regarding enrichment. President Ahmedinejad replaced his seasoned top nuclear negotiator, Ali Larijani, with a less experienced hard-liner, Saeed Jalili, on the eve of new talks in Rome with Javier Solana in October 2007. Larijani accompanied his successor to the talks, but no progress was reported on the key EU demand for suspension of enrichment. In the wake of the talks, President Bush announced new U.S. sanctions against key Iranian institutions such as the Revolutionary Guard and the British foreign office announced that new UN sanctions were being planned. The November 15, 2007, IAEA Report by the Director General (IAEA, 2007c) recognized Iran for cooperation according to the August work plan and explained what information it had received from Iran, and what concerns remained to be clarified. The Western powers seized upon the negative part of the report to begin the push for more sanctions, while Iran pointed to the IAEA's ongoing inspections, Iranian cooperation, and provision of documentation to the IAEA as evidence that it was doing everything required of it under the NPT.

The year 2007 closed with the puzzling disclosure of the U.S. intelligence assessment indicating that Iran had abandoned its weapons program years earlier (NIC, 2007). In early 2008 IAEA director general el-Baradei announced that the IAEA had clarified "all the remaining outstanding issues" regarding Iran's enrichment program, with the exception of a set of "alleged studies" conducted by Iran on "weaponization" (IAEA, 2008c). Nevertheless, the UN Security Council imposed its third round of sanctions on Iran in March, reiterating the call for Iran to suspend enrichment within ninety days, and reiterating the offer to negotiate based on the 2006 E3+3 proposals (UNSC, 2008). The pattern of Iran's cooperation with the IAEA and the ongoing need for deeper and more complete disclosures by Iran continued. By June 16, 2008, the Iranian government conveyed a new offer to negotiate on a variety of issues, and added the idea of establishing fuel enrichment consortia in various parts of the world "including Iran" (IAEA, 2008a), but it did not halt its enrichment work. In June 2008 Javier Solana wrote a letter to the Iranian minister of foreign affairs, signed also by his counterparts from China, Russia, the United States, France, Germany, and the UK, in which he reiterated the principles of the 2006 E3+3 offer, and proposed the resumption of negotiations contingent on the suspension of enrichment (IAEA, 2008b). Enrichment continued throughout 2008, as did the stalemate on additional IAEA discovery of alleged weaponization studies conducted by Iran in the past.

The November 2008 election of Barack Obama as President of the United States appeared to open new possibilities of engagement with Iran, and shortly after his inauguration, he made a direct video appeal to the Iranian nation on the occasion of the Persian New Year: "My administration is now committed to diplomacy that addresses the full range of issues before us" (White House, 2009). President Obama's efforts were made difficult by the events surrounding the June 2009 reelection of President Ahmedinejad. Popular protests and allegations of electoral fraud devolved into violence and the killings of protestors by Iranian forces. A second, previously undisclosed facility for uranium enrichment near the city of Qom, was revealed by Iran to the IAEA in September 2009, further raising concerns about its nuclear intentions.

However, in October, the IAEA announced that Iran had requested its assistance on a new nuclear issue. Iran wanted help in facilitating an agreement on the provision of nuclear fuel for its Tehran Research Reactor, which the IAEA declares is used for medical purposes. The reactor would need fuel enriched at a higher level than Iran was currently producing. Just prior to the end of his tenure as IAEA Director General, el-Baradei seized upon this opportunity to mediate a smaller technical issue and establish some international cooperation with Iran. He brokered a draft agreement on this issue among France,

Russia, and Iran, separate from the ongoing political stalemate over enrichment. However, this potential breakthrough fell victim to the overarching dispute, with the international community and Iran each blaming the other for its failure to be implemented.

The February 2010 Report by the IAEA Director General concluded on a relatively negative note: "While the Agency continues to verify the non-diversion of declared nuclear material in Iran, Iran has not provided the necessary cooperation to permit the Agency to confirm that all nuclear material in Iran is in peaceful activities" (IAEA, 2010a), raising the specter of undisclosed past or even current weapons-related nuclear activities. In March 2010, Iran tried to explain why it lacked confidence in U.S. and European pledges to supply Iran with nuclear fuel. It released a detailed description of past transactions with American and European companies. Iran paid for enrichment services and uranium while the Western companies in some cases kept payment from Iran, but their governments used the fall of the Shah's government to block contract compliance and deliveries of materiel (IAEA, 2010b).

Anxious to help Iran replace the depleted fuel for its research reactor, Brazil and Turkey announced a plan to have Iran deposit 1,200 kilos (half of its stockpile at the time) of low enriched uranium (LEU) in Turkey while seeking an arrangement in which the United States, France, and Russia would resupply Iran with 120 kilos of highly enriched uranium (HEU) for the research reactor. The IAEA announced the Brazil-Turkey-Iran proposal and shared it with the United States, France, and Russia in May 2010. However, in June, the fourth and most recent round of UN sanctions was imposed on Iran, and the U.S. Congress approved further unilateral sanctions against the country. During July and August 2010, Iran declared its willingness to forgo its own efforts to enrich uranium to the levels needed for the Tehran Research Reactor if an international fuel exchange could be arranged. Russia, for its part, and despite its support for each round of sanctions, began loading fuel into a nuclear reactor it built for Iran at Bushehr, as part of efforts to make the reactor operational.

Both the international community and the Iranian government continuously declare their willingness to restart negotiations. However, each side also declares opening positions that the other side will not contemplate. The Iranians have not tired of reiterating that they will never suspend enrichment (even if they sometimes have offered to limit themselves to LEU enrichment), a declaration that has the effect of significantly reducing or eliminating any possibility of agreement along the terms the parties entertained during prior years. They point to a long record of broken contracts and foreign interference in their internal affairs. The EU, as lead negotiator for the international community, and citing a long history of Iran's concealment of its nuclear activities, including some related to nuclear weapons research, want Iran to prove beyond the shadow of doubt the peaceful intentions of its program, and as a token of good faith, consistently demand the suspension of enrichment, as a precondition for further negotiations. Without any wavering from these core positions, it appears clear that negotiations will not progress. By the end of August 2010 (as this essay went to publication) none of the negotiations or coercive attempts to influence them had succeeded in halting or even slowing Iran's enrichment activities. Iran continues to state its opposition to the acquisition or development of nuclear weapons, but instead of restoring the trust of the international community, it has seen the nascent trust evaporate.

AMBIGUITY, INCREMENTALISM, AND ZOPA IN NEGOTIATION

Why have these overlapping sets of negotiations so far failed to result in a long-term, comprehensive agreement? Numerous variables help explain it. Three have been singled out here: the construal problems related to the ambiguity of EU offers and clarity of demands made of Iran, the incrementalist negotiation processes used, and the consequently narrow or absent zone of possible agreement.

The dilemma with incrementalist negotiations is precisely this: if early agreements are meant to generate breakthroughs and build confidence gradually, any real or perceived failures or lack of compliance by the parties will greatly erode confidence and trust, and leave the parties worse off than before the negotiations. The principles embedded in the Tehran Declaration and the Paris Agreement were sufficiently general as to be acceptable to all the parties, but not specific enough to build the confidence each side required of the other. Iranian and EU rhetoric, not to mention the commentary of countries such as the United States, has over the years amounted to a series of mutual recriminations, with each side blaming the other for failing to do what it was supposed to do during the interim phase.

The Framework for a Long Term Agreement also seemed unnecessarily tentative, rather than being a fully comprehensive draft. This was surprising, given the time that had passed from the initiation of the negotiations until the delivery of the proposed Agreement. Nevertheless, this incrementalism had as a consequence the absence of a shared vision of the final outcome of the negotiations. A narrow focus on fragile interim negotiations is predicated on the need to move slowly toward comprehensive settlement negotiations, building trust but not necessarily a shared goal along the way. The fundamental divergence over what diplomacy was supposed to achieve continued to be embedded throughout successive international offers, including the E3+3 proposal of 2006.

Numerous actions by Iran, the EU, and the mostly absent party, the United States, helped to reduce or eliminate a zone of possible agreement. The parties also seem to have failed to understand the fundamentals of uncertainty and ambiguity as they affect negotiations. The EU mistakenly concluded that Iran would permanently forgo the development of a nuclear fuel cycle in exchange for the opportunity *to apply to the* WTO *and to negotiate trade and other accords with Europe.* The open statements of Iran consistently contradict any willingness to give up something so certain for something so tentative. It seems reasonable to assume that Iran was not simply courting deadlock by seeking better terms. The election of a hard-line president during the negotiations period, as well as the reactions of some elements of Iranian civil society and the parliament, all reflect a strong interest in self-sufficiency in terms of nuclear fuel supply. Nowhere does one find any wavering on this central item.

Similarly, the Iranian side at no time appears to have appreciated that the E3/EU were not contemplating *any* long-term arrangements in which Iran controlled the entirety of its own fuel cycle. More recent negotiation proposals, particularly those advanced by Russia, appear to have modified this and even hinted at a limited Iranian enrichment capacity. The goodwill shown by all sides early on was necessary perhaps, but not sufficient to create a true zone of possible agreement in which nuclear self-sufficiency for Iran could be combined with robust nonproliferation measures.

Given the choice between uncertain cooperation with past adversaries and certain mastery of the nuclear fuel cycle, it should not surprise us that Iran preferred the latter. Similarly, given a choice between the uncertain lifting of U.S./UN sanctions and the certainty of enrichment, the same conclusions hold. (Recall, for example, the conflict between "suspension" versus "termination.") Facing these choices with some degree of simultaneity and thus evaluating them in comparative fashion, the degree of ambiguity in the U.S. and EU "offers" only intensifies, and we could expect Iranian confidence in its preferred path to only increase. What is surprising is that EU and U.S. diplomats would have believed their inducements (EU) or coercion (United States) could otherwise persuade Iran. The determination and widening of the ZOPA are a critical activity for negotiators from all sides of a conflict and require proactive attempts to alter the perceptions of the parties and discover optimal possibilities of agreement.

The analysis contained in this chapter does not prejudge the good faith and intentions of the negotiators. It is not, however, surprising that they have not reached a comprehensive agreement to date. The failure of the E3/EU-Iran negotiations presages a long-term stalemate. At the same time, it is not at all inevitable that the current state of affairs will lead inexorably to further confrontation. Breakthroughs are still possible given political will, creativity, and skill in negotiations in which the parties discover that their interests in international peace, disarmament, energy security, sovereignty, and multilateralism are indeed complementary.

NOTES

The author would like to recognize the research assistance of Christoff Luehrs, Sara Cady, Camilo Zambrano, and Bob Schlehuber as well as the helpful comments of Christophe Dupont, Guy Olivier Faure, Franz Cede, Darren Kew, Bill Zartman, Claudia Rosati, and two anonymous readers. Errors and omissions, of course, remain the responsibility of the author.

1. The capacity to create and manage a nuclear fuel cycle refers to the ability to obtain, extract, and enrich nuclear fissile materials, such as uranium, so that they can be used to generate nuclear energy. The cycle also includes the ability to store, transport, reprocess, and dispose of depleted nuclear materials and waste generated by the creation of nuclear energy. Enrichment is the process of purification of the fissile material. The technological gap between civil and military enrichment purposes is large, encompassing scale and scope, and Iran is not believed capable of quickly bridging this gap.

2. "We judge with high confidence that in Fall 2003, Tehran halted its nuclear weapons program. . . . We judge with high confidence that the halt lasted at least several years. . . . We assess with moderate confidence Tehran had not restarted its nuclear weapons program as of mid-2007, but we do not know whether it currently intends to develop nuclear weapons. . . . We continue to assess with moderate-to-high confidence that Iran does not currently have a nuclear weapon" (Key Judgments, NIC, 2007).

3. Treaty on the Non-Proliferation of Nuclear Weapons, 729 UNTS 161, July 1, 1968 (entered into force March 5, 1970).

4. Enrichment is part of the process of converting uranium from its natural mined state into a usable nuclear fuel, whether for peaceful or military purposes.

5. U.S. covert plans to invade Iran and topple the regime were also reported by archival historian James Bamford, known for his two exposés on the secretive National Security Agency (Bamford, 1982 and 2001). According to Bamford, civilians at the Pentagon were working with pro-Israel lobbyists to promote a policy of regime change at the White House, until they were arrested by the FBI and indicted by federal prosecutors (Bamford, 2006).

The Cyprus Conflict

Will It Ever End in Agreement?

RAYMOND SANER

The goal of this chapter is to describe factors that have contributed to the persistent failures of peace negotiations on Cyprus. Although there are several causes of this protracted deadlock, such as identity issues (see P. Terrence Hopmann's chapter, "Issue Content and Incomplete Negotiations"), and the power issue for the two communities, this chapter attempts to delineate an essential impact that multiple and competing external stakeholders (influential foreign powers, supranational institutions, intergovernmental organizations, and NGOS from various countries) have had on the peace process. Then, to show how these third parties (first level Greece and Turkey; secondary level United States, UK, EU, and UN) have used the Cyprus conflict for their own strategic aims and secondary gains by offering their influence to the two conflict parties (Greek Cypriots and Turkish Cypriots). As a result of these ongoing external stakeholder interferences, the Cyprus conflict has persisted and the negotiation behavior of the primary conflict parties became characterized by opportunistic tactical maneuvers that have prolonged and deepened nonagreement ever since the peace-enforcing presence of UN forces on the island started in 1974 and has lasted up to the writing of this chapter.

THE CYPRUS CONFLICT 2002–JANUARY 2006

In January 2002, direct talks under the auspices of UN secretary-general Kofi Annan began between Republic of Cyprus president Glafcos Clerides (Greek community) and Turkish Cypriot leader Rauf Denktash.[1] In November 2002, Annan released a comprehensive plan for the resolution of the Cyprus issue, which was revised in early December. In the lead-up to the European Union's December 2002 Copenhagen Summit, intensive efforts were made to gain signatures of both sides to the document prior to a decision on the island's EU membership. Neither side agreed to sign. The EU invited the Republic of Cyprus to join on December 16, 2002.

Following the Copenhagen Summit, the UN continued dialogue with the two sides with the goal of reaching a settlement prior to Cyprus's signing of the EU accession treaty on April 16, 2003, and a third version of the Annan plan was put to the parties in February 2003. That same month the secretary-general again visited the island and asked that both leaders agree to put the plan to referendum in their respective communities. Also in February 2003, Tassos Papadopoulos was elected as the fifth president of the Republic of Cyprus. On March 10, 2003, this most recent phase of talks collapsed in The Hague, Netherlands, when Denktash told the secretary-general he would not put the Annan plan to referendum.

In February 2004, Papadopoulos and Denktash accepted the secretary-general's invitation to resume negotiations on a settlement on the basis of the Annan plan. After meeting with Annan in New York, talks began on-island on February 19, 2004. The two community leaders met nearly every day for negotiations facilitated by the secretary-general's Special Representative for Cyprus, Alvaro de Soto. In addition, numerous technical committees and sub-committees met in parallel in an effort to resolve pending issues. When this stage of the talks failed to reach an agreeable settlement, Rauf Denktash refused to attend the next stage of meetings, which were scheduled to take place in Bürgenstock on March 24, 2004, and sent Mehmet Ali Talat, then prime minister of the Turkish Republic of Northern Cyprus (TRNC), and Serder Denktash, son of Rauf Denktash and then TRNC deputy prime minister and TRNC minister of foreign affairs, as his agents. The talks collapsed and the two communities did not reach any agreement. The secretary-general then stepped in as arbitrator, and on March 31 presented to the two sides a proposed final settlement. Rauf Denktash rejected Annan's proposal immediately, and Tassos Papadopoulos, the fifth president of the Republic of Cyprus, rejected the plan a week later, while Mehmet Ali Talat supported it. The plan was placed before the two communities in a simultaneous vote in the reunification referendum of April 24, 2004. Although the proposal received a 65 percent favorable vote from the Turkish community, the Greek Cypriot community rejected it by three to one. Since implementation of the plan was dependent on its approval by both communities, reunification did not take place. Had there been a positive vote on both sides, a unified Cyprus would have acceded to the European Union on May 1, 2004; instead, Cyprus joined the EU without the northern part populated by the Turkish Cypriots. Since then, low-key talks have started again between the newly appointed UN Under Secretary-General for Political Affairs, Kieran Prendergast, and leaders of both communities; on June 16, 2005, the UN Security Council unanimously adopted resolution 1604, thus renewing the mandate of the UN Peacekeeping Force in Cyprus (UNFICYP) for a further six months, until December 15, 2005.

On October 3, 2005, membership negotiations were symbolically opened with Turkey, which has been an associate member of the EU since 1963 and an official candidate since 1999. The historic decision on December 17, 2004, by the European Council was confirmed by the European heads of state and government on June 17. On June 29, 2005, the commission presented its negotiating framework to Ankara, and after a full day of intense negotiations, the EU-25's foreign ministers finalized the document on October 3, 2005. Within hours, Turkey accepted the terms. Amid a flurry of controversy over Turkey's latest "action plan" on Cyprus, the UN announced its intention to start a new round of Cyprus peace talks in May 2006. This came about after Turkish prime minister Recep Tayyip Erdogan called for a meeting on the Cyprus conflict to be held "in May or June 2006" with the participation of representatives from Turkey, Greece, and the Turkish and Greek Cypriot communities. Meanwhile, Kofi Annan's spokesman George Lillikas said that the UN would resume its peace efforts in Cyprus after the May 2006 parliamentary elections in the Republic of Cyprus. "Our effort is to avoid a hasty new process of negotiations, which would fail in no time," said Lillikas. In its latest "action plan" revealed on January 24, Ankara said that it would open its ports and airports to Greek Cypriot carriers on the condition that they reciprocally end restrictions on Turkish Cypriots. The initiative was welcomed by the EU, the United States, and the UN, but it was immediately rejected by Greek president Papadopoulos and the Greek Cypriot leaders as a rehashing of earlier inconclusive proposals.

EU enlargement commissioner Olli Rehn appointed Jaakko Blomberg, former Finnish envoy to Cyprus, as EU Commission special adviser on Cyprus in June 2005. All looked set for another round of informal talks, quasi negotiations, and initiatives with uncertain outcome for all parties concerned, but with a nagging wink to the French proverb that says: "plus ça change, plus c'est la même chose."

PROBLEMATIC CAUSE-AND-EFFECT TIME LINE
OF CYPRUS CONFLICT

For many experts and scholars, the international conflict over Cyprus started with the attempted coup in 1974 by Greek Cypriot Sampson against then-president Makarios. Sampson's violent coup was supported by the military junta then in power in Greece with the aim of achieving *enosis* (unification of Cyprus with Greece). This attempted overthrow of the Cypriot government led subsequently to military interference by Turkey, one of the guarantor states of the newly independent Cyprus, ostensibly to protect the Turkish Cypriot minority from possible violent acts by the majority Greek communities, although the Turkish forces stationed on Northern Cyprus have yet to retreat to Turkey.[2] What remains puzzling is the inactivity of the UK, the third guarantor nation of Cyprus. Greece, being temporarily paralyzed by the collapse of the military junta and their return to democracy, was in no position to intervene militarily on the island. This was not the case for the UK, which had troops stationed on its two extraterritorial military bases. The military inactivity led to speculations as to the intention of the UK government and by extension of the United States, speculations that were recently rekindled by the release of the Callaghan report that seems to suggest that former secretary of state Henry Kissinger was intent not to intervene nor suggest intervention by the UK forces in order to not oppose Turkey's goodwill in relation to U.S. policy in the area.[3]

The ensuing war and partition of the island led to the intervention of the UN, who dispatched peace-enforcing military forces, the UNFICYP, stationed between the two sides along the so-called green line dividing the island into the Greek Cypriot controlled South and the Turkish Cypriot controlled North, with both sides' military forces being supported by Turkish and Greek army units. The largest foreign force, though, are the Turkish army units stationed on the northern part of the island since 1974. Pointing out the discrepancy between the UN force's success in keeping peace but on the other hand not being able to fulfill its mandate of "bringing a return to normal conditions," Evriviades and Bourantonis (1994) suggest that the UN peacemaking efforts were fundamentally flawed, since they led to a freezing of a status quo on the island. Some scholars attribute the cause of the 1974 violence and inability of both sides to peacefully reunite to earlier disputes and related violence. Diana Weston Markides (2001), for instance, goes back to colonial rule by the UK and suggests that the inability of both communities and of the British administration to create functioning municipal administrations acceptable to both communities was a key factor of subsequent division of municipalities along ethnic lines, leading further to a full breakdown of cooperation between both communities at the central government level in 1963, only three years after Cyprus achieved independence from the UK. Until 1957, the main towns of Cyprus were run by councils elected on the basis of communally based proportional representation, which inevitably resulted in Greek-dominated bodies run by Greek Cypriot mayors. With independence from Britain looming and facing a power imbalance at the municipal level, some leading members of the Turkish Cypriot community requested that at the time of British withdrawal, Cyprus should be retroceded to Turkey from Britain, who had taken control of the island in 1878. The orders given to their respective Turkish Cypriot communities were to withdraw from any official participation in municipal administrations. Other scholars suggest that causes of the conflict go much further back in time, alluding, for instance, to the cruelties committed during the invasion and subsequent rule of the Ottoman empire; the various wars, sacking, and pillaging through the period of the Christian crusades; and the competition between the Venetian and Genovese forces during their colonial intrusions into the region.[4] As Alvaro de Soto, previously the UN secretary-general's Special Adviser on Cyprus, stated:

> Regrettably, as Churchill said of the Balkans, Cyprus has more history than it can digest. Trying to capture what happened in a few paragraphs is the diplomatic equivalent of walking through a minefield. For the Turkish Cypriots, the problem began in 1963 when Greek Cypriots hijacked and tried to Hellenise Cyprus, undoing the partnership enshrined in the 1960 constitution, corralling them in a small number of villages out of fear for their lives. The Greek Cypriots tend to fast-forward to 1974 and say that the problem started with the Turkish invasion and continues with its occupation. (2005)

Looking at the region from a historical point of view and reflecting on the wrangling for power over the territories of the former Ottoman empire by the UK, France, Russia, and Greece and Turkey, it is very instructive to follow in more depth the conflicting strategic interests of the big powers around the time of the Lausanne conference of 1922–23 (Goldstein, 2003). Taking this conference as an early indicator of what was to come later in regard to the Cyprus conflict, Goldstein's article gives a picture of how third parties can decisively influence the outcome of international negotiations. Another frequently mentioned perspective is the one concerning the role of the EU. For instance, Oliver Richmond suggests that the EU expected to "act as a catalyst for the settlement of the Cyprus problem without becoming a direct mediator" (2006b:154), but by allowing Cyprus to become a member of the EU before reaching an agreement with the Turkish Cypriots, "the EU . . . had effectively become a party to the conflict" (163). Related to the above, fault has been attributed to the UN secretary-general and his team of negotiators who lost their neutrality by making use of the UN mandate to act as arbitrator when faced with no agreement after the failed Bürgenstock negotiations in 2004. By imposing a "UN solution," authors close to the Greek Cypriot position declared the UN mission of good office as a debacle (Palley, 2005). While such an observation is worthy of a longer discussion, attacking experts of the UN team as being of dubious intention reveals the suspiciousness and animosity that have always characterized the Cyprus negotiations.[5]

Finally, observations have been made about the fact that both sides of the conflict enjoy higher GDP per capita than their respective motherlands (Saner and Yiu, 2002). This could be due to the ingenuity and hard work of the two communities. It could also be due to the fact that both sides receive support from Greece and Turkey respectively and from third parties such as the UN (e.g., UNDP) and bilateral donors. Long-lasting conflicts tend to attract parallel economies (Wennmann, 2005) and result in duplication of governmental structures that in turn require additional resources of sometimes dubious origin.

PARTIES, STAKEHOLDERS, AND MEDIATORS

When mentioning the Cyprus conflict, most often allusion is made to the intercommunal conflict between Greek and Turkish Cypriots going back to pre-independence times, as described in the previous section. However, due to the fact that three guarantor countries (the UK, Turkey, and Greece) have the constitutional right to intervene unilaterally if seen as needed, the intercommunal conflict was immediately raised to the level of conventional war (e.g., Turkey's landing of troops on the island in 1974 leading to war with the forces of the official Cypriot government). In addition, subsequent to the conventional war between official Cyprus and Turkey, the Security Council of the UN, following multiple resolutions passed by the UN Assembly, gave a specific mandate to the UN secretary-general and his office to create a peace-enforcing group of UN soldiers to interpose themselves between both belligerent parties (green line) and to initiate diplomatic efforts that should lead to reconciliation and reunification. From a conflict theory point of view, one could hence classify the Cyprus conflict as consisting of a bilateral conflict (Cyprus-Turkey) mediated by a third party, namely the UN secretary-general, and influenced by multiple stakeholders (e.g., two remaining guarantor countries of Greece and the UK; the EU as political supranational umbrella representing Greece and the UK; since May 2004 Cyprus [Southern Cyprus] and all the other EU member countries).

Figure 2 gives an overview of the multiple coalitions that have a direct or indirect impact on the outcome of any negotiated solution of the Cyprus conflict, if one can ever be achieved at all. Third parties to the conflict can try to be constructive and help bring about a resolution of the conflict, or they might be interested in using the conflict to obtain concessions elsewhere. Several interest alliances are known to be influential in the region and linked to the Cyprus conflict. On one hand there is a configuration of countries tied to one another through various pacts and cooperation agreements ranging, for example, from cooperation in the military sector (Turkey, Israel, the United States) to alliances against a common enemy or competitor, such as Turkey and Israel together against Syria, Lebanon, and Iraq's former Saddam regime.

On the other hand, a very old alliance exists among fellow Christian orthodox countries such as Greece, Serbia, and Russia (formerly Soviet Union) against Macedonia, Kosovo, Albania, and Turkey and a strategic alliance going back to the Cold War with Syria against Turkey and later on Israel (as ally of Turkey). Another link based on common interest and years of active cooperation exists between the UK and the United States. The two bases ceded in perpetuity to the UK are used for high-tech espionage work covering the Near East, the Black Sea, and the Caucasus area. The airbase was used during the Iraq war and is intended to be at service for any other armed conflict situation. A fully reunited and harmonious Cyprus could question the legitimacy of the two bases and even ask the UK to retrocede them to the sovereign country of Cyprus.

The UN secretariat has its own concerns and tactical alliances. The Cyprus conflict has meant continuous expenditures, troop presence, and a mandate to

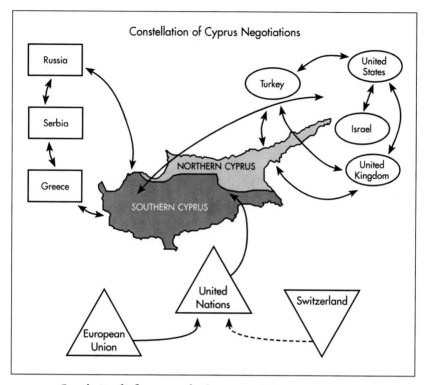

FIGURE 2. Complexity of influences on the Cyprus negotiations.

be a conciliator of this old conflict. Having had to face increasing criticism especially from the United States and the UK, it is perfectly understandable that the UN SG would like to see an end to the Cyprus conflict. Not to find a solution means continued expenditures that are actually needed elsewhere. Also, not being able to find a solution represents the risk of negative PR with third parties.

The alliance network depicted in figure 2 is not exhaustive. It solely serves to illustrate the complexity of the Cyprus conflict and the obvious links to other business that countries might have with one another or with other groups and where a solution or the withholding of a solution on the island could be in the best interests of these third parties but to the detriment of the concerned two communities. A classic case of such opportunistic use of conflicts is, for instance, the use of veto power by Greece to block internal EU and NATO decision-making processes. To opt for a negotiators' behavior called the "nuisance factor," third partiers can score points for their protégé (here Greek

Cyprus) as well as use their blocking power to bar entry of Turkey to the EU until Turkey, for example, makes concessions in other domains. It is unrealistic to expect a solution to the Cyprus conflict without a simultaneous package deal covering all the additional external conflicts described above. In other words, a solution to the Cyprus conflict necessitates a comprehensive solution covering the conflict but also the other stakeholders' interests.[6]

CONFLICT COMPLEXITY IN ACTION: INFLUENCE OF
THIRD PARTIES ON MALIGNANT CYPRUS CONFLICT

Cyprus has been called "the graveyard of well-intentioned mediators." Over the last nearly forty years, a multitude of peace initiatives have resulted in failure. The list of failed attempts of official and nonofficial third-party interventions is long (see Diamond and Fisher, 1995; Dodd, 1998). What follows is the list of the main causes that led to a failed Track III attempt to bring the two communities together through a so-called confidence-building project.[7] The case itself is described in detail elsewhere (Saner and Yiu, 2002).

The basic idea of the endeavor was to create joint projects in the economic sphere that would offer mutually beneficial incentives to both sides. The proposal was based on the assumption that a Swiss NGO could provide a neutral arena, in contrast to the UN auspices of the secretary-general, who was at different times seen as being biased by either of the two parties or sometimes by both for different reasons, or to a UK- or U.S.-based NGO because of their affiliation or perceived allegiance to their respective governments who were in fact actively intervening as behind-the-scenes external stakeholders. Only a new approach that had not been tried before could succeed — the involvement of both sides' economic interests in order to develop sufficient common ground for future intercommunal cooperation. What seemed possible was a nonofficial third-party intervention, which would not jeopardize the ongoing political efforts of the UN. The key to success would be to sidestep the political big picture discussions and to focus instead on the common economic interests of both communities. If the economic cooperation project succeeded, both sides would gain sufficient confidence to tackle the more complex political issues at a later stage. Switzerland was willing to extend financing for the project under conditions that the UN would welcome the project and support it, and that a second country would join the initiative.

The project did not become operational for various reasons. It could be said that the time was not ripe for such an intercommunal project since each party involved was still trying to "win," which by definition was unacceptable to the other party. From a position of Realpolitik, one could indeed say, "Don't force cooperation if there is no will to cooperate" — in other words, the international community should allow the opponents to be separated from each other and to accept the inevitable division of Cyprus into two distinct and independent states. While this seems to be the solution preferred by many Cyprus experts, at the time of the project proposal it did not seem that all efforts had yet been tried, and that the will toward reconciliation was not yet exhausted. On the contrary, it seemed that the majority of the citizens of both communities favored reconciliation, not separation. But the main cause for the failure of this project was the multitude of interferences by third parties, who influenced the members of both communities according to their own strategic designs leading to paralysis. The paralysis came about because of the destructive impact of competition between external and internal parties and institutions who are all stakeholders to the conflict, but who at the same time could not cooperate. Their competition often led to confusion and dangerous instability, since they at times tried to manipulate the two sides' officials and populations, while at the same time they also became the victims of manipulations by either side's officials and opinion leaders.

The main forms of third party interferences were (Saner and Yiu, 2002):

- Interferences due to contradictory strategies of key external stakeholders

- Interference due to local stakeholder prerogatives

- Interference due to historical distrust of main conflicting parties

- Interferences due to the use of the "Cyprus card" for secondary gains elsewhere

- Interference due to competing agenda of institutional stakeholders (the United Nations Secretariat, the United States, the European Union, the United Kingdom)

- Interferences due to bilateral tensions between Greece and Turkey

- Interferences due to competition between local leaders

- Interferences due to secondary gain of current impasse

RECENT PRESSURE TACTICS BY THIRD PARTIES
TO THE CYPRUS CONFLICT

Annan V

The Annan plan for Cyprus in fact evolved over time, starting with Annan I (October 11, 2002), moving to Annan II (December 10, 2002) and on to Annan III (March 8, 2003). Annan IV was a short-lived trial version before the final Annan V (March 31, 2004) which was presented to the public a few days before the referendum took place in both communities, consisting of several thousands of pages.[8] Based on the limited access to documented texts, it appears that the UN team, in unison with the EU, U.S., and UK delegations, hoped to accommodate Denktash's objections by progressively adding concessions to the benefit of the Denktash position and to the detriment of the Greek Cypriot position. At the same time, the UN team, together with the EU Commission, the United States, and the UK, assumed that presenting the Greek Cypriot side with a last-minute complex deal a few days before the referendum and four weeks before official acceptance as EU member would be too much to reject for the Southern Cypriot leadership and people.

The opposite was the case. The negotiation behavior of the UN and the three big powers was seen as "take it or leave it" pressure on a subject that was too crucial for both communities. Too much was at stake for the Greek community to expect them to almost blindly trust that the complicated text would be in their interest. Holding a quasi monopoly in the official media, President Papadopoulos was easily able to highlight the negative aspects of the deal while downplaying the potential benefits. When under pressure and facing uncertainty, most people reject experiments they cannot control or whose implications they cannot anticipate. Adding to this uncertainty came anger when it became known that the Turkish settlers would be allowed to vote, in contrast to a comparable vote in East Timor, where Indonesian settlers were not allowed to vote during the crucial vote on independence (Evriviades, 2005:5).[9]

Ambassador Ziyal's "Final Points"

Another example of high pressure of time and demands was the list of ten points presented by Ambassador Ziyal, Turkish representative to the UN, on March 26 at the beginning of the Bürgenstock meeting, which was attended by the presidents of Turkey, Greece, and Cyprus (Greek Cypriot); the UN secretary-general; U.S. secretary of state Colin Powell; and other world leaders. However, Turkish president Denktash opted to stay at home and to be replaced by Mehmet Ali Talat, then holding the function of Prime Minister of the TRNC, and his son Serdar Denktash in the role of TRNC Minister of Foreign Affairs.

Being absent from the meeting, Denktash did not have to submit to pressure nor extend any concessions. As his son's and Talat's mandate for negotiations and possible give-and-take concession making were seriously limited, there was not much hope for the Greek Cypriots to be able to trade concessions. To this one-sided situation came the sudden presentation of ten "final points" of Turkey presented by Ambassador Ziyal to the UN and addressed to the Greek Cypriot representatives. Again, the pressure of a last-minute surprise demand, similar to the Annan V "last minute proposal." The ten points consisted of the following:

1. The percentage of the Greek Cypriots returning to the North should be reduced from 21 percent to 18 percent. This percentage is the least we can accept.

2. The Turkish Cypriot proposal regarding the property issue (1/3) should be accepted.

3. Bi-communal/bi-national configurations, such as that twenty-four Turkish Cypriot and twenty-four Greek Cypriot senators should be properly reflected in the plan.

4. The restriction of fifty-five years to be applied to the Turkish citizens to establish residence in Cyprus even after Turkey's accession to the EU should be lifted, since Turkish citizens would be treated as members of the EU and could hence take up residence anywhere within the EU.

5. Inclusion in the plan of the understanding of neither side claiming jurisdiction and authority over the other side.

6. Individual applications of Greek Cypriots to the European Court of Human Rights (ECHR) should not be encouraged. The United Cyprus Republic should be the sole responsible addressee for these cases.

7. Expectations regarding security and guarantees should be fully met.

8. Preservation of Greek and Turkish military presence on the island even after the accession of Turkey to the European Union. (The contingents provided by the Treaty of Alliance should be maintained.)

9. Measures should be developed for effective preservation of bi-zonality.

10. Turkish Cypriot citizens originating from Anatolia should not be discriminated against within the framework of a comprehensive settlement.[10]

COMPLEXITIES IN RETROSPECT

Both examples of interventions by external parties shed light on the complex situation of the Cyprus conflicts. Gaining a point, even if beneficial at first glance for the ally, here Northern Cyprus, means oftentimes scoring a point at home or signaling a message to third-, fourth-, even fifth-level parties outside the immediate Cyprus conflict "zone." Taking, for example, the tough stance of Turkey during the Bürgenstock negotiation, one can also imagine that scoring points there was equal to gaining points at home in Turkey and getting messages across to friends and enemies as well. Some of the motivations behind Turkey's tough stance might be related to the following concerns. Turkey has been working hard on making political and economic reforms required for EU membership. It passed the hurdle of being accepted as an EU candidate only in 2004. With Cyprus (Southern Cyprus) having become an EU member in May 2004, Turkey faces a situation whereby its own future EU membership application could be vetoed by Southern Cyprus, since EU membership decisions are taken by consensus. Southern Cyprus as a new EU member could hence block Turkey's EU ambitions indefinitely, an unacceptable possibility for Turkey's political and economic leadership.

At the same time, the U.S. government's antiterrorist campaign and remodeling of post-Saddam Iraq is resulting in increasing pressure on Turkey to cooperate. Such an eventuality worries Turkish leaders since the defeat of Saddam has rekindled hopes in the Kurdish-held territories of an independent Kurdish state in the northern part of Iraq. Turkish political and military leaders fear such an eventuality: an independent Kurdish state might reignite Kurdish rebellion in Turkey, and, even more worrisome, it might lead to new calls for Kurdish separation from Turkey. On the other hand, Turkey does not want to be seen as obstructing the U.S. geopolitical aims and strategies in the Middle East. Tensions are further kept high due to Southern Cyprus's continued threat to install the s-300 PMU-1 Missile System bought from Russia, which, if installed on the island, would alter the current military balance and possibly threaten Turkish airspace, including parts of Turkey inhabited by the Kurdish minority unhappy with its status and treatment by the majority Turkish government. Southern Cypriot authorities promised to withhold the installation of the missile system but not to relinquish its right to do so at a later stage. All this is, of course, not helped by recent statements of the Turkish chief of general staff Hilmi Ozkok, who declared in his new year statement of 2006 that Turkey should be "defending our rights and interests on Cyprus, which constitutes the cornerstone of our security in the Eastern Mediterranean" (Ozkok, 2006).

Among the multiple causes of this especially long-lasting deadlock are the extreme level of distrust between both parties, their constant change of positions in an often less and less cooperative way, and finally a refusal to even consider objective facts on the problem. These are as many obstacles to crack in the elusive Cyprus stalemate.

Extreme Level of Distrust

Bad faith, suspicion, and an extreme level of distrust characterize the overall situation. For instance, in March 1986, UN secretary-general Javier Pérez de Cuéllar presented the two sides with a draft framework agreement. The plan envisaged the creation of an independent, nonaligned, bicommunal, bi-zonal state in Cyprus. However, the Greek Cypriots shifted their position. They argued that the issue of the presence of Turkish forces was not addressed, nor was the repatriation of the recent Turkish settlers on the island. Finally, they pointed out that the proposed state structure was confederal in nature and as such not acceptable. De Cuéllar later blamed the failure of the talks on Denktash, because of the Turkish Cypriot leader's demand for equal sovereignty and a right to secession for the two communities.

Demonization of the other side legitimates refusals, deadlocks, and the systematic use of the "nuisance power." This built-up perception of the other entails an absolute lack of goodwill on both sides and has already worn out five UN secretary-generals.

Secretary-General Boutros Boutros-Ghali, when in charge, proposed eight confidence building measures (CBMs). These included reducing military forces on the island, reducing restrictions on contacts between the two sides, undertaking an islandwide census, and conducting feasibility studies regarding a solution. The Security Council endorsed the approach. Denktash accepted only some of the proposals but did not agree to the package as a whole, which was the condition for success. He stated that he was "willing to accept mutually agreed changes," which clearly meant nothing. On his side, Greek Cypriot Clerides refused to negotiate any further changes to the former proposals, which put an end to any possibility of moving on (Migdalovitz, 2005).

Close to two hundred thousand Greek Cypriot refugees have been isolated from their homes by the Turkish control of the northern sector of the island. The issue of the restitution of their property has been a fundamental claim of the Greek Cypriot side. However, the Turkish Cypriots argue that the complete return of all Greek Cypriot properties to their original owners would be incompatible with the functioning of a bi-zonal, bicommunal federal settlement, again leading the whole negotiation process to a dead end. UN special adviser Alexander Downer raised the question to the two sides to make clear whether they wanted a solution or not. "The parties have exhausted all their arguments and counter-arguments," he added. "What is missing now is the political will." In March 2011, UN secretary-general Ban Ki-moon reported, "The negotiations cannot be an open-ended process, nor can we afford interminable talks for the sake of talks" (Kambas, 2011).

Unstable Positions

Shifts in positions that are often inexplicable have made all solutions less and less credible. Initially the two sides strongly disagreed on the concept of "bi-communality." The Turkish Cypriots considered that their state should be exclusively Turkish Cypriot and that the Greek Cypriot state should be exclusively Greek Cypriots. The Greek Cypriots contended that the two states should be predominantly, but not exclusively, made up of a particular community. Later, the Greek side changed position on its understanding of bi-communality, and this attitude raised more suspicion than satisfaction on the Turkish side.

In December 1993, Greek Cypriot leader Glafcos Clerides proposed the demilitarization of Cyprus. Denktash, the Turkish Cypriot leader, dismissed the idea, but the next month he announced that he would be willing to accept the CBMs "in principle." These CBMs included the gradual demilitarization of the island. Then, Clerides said that he would be willing to accept the document if the Turkish Cypriot did. Then, Denktash refused, arguing that it would upset the balance of forces on the island.

Furthermore, Denktash announced that he would no longer accept federation as a basis for a settlement. In the future he would only be prepared to negotiate on the basis of a confederal solution. His successor, newly elected Northern Cyprus prime minister Mehmet Ali Talat, accepted the bizonal bicommunity federation in final UN-led negotiations in 2003, only to have the Annan plan rejected by the Greek Cypriots in the April 24, 2004, referendum. Such a continuous dance leaves all mediators and observers wondering what can be taken seriously in these ever-changing positions. No solid and reliable base for building up a sustainable agreement has been established. What is at stake is nothing less than the credibility of all statements.

Denial of Objective Facts

In December 1996, the European Court of Human Rights delivered a ruling that affirmed that Turkey was an occupying power in Cyprus. The Turkish Cypriots did not accept the sentence, arguing that the court was politically biased. Another important problem is that the Greek Cypriot side has asked that the UN or another international organization organize, supervise, and execute a simultaneous census on the whole island. The Turkish Cypriots rejected this demand. It is a major problem if there is already a disagreement on objective facts or on attempts to collect objective data, for durable agreements have to be built from realities.

CONCLUSION

The objective of this chapter has been to shed light on the impact of external stakeholders' interferences on a protracted conflict, in this case the Cyprus conflict. We contend that the impact of persistent interference by external stakeholders is a topic that has not received sufficient exposure in the conflict literature. The objective here was hence to illustrate such third-party interference in the case of the long-lasting Cyprus conflict and to describe the diverse forms of interference used by the third parties and how these multiple interferences have turned the Cyprus conflict into a malignant, seemingly intractable conflict as long as third-party interests remain high and secondary gains too important to maintain for other purposes elsewhere.

NOTES

1. Public domain U.S. State Department background note on Cyprus, April 2004.

2. Both sides describe this situation differently, namely as an "intervention" by Northern Cyprus and Turkey based on the legal argument that Turkey had a unilateral right and obligation based on the 1960 constitution, and as an "invasion" by Southern Cyprus and Greece based on the argument that Turkey has violated international law by not having withdrawn its forces from Cyprus, and frequently making comparisons between the Cyprus conflict and, for instance, the invasion of Kuwait by Iraqi forces.

3. Reference is made here to the release by James Callaghan, former UK secretary of state for foreign and commonwealth affairs, which supposedly has been released for publication according to the thirty years rule (see http://www.cyprusembassy.net, February 20, 2006).

4. For an insightful analysis of conscious and unconscious motivations of members of both conflict parties, see Volkan (1979).

5. Palley, for instance, insinuates the partiality of Didier Pfirter, Swiss delegate to De Soto's team, by mentioning that he has studied philosophy and Islamic studies (Palley, 2005:19).

6. Yesilada and Sozen (2002), for instance, offer a very well argued analysis of the Cyprus conflict based on game theory and the prisoner dilemma concept. While such game's theoretical perspective offers interesting insights, it is also insufficient since it reduces real complexity of multistakeholder interferences to a purely bilateral conflict between Greek and Turkish Cypriots.

7. For clarification, Track I refers to government, Track II to nongovernment/professional, and Track III to business or peacemaking through commerce.

8. For detailed analysis of how the four Annan proposals evolved over time, see Palley (2005:275–314).

9. For many scholars following the Cyprus conflict, it was a surprise that the EU would allow membership of a country that did not have full control of its territory. It was, however, often insinuated that without Cyprus being given EU membership status Greece would not have agreed to NATO enlargement.

10. Palley (2005:19, 128–29) describes how many of the points were accommodated by the UN team as reported from a pro–Greek Cypriot perspective.

The Biological Weapons Convention

JEZ LITTLEWOOD

The Biological Weapons Convention (BWC) entered into force in 1975. It was negotiated in Geneva during the period 1968–71. The negotiations were multilateral, but they occurred during the Cold War. A deal between the United States and the Soviet Union in mid-1971 presented other states with a fait accompli on the text of the convention through the submission of identical texts of the BWC in September 1971 (Chevrier, 2006:325). While a number of states were unhappy with the text of the convention (Myrdal, 1976:272–75), the BWC was adopted by the United Nations General Assembly in December 1971 and opened for signature in 1972 in London, Washington, and Moscow.

During its thirty-year life to date the BWC has been both lauded and derided (Littlewood, 2005:16–37). As Croft noted, any arms control agreement is a product of the international political culture and context of the time (Croft, 1996:31), and while the BWC was hailed as the first disarmament treaty for a weapon of mass destruction, its relative weaknesses were due to the fact that it contained no verification mechanisms. Implementation relies almost exclusively on mutual trust between the states parties. Trust between states diminished against a background of the failure of détente in the late 1970s, allegations of noncompliance involving the Soviet Union's offensive biological weapons program up to 1992, and proliferation concerns following the Iran-Iraq War (1980–88), the first Gulf war (1990–91), and the end of the Cold War. However, unlike the Nuclear Non-Proliferation Treaty of 1968 — which defined and legitimized China, France, UK, the United States, and the Soviet Union as the five legal nuclear weapon states — the BWC was nondiscriminatory. All states were bound by the same obligation: biological disarmament within nine months of the entry into force of the convention. The convention and its evolution since 1975 therefore has implications for understanding how states negotiate in the post-agreement phase of a treaty and how agreements evolve to address and resolve problems unforeseen during the original negotiations.

One result of some states parties to the BWC being unhappy with the final text of the convention has been that throughout its life, efforts have been made to strengthen the BWC. Most of these efforts failed to deliver significant progress. In particular, during the 1990s extensive efforts were made by the states parties to the BWC to negotiate and agree a new legally binding instrument to supplement the convention: the BWC Protocol. These efforts collapsed during the period of July–December 2001.

Although acceptance of the agreed text of the BWC Protocol would have been undertaken at, and by, a special conference of the states parties, the process was expected to culminate in affirmation of acceptance of the protocol at the scheduled Fifth Review Conference of the BWC in late 2001. The subsequent failure of the Fifth Review Conference is inextricably linked to the failure of the Ad Hoc Group to agree a protocol. Nevertheless, the Fifth Review Conference did produce an agreement in 2002, and it is the failure of the Ad Hoc Group and the collapse of the negotiations on the BWC Protocol that are of most interest to any study of why negotiations do not end in agreement. The Fifth Review Conference is therefore not considered in this case study. In this chapter I briefly assess the background to the negotiations on the BWC Protocol between 1995 and 2001 and the failure to reach agreement on the protocol, before assessing possible explanations for why the negotiations collapsed.

THE BIOLOGICAL WEAPONS CONVENTION

It is widely believed that when the BWC was negotiated, four states were pursuing biological weapons programs, whereas by the end of the Cold War the United States intimated it had suspicions about up to ten states (Leitenberg, 1996:12). Evidence began to emerge from the early 1980s of noncompliance with obligations not to develop, produce, or stockpile biological or toxin weapons. This compliance problem was the key driver of efforts to negotiate additional politically and legally binding measures intended to strengthen the BWC. In that regard, although work on the BWC Protocol began in 1995 the negotiations represented a change in the direction and speed of a continual evolution of the convention. Indeed, the period 1985–90 can be viewed as preparing the ground for decisions and proposals made in 1991. The negotiations on the BWC Protocol stretch over a decade (1991–2001), and the process includes pre-negotiation phases (1991–94) and what can be viewed as overlapping diagnostic (1992–96), formula (1995–97), and detail (1998–2001) stages in the negotiations (Zartman and Berman, 1982).

By 1986, states parties reacted to an erosion of confidence in the BWC by extending their understandings about implementation and adopted a series of confidence-building measures (CBMs). This relatively minor measure was important in that it indicated a willingness to negotiate additional mechanisms to implement the convention. The convention was no longer viewed as a fixed agreement: while there was no support for formally amending the convention, there was increasing support for the creation of mechanisms relating to implementation and compliance. Those calling for change in the actual implementation of the BWC between 1975 and 1985 were "no longer crying in the wilderness" by 1986 (Sims, 1990:283). A convergence of factors in 1991 resulted in a greater support for a more-thorough attempt to strengthen the BWC beyond the politically binding mechanisms used to date. These factors included scientific and technological developments that hinted at greater availability of the equipment, materials, and knowledge to develop and produce biological weapons, a more propitious international political climate following the end of the Cold War, a more aroused public opinion in the form of a growing epistemic community of nongovernmental and other organizations concerned about biological weapons, and a more enlightened approach among some states parties to the convention (and in arms control agreements generally). At the Third Review Conference of the BWC in 1991 a number of states parties proposed that a protocol to the BWC be agreed to add verification provisions to the convention. Although states parties failed to reach agreement on the proposal for negotiation of a verification protocol in 1991, they established a group of Verification Experts (VEREX), who met between 1992 and 1993 to consider the scientific and technical possibilities of verifying the BWC. The omission of political issues related to verification of the BWC was deliberate; hence the VEREX process had a limited mandate for action (United Nations, 1993:1–2).

A special conference was held in 1994 to consider the work of VEREX and decide on further action. Critical to further action was the attitude of one particular state party: the United States (Littlewood, 2005:54–59). In the early 1990s the United States had opposed the negotiation of a formal verification protocol (Lehman, 1991; U.S. Congress, 1993:74). A similar U.S. position in the ongoing CWC negotiations required effective verification under the CWC, but that requirement was altered by the administration of President George H. W. Bush. As Robinson et al. noted, "the importance of this change lay in its express recognition of what had been the case, that no international ban on chemical weapons could ever be fully verifiable" (Robinson, Stock, and Sutherland, 1994:715–16).

The U.S. position on the BWC changed with the advent of the Clinton Administration, which "fully supported the preparation of a protocol containing a regime to strengthen the BWC" (United Nations, 1994:88). The discourse was significant because the objective and purpose of the BWC Protocol for the United States was not verification (Littlewood, 2005:56). The envisaged legally binding protocol would not verify whether states parties were complying with the BWC; rather the new agreement would strengthen the convention and establish mechanisms by which states parties could address suspected noncompliance (investigations) and demonstrate their compliance with the obligations under the BWC through a series of formal declarations and related on-site compliance assurance mechanisms (visits).

Through its change of policy the Clinton Administration effectively tipped the balance of power in the BWC to those favoring new negotiations. As a consequence, the 1994 Special Conference agreed to "Establish an Ad Hoc Group, open to all States Parties. The objective of this Ad Hoc Group shall be to consider appropriate measures, including possible verification measures, and draft proposals to strengthen the Convention, to be included, as appropriate, in a legally binding instrument, to be submitted for the consideration of the States Parties" (United Nations, 1994:9).

The mandate was a hard-won compromise between the United States, China, India, Iran, and the European Union member states and as part of the agreement the states parties were to consider the issues of definitions of terms, confidence building measures, compliance measures, and measures to promote peaceful cooperation among the states parties. The negotiations in the Ad Hoc Group began in 1995; they ended in 2001.

THE BWC PROTOCOL NEGOTIATIONS

The expectation was that the Ad Hoc Group would submit the protocol to the states parties in 2001 for consideration and adoption. An initial target date had been set as 1996 — the Fourth Review Conference — but this proved to be too ambitious.

The Breadth of Issues under Consideration

As was clear by the mandate of the Ad Hoc Group there was not one issue that states parties had to negotiate and agree upon, but many. In addition, other elements of this process make it potentially more complex than other arms control negotiations. To begin with, it was important to note that the BWC Protocol was an additional legal instrument to the BWC itself. The states parties had no mandate to formally alter the BWC itself (i.e., amendment of the convention). Equally, whether or not the negotiations on the protocol succeeded or failed, the legal status of the BWC remained unchanged. If a protocol was agreed and later entered into force, states parties to the BWC would have to sign and ratify the protocol itself in order to be bound by it. The prohibitions on production, development, and stockpiling of biological and toxin weapons in the BWC would remain unchanged regardless of the outcome of the protocol negotiations. Of equal import, the prohibition on the use of biological weapons (and chemical weapons) under the 1925 Geneva Protocol would remain unaltered by the outcome of the BWC Protocol debate. Thus, unlike the Nuclear Non-Proliferation Treaty Review and Extension Conference in 1995, there would be no legal implications of failure of the BWC Protocol negotiations (Albin, 2001:185).

A second issue underlying the negotiations was the range of topics covered by the 1994 mandate. The relationship of disarmament and development to disputes along a north–south axis of conflict were readily apparent. The legitimacy of export controls, central to nonproliferation obligations under the BWC, was also contested by developing states. The intrusiveness of compliance and verification mechanisms remained contentious among many states, including Western, Eastern, and Non-Aligned, and disputes over definitions and the establishment of objective criteria to assess compliance were problematic throughout the negotiations (Kervers, 2003; Littlewood, 2005; Ward, 2004).

The third issue not dominant during the negotiations themselves, but evident under the mandate, was the final outcome of the negotiations. While the mandate required agreement on a legally binding agreement, it did not necessarily require a single legally binding agreement covering all the topics identified for consideration of the Ad Hoc Group: definitions, compliance mechanisms, CBMs, and peaceful cooperation. Had it so decided the Ad Hoc Group could have developed a range of measures and agreements to be adopted by states parties including a legally binding agreement, but also perhaps more than one, and politically binding agreements as the outcome of the negotiations? While a range of possible outcomes could have been envisaged, only one — a single legally binding agreement — was the preferred outcome of the negotiations, not least as this was the only identifiable way to link issues considered by states parties as important. This interpretation has implications in terms of how success or failure would be judged by the states parties.

Finally, during the life of the BWC specific noncompliance problems with the convention and the proliferation of biological weapons had been addressed by mechanisms outside the actual framework of the convention. Noncompliance of the USSR had been partially addressed under a separate 1991 Trilateral Agreement between the United States, UK, and the USSR (Kelly, 2002). Concerns about proliferation of materials and technology were addressed via the Australia Group from 1991 onward. The Iraqi biological weapons program was addressed under the United Nations Special Commission (UNSCOM) and later the United Nations Monitoring, Verification, and Inspection Commission (UNMOVIC). Only in one case, Cuban allegations of U.S. use of biological weapons, did the states parties to the BWC address a specific compliance issue under the BWC and its consultation and cooperation mechanisms. The importance of these developments lay in the prospect of maintaining a functioning BWC via the use of specific and discrete mechanisms exogenous to the convention itself.

The Phases of Negotiating the BWC Protocol

As in other negotiations, an examination of the BWC Protocol reveals that the negotiations moved through distinct phases (Druckman, Husbands, and Johnston, 1991:56; Pruitt and Rubin, 1986:137; Zartman and Berman, 1982). At face value the early contentious phase of the negotiations settled down into problem-solving approach from 1997, but equally, Zartman and Berman's diagnostic, formula, and detail phases are also in evidence. In addition, in the BWC Protocol we can identify pre-negotiation between 1991 and 1994 that established the coalition of states, most notably including the United States, in support of the protocol and agreed the mandate for the negotiations. Disputes over the mandate of the Ad Hoc Group nearly derailed the Special Conference, which only reached agreement late into the night of its final day (Ward, 2004:1–4). Evidence indicates that China, India, and Iran opposed new negotiations and extracted from the United States and others in the Western Group a package deal that addressed not only issues related to compliance and verification, but also peaceful cooperation and the prospect of bolstering existing mechanisms such as CBMs (Littlewood, 2005:54–58). This "package deal" may have given rise to the balanced agenda essential for negotiations to begin (Albin, 2001:205), but states parties to the BWC did not collectively enter new negotiations united in their objectives, visions, or belief in the value of a new negotiation process. Strong differences of opinion are evident from the beginning of the negotiations on the BWC Protocol.

Between 1995 and mid-1997 the first formal phase of the negotiations repeated much of the scientific and technical analysis of possibilities undertaken by the VEREX group. This repetition was not wholly without merit, but the principal addition to this debate was the overt political considerations that influenced the negotiations. During this period most of the points of principle were identified by the states parties. Between 1997 and mid-2000 the negotiations shifted from the principles to the identification of key issues to flesh out the agreement. From mid-1997 the Ad Hoc Group made the transition to negotiations based on a "rolling text" of the draft protocol, akin to the single negotiating text commonly identified in negotiation literature (Fisher and Ury, 1981:118–22; Raiffa, 1982:205–17). From that point the rolling text served as the sole basis of the negotiations, and it shifted through a further fifteen iterations during the course of the negotiating sessions between July 1997 and April 2001 (the seventh to the twenty-second sessions of the Ad Hoc Group). As the differences between the states parties were narrowed, the negotiations shifted toward the endgame through the circulation of a chairman's text (the so-called composite text of the BWC Protocol) in March 2001. That transition was intended to signal the final phase of the negotiations during the period April–August 2001. The Ad Hoc Group had scheduled no further sessions after July–August 2001.

The Negotiating Process and Procedure

From the beginning of the negotiations the chairman, with consent from states parties, separated the issues into discrete negotiation topics. The negotiations began with four Friends of the Chair and ended with twelve Friends of the Chair. The increase in the number of Friends of the Chair reflected the addition of topics under negotiation as the text of the agreement progressed. Thus, the initial four Friends of the Chair dealt with the issues identified in the mandate of the Ad Hoc Group: definitions of terms, confidence-building measures, measures to promote compliance, and measures related to peaceful cooperation (Article X of the BWC). As the negotiations progressed, additional Friends of the Chair were appointed to cover discrete topics.[1]

By mid-2000 the chairman and the Friends of the Chair had identified forty-one remaining problems where states parties still held strong conceptual differences over the form of the final text (Littlewood, 2005:209–10; Pearson, 2000:15–23). Within the rolling text over fourteen hundred differences could be identified through the square brackets that denoted where consensus was lacking. As the discrete approach began to deliver fewer compromises, because of the interlinked areas of disagreement across the protocol as a whole, the negotiating format of using the rolling text and taking each remaining dispute line by line became less useful. The chairman had initiated private, invitation-only, informal sessions on certain issues in 1999 designed to explore approaches to taking forward the text of the protocol in discrete areas. These gradually increased in number, together with Friends of the Chair breaking out of formal sessions into informal exploratory discussions. In addition, the Friends of the Chair began circulating in 1999 formal proposals for compromises in what became known as the "Part II" rolling text; thus, at the end of every session of the Ad Hoc Group states parties would leave with two documents: the updated version of the rolling text and formal proposals from the Friends of the Chair for compromises at the next session, thus giving states parties something to work with during intersessional periods. By the second half of 2000 it was necessary to conduct and manage the negotiations in a more holistic manner. The transition to a compromise, square–bracket free chairman's text became increasingly necessary. The chairman's text was developed in the latter half of 2000 and finalized in Budapest in March 2001. By the time of its release to states parties, it had itself been through over thirty iterations, and fewer than a dozen individuals had likely seen the text in its entirety before its release on March 30, 2001.

With the release of the chairman's text, states parties appeared to be moving toward consensus agreement that the draft chairman's (composite) text of the BWC Protocol would be the basis of the last phase of their negotiations in August 2001. The final draft of the protocol in 2001 reflected the outcome of negotiations over seven years. As in many negotiations, the outcome was not necessarily a lowest common denominator solution, but it certainly was made up of an extensive number of compromises. The draft certainly fitted the idea that an arms control agreement reflected a "fragile construction of compromises and a minimum consensus related to highly controversial issues" (Ipsen, 1991:77).

By the consensus rule, in the negotiations any state could block progress and prevent agreement. The maxim "nothing is agreed until everything is agreed" was often invoked publicly by delegations, and many of the compromises in the text were undertaken on an ad referendum basis. Hence, there is ample evidence throughout the negotiations of states asserting their authority and wielding their power of veto as a means to achieve their objectives (Kervers, 2003:197). Unlike the BWC itself, which was a superpower deal presented to other states in the CCD as a fait accompli, the BWC Protocol of 2001 was truly a multilateral exercise, and the text reflected the objectives of many states parties, including the United States, Russia, Canada, France, the UK, Germany, Sweden, South Africa, Australia, New Zealand, Japan, China, Iran, India, Pakistan, Cuba, Brazil, and other NAM states, as well as other Western Group and Eastern Group states parties (Littlewood, 2005:205).

Prior to the final scheduled session of the Ad Hoc Group states parties had been requested to submit their comments and any requests for revisions to the draft text. While it is correct that more than fifty states parties did signal their agreement to negotiate the final changes to the BWC Protocol on the basis of the chairman's text (Dando, 2002:174), this has been characterized incorrectly as indicating fifty or more states parties had few concerns with the BWC Protocol as it existed. That interpretation is erroneous. By the end of July 24, 2001, close to three hundred comments, views, and requests for changes had been recorded: in total twenty-eight states parties explicitly requested eighty-seven changes to the composite text, most of them incompatible with one another. Moreover, the list of requests was expected to increase, not diminish, in the near term (Littlewood, 2005:211–12).

Requirements for changes, even those opposed to each other, did not present insurmountable problems. In addition to concerns about the commitment of the United States to the negotiations (Rosenberg, 2001:1), China, Cuba, Iran, Indonesia, Libya, Pakistan, and Sri Lanka attempted to reject the chairman's text by calling for a return to negotiations based on the rolling text in May 2001. They were rebuked not by overt means but by other states parties ignoring their formal written proposal — contained in a working paper — and, thereby, implicitly challenging them to translate that proposal into an actual request to the chairman. The seven did not publicly do so. However, with concerns about the U.S. commitment to the protocol, the attempt by the seven to derail the chairman's text, and perceptions that the proponents of the protocol were reaching the limits of their willingness to offer further compromises to hard-liners and holdouts, the envisaged final stage of the negotiation process in mid-to-late 2001 was about holding onto existing strengths in the draft protocol, reducing the remaining contested provisions to a minimum, and preventing the rejection of the chairman's text.

THE COLLAPSE OF THE PROTOCOL NEGOTIATIONS

Much has been written about the rejection of the protocol by the United States (Dando, 2002; Feakes and Littlewood, 2003; Kervers, 2002 and 2003; Littlewood, 2005; Roberts, 2003; Rosenberg, 2001; Ward, 2004). In terms of the impact on the negotiations themselves, the U.S. rejection of the protocol was comprehensive and final. In its formal statement, the United States concluded that "the current approach to a Protocol to the Biological Weapons Convention . . . is not, in our view, capable of achieving the mandate set forth for the Ad Hoc Group. . . . [W]e will therefore be unable to support the current text, even with changes, as an appropriate outcome of the Ad Hoc Group efforts" (Mahley, 2001:2). Furthermore, the United States intended to explore new ideas and alternative approaches to the strengthening of the BWC (Mahley, 2001:4).

The United States rejected not only the text offered by the chairman for the final phase of the negotiations but also the negotiation process itself. Without the prospect of consensus the negotiations could not continue and hope to reach agreement. Furthermore, the United States was not leaving the negotiations; it was staying at the table. Had the United States walked away, this would have, in theory, permitted others to continue to craft an agreement among those remaining at the negotiating table.

A broader assessment of the BWC Protocol indicated that it was not embraced by any state party or anyone in industry, the NGO, or the academic community, with great enthusiasm (Littlewood, 2005:206–15). The protocol negotiations did not fail to reach agreement only because of the U.S. position. To suggest otherwise is to underplay the remaining problems in 2001, the dynamics of the negotiations, and the reluctance of more than one state party to see an agreement enter into force. Yet, with the U.S. decision there was now no possibility of reaching consensus on the draft text, and the process of negotiations in the Ad Hoc Group had come to an end.

WHY DID THE BWC PROTOCOL NEGOTIATIONS FAIL?

At face value, one answer to the question of why the BWC Protocol negotiations failed is because the United States rejected the draft protocol text and the negotiating process of the Ad Hoc Group. The United States determined that the negotiations themselves, whatever the outcome, could not fulfill the objective of strengthening the BWC. There are complex issues behind the change in U.S. position that need both further exploration and explanation. Without doubt, the internal political changes in the United States played a very important role in the U.S. decision to reject the text, and existing negotiation theory can shine a light on the rationale(s) and processes that led to that decision (Carter, 1989; Druckman, 2004; Hampson and Hart, 1995; Hopmann, 1996; Iklé, 1964; Putnam, 1988; Raiffa, 1982:12–25; Strange, 1992).

Two questions have to be posed about the U.S. decision and its impact on the negotiations. First, why did the United States reverse policy in 2001 and remove its support for the Ad Hoc Group negotiations? Second, if the United States had not withdrawn support for the Ad Hoc Group, would the negotiations have culminated in an agreement among the states parties? The second question is counterfactual, and no one is in a position to claim categorically there would have been an agreed outcome from the negotiations. It is true to claim that the expectation was that agreement would be reached in 2001 or within the next year, but on the available evidence it is not certain consensus was attainable. The draft of 2001 had few champions, and had further concessions been required, other states parties may well have decided that the effort was not worthwhile.

Cultural and Institutional Explanations

Cultural and institutional explanations do not appear to offer adequate explanations for the failure to reach agreement. In part this is due to the professional cultural context of arms control, in part because of the length of the negotiations — over a decade if we factor in the pre-negotiation and agenda-setting phases — in part because of the role of epistemic communities, and due to the creation de facto of institutional support for the Ad Hoc Group. It is also true that in this multilateral negotiation context, which usually involved fifty or more states at each session of the Ad Hoc Group, there is insufficient empirical evidence available on the cultural factors that influenced every delegation (assuming they did) on which to make a judgment.

Arms control negotiation is a team endeavor in the larger delegations — mixing diplomats, experts from capitals, scientists, and so forth — and even though studies have identified specific attributes to certain states (USIP, 2002), as Lang noted, "negotiators, as a rule, do not act on their own behalf; they act on behalf of those who issue instructions" (Lang, 1993:41–43). This professional culture may subsume the various other cultures in existence in the negotiations. A professional culture in the BWC Protocol certainly existed, similar to the professional culture in most negotiation processes (Kremenyuk, 2002:36). The BWC Protocol negotiations followed established rules of procedure. Negotiations took place in Geneva, home of the Conference on Disarmament (CD). Many delegations in the Ad Hoc Group were composed of a mix of experts from capitals and diplomats based in Geneva for the CD (and other UN missions). Delegations and individuals were familiar with one another; between 1991 and 2001, states parties met over thirty times. The rules and rituals of the negotiations in the Ad Hoc Group were based on long-standing practice (the rules of procedure being handed down from previous BWC Review Conference and other meetings, mutatis mutandis, and which were themselves based on other arms control fora rules of procedure).

If culture is an explainable (identifiable) factor in the failure of the Ad Hoc Group, then conversely it must also be an explainable factor in the success of concurrent negotiations in the 1991–2001 period related to arms control and disarmament, not least the CWC (1993), the extension of the NPT (1995), and the completion of the CTBT (1996). No immediately identifiable cultural changes occurred between 1997 and 2001 to explain why negotiators were unable to reach agreement. While cultural influences cannot be dismissed out of hand, separating a cultural influence from another influence is not possible here with the available evidence to date. If for no other reason than lack of data and evidence, cultural factors have to be put on one side.

The institutional approach to negotiating success or failure is also not entirely convincing in this case study. The BWC does not, as Boyer ("Institutions as a Cause for Incomplete Negotiations," this volume) and others (Sims, 1988 and 2002) have noted, have a formal institutional support network or a dedicated organization to support it. The proposition Boyer postulates, however — that the more complex multilateral negotiations are in terms of issues, parties, and expectations, the more elaborate micro-level institutions will have to be to service the regime and promote constructive negotiation processes — does not entirely hold in the BWC Protocol case. The BWC Protocol was fairly low level and expert based. It also had two factors that added some stability to the negotiations. The first was a long-serving chairman of the negotiations, Ambassador Tibor Tóth of Hungary, who had represented Hungary in Geneva on biological weapons issues in the late 1980s, chaired the VEREX negotiations in 1992–93, and went on to be Chair of the Ad Hoc Group throughout its existence (1995–2001). The continuity and institutional negotiation memory Tóth held in the Ad Hoc Group was therefore an important factor. One consideration that has received no detailed attention in the public domain is whether or not the Chair of the Ad Hoc Group played a role in the failure of negotiations. As Albin noted ("Explaining Failed Negotiations," this volume) the chair has to "steer a chaotic and competitive process toward a balanced package agreement with benefits for all." The reaction of delegations to the chair's text was mixed, but aside from the halfhearted attempt to reject the text by China and others, it was viewed as the best means to finalize the negotiations. At face value, therefore, the chair would appear to have steered the Ad Hoc Group to a balanced outcome. In addition, Tóth created institutional support mechanisms for his work upon the transition to a rolling text of the protocol: a de facto secretariat emerged from 1997. The states parties paid for additional support to the chair beyond the support provided by the United Nations Department for Disarmament Affairs, beginning with one additional member of staff dedicated to the BWC Protocol and its chair in 1997 and adding another in 1999. Administering the Ad Hoc Group sessions in

Geneva was relatively straightforward, the rules of procedure and other procedural issues were by and large uncomplicated, and the interaction between the
delegations, Friends of the Chair, chair, and the secretariat were largely problem free. By late 1999 an almost complete picture of every state party's known
(stated) position on every issue under negotiation was available to the chair.
A large, electronic repository of information existed and was used extensively
by the chair (and a few delegations) in attempts to bring the negotiations to a
successful conclusion. Boyer does point to important factors that may have a
role in other negotiations, but in the case of the BWC Protocol, the institutional
explanation is not sufficiently convincing.

Too Complex to (Re)solve?

A further factor in considering the failure of the Ad Hoc Group was the
complexity of the topic under negotiation. Complexity (Mermet, "Managing
Complexity," in this volume) in this context cannot be understood as the topic
of "biological weapons" being too complex; after all, the use of such weapons
had been prohibited in war since 1925 under the Geneva Protocol, and disarmament was agreed in 1972 under the BWC. Rather, in the BWC Protocol the
range of issues, the linkage of issues seemingly unrelated to biological weapons, the number of players (delegations) in the room, and the differing levels
of scientific, technical, and political expertise allowing delegations to make a
constructive contribution to the multilateral negotiations all played a role. The
large number of actors and issues under consideration in multilateral negotiations make the task of reaching agreement even more difficult (Hampson,
Osler, and Hart, 1995; Hopmann, 1996; Zartman, 1994b). However, other negotiations, such as the Chemical Weapons Convention, successfully overcame
and dealt with similarly complex issues during the period 1980–92, so "complexity" per se cannot be considered the cause of failure. The negotiations were
complex, but the negotiations collapsed at the point when many observers expected states parties to complete their task. Up to mid-2001, despite the complexity of the issue under discussion, the negotiations in the Ad Hoc Group
could be characterized as rather successful. Over the course of seven years of
negotiations, building on a wealth of historical experience, bringing in relevant
lessons and solutions from other areas — and, importantly, rejecting solutions
from other areas — the negotiators in the Ad Hoc Group were able to translate
the complexities of biological disarmament into broadly agreed language —

the draft protocol — by virtue of the mandate given to them in 1994, known aims, a defined outcome, and institutionalizing and procedural methods, together with specific know-how of key individuals and delegations.

Psychological Explanations

Jönsson's analysis ("Psychological Causes of Incomplete Negotiations," in this volume) notes the inherent complex and multidimensional complications of bargaining situations that involve managing uncertainty. Disputes and uncertainty were at the center of the negotiations and, as Jönsson notes, this moves psychological consideration from the periphery to center stage. An assessment of the BWC Protocol negotiations can certainly point to examples and practice of being resistant to change — belief perseverance in George's terminology (George, 1980:73–74) — in the way states hold on to positions. Classic strategies, such as "anchoring," played a role with the creation of baseline positions from which to negotiate. Risk aversion was evident, with a high propensity to highlight losses and play up concessions and compromises on each side (Jönsson, this book; McDermott, 2004:139). Perhaps inevitably, as coalitions formed to overcome discrete problems, groupthink had to play a role in holding the coalition together but also moving it forward to further refine the policy in order to keep things progressing. Belief perseverance may warrant particular attention in this regard, coupled with the political changes in the United States between 1991 and 2001. The United States initially did not believe that the BWC could be verified, and its position on verification blocked negotiations in 1991 (Chevrier, 1990:96–98). When the term "verification" was put aside by the United States in 1994, negotiations were able to begin. While many referred to the BWC Protocol as a "verification protocol," the actual word "verification" was expunged from the text of the protocol because of U.S. objections to it, and "verification" did not appear in the final draft. Yet, in its rejection of the BWC Protocol the United States reintroduced verification problems as one of its principal reasons for rejecting the text and the process itself. As Gallagher has noted, arguments about verification in the United States have significance, and verification issues shape pre-negotiation strategy and assessment of the final outcome to significant degrees in the United States (Gallagher, 1999:3–26, 56–90).

Differences within the Western Group, especially, led to uncertainty among key delegations that were attempting to drive the negotiations forward. Thus, the UK and others struggled against both one of their closest allies and more hard-line elements in the NAM. To paraphrase Jervis, the lack of a coherent Western Group position in these negotiations meant that many U.S. allies could not rely on the belief or assumption that their closest and most important ally would actually support their goals (Jervis, 1976:116–17). Intra-caucus and intra-coalition disputes were as important in understanding the progress, or lack of, in the negotiations as intercaucus and intercoalition disputes among the states parties.

Kydd ("A Failure to Communicate," in this volume) points to three types of uncertainty concerning lack of knowledge about the other side(s) bargaining positions, mistrust between the parties, and uncertainty about the state of the world. Examples of each kind of uncertainty can be found in this case. No one can ever know everything about the other side's position. Mistrust was evident throughout the negotiations, not least because noncompliance with the BWC itself was the underlying rationale for strengthening the convention and there was no guarantee further noncompliance would be addressed by the protocol. In addition, with the end of the Cold War, the decade of the negotiations occurred against a background of a changing global order. Uncertainty was rife not only in the background, but also in terms of solutions offered to particular problems.

Throughout the negotiations we can also see evidence of framing and loss aversion on issues. While common in negotiations, in this case the disputes over the relative importance of aspects of the mandate of the Ad Hoc Group led to overemphasis on the disarmament-development linkage inherent to the position of the NAM and the security-first/development-second approach of the Western Group as a whole. Thus, in the area of peaceful cooperation, Western states were particularly averse to any concessions, whereas NAM states tended to be particularly averse to the lack of progress in the development context. Both caucus groups threatened to hold the negotiations hostage to further concessions related to development and peaceful cooperation mechanisms. In the case of the BWC Protocol, for the NAM the recently concluded CWC was unsatisfactory in terms of development and, especially, the issue of export controls (Littlewood, 2005:147–57). Perhaps, for key NAM states, perceiving that they had conceded too much previously (in the CWC) there was a greater determination not to concede without increased gains and more concessions this time around: anchoring, loss aversion, groupthink, and belief perseverance all had a role to play.

Groupthink was also a problem in the negotiations, in part because arms control and disarmament negotiations tend to build on their successes. To use Myrdal's phrase, "the game of disarmament" (Myrdal, 1976) can be repetitive. Where possible, negotiators transfer similar approaches, processes, and mechanisms to other problem areas in the hope of resolving differences. It was a common complaint of the United States that attempting to replicate the mechanisms in the CWC was a flawed approach. There was, and is, certainly an element of truth in this, but while the recognized scientific and technological experts may have been able to distinguish between what was appropriate and what was not from the CWC, many delegations were simply not equipped with the scientific and technical expertise to make informed choices. They relied on others and tended to believe that what worked in one arms control agreement would likely work in another. At the generic level this does tend to hold true — with very important exceptions — but it cannot be relied upon as a means to develop policy in a complex negotiation.

Psychological explanations for the failure of the Ad Hoc Group probably deserve greater attention. Their impact and role in the wider context — how negotiators interacted, belief perseverance, the role of groupthink, the framing of issues, and so forth — all offer explanations of why the negotiations dragged on for seven years. With hindsight, that time factor was important, and thus psychological factors cannot be disregarded out of hand and may be viewed as contributing to any explanation of why the BWC Protocol negotiations failed.

Timing and Staging Factors

Theories about the importance of time and timing have resonance in the context of the Ad Hoc Group. Seizing the "historical moment," the "window of opportunity," and the available "momentum" were terms all equated with the negotiations in Geneva (Matthews, 2000; Tóth, 1997 and 1999). Equally valid is the claim that bargaining, dialogue, and negotiation are shaped by actors' experience of time (McDuff, 2006:37), and there were frustrations at the pace of negotiation among states parties. Cohen's work relating to monochromic and polychromic cultures, also has salience in this case study (Cohen, 1991). The constant refrain among some delegations of the need to "refer that to my experts in Capital" served as a stalling device in later stages. Linked to this, some delegations rejected any attempts to set "artificial deadlines," such as completing the protocol before the end of 2001. As both Jönsson and Boyer note (see their respective chapters in this book), multilateral negotiations tend to overrun and turn into marathons. An early complaint of the BWC Protocol's strongest proponents was the unwillingness of some states to find the time to negotiate. Strengthening the BWC was not the major arms control issue on the agenda in the mid-1990s. Again, the fact that the BWC already existed and that the BWC Protocol was an additional element to it reduced its standing in the list of priorities (Duncan and Matthews, 1996:156). Controlling negotiating time, apathy among states parties, changing priorities in the arms control calendar, changing political situations and events, and attrition through slow negotiation were allies to those states parties negotiating for side effects in the BWC Protocol.

The stages of the negotiation would appear to have followed a pattern familiar to other negotiations. Rather than the stages themselves, it was the length of time between them that was problematic. The first two years of the Ad Hoc Group were a rerun of previous debates; the shift to the rolling text in 1997 locked the Ad Hoc Group into a negotiation format that prevented other mechanisms from emerging until the last possible moment. Many felt a chairman's text should have appeared in 2000; certainly, after the twentieth session of the Ad Hoc Group (July–August, 2000) the rolling text was no longer a useful means on which to base negotiations, but a chairman's text did not appear until March 2001. Reluctance to abandon the rolling text, and as a consequence permit some states parties to avoid making invidious decisions, meant the chairman could not be totally sure of support for the transition to a new text until it became inevitable (February, 2001).

Epistemic communities and stakeholders also interfered in the negotiations, thus external influences were felt in Geneva, via stakeholders, institutions, history, tactical alliances, and strategic incoherence and tensions, all of which were identified by Saner ("The Cyprus Conflict," in this volume) in the case of Cyprus. Equally contending views on solutions to problems in the BWC were evident from a range of experts. As Kydd noted, "for every epistemic community there is a countercommunity making opposite claims" (Kydd, "A Failure to Communicate," this volume), and many scientific disputes over technical solutions proffered during the negotiations were never resolved.

Strategic Causes for Failure

Albin's observation that "the tension between claiming and creating value is particularly sharp in international negotiations and frequently explains their failure or poor results" (Albin, "Explaining Failed Negotiations," in this volume) has resonance for this case study. Albin also points to three factors that influence international economic negotiations: changing international political conditions; negotiators' beliefs; domestic politics (Odell, 2000). These factors can certainly be used as one lens through which to view the BWC Protocol negotiations, because the changed international political environment and domestic politics were important factors which led the United States to the negotiating table in 1994 and resulted in it rejecting the negotiation process in 2001. Changing international political conditions also played a role for other states: as the chair of the negotiations remarked, "the political climate had changed since the CWC negotiations were concluded, and States Parties seem to have become less willing to accept international on-site inspection and monitoring" (Tóth, Geissler, and Stock, 1994:74).

It is possible to identify specific examples of a value-claiming strategy throughout the negotiations on the BWC Protocol by many states parties. Indeed, even if just posturing or positional play, value claiming increased publicly from mid-2000 onward as the target (or deadline) of the end of 2001 began to loom. Behind the scenes, however, value-creating strategies also occurred. There are enough individual examples recorded of problem-solving behavior, enlightened self-interest, and concessions made by key states to indicate the majority balanced their value-claiming and value-creating strategies.

A further factor worth considering is the actual mandate of the Ad Hoc Group. At least one U.S. commentator (and former negotiator) on the Ad Hoc Group believes the mandate agreed to after much hard bargaining in 1994 doomed the negotiations from the very beginning (Ward, 2004). The negotiation of the actual mandate is a classic case of perceptions about justice and fairness in negotiations and the importance of agenda-setting (Albin, 2001:30). Had the mandate not been a package deal, the negotiations would have never begun, but some viewed it is as detrimental to the negotiations from the very beginning.

An Insufficiently Mutually Enticing Opportunity to Resolve a Mutually Hurting Stalemate?

The concepts of a Mutually Enticing Opportunity (MEO) and the existence of a Mutually Hurting Stalemate (MHS) (Zartman, 2000) have relevance in understanding the failure of the BWC Protocol both in terms of when, and how, the negotiations began and when, and how, the negotiations collapsed. Translating these concepts into pertinent questions for this case study, we can ask: was the final draft text of the BWC Protocol a sufficiently enticing solution to a problem that was hurting a sufficient number of states? Put this way, the reasons for the failure of the Ad Hoc Group become more apparent in a broader context. In particular, the problem of biological weapons was not that great in the period 1995–2001. Biological weapons have not been used to great effect or on a systematic basis by any state in recent history. Most states, such as Iraq, had failed to develop sophisticated biological weapons programs, and a range of measures external to the BWC had been used to address specific issues. Based on this view the United States could bring about the end of the negotiations without serious (hurting) consequences, while leaving open its options for the future. Thus, it might be argued, the United States could not find a formula or solution preferable to the status quo or a unilateral approach to the problems and threats posed by biological weapons: that is, no BWC Protocol (Zartman, "Process Reasons for Failure," in this volume).

This is in contrast to the situation with regard to chemical weapons prior to completion of the CWC in 1993, and nuclear weapons prior to the completion of the CTBT in 1996, and the extension of the NPT in 1995. Failure to extend the NPT in 1995 would have altered the status quo and raised difficult legal questions relating to nuclear weapons (Albin, 2001:185). The failure to agree the BWC Protocol had no real effect on the status quo, did no legal harm to the BWC, and did not preclude other solutions (legal, multilateral, or other) from emerging or being proposed in the future.

The most salient fact may be that the United States did not need the BWC Protocol. Of the problems with biological weapons, the USSR–Russia transition and highlighting of noncompliance was addressed at least partially by the Trilateral Process between the United States, USSR, and the UK and not by the BWC states parties. The problem of Iraqi biological weapons was addressed via the United Nations until 1998, by containment and sanctions between 1999 and 2002, and further attempts by the UN, and then war in 2003. Other cases, such as Libya, were resolved by other means in 2003. Terrorist threats from biological weapons were not, at the time, viewed as pertinent to the BWC. Perhaps the best explanation in this case builds upon Zartman's observation that "negotiations may fail because parties prefer the status quo even when an objectively good and fair agreement is possible" (Zartman, "Process Reasons for Failure").

Also relevant in this case is the long-standing aspect of negotiations: they are not always intended to succeed. In the context of Iklé's negotiation for side effects this makes sense, but there is an important nuance in that a failure of negotiation indicates a successful strategy for those who are willing to negotiate but view an agreement as undesirable. Central to the collapse of the Ad Hoc Group and the rejection of the process of negotiations on the BWC Protocol was the change in policy in the United States in 2001. It has been noted that the Clinton Administration overturned the previous U.S. BWC policy to permit negotiations on the BWC Protocol to proceed. This 1993 change in U.S. policy was itself reversed in 2001 with a reversion to the previous policy. As an aside, proponents of the BWC Protocol should not take comfort from a belief that had the negotiations been completed with an agreement during the Clinton Administration, the protocol would now be in force: as the U.S. failure to ratify the Comprehensive Test Ban Treaty indicates, and the willingness of the United States to remove its signature from an agreement—as the Statute on the International Criminal Court attests—a successful outcome may be transient.

CONCLUSION

The change of policy within the United States is central to understanding the demise of the negotiations, but based on the status of the protocol in mid-2001, it cannot be stated categorically that the Ad Hoc Group would have reached agreement even if the United States had not altered its policy to the protocol. Ultimately, there is likely to be no agreement on which factor(s) was the most influential in causing, or explaining, the failure of the Ad Hoc Group.

Nevertheless, the United States determined the fate of the Ad Hoc Group and the BWC Protocol. In line with the observations of the USIP Cross-Cultural Negotiation Project (USIP, 1992:3), at the most critical point the U.S. negotiation stance was perceived as domineering, insistent, and uncompromising. Recognizing that others in the Ad Hoc Group could or would not be persuaded by its views the United States acted on its own. A unilateral decision to abandon the negotiation process became the U.S. policy.

Direct participation and leadership by the President of the United States is essential to the successful conclusion of arms control negotiations (Bunn, 1992:171). President Clinton lacked this direct involvement in the BWC Protocol. In contrast, President George W. Bush (and opponents of the BWC Protocol) did not. Interests shift as a result of changes in the electoral landscape (Hopmann, 1996:155), and in 2001 a new presidential administration in the United States was a precipitant: it was followed by a departure (decision) by the United States with regard to the utility of the BWC Protocol negotiations that had significant consequences on the negotiations (Druckman, 2004). Following this, the outcome of the Ad Hoc Group could not be altered by other states in the negotiations.

Such single-state opposition to a multilateral arms control agreement is not unique. The CTBT negotiations nearly fell at the final hurdle when the CD failed to adopt it. As Kumin noted, "This happenstance . . . was not due to the nature or quality of the communication and negotiation process nor the fault of the professional cultures involved, but a consequence of some overriding political considerations of one single country [India] which was of the view that its vital interests might be jeopardized by this treaty" (2003:125). In a wider context, a new U.S. view on security issues in the post-post Cold War period emerged before September 11, 2001 (Steven Miller, 2002). New eras require new approaches, and as Lall observed, "The stronger the conviction of a country that is riding the advancing tide of history, the more narrow and rigid its negotiating postures in regard to international disputes or situations in which it is involved" (1966:246).

The failure of the BWC Protocol may not, however, be taken as the final word with regard to negotiations on biological weapons issues. The future remains open and even "highly unsatisfactory negotiations," like the INF talks between 1981 and 1983, may result in, or create the ground for, more satisfactory (successful) negotiations at a later date (Carter, 1989:259).

NOTES

1. Friends of the Chair were created for the following areas: Preamble, General Provisions, Definitions of Terms and Objective Criteria, Compliance Measures, Investigations, Confidentiality Issues, Legal Issues, National Implementation and Assistance, Peaceful Cooperation, The Organization, Seat of the Organization, and Declaration Formats. The chair of the negotiations oversaw the discrete areas of "The Organization" and "Confidence-Building Measures."

The Negotiations on the Status of Belgium

London Conference, 1830–1833

DANIELLA FRIDL

History teaches us that at times a small power, due to its geographic location and relevance, can play a key role in international politics. Nineteenth-century Belgium was a rare "jewel of Europe," a battlefield, the most sought after "prize," and an intriguing puzzle for both eager conquerors and presumptuous European diplomats.[1] Due to its appealing strategic geographic location, this "crossroads of Europe" and "keystone" was the easiest path between France and Germany and the best avenue for entry of British goods to the Continent.[2] This paper will analyze Belgium's turbulent fate in the nineteenth century, when the country found itself in the hands of great powers, serving their strategic purpose within the balance-of-power system. The primary purpose of this study is to analyze the process of contentious negotiations that took place at the London Conference in the period from 1830 until 1833, after which it was suspended, and determine the answer to the question of why the negotiations did not result in an agreement. By analyzing the process that took place and explaining the outcome through negotiations theory, this paper seeks to provide valuable lessons and tools for future negotiations.

HISTORICAL BACKGROUND

Throughout its history, the Belgian Provinces remained a persistent object of contention between the French to the west and the Germans to the east, and both Spanish and Austrian monarchs ruled the provinces from 1556 to 1792. The French, however, remained the fiercest and most adamant claimants of Belgian territories. They captured the Belgic Provinces in 1792 and lost them the following year, only to regain and annex them in 1794 (H. Thomas, 1959:5). In addition, the period between 1776 and 1790 was characterized by instability and a series of insurrections and revolutions that broke out in Europe.[3] This period of volatility ended in 1814 with the disintegration of Napoleon's empire, which placed Belgium's future in the hands of European powers. Napoleon's defeat at Waterloo and the loss of the Belgic Provinces, even though it caused heartache for the French, did not discourage them from pursuing their dream of reannexing Belgium.[4] A French ambassador at the time of Louis XIV commented, "The English will give the shirts off their backs to prevent the French from penetrating into the Low Countries" (Linden, 1920:161).

Both the French and the British maintained a close interest in the fate of the Belgic Provinces.[5] For military and economic reasons, the Northern Netherlands also had a great stake in Belgium's future. In the eighteenth century, long fortresses stretched along the border between the Habsburg-owned Austrian Netherlands (Belgium) and France. It soon became apparent that fortification did not represent enough of a barrier to stop the northward expansion of the eager French troops (Ernst Haas, 1952:7–8). As a result, "during the height of the allied offensive against Napoleon in the fall of 1813, the stadtholder-in-exile, later King William I of the Netherlands, requested the cession of all Belgium to Holland in order to build a new barrier against French aggression."[6] The Kingdom of the Netherlands that was created at the end of the Napoleonic Wars was one of "the most deliberate and carefully motivated decisions of the Quadruple Alliance of 1814" (Ernst Haas, 1952:7). The unhappy union of the United Netherlands consisted of Belgium, Luxembourg, and the Northern Netherlands.[7] The powers disposed of the Southern Netherlands first at the Peace of Paris on May 30, 1814, and later by the Final Act of the Vienna Congress on June 9, 1815. William I was appointed as the new legitimate king and accepted this disposition on July 21, 1814, and commenced his rule of the amalgamated kingdom on March 16, 1815.[8] The Treaty of Vienna never consulted the Belgians about the decision to unite them with Holland in order to form a barrier against any French expansion and to preserve peace in Europe. The central goal of European powers at that time was buttressing the well-established balance of power determined at Vienna, regardless of the cost this effort entailed (Meeus, 1962:262). Between 1815 and 1848 intervention was a device used by the great powers (Austria, Great Britain, Russia, and Prussia), who perceived themselves as the guardians of peace, to control and assist the governments of weaker states.[9]

While the strategic plan for the Kingdom of the Netherlands appeared to be a great masterpiece on paper, in reality the differences between the two peoples were only exacerbated by the deep inequality imposed by King William's ignorant policies. The antagonism between the Belgian and the Dutch people was evident with respect to the diversity of commercial and agricultural interests between the two parts of the kingdom, as well as on differences of religious principles.[10] In response to the threat posed by Napoleon's return from Elba, William I appointed a select commission of Belgians and Hollanders to consider codifying the Fundamental Law of the Kingdom.[11] Another point of contention and Belgian frustration was the fact that they had a greater burden in paying taxes.[12] Belgian notables decided to reject the modified Fundamental Law, and as the bourgeoisie of Belgium increased in economic power, they demanded a greater role in solving political and social questions. Instead of trying to accommodate the Belgian demand, William I disregarded their claim and proclaimed the law as accepted.

The fact that the Dutch always thought of Belgium as a territory annexed to Holland rather than as an equal part of the state did nothing to alleviate Belgian grievances.[13] Failing to recognize the signs of growing displeasure, King William made an attempt to promote a national feeling of unity by urging the acceptance of Dutch as the national and official language, which he made official in 1822. This caused not only an outrage but a problem for Belgians who spoke French or Walloon, which included nearly all the professional men and leaders of society. Even though some concessions were made in 1829, by then a majority of the leading figures of the South, receiving considerable support both in Flanders and in Wallonia, were demanding for autonomy from Dutch rule (Helmreich, 1976:12; see also Strikwerda, 1997:27–30). It was only a matter of time before Belgian grievances would turn into violent protest.

The Belgian Revolt

The riots erupted on August 25, 1830, following the performance of a patriotic opera *La Muette de Portici* in Brussels (Rooney, 1982:1). Even though William's overconfident temperament and political ideology played an important part in the causes of the revolution, they provide insufficient explanation of the events that unfolded. The basic causes of the eruption of 1830 were the deep sentiment of "separateness" of each people and Belgians' displeasure and protests over the fact that the Dutch were "running the country solely to their own benefit" (Helmreich, 1976:12). In the beginning, the Bruxellois did not plan on demanding separation from Holland (13).[14] Instead of the anticipated and much feared French oppression in September of 1830, the European powers faced the challenge of internal revolution. Berlin, London, Vienna, and St. Petersburg were confronted with the decision of whether to lend armed aid to Holland to maintain the status quo, or whether they should pursue a different course of action (Ernst Haas, 1952:16). Each of them individually considered what was in the best interest for their countries. Tsar Nicholas I of Russia was interested in the success of the Netherlands for military, dynastic, and economic reasons, and he profoundly feared French expansion. The foreign minister of the new French government, Count Mole, faced a dilemma regarding the issue of whether France should allow the dispatch of British and Prussian troops to Belgium to restore order or whether the proper policy should be to give aid to the insurrection. Another option for the French was to stay neutral in this matter and leave things up to the other European powers. During the rebellion, the British seemed to support the Belgian efforts to challenge the existing order and break into the European system. At first, London's reaction to the riots was nonchalant, as the British Foreign office was convinced that the Brussels affair centered on local grievances.

The Tory prime minister at the time of the revolt, the Duke of Wellington, regretted the disruption of the Vienna system, but at the time he did not want to pledge British military aid to King William I, partly because he regarded him as a weak ruler and partly because Britain was militarily weak. England's primary interests required stable relations with France. When Mole indicated that France wanted arrangement of the Belgian matter, the duke acquiesced.[15]

On October 5, 1830, King William I made an appeal for help to end the rebellion, basing his request on the Treaty of the Eight Articles, which had made the victorious powers guarantors of his dominions. The French government was the first to take the initiative by appointing the experienced diplomat Charles-Maurice de Talleyrand-Périgord as the new ambassador to the Court of Saint James. His task was to persuade the British government to call a conference of all the interested powers to resolve the issue (Helmreich, 1976:18–19). On the ground, Belgians fought fiercely and defeated the Dutch outside the Brussels palace in a battle that lasted for three days. On September

27 the Dutch withdrew. The Belgians rather quickly formed a provisional government, which declared independence on October 4, 1830. On November 3,
a National Congress was formed by an electorate of thirty thousand men, and
on November 18 the National Congress of Belgium declared its independence
(Juste, 1850:54–55).

   Belgium's declaration of independence was the starting point for negotiations about its future among the great powers.

The London Conference Negotiations

The Conference of London opened on November 4, 1830, and was crucial in
determining the future of Belgium.[16] The great powers, rather than Belgium
and Holland, occupied themselves with establishing the arrangements to "combine the future independence of Belgium with the stipulations of the Treaties,
with the interests and security of other powers, and with the preservation of
European equilibrium" (Rooney, 1982:183–84). The plenipotentiaries of Great
Britain, Austria, Prussia, Russia, and France declared at its first session that re-
uniting the two countries without war would be impossible (Rooney, 1982:183).
The rivalry at the conference was mainly between England and France, and
both took the initiative in determining the future of Belgium. It was Lord
Palmerston, one of the ablest foreign secretaries England ever had, and the
French ambassador Prince Talleyrand, the most prominent figure in European
diplomacy of that time, who gave Belgium its status among the European nations, naturally to suit their own countries' purposes. On its first day, the conference issued the first of its seventy protocols. It ordered the establishment
of an armistice and the evacuation by both parties of all areas that had not
formed a part of their respective territories before May 30, 1814 (Ernst Haas,
1952:20). The first protocol declared the withdrawal of all troops.[17]

   A change of British governments did not work in favor of the Dutch, as
even before Palmerston replaced Wellington the Belgians made a gain when
the conference proposed an armistice based on the borders given Holland by
the Treaty of Paris of 1814. The protocol further benefited the Belgians by referring to them not as rebels but as recognized belligerents, which significantly
promoted their cause in further negotiations (Helmreich, 1976:15). Some of
the main problems that arose at the conference were related to the questions
of boundaries, the division of the national debt, and the navigation of rivers
and canals. The international aspects included a buffer between France and

Belgium, and noted the problem of the balance of power and general security (20). There was a uniform belief among the European powers that a monarchy rather than a republic would be a preferred form of government for Belgium (Cammaerts, 1939:15).

Russia, Austria, and Prussia opposed Belgian independence. The simultaneous outbreak of revolution in Poland prevented a Russian-Austrian-Prussian military intervention in support of William I against the rebellious provinces. However, Lord Palmerston's new government wholeheartedly supported recognition. It was precisely the Franco-British coalition that imposed a reversal on the London conference, affording Belgium its official independence in January 1831 (Cammaerts, 1939:15). The initiative and formal motion that initiated the process of recognition was introduced by Lord Palmerston and seconded by Prince Talleyrand on December 18, 1830 (Ernst Haas, 1952:22).

As pointed out by one distinguished Belgian international lawyer, the future independence of Belgium was stated in strict terms that had to be abided by: "The preservation of the balance of power; the principle of security of the other powers; and the principle of maintaining the treaties of 1815 which tied Belgium to the security system of the victor powers" (Deschamps, quoted in Ernst Haas, 1952:7).

William strongly protested against a new disposal of Belgian provinces by the powers by claiming that it was against the principles of international law for the powers to revoke their decision.[18] During January 1831, the main topics that were discussed were the conditions, limitations, and qualifications to full national sovereignty, which the conference pointed to in its seventh protocol. In two key protocols, the so-called Bases of Separation of Belgium from Holland, or the Eighteen Articles, were defined, and the main points of contention between the two entities were addressed, though not to everyone's satisfaction. First, the conference prefaced the fixing of the borders and the division of the public debt with another declaration concerning the European obligations of the two nations. It also indicated to Brussels that any future arrangements would be subordinated to the rights of the conference members. The plenipotentiaries made it crystal clear to the Belgian authorities that no new Belgian conquests or territorial aggrandizements were to be made at the expense of Holland.[19] The plenipotentiaries also added a condition of neutrality that was to be achieved with Belgian independence.[20] One week later, the conference issued anther protocol, which stated, "Belgium assumes 16/31 of the total public debt of the former Kingdom of the Netherlands;

that while the final debt settlement was worked out by bilateral negotiations, Belgium pay its share of the service charges; that Belgium should enjoy free and unhampered trading privileges with the Dutch colonies."[21] The provisional Belgian government rejected the territorial and the financial "Bases of Separation" and refused to ratify these proposals (Ernst Haas, 1952:32). London warned that in the event of Belgian failure to accept the separation plan, the powers would break off relations with Belgium and refuse to recognize its independence.[22]

The choice of the new king was also a subject of great debate. Lord Palmerston took measures to prevent such a possibility by introducing a proposal according to which no prince of the ruling houses represented at the conference would be eligible for the Belgian throne. After a couple of eliminations, the British Cabinet obtained on June 4, 1831, the election of its own protégé, Prince Leopold of Saxe-Coburg and Gotha, who had been married to the late Princess Charlotte of Great Britain and Ireland and was known to contemplate a second marriage with Louise of Orleans, daughter of the King of France (Fuehr, 1915:6).

Sponsored by the conference, Leopold had been negotiating for weeks with a Belgian deputation in London. The basis of the talks was the acquisition of Luxembourg for the choice of Leopold as king and the acceptance of the remaining articles of the Basis of Separation.[23] Leopold's close adviser, Baron Stockmar, confirmed that the powers were willing to accept this deal, since by June they were desperate for some sort of Belgian settlement (Ernst Haas, 1952:33–35). After the Treaty of Eighteen Articles was announced on June 26, 1831, the Belgian National Congress not only speedily elected Leopold king, but on July 12, 1831, accepted the Eighteen Articles (33–34). It appeared that the armistice was finally achieved and that Europe was on its way to a solution to the Belgium problem. However, King William flatly refused to even consider these terms.[24] On August 2, 1831, William sent the Dutch troops to invade Belgium (Rooney, 1982: 62).[25] Paris, without consulting the conference, but with British approval, reacted by sending an army of fifty thousand soldiers into Belgium. To avoid risking an engagement with the French troops, the Dutch commander rapidly withdrew his forces (36–39).

As soon as the armistice had been reestablished the plenipotentiaries returned to finding a final settlement that would be acceptable to both parties. It was becoming apparent that there was no hope that Holland would accept the Eighteen Articles, nor could the status quo be permitted to last indefinitely, as Belgium or Holland would return to fighting particularly over the bitter Luxembourg question. Threatening Holland with a naval blockade to prevent further hostilities, the powers extended the treaty draft on November 14, 1831, to a definite and irrevocable instrument, to be adhered to not only by the two main parties, but also by the conference powers themselves. Through this means, the final and definite separation of the two countries was to be made binding on all the major powers, who became the guarantors of the arrangement.[26] This was the famous Treaty of the Twenty-Four Articles, which, despite a seven-year-delay, was destined to be the final arrangement. The treaty established the independence of Belgium, defined the borders, and regulated the relations between not only Belgium and Holland but also of Belgium and the rest of Europe.[27] The second major provision dealt with mutual transit, navigation rights, and the partition of debt (Ernst Haas, 1952:42). In contrast to their earlier position, the plenipotentiaries now ruled that the Belgian share of the joint debt would amount to 8.4 million florins of total annual charges, with Belgium being freed from any payments pending the creation of the machinery for transferring the money. The remaining fund of the Kingdom of the Netherlands was to be divided equitably through a bilateral agreement (42). In addition, not only was the territory and the neutrality of Belgium guaranteed, but the financial, transit, and miscellaneous articles were placed under the protection of the conference as well. The Belgian government expressed readiness to ratify, but The Hague refused. Berlin, Vienna, or St. Petersburg seemed just as disinterested, and London and Paris did not exchange ratifications with Belgium either (43).

The fruitless and tiresome negotiations continued during the summer of 1832. Immediately after the French troops were safely pulled out of Belgium, Britain and France reopened negotiations with the Dutch government. Their ultimate aim was the full acceptance of the Twenty-Four Articles by The Hague, but having as a minimum objective the conclusion of some sort of a provisional arrangement, pending the conclusion of a mutually acceptable final treaty. On December 31, 1832, Palmerston and Talleyrand proposed to the Dutch an interim agreement that provided for "evacuation of all territory still occupied by each party in defiance of the borders drawn by the treaty, opening of navigation on the Meuse and the Scheldt, the granting of amnesties and the exchange of prisoners, the opening of the Sittard trade route to Germany, mutual arms reductions, to be followed by raising the blockade and embargo still in effect against Dutch trade" (Goblet, 1864:137–38).

Britain and France demanded an unlimited armistice and full Dutch recognition of Belgian neutrality. On March 9, 1833, a treaty was concluded at Berlin in which it was provided

> 1) that the London Conference should be reconstituted after the cessation of all coercion measures; 2) that the Twenty-Four Articles should be the basis of an entirely new negotiations, in which the Belgian and Dutch governments should participate as equals; 3) that the consent of the German Bund to the Luxembourg-Limburg arrangements of the treaty of November 15, 1831 was an essential condition; 4) and the three monarchs agreed that any new arrangement could not put more onerous conditions on Holland than those already agreed to that the new negotiations would be broken off if a new attempt at coercing Holland was to be made and finally the three rulers predged themselves to assist Holland if her territory were attacked or if Britain and France were to act contrary to these stipulations. (Martens, cited in Ernst Haas, 1952:56–57)

The new negotiations would be broken off if a new attempt at coercing Holland was made. Finally, the three rulers pledged to assist Holland if its territory were attacked or if Britain and France were to act contrary to these stipulations.

The conference reopened in London, and during the summer and fall of 1833 attempted to work out a new treaty that would satisfy the wishes of the Dutch in the disputed transit and navigation clauses of the Twenty-Four Articles. The demands of Holland clearly indicated that they had no wish for a final treaty, and the negotiations made no progress. In November of 1833, upon learning that King William had not taken any measures to obtain the consent of the German Bund to the proposed division of Laxenburg and Limburg, Palmerston declared the conference suspended until The Hague would give evidence of being ready to accept the Twenty-Four Articles (Ernst Haas, 1952:54–58). Amazingly, no such signals were given for the next five years, which ensured suspension of the conference over those years.

REASONS FOR NONAGREEMENT

There are a number of reasons that contributed to negotiations ending in nonagreement in 1833.

Perceived Power Asymmetry

One of the reasons is the issue of perceived power asymmetry. In the negotiations theory perceived asymmetries, whatever their bases may be, produce different attitudes and strategies in the exercise of power by the strong. The party perceived as stronger typically attempts to dominate the exchange and adopt a take-it-or-leave-it strategy toward its negotiation partner (Zartman and Rubin, 2000:276). At the London Conference, not all issues pertaining to the conference were debated at the foreign office. Many crucial matters were discussed and decided in the countryside. Talleyrand spent weekends with Wellington and Aberdeen, the English minister for foreign affairs, and, after the Whigs came to power, with Palmerston and Grey. In addition Palmerston, Lord Grey, and Prince Leopold spent several days in the country before proposing Prince Leopold's candidacy for the Belgian throne. Leopold himself gave a politically important dinner before accepting the Belgian throne, at which he entertained Talleyrand, Palmerston, and the Belgian delegates. This practice indicated the concentration of power in a small circle of leading members of the great powers. It was apparent that in London, the central figures of power and the decision makers were Wellington, Palmerston, and Talleyrand, the leaders of the Anglo-French entente. With this nucleus of influence it was possible for Talleyrand and Palmerston to seize the initiative on select issues and, by an adept sense of timing, dictate both the agenda and the pace of negotiations.

They used their power and influence to force those decisions on the Eastern powers. The power was self-perceived by Talleyrand and Palmerston and used to dominate negotiations in order to fulfill their self-imposed responsibility of maintaining peace in Europe. For them this was a greater good far more important than the wishes of individual states, which in this case represented the Dutch and the Belgians. It was apparent the Dutch were not involved in those negotiations but were rather only informed of the decisions once they had already been made. This played an instrumental role in King William's feeling helpless and powerless. He failed to recognize that he did indeed possess the power; however, he needed to adopt an appropriate counterstrategy in order to borrow sources of power and move the great powers into the direction in which he would like the negotiations and outcome to go (Zartman and Rubin, 2003:277).

The Mediator's Role

The great powers' role with respect to the negotiations is questionable. The conflicting parties call on or, rather, allow mediators into negotiations because they are seeking a better solution to their conflict than they are able to achieve themselves (Touval and Zartman, 1985:260). The mediator's role is to invent outcomes and help move parties toward reaching a jointly acceptable outcome. Furthermore, one of the key goals of mediators is the ability to redefine the problem and expand the possibilities around the contested issues, to include items that can be traded against each other (268). For example, a mediator can initially help the parties reach agreement on matters that are not considered of vital importance and help the parties define the subject of the negotiations in a manner that "allows the circumvention of vital issues on which no compromise is possible" (267). The great powers, however, developed their own formula for negotiations. Most of the Bases of Separation Agreement, the Eighteen Articles, and the subsequent Twenty-Four Articles Agreement were drafted by the powers without consulting the Dutch or the Belgians. Rather than assuming the role of mediators and facilitators, the great powers were conducting negotiations amongst themselves, consulting the two conflicting parties only to present final agreements. In addition, when the parties refused to accept the agreement, as Belgium did with respect to the Bases of Separation agreement, instead of searching for a compromise solution or finding a solution that better matched Belgian interests, the powers immediately issued an ultimatum. The great powers never managed to broaden the spectrum of options and possibilities, nor did they try to change the perspective and perception of negotiations that each party had. In being so adamant about following a strict formula the great powers only decreased the chances of bridging the gap between the two parties and helping them reach an agreement.

Strategic Issues

Also related to the matter of the mediator's role were the strategic issues that played a significant role in the outcome of negotiations. This is evident in the perception of the outcome of the London Conference. However, some have claimed that the conference was one of the greatest victories gained by the Concert of Europe in the nineteenth century. From the perspective of the two negotiating parties, the events and negotiations were perceived as far from successful. For the Dutch the year 1830 represented the low point in their history, as they lost the Southern Netherlands. This shook the nation's confidence and put into question their ability to continue their role as a strong nation on the international stage. For the Belgians, the proceedings in London were a frustrating and even humiliating experience, as they had to abide by the terms of the great powers. They indeed achieved independence, but just like the Dutch they were subject to the wishes and terms of the great powers. The former Belgian delegate to the London Conference, Sylvain Van de Weyer, described Belgian independence as a "European transaction" (Van de Weyer, 1873:317).

This was evident in the negotiations, during which the great powers only focused on achieving their own objectives, which were strategic in nature and involved maintaining the status quo in Europe and preventing major wars from erupting. Hence, their goals stood in the way of the negotiations as they proposed a formula and pressured the two parties to abide by it. This caused dissatisfaction and aversion of the parties toward the mediator, and in turn eliminated some of the opportunities that could have been pursued if the powers had shown more flexibility and concern for the interests of the parties.

Lack of Trust

Another reason for the incomplete result of the negotiations was the lack of trust among the parties and toward the great powers of Europe. Trust as well as credibility in negotiations is imperative in order for each side to feel certain of the other side's desire to reach a negotiated outcome (Zartman and Berman, 1982:27–41). The Belgian people did not trust the Dutch king, as they perceived him as a selfish and single-minded ruler concerned only about maintaining his power. Even though he made promises of equality between the Dutch and the Belgian people, his actions clearly indicated that he wanted to assimilate the Belgian people into Dutch culture. On the other hand, King William did not trust the great powers. In his eyes, the powers lost all credibility when they decided to abandon their decisions from 1815. From the beginning he protested against a new disposal by the powers of Belgian provinces and argued that according to international law the great powers had no right to revert their decision made in Vienna. Throughout negotiations, the great powers never attempted to reestablish trust among negotiating parties nor between the parties and themselves.

In negotiations there are numerous ways in which the mediator or mediating parties can assist in enhancing trust. This can be achieved by improving mediators' capacity to understand the problem, by following up on promises, by demonstrating a genuine interest in trying to help the two sides reach their objectives, by not using threats or ultimatums, or by making concessions and showing the two sides that they can gain from negotiations more than by not negotiating at all. The great powers, however, never established an environment conducive to enhancing trust among negotiators.

FORWARD- VS. BACKWARD-LOOKING OUTCOMES

Another reason was King William I himself. Initially he appealed to the great powers to support his fight against the revolution and to "rescue" the kingdom that they established in 1815. He expected the great powers to side with him and assist in "mending" the kingdom to bring it back together. When he realized that the goals of the great powers did not coincide with his own, he refused to negotiate. Instead of focusing on the benefits he could gain from negotiations, King William was strictly focused on losses compared with his past situation. He was hanging on to a notion of his past-based rights, ignoring the new present-based claims on rights based on feelings of nationality. By looking backward to the time when he was the ruler of the great kingdom, he was not able to divorce himself from his perception that he would lose the kingdom. He was disappointed to find out that the goals of the great powers were mainly to prevent any revolutions from turning into major wars, even if that meant revising their earlier decisions. William was outraged by this realization to the point that even after his short military campaign, which afforded him more equitable conditions as outlined in the Twenty-Four articles of October 1831, he took no advantage of them. He turned into a "spoiler" in the negotiations, not realizing that the refusal of this agreement only hurt the Netherlands, which was driven into complete diplomatic isolation.

In negotiations forward-looking outcomes look for mechanisms to prevent future violence as they "seek outcomes that reach beyond the conflict to opportunities for cooperation and problem solving, and try to prevent the resurgence of the old conflict in a new, later form by resolving its underlying causes" (Zartman and Kremenyuk, 2005:3). This is precisely what the new arrangement that entailed neutrality on Belgium promised. It was a mechanism that was implemented to prevent future conflicts from occurring in the whole region. However, William's shortsightedness prevented him from seeing the long-term benefits and gains of negotiations and the proposed formula.

Mutually Hurting Stalemate and Mutually Enticing Opportunity

As the negotiations in London progressed, it became obvious that there was neither a Mutually Hurting Stalemate (MHS) nor Mutually Enticing Opportunity (MEO). MHS is a situation in which the parties are locked in a conflict from which they cannot escalate to victory, the deadlock is painful to both of them, and they see a way out (Zartman, 2000:228). The point at which they decide to do something about their situation is upon realizing that that pain will only increase unless something is done about it. However, at the London conference there was never a point at which both parties felt they were "hurting." One of the tasks of the mediator is to balance the parties in the conflict in such a way as to produce the hurting stalemate if it does not naturally occur by the existing circumstances that the parties find themselves in. The key is to do so in a way so that the parties do not perceive the mediator as taking sides but rather as an impartial player (Zartman, 2000:264). The great powers never made such an attempt. Similarly, there was no MEO, a concept defined as a scenario and a point in time when both parties perceive an attractive opportunity that pulls them out of a stalemate and eventually leads them to an agreement. Surprisingly, in 1831, William still expected Belgium to revert to him in the future, and he did not want to compromise his position by abandoning his sovereign rights over his southern provinces. This is due to the fact that he did not believe that the powers would betray the Vienna arrangement; thus, he undermined the credibility and sustainability of the "artificial equilibrium" created in 1830 (Kossmann, 1978:160). Therefore, a combination of the lack of trust in both the powers and their intentions as well as in the viability of the system the powers created caused William to refuse the agreement and wait for a better offer. When that offer never arrived and Belgium established its viability as a state, in March of 1838 William finally declared his willingness to accept the articles. The revised Twenty-Four Articles were signed by Belgium in May and ratified early in June 1839. The signed agreement was not significantly different from the one proposed in 1831.

NOTES

1. Central Belgium consisted of a corridor that extended from the Aachen area in western Germany to the Lille-Maubeuge region of northern France.

2. Its centrality is evident in an incredible historical record of 32 battlefields within the present Belgian boundaries during ancient times, 352 in the Middle Ages, and 618 between 1500 and 1932 (Winter, 1919:26–27, 51–54, 105–10).

3. These included the American Revolution of 1776; revolutions in Holland, Sweden, Ireland, and Geneva; as well as the Brabant Revolution, the Liege revolution in 1789, and finally the French Revolution (De Mee, 1962:236).

4. The French were encouraged by the fact that the majority of Belgians spoke French and had already accepted French institutions. French authorities came back to the idea in 1829 and made an unsuccessful pursuit of annexing Belgium. This was part of a scheme of Prince Jule de Polignac, who became foreign minister and minister of war. The council of state decided to propose that the French annex Belgian provinces and the Prussians take the Dutch provinces. The British were to be offered the Dutch colonies. If they refused, Britain would face a coalition of the other powers. Fighting in the Balkans ceased before the French revealed their plan (Ward and Goosch, 1922–23:122–23). See also Alfred Stern, 1905:189.

5. The main reason behind this was Britain's strong belief that possession of the provinces by France or any other country in Europe would upset the balance of power and pose a threat to the British Isles. They were fully aware of the danger implied by the shrewd comment made by Napoleon: "Antwerp in the hands of a strong France was a pistol pointed at the heart of England" (Sir James Headlam-Morley, cited in Daniel Thomas, 1959:6).

6. William I to Castlereagh, November 9, 1913, and Castlereagh to Aberdeen, November 23, 1813 (cited in Renier, 1930:205–7).

7. Arthur Wellesley Wellington, Dispatch, Correspondence, and memoranda of Field Marshal Arthur, Duke of Wellington (London, 8 vols., 1867–80), "Statement of the Expenditure on the Fortresses of the Pays-Bas during the year 1829," and "Statement in English Currency of the Expenditures on the Fortresses in the Netherlands to 31st December, 1829." These enclosures are attached to the letter of Colonel Jones to the Duke of Wellington, May 12, 1830, cited in Rooney, 1982:1.

8. The primary goal of the Congress of Vienna was to establish a new balance of power in Europe that would prevent imperialism within the continent, and maintain the peace among the great powers. Moreover, it was hoped that it would prevent political revolutions such as the French Revolution and maintain status quo (Ernst Haas, 1952:6).

9. This principle was evident in the words of Austrian minister Klemens von Metternich, who asserted that "when domestic social unrest makes it impossible for

a government to meet its treaty obligations that bind it to other countries, the right to intervene belongs as clearly and indisputably to every government which finds itself in danger of being drawn into the revolutionary maelstrom, as it does to any individual who must put out a fire in his neighbor's house if it is not to spread to his own" (Kalevi Holsti, 1992:261).

10. With respect to economy the Dutch had the traditional economy of trade and was very open, while Belgians had less-developed local industries. The Dutch called for free trade, while the Belgians asked for the protection of tariffs. Religion and language also pointed toward significant differences between the French-speaking Roman Catholic South and the Dutch-speaking Protestant North. Belgians demanded a higher role for the Church in the government, which was opposite of what the Dutch wanted. These differences were probably not sufficient to cause a riot, but the worsening situation within the kingdom and the oppression of the Belgian population awakened nationalistic feelings. This assisted the Belgian people in developing a strong sense of national identity and unifying them in their fight for freedom. In addition, King William's rule proved to be a grave disappointment to the Belgian people (Metternich, 1830:35–36).

11. Ministers were responsible only to William; in addition, the king appointed over half of the Senate, and the Second Chamber could only reject or approve but not amend legislative proposals. A problem came about with respect to representation in the chamber. The Belgians, whose region possessed 3.4 million inhabitants compared with Holland's 2 million, insisted that representation be proportionate to the size of the population (Edmundson, 1902:521).

12. Even though the two regions were to share their joint debts, the Belgians' liabilities amounted to thirty-two million florins while those of Holland were two billion. The Belgians thus were obliged to pay taxes to finance a debt which was mostly not theirs (Helmreich, 1976:10).

13. From the very start, the Dutch made clear their intention to keep control of most governmental and administrative posts. The home ministry employed 117 Dutch officials, compared to 11 from Belgium in 1830; of the army's approximately 2,500 officers, less than a fifth were Belgian (Edmundson, 1902:525).

14. "An assembly of notables met three days after the outbreak of the riots and sent a delegation to ask the king to consider Belgium's grievances and to discuss them with the States General. A Committee of Public Safety was formed, of which the majority were moderates. Revolutionary groupings did call for a provisional government, but until September 20 it was all in vain" (Helmreich, 1976:13).

15. Mole told the Prussian ambassador in Paris, Werther, that France would refrain from any intervention in any country on its borders, as long as no other major European state intervened first. By announcing this, France proclaimed that any entry of Prussian troops into Belgium would be followed immediately by the involvement of

the French army as well. This policy became known as the "non-intervention doctrine." This decision/doctrine was rejected by the European powers, and only the British cabinet expressed conditional agreement. The Prussians had mobilized immediately and were prepared to march into Belgium (Haas, 1520:17).

16. There was much debate regarding the location where the conference should be held. During the month of October 1830, there were three possible locations: The Hague, proposed by King William; Paris, which was favored by the French government; and London, which was insisted upon by the Duke of Wellington. It was Talleyrand's and Wellington's insistence on having it in London that prevailed at the end (Fishman, 1988:62–63).

17. The protocol stated: "The troops of both parties shall withdraw behind the line which before the treaty of May 30, 1814, separated the territory of the Sovereign Ruler and the United Netherlands from the provinces added to his dominions to form the Kingdom of the Netherlands" (Rooney, 1982:25).

18. William declared: "Having once for all determined the fate of the Belgian provinces, you have not according to international law, the right to rescind your decision: to sever the ties binding Holland and Belgium, is outside the sphere of your competency, the more so as this increase of Dutch territory was granted on certain burdensome conditions. . . . At the expense of several colonies and considerable financial sacrifices. The Conference of London, it is true, met at my request, but this circumstance does not give it the right to give to its intervention an effect, diametrically opposed to the purpose for this it was requested" (Ernst Haas, 1952:7).

19. Protocol No. 10, Annex B, January 18, 1831, BFSP, XVIII, 756–58, cited in Ernst Haas, 1952:23–24.

20. "Belgium, within the limits described above . . . will be constituted into a perpetually neutral state. The five powers will guarantee it this perpetual neutrality, as well as the integrity and inviolability of its territory, within the limits mentioned. By a just reciprocity, Belgium will be constrained to observe the same neutrality toward all other states, and not to disturb in any way their internal or external tranquility" (Protocol, No. 11, January 18, British and Foreign Papers [Foreign Office, London], 18:759–61, cited in Ernst Haas, 1952:23–25).

21. Protocol No. 12, March 17, 1831, Annex A, 785–88, January 27, 1831 (British and Foreign Papers), 18:761–65, cited in Ernst Haas, 1952:25.

22. Protocol No. 22, April 17, 1831, 794–96.

23. Even though the question of who would be the sovereign was never a part of formal discussion, as early as December 14, 1830, Palmerston and Talleyrand agreed on their choice of Leopold of Saxe-Coburg as monarch, much before the Belgians chose him (Fishman, 1988:71).

24. Protocols Nos. 27, 28, and 29, July 25, and August 4, 1831.

25. Concurrently, the whole of Europe continued to be an arena for revolution. The French government was in disagreement with the courts of the Holy Alliance on a number of issues. In Poland, a bloody war was already raging, and Italy seemed about to be engaged. Britain was thought to be anxious above all to keep the French out of Belgium.

26. Protocol No. 52, November 14, 1831, 913–14, Ernst Haas, 1952:41.

27. The French-speaking section of Luxembourg, roughly three-fifths of the original territory of the Grand Dutchy, was added to Belgium, while the remaining portion was to form a part of the German Bund under the personal rule of the House of Orange. The Belgians were obliged to cede the northern sector of the province of Limburg, containing the important fortresses of Venloo and Maestricht, as compensation for their acquisition of parts of Luxembourg. The question whether this area of Limburg should belong to Holland outright or be ceded to the German Bund and then given to the House of Orange was left undecided by the conference. The conference preferred not to leave the exchange of enclaves to the parties, and instead to distribute them itself (Ernst Haas, 1952:40–41).

Two Hostage Negotiations

Waco and the Munich Olympics

DEBORAH GOODWIN

Any incomplete negotiation can be frustrating and disappointing and can often result in a sense of failure for all concerned. This outcome may be politically detrimental or personally demoralizing, but often the scope for renewed initiatives at some future date will continue to exist. But there are some negotiation situations where an inability to resolve the dilemma cooperatively can, and does, result in destruction and loss of life as the ultimate consequence. Siege situations, hostage-taking incidents, and any circumstance that explicitly involves a threat to life are replete with both the urgent drive to resolve the crisis cooperatively and the pernicious reality of the difficulty of so doing. This chapter will investigate the seeming antithetical nature of hostage taking and creative crisis negotiation resolution, together with main stumbling blocks to effective negotiated solutions with particular reference to the Waco Siege 1993 and the Munich Olympics hostage taking in 1972. Before analyzing some of the nuances and dynamics of these incomplete and unsuccessful crisis negotiations, a summary of the respective events will prove beneficial.

THE WACO SIEGE, 1993

The Branch Davidian Sect, based at New Mount Carmel in Waco, Texas, was a Bible-based religious community led by David Koresh. From the mid-1980s onward Koresh had shown himself to be an able organizer and articulate evangelist, developing and proclaiming a belief in an imminent Armageddon based on the apocalyptic revelations in the Bible, with Koresh himself being the "Lamb of God" personally receiving advice from the Lord. This conviction drew many converts, and along with furthering their religious beliefs, the Branch Davidians established many commercial ventures, ranging from repairing cars to selling guns. Koresh fathered many children within the established community, and there was a strong acceptance of his leadership of the group.

On the morning of Sunday, February 28, 1993, agents of the U.S. Bureau of Alcohol, Tobacco, and Firearms attempted to search the Branch Davidian Compound in order to arrest David Koresh. A firefight ensued, resulting in the deaths of four ATF agents and an undetermined number of Branch Davidians. Very soon after these deaths the FBI became the lead agency for resolving the resultant standoff, with their Hostage Rescue Team (HRT) arriving on site and initiating telephone negotiations the same afternoon. President Bill Clinton implicitly endorsed a negotiated settlement to the situation, given that a large number of women and children lived at the compound and were perceived to be at risk.[1]

By the following morning effective negotiations were proceeding (led by Byron Sage of the FBI), and ten children were sent out of the compound. Talks continued into the early hours, and Koresh made an audiotape of his teachings with an opening statement that promised surrender if the tape was aired nationally. At 1:30 p.m. the audiotape was played on the American Christian Broadcasting Network, but at 5:58 p.m. Koresh informed the negotiators that God had told him to wait. At this juncture Acting Attorney General Stuart Gerson stated that the response was to "talk them out, no matter how long it took." However, President Clinton did agree to deploy military vehicles for safety purposes.

Wednesday, March 3, saw Koresh becoming more actively involved in the negotiations in terms of describing the Branch Davidian "world picture" to the FBI negotiators. He made references to dealing with God rather than "your bureaucratic system of government," and explained his interpretations about the end of the world at length. By the late evening Koresh noticed armored vehicles moving around the compound and warned the FBI that they would have to "look at some of the pictures of the little ones that ended up perishing." Undoubtedly, this comment would have been seen as an explicit threat to the lives of the children, reinforcing the authorities' view that this was a serious hostage situation. Despite this, negotiations remained

conciliatory over the next two days. The FBI was compiling detailed information about Koresh and the sect away from the negotiations, though; two
FBI psychological profilers concluded that a strategy of negotiations, together with escalation in a tactical response initiative, would be destructive and liable to result in loss of life, and information from experts concerning Davidians and preference for suicide proved "inconsistent." The
FBI also worked out that the Davidians had food supplies that would last
a year.

By Saturday, March 6, all parties were becoming increasingly agitated and
suspicious. The FBI voiced frustration at being unable to negotiate effectively
with Koresh, who, in his turn, was concerned that the compound might be
burned down to destroy evidence. Negotiators refused to deliver milk for the
children unless more were released, but Koresh countered by saying that they
were all his biological offspring. The psychological profilers urged the FBI negotiators to establish trust with Koresh, and predicted an assault on the compound would result in mass suicide. However, the succeeding days saw the
escalation continue; on Tuesday, March 9, the electricity was cut off, resulting
in the response from Koresh that he would not negotiate unless it was put back
on. It was, though HRT members were alarmed to see weapons being placed
at the windows inside and firing ports being cut out. The power supply tactic
was used repeatedly from this time onward, along with the use of constant
bright lights on the compound buildings, and often despite objections by the
HRT negotiators. This was particularly the case on March 12, when the power
supply was shut down for good by the authorities. This was a huge setback
for the negotiations and instantly stopped several members of the sect from
coming out that day as had been agreed. Tactical commanders were increasingly making decisions that superseded the more conciliatory actions of the
negotiators, and these had a direct impact on the initiatives possible through
negotiation.

On Monday, March 15, the FBI reviewed its negotiation strategy by deciding
to continue to seek to talk but also refusing to listen to any more "Bible bab-
ble." The immediate effect was to significantly decrease the time spent negotiating daily (only forty-six minutes on March 16). A few adult Davidians did
come out over the next few days, but tactical command insisted on another
escalation of hard-line moves, playing loud music over a loudspeaker system
into the early hours and, later, relaying messages from those who had exited
already.

The siege was to prove painfully protracted, lasting until April 19, 1993, with an ebb and flow of action/inaction and negotiation/escalation/negotiation throughout this time. Ultimatums were issued on several occasions by the FBI, particularly between March 25 and 28, moves that were reinforced by armored vehicles moving forward and the further use of spotlights and loud music. Koresh's response was a refusal to negotiate for three straight days, and many days of stalemate subsequently followed.

Eventually, official frustration grew at this lack of resolution. Various authorities informed Attorney General Janet Reno that negotiations had reached an impasse, and so she met with Delta Force commanders to review an action plan on April 14.

On April 15 even the HRT negotiators personally voiced their fears that there could not be resolution through negotiation, so plans were formed to use tear gas to expel the occupants. After a warning, at 6:02 a.m. on Monday, April 19, two FBI vehicles began to gas the building. The Davidians started to shoot back, and the melee continued for several hours. By 12:07 p.m. the Davidians were seen starting several fires, and nine Davidians ran for safety, but at 12:25 p.m. the FBI heard "systematic gunfire," indicating that the Davidians were either killing themselves or each other. At 12:41 p.m. HRT teams entered the fiery building to try to find survivors, especially the children. They did not succeed.

So, the protracted siege had ended in the use of force and extensive loss of life. Over the course of fifty-one days, more than forty officers had participated in the negotiations that had the goal of persuading the Davidians to leave the complex peacefully. They had made many concessions during that time (the broadcast of Koresh's tape, allowing Davidians to exit to bury one of their members and to retrieve Bible material from cars, sending in milk, supplying legal documents as requested, and allowing communication with family members outside). But these initiatives were increasingly undermined by tactical response measures as described, and any early negotiated success eventually turned into tactical disaster.

MUNICH OLYMPICS HOSTAGE TAKING, 1972

Some twenty years before Waco, events at the Munich Olympics took a deadly turn on September 5, 1972. The international television cameras that were following the games daily were suddenly capturing the storming of the Olympic village by Arab "Black September" terrorists and their seizure of eleven Israeli athletes in the early hours of that day. Holed up in the athletes' chalets, makeshift negotiations ensued between the terrorists and an intriguing group comprising the Bavarian interior minister Bruno Merk, Munich police chief Manfred Schreiber, and the mayor of the Olympic village, Walter Troger (the Germans had no professional HRT at this time).[2] Throughout the course of the day the Germans fielded this eclectic mix of negotiators at different times — adding a representative from the Arab League; West German Interior Minister Hans-Dietrich Genscher; the vice president of FINA (International Swimming Association); A. D. Touny, an Egyptian member of the International Olympic Committee; and an unnamed female official — to the original "triumvirate" of negotiators.

Terrorist demands centered on the release of two hundred Arab prisoners held in Israel and the provision of an escape aircraft with a range of three thousand kilometers and room for twenty-six people. Essadafi (Issa), the leader of the terrorist group, spoke directly to the negotiators on several occasions while holding a primed grenade as an explicit threat. All of these encounters were captured on camera — there seemed to be no embargo on media coverage — and it later emerged that the terrorists had kept the television on throughout as a useful method of information gathering. For example, at 11:20 a.m. an interview with Shilon, the chief Israeli sports editor, was broadcast on West German television where he stated, "We have received word that the safety of the Israeli Olympic athletes is guaranteed." Also, at 4:18 p.m. Schreiber appeared on television to restate the terrorist demands and to add that every offer of money and the substitution of hostages had been vehemently refused.

The terrorists set a deadline for 12:00 p.m., after which an athlete would be shot every hour if their demands were not met, but ongoing negotiations guaranteed an extension. At 1:35 p.m. a declaration from the Black September organization was publicly broadcast: "Our revolutionary strike force has stormed the Israeli Headquarters in the Olympic Village to protest against the Israeli regime of terror." Negotiations continued over the next few hours, with the Germans attempting resolution by proposing a handing over of money or exchanging prisoners, but all of these offers were refused, as Schreiber later stated on television. Negotiators were seen openly talking to the terrorists and some of the hostages who were brought out onto the balcony, and they even managed to enter the besieged apartment. It then became apparent that there had already been a fatality.[3]

Between 4:35 and 7:12 p.m. there was a flurry of negotiation ranging from overtly aggressive encounters between the terrorist leader and Merk to casual chats while smoking.

Throughout the day armed police had moved into position in the village (but their presence was broadcast by a news team, and the terrorists probably saw this on their television), and official discussions had been held concerning the eventual choice of resolution. At 4:54 p.m., Defense Minister Leber appeared on television to announce that no sharpshooters were involved in the proceedings (an indication that the authorities wanted to make this message clear to the terrorists, and that they now knew the television was being monitored).

Negotiations ensued about the transportation of the terrorists and the hostages out of the Olympic village, with obvious anxiety being shown by the terrorists themselves concerning the logistics and possible ambush setups (which the Germans tried twice throughout the day, but bungled). At 9:53 p.m. an official addressed the leader from a distance, saying, "You will be shortly be taken away . . . you're on your way . . . you'll be informed, wait there." For the first time the terrorist leader was carrying a machine gun, rather than a grenade, and was obviously annoyed at this point.

However, at 10:20 p.m. all the terrorists and their hostages were transported by bus and helicopter from the village to the Furstenfeldbruck Airport. When they arrived at the airport a German armed rescue was attempted, using five snipers, an insufficient number given the number of terrorists. This was a result of the authorities having never correctly established the number of terrorists involved in the hostage taking at the village, and so they were forced to make an educated guess. But this guess resulted in the deaths of all the Israeli hostages at the hands of the terrorists, and of five of the eight hostage-takers at the scene after a fierce firefight. The surviving terrorists, and the related leadership, viewed the entire day as having been a success.

ANALYSIS

Although these two incidents initially seem different in their scope, agendas, and modus operandi, both were adversely and grimly affected by failed or incomplete negotiations. There are some distinct elements in both situations that indicate a commonality of failure, or that might be seen as clear indicators that flagged a failing negotiation dynamic. These factors can be broadly delineated as follows:

- Poor phase development and different perspectives

- Mixed messages and poor strategies

- Power issues

- The "bigger boss syndrome"

Poor Phase Development and Different Perspectives

Essential to effective negotiation tactics is the development of the phases, or "life cycle," of strategic interplay. For example, the movement away from original positions early in the dynamic is crucial (otherwise deadlock or stalemate will ensue), the generation of option creation, the exploration of the Zone of Possible Agreement, the avoidance of choosing to act aggressively rather than continue to negotiate, together with a sustained developmental ethos implicitly and explicitly expressed throughout the negotiation (for more discussion, see Fisher, Borgwardt, and Schneider, 1994; Lewicki, Saunders, and Minton, 1997; Thompson, 1998; Tversky and Kahneman, 1974). Progression in the dynamic can be best effected through constructive communication, empathetic response, lateral thinking, and the recognition of motivational interests. Effective progressive negotiation is also reliant on the affirmation of one disputed factor before moving on to the next.[4]

J. A. Call (1999) has highlighted some key characteristics of crisis negotiation, and these are useful in the analysis of why Waco and Munich failed as negotiations:

- Use of force on both sides

- Bargaining for high stakes

- Focusing on one option

- High degree of emotion

- Preponderance of "face-saving" issues

- Feeling of urgency

- Lack of complete information

- Failure to work out a detailed implementation plan (see J. Call, 1999)

All of these characteristics are necessarily negative and potentially destructive to any effective negotiation process, and if the negotiator is either not aware of such a working context or at a loss as to how to remedy such dilemmas, then a negotiation in such circumstances is likely to fail. In both the Waco and Munich case studies, all of Call's characteristics can be clearly observed, plus the resultant negativity in terms of handling the respective negotiations.

At Waco it is remarkable that the negotiations, albeit lengthy, substantially failed to move beyond the agenda-building or meta-negotiation phase, and rarely into constructive option creation. This was most noticeable in the attitude of the Branch Davidians, whose framing of the situation was markedly different from that of the FBI. Koresh and the Davidians perceived the situation as a "state to state" and "citizen to government" encounter and wished to shape an agenda accordingly, whereas the FBI viewed the same situation as a "state to individual/hostage-taker" encounter.

> We don't want anything from your country. (Feb 28: Branch Davidian Wayne Martin to FBI negotiator Lt. Lynch)[5]

> The extraordinary discipline that Koresh imposed on his followers . . . made him far more threatening than a lone individual who had a liking for illegal weapons. The Compound became a rural fortress, often patrolled by armed guards . . . were [he] to decide to turn his weapons on society, he would have devotees to follow him, and they would be equipped with weapons that could inflict serious damage.[6]

This respective framing of the situation never changed, and thus formed a substantial block to progressive phase development in the negotiations.[7] The Davidians viewed themselves as a separate state within the United States and wanted negotiations to proceed on that basis, while the government/FBI always saw the situation as an armed siege with lives at risk, with a pursuant reliance on tactical armed response measures as required.

Also, discussions rarely moved away from two key areas; for the Davidians there was a constant imperative to teach the FBI/U.S. state about their religious beliefs and attempt to convert them (which left the FBI negotiators baffled and frustrated), and the FBI repeatedly demanded the release of "hostages" (a term that baffled the Davidians) (see also Ross Ward, 1994). So, there was little progression thematically, and the perceptions of the situation were markedly opposed.

At Munich, there were more obvious signs of phase progression throughout the day. The framing of the essential situation was more easily perceived; with the authorities acknowledging an "authorities versus hostage-taker" encounter and the terrorists a "group versus state" encounter (as expressed in their media statement cited above):

0920   Negotiations in front of the apartment between the leader
        and a delegation comprising Schreiber, Merk, and Troger. The
        leader passes a list to them and explains it. . . .

1030   The female official resumes contact with the terrorist leader
        through hand signals. . . .

1115   Schreiber, Troger . . . come to negotiate. They are greeted
        by the leader with a hopeful handshake. It appears that
        an agreement has been reached over the extension of the
        ultimatum. . . .

1702   Genscher and Troger go into the besieged apartment with the
        terrorist leader.[8]

One of the first things that Schreiber realized was that negotiation could only be advanced by the involvement of the government of Israel, as the local authorities could only ever be "middlemen," and he attempted to effect progress in this way (see Boltz, Dudonis, and Schulz, 2002). After the initial stages of the siege, with positions quickly revealed, deadline issues were dealt with effectively at the local level and some option creation initiated. However, rejection of options meant that a stalemate was soon reached with an explicit threat of escalation by both sides as the hours ticked by.

Mixed Messages and Poor Strategies

One of the key elements of successful negotiation is an ability to create links between the conflicting parties, particularly by and for the professional negotiator, in order to understand motivations, drives, and interests, and hence predict reactions and possible responses as the situation develops. Inability to achieve this open-mindedness and perceptiveness results in an encounter that cannot achieve effective mutual responsiveness, but merely a communication that runs in parallel throughout, rather than converging as necessary.

As Zartman has stated, "Negotiators need to construct legitimacy for a negotiated agreement and build the terrorists' independent decision making capabilities to think in terms of lowered expectations and thus of lowered demands. Treatment as equals, development of the legitimacy of a solution, and expansion of options are all ways of moving the hostage-takers off positional bargaining and opening up the possibility of a fruitful search for mutually satisfactory solutions by newly defined standards" (2005b:3).

At the heart of both these events was the failure to move away from positional bargaining and the successful implementation of integrative strategies and options. As is well recognized, positional bargaining is fundamentally flawed, negative, and destructive as an effective negotiating strategy, and failure appears inevitable if this course is sustained.

At Waco the framing of the entire situation, the belief systems of the respective parties, and the perceptions of one another all meant that there was constant competition and negativity in the jarring and nonprogressive negotiation dynamic. For example, the Branch Davidians characterized all their actions as "fatalistic" and being dictated by a higher entity, while the FBI were thoroughly goal-rational and task-oriented. Koresh spoke in an autobiographical manner, often using explanatory narratives, while the HRT employed visionary stories based on conceptualizing the end of the siege, with both types of narrative blaming the other party for matters not proceeding. The Davidians believed in a degenerative view of history (a negative future), while the authorities represented and voiced the generally accepted socially progressive view of history (a positive future), and both parties constantly sought to convert the other, to no avail. This truly was a dialogue of the deaf, and a fundamental element in the "incomplete" nature of the negotiations at Waco.

When an entrenched negative perception of the future cannot be affected or altered, then there is very little scope to create a positive outcome to the situation or to make it mutually appealing. This also links with the concept of Attribution Theory, where it is postulated that communications are understood through the perception of their intent, and thus sincerity and understanding are key facets in mutual appreciation, and for sustainable negotiation (see Woodward and Denton, 1996). Another applicable tactic would have been the overt use of Social Judgment Theory tenets at Waco, where the effectiveness and attractiveness of communications are based on how close they are to personal belief systems. The closer the proposal made is to the core belief then the more likely the potential to change or alter response (Woodward and Denton, 1996). This concept effectively explains the communication gulf apparent between the authorities and Koresh and, if used proactively by the negotiators, might have proved beneficial in moving the negotiation into an integrative phase. In addition, Masterson, Beebe, and Watson (1989) made a very valid argument that when we listen to a speech/dialogue that is radically different from our own beliefs then we do not evaluate or actively listen, but constantly internally criticize. This is, of course, extremely detrimental to successful dialogue.

Munich witnessed a very haphazard negotiation organization, as evidenced by the random choice of negotiators, their large number, and their inconsistency of approach and understanding. Since there was no official HRT to call upon in this circumstance, officials remained at a loss as to how to proceed through negotiation but appeared to remain unrealistically optimistic about the eventual outcome.

Negotiators in Munich did not obtain basic information concerning the number of terrorists (and this could have been achieved through discussions over the number of meals needed, for example), fatalities, and circumstances in the rooms and suchlike. A major error was the sustained availability of the television in the hostage rooms; here was a case for shutting off the electricity swiftly. Also, since none of the negotiators was professionally trained as such, the transcripts reveal that they wandered around, chatted with the leader on the balcony, in the room, or at a distance. This all indicates that they were being dictated to by the terrorists rather than trying to shape the situation to their own advantage. Strategies and tactics altered throughout the day, dependent as they were on external decision makers, but the dearth of information was always going to prove problematic in respect to any creative negotiations and probable attempted assault at some stage.

However, there are effective strategies that can be, and are, used in similar crisis situations in order to attempt to avoid deadlock or catastrophe. One notable technique is the use of the Perceptual Contrast Principle (PCP), which involves the negotiator's recognizing, and exploiting, known patterns of behavior to both influence and obtain compliance. This principle works on the basis that if two items are presented to us that are different from one another, then we tend to view them as being more different than they actually are (for example if we lift a light weight followed by a heavier weight, we would then tend to gauge the heavier weight as being heavier than it really is). So, by using this principle in negotiations, the negotiator can offer up options that appear markedly diverse, and present initiatives that, if following the PCP pattern, will appear more profound than they might be in reality, and thus more appealing to the other party (for full details, see Cialdini, 1984 and 1993). This might have proved a viable tactic at Munich, for example.

Also missing from both Waco and Munich was the effective use of a Rule of Reciprocity strategy. If someone does us a favor, then we tend to seek to return that favor at some stage. This rule tends to work best when parties do not know each other, or even dislike one another, a fact that is self-evident in crisis negotiations. Research has revealed that even small favors being given, or even perceived to have been given, tend to result in larger paybacks (Cialdini, 1984 and 1993). For example, leaving the electrical power on can be used to extract the release of hostages (attempted, but not successful, at Waco), as can the delivery of food (so woefully ignored in Munich). Another element of this rule of reciprocity is the technique of "reject then retreat" where a large demand is made by the negotiator, and then retracted, and the true demand ultimately stated (that is often less demanding). This can lead the other party into a more concession-making frame of mind that, with the implications of PCP also at work, will usually result in movement in the negotiation. What tends to happen also is that the hostage taker starts to perceive himself as acting agreeably and cooperatively with the negotiator, and this dynamic is likely to remain throughout the event unless the negotiator undermines this perception through deliberate antagonistic behavior (for greater detail, see McMains and Mullins, 2001:208).

One of the most established strategies for effective persuasion in these circumstances is the Stimulus-Response Theory (SRT), where the negotiator wants the other party to link certain emotions with particular communications and to construct this new emotion as the new response; for example, removing aggressive reactions when there is talk of surrender. A powerful strategy is to discuss such emotive topics when the situation is calm for both parties, and at no other time, so that a precedent is set and then expected (McMains and Mullins, 2001:213). There were ample opportunities to attempt this throughout the lengthy Waco siege; however, this strategy does not appear to have been used to good effect there, if at all, or in Munich. A reason for this might lie in the ignorance of negotiators concerning how to employ such strategies (especially in Munich), or a reluctance to do so.

Thus, the main approach made by the authorities in both instances centered mainly on a "watch and wait and then react" strategy, rather than seeking to be consistently proactive in order to progress effectively. This failed to allow the dynamics in both situations to progress in a more positive and potentially constructive manner.

Power Issues

The power dynamics in both case studies are complex and replete with impact and consequences. The concept of "power" was also perceived by all parties in a variety of ways, ranging from the idea of "the value added to a particular outcome" to asymmetry issues (Schelling, 1960; Zartman, 1974). As Zartman and Rubin stated, "High power symmetry brings together two parties experienced in dominating behavior; it allows each party to hold the other in check; therefore it makes them primarily concerned with maintaining their status — locking in their side of symmetry — rather than reaching an agreement" (2000:272).

At Waco power was used, and perceived, in markedly different ways between the parties involved. As for Koresh, he believed he was "armed" and was ready to use "power rhetoric," as heard in his numerous, lengthy declamations concerning the beliefs and the unity of the sect when under threat. Personal power also came from the evidently devoted discipleship of his followers. For the FBI, power came through the ability to escalate the dynamic, to increase fear, and to cause physical discomfort. But physical threats were unlikely to succeed with a group so fixed upon the life hereafter and a ready acceptance of necessary apocalyptic events prior to death. So, although in logistical terms it might have appeared that the authorities had the upper hand in power dynamics, the reverse was closer to reality with the Branch Davidian imperatives to save face, deny hostile intent, and employ pugnacious rhetoric proving influential. The culmination of this verbal interplay meant that the FBI immediately perceived any of the Davidians' warnings as explicit threats, and thus the warnings assumed significant impact and reactive response. It has to be recalled that the sect had shot four ATF agents already.

At Munich, practical and perceived power lay with the hostage takers from the start. In concrete terms they were armed, prepared, focused, and willing to do whatever was necessary to achieve their demands, as evidenced by the killings. They never really lost this superiority, even when finally attacked at the airport, due also to the disorganization of the authorities and the lack of any coherent response throughout the day. The authorities essentially remained reactive throughout the siege, rather than proactive, and since none of the multiple negotiators had any real decision-making authority, their status as effective negotiating partners was severely undermined.

In both situations it can be argued that all protagonists perceived the power issue as the ability to use force, either to influence the other party or to cause a preferred outcome. The problem with this perception is that subsequent tactics then tend to move toward polar opposites, or result in the view that either negotiation or force can be used, but never the twain shall meet.[9] Henry Kissinger commented upon this weakness very perceptively: "Treating force and diplomacy as discrete phenomena caused our power to lack purpose and our negotiations to lack force" (1982:62).

Thus, authorities can find themselves in a cyclical power "game" that results in predictable disaster.

The "Bigger Boss Syndrome"

In both case studies the most striking element is the extent to which the impact of external decisions affected both negotiations and their resultant ultimate failure. On-the-scene negotiators were constantly undermined by "superior" parties who were remote but influential, and such interference is inherently disruptive and potentially destructive.

Both these case studies involved state/terrorist interaction. In this case, the decision as to whether to negotiate at all or choose some other response is necessarily political, and, as Abraham Miller alludes, "it is also subject to the forces in the political environment. It is this situation that plays an important role in the drama between terrorists and nation states, in the former's selection of targets and the latter's selection of responses" (1980:31).

This dynamic inevitably also demands that credibility, particularly for the nation-state and authorities under "attack," remains intact: a permanent necessity for those sustaining power through popular franchise or approval. Thus, a drive to sustain state credibility is very likely to result in multilayered decision-making that will tend to conflict, countermand, and ultimately stall conciliatory moves on the ground.

The length of the Waco siege caused frustration, possible embarrassment, and a perceived loss of face for the authorities and, as a result, together with the growing intransigence of Koresh, caused superior commanders to interfere and to impose actions and decisions increasingly. Forty negotiators had been used throughout the siege, a fact in itself that led to a lack of continuity, loss of trust, and little chance of relationship building, but the entire situation was further affected by the all-pervading presence of the media, the government, and public accountability. Koresh had only one higher authority to whom he deferred, God; but the negotiators were receiving orders from many levels of command superior to themselves. This "big boss syndrome," replete with a plethora of interests that ran counter to the original goal of achieving a peaceful, speedy resolution, finally overwhelmed the HRT and caused them to doubt their abilities to negotiate a safe outcome. This might have been true, yet the pressure from outside agencies upon the entire dynamic cannot be overlooked or underestimated. It is important to note that the FBI developed its "Negotiations Concepts Course for Commanders" as a direct result of the Waco Siege and from the recognition that the commanders did not actively consider the advice that came from the tactical negotiators, nor did they correctly understand the crisis negotiations perspective (see Noesner, 1999).

Similarly, as Schreiber recognized, the resolution of the Munich situation was dependent on so many authorities external to the crisis itself. The governments of Israel, West Germany, and the Middle East states all played their part in imposing strictures on the potential to negotiate, as well as the Olympic community, the Black September group, and the watching world. These factors were all influencing the potential for decision-making on the ground, explicitly and implicitly, and they resulted in a complicated and unclear strategy that untrained negotiators found difficult to interpret and conduct.

Each of these incidents undoubtedly suffered from "too many cooks" affecting the decisions made both at the scene and remotely, and this factor was another crucial component of the ultimate failure in negotiation in both instances.

CONCLUSION

In these two case studies the potential for a negotiated outcome appeared possible and viable, particularly at Waco, but due to both internal and external factors, negotiation was ultimately abandoned or proved futile. Incomplete negotiations in a crisis situation often result in escalation, destruction, and death, as happened at Waco and Munich.

There are also problems with defining "success" in hostage situations; for example, whose terms of reference should be used to judge the successful outcome of such an event? The Davidians achieved their "ultimate" spiritual goal through death, and so success might be insinuated from this fact, but the U.S. government, FBI, and media audience saw the events as a marked failure both for negotiation tactics and slipshod armed tactical response. Munich was overtly a tactical disaster for the authorities, but for the terrorists it represented a significant success for their cause, a claim that was upheld by one of the surviving terrorists.

Pressures upon negotiators in such settings are significant, multiple, and potentially damaging, and the situation itself is highly charged and emotionally draining. However, while people continue to talk, then hope remains, and hope is only extinguished in these crisis circumstances when silence reigns and despair takes over. Incomplete negotiations in crisis situations can cause chances to be lost, and lives also, when any lingering potential to negotiate is destroyed by the finite sound of gunfire.

NOTES

The views expressed are those of the author and do not represent the views of the Ministry of Defense, or any other organization or individual.

1. Detailed chronologies of the lengthy siege and negotiations can be found in two main documents from the U.S. Justice Department: "Report to the Deputy Attorney General on the events at Waco, Texas, February 28 to April 19, 1993" (compiled by Richard Scruggs), and "Evaluation of the Handling of the Branch Davidian Stand-Off in Waco, Texas, February 28 to April 19, 1993" (compiled by Edward S. G. Dennis Jr.).

2. Details of this siege and the negotiations are taken from the original German DDR Ministry for State Security file MfS HAXX/3–505. Translated for the author by Alexander Paterson, December 2004.

3. This was Moshe Weinberg, a wrestling coach, who had leaned against the door in the vain attempt to stop the terrorists entering the room. He was shot through the door and his body left in front of the remaining bound hostages for the rest of the day.

4. Zartman (1976) has identified eight main approaches taken by social scientists toward negotiation per se: historical, contextual, structural, strategic, personality-type

analysis, behavioral skills, process variables analysis, and experimentation and simulation.

5. For full details of the siege and the negotiations, see Docherty, 2001.

6. Treasury report quoted in Dean M. Kelley, "Waco: A Massacre and Its Aftermath," *First Things*, May 1995, http://www.firstthings.com/article/2008/09/001-waco-a-massacre -and-its-aftermath — 12.

7. A detailed analysis of the creative-processes model is to be found in Pruitt and Carnevale, 1993.

8. DDR Ministry for State Security file MfS HAXX/3–505.

9. A full discussion of the negotiator with force capability can be found in Goodwin, 2005.

PART THREE

Actors as a Cause for Failure

Psychological Causes of Incomplete Negotiations

CHRISTER JÖNSSON

Rational actor models loom large in the study of international relations. When rational actors engage in bargaining and negotiation, such exchanges are then understood in terms of game theory. Some of the pioneering theory-building efforts in the field of international negotiation in the 1960s drew heavily on game theory. To be sure, game theory remains an important source of inspiration for students of international negotiation. Yet it is noteworthy that one of the most influential early works, Thomas Schelling's *The Strategy of Conflict* (1960), supplements game theory with psychological insights.

Later approaches to international negotiation emphasize the structural uncertainty experienced by negotiating parties; that is, "the nature of the possible outcomes and not just the probability associated with different outcomes is unknown" (Winham, 1977:101). Trial-and-error search, information processing, and uncertainty control are basic elements in such an understanding of negotiations. Reducing the variety inherent in complex and multidimensional bargaining situations becomes a fundamental aspect of international negotiations. The management of uncertainty involves human judgment; hence, psychological considerations move from the wings to center stage.

My discussion of psychological aspects of uncertainty control, bearing on negotiation failure, should be prefaced by two caveats. First, uncertainty is a multidimensional concept, and we cannot take for granted that there is always a common understanding within and between negotiating teams as to what kind of uncertainty is to be reduced. For instance, with the increasing presence of scientific experts in delegations negotiating complex technical matters, such as environmental protection, food safety, and health, the difference between scientific and lay notions of uncertainty becomes pertinent. Scientists commonly discuss uncertainty in terms of risk; in other words, possible outcomes are understood to be known as well as their probabilities. Risk calculations are frequently made in quantitative terms. Politicians usually rely on more intuitive notions of uncertainty and worry about unknown developments, where neither possible outcomes nor their probabilities are known. They point to the risk of not doing anything in areas where they fear highly uncertain but potentially disastrous outcomes.

Second, the application of psychological theories and insights to political processes is problematic in several ways. Are we justified in applying concepts and theoretical ideas derived from the study of individuals to collective entities such as states? What kind of data can be used to gain insights into the cognitive and emotional processes of political actors? How much explanatory power can be assigned to psychological as opposed to other factors?

One common — and weighty — argument against psychological explanations in the context of international negotiations is that negotiators are representatives of larger collectives. Certain functions are delegated to them as agents of their principals. They always negotiate on behalf of others, carrying out instructions from principals — governments in the case of negotiators representing states. Hence, their individual traits carry little weight in relation to their role requirements, and psychological factors can only have a marginal impact in encounters between agents or representatives with restricted mandates. Two kinds of counterargument can be adduced. First, many multilateral negotiations today turn into marathons, where the same negotiators meet over a period of years and sometimes decades. Interpersonal relations then assume greater importance, especially since instructions to negotiators are seldom detailed and give considerable leeway. Second, as shown in several studies by authors such as Robert Jervis and Alexander George, psychological factors and mechanisms apply to collectives as well as individuals. At least by analogy, governments and other cohesive collectives are prone to the same cognitive and emotional biases as individuals (see Cristal, "Camp David, 2000," in this volume).

Proceeding from the centrality of uncertainty reduction and control in international negotiation, I will discuss in this chapter some prominent psychological factors that (a) set limits to rational choice, and (b) tend to obstruct coordination and contribute to failed negotiations. Political psychology has become an established subfield, studying the multiple ways in which politics and psychology interact in the realms of domestic and international politics. The relationship between political science and psychology can be described as a one-way street, insofar as political scientists have borrowed from psychologists to a far greater extent than the other way around (McDermott, 2004:45, 263). Theories from social and cognitive psychology have been most influential and widely used, including attribution, judgmental heuristics, and prospect theory. Moreover, recent neurocognitive work on emotion promises to be of relevance to international politics in general and international negotiation in particular (cf. McDermott, 2004:50).

My discussion of the relevance of psychological theories and insights to negotiation failure will be divided into three subsections, dealing with perception or judgment, decision-making, and emotions, in turn. Perception or judgment, on the one hand, and decision, on the other, are related but not interchangeable concepts: "Judgment happens prior to decisions. Judgments involve assessments of the external world; decisions are choices based on those judgments as they are evaluated with reference to internal values and beliefs" (McDermott, 2004:58).

The individual and joint decisions of negotiating parties, as noted above, are based on perceptions made under conditions of uncertainty, which opens up for subjective, personal, or idiosyncratic factors. The role of emotions in international negotiations, finally, is a largely uncharted territory. Yet it deserves inclusion in light of new psychological insights, which suggest the direction for possible future research.

Selective perception of the counterparts' attitudes may lead to misinterpretations, wrong attributions, suspicion, even demonization. Unconscious, self-serving biases may anchor positions to such an extent that additional moves become unthinkable. Stereotypes may play their part in feeding distrust and hampering the negotiation process.

Suspicion may, for instance, induce distrust and tough attitudes that will tend to be reciprocated by the counterpart. Thus, the way is paved for a self-fulfilling prophecy. The Cyprus case is a good example of such a process.

Perceptions of the situation, of what could be negotiated, play an essential role in devising an appropriate strategy to deal with the problem. If the situation is perceived as a zero-sum game, negotiators will play win–lose and the whole process may end up deadlocked.

Judgments derive from perceptions and orient behaviors. They may be biased by referring to seemingly identical situations, drawn from previous experiences, especially upsetting ones. Negotiators may tend to first protect themselves and take no risk, thus reducing options and freezing the discussions.

Another type of psychological causes is related to decision making. Group processes may produce wrong decisions as shown by the research on groupthink (Janis, 1972). Smart people put together may end up with sub-optimal decisions that will put the negotiation process on the wrong track and make any potential agreement hardly reachable.

Rational behavior can also be seriously challenged by emotions, sometimes to a larger extent than cognition. Mistrust can, for instance, be understood as an emotional dimension. Negative emotions, memory remnants of past traumatic events feed judgments, lead negotiators to act defensively and then impede their chances of developing win–win outcomes.

PERCEPTION OR JUDGMENT

Cognitive psychology offers two crucial points of departure. First, all human perception is selective and theory-driven. We all process information through preexisting "knowledge structures," without which "life would be a buzzing confusion" (Nisbett and Ross, 1980:7). These knowledge structures or theories, whether conscious and formalized or not, represent good cognitive economy, insofar as they allow us to sort out what to pay attention to in the overwhelming flow of stimuli. They are like floodlights that illuminate one part of the stage but, by the same token, leave other parts in the shade or in the dark. Our preconceptions, in short, help us structure, but may also distort, what we see, understand and remember.

Second, these knowledge structures tend to be resistant to change. The human tendency to adhere to preconceived beliefs in the face of contradictory evidence was noted already by Francis Bacon in 1620 (see Nisbett and Ross, 1980:167) and has since been well documented in empirical research. For instance, Robert Jervis (1976:291–96) identified several psychological mechanisms that tend to make beliefs resistant to change. Belief perseverance, it has been noted, applies not only to individuals but to collective political actors as well (George, 1980:73–74).

The uncertainty inherent in international negotiations limits the usefulness of rational utility-probability calculi and broadens the scope for human judgment based on preconceived knowledge structures. The success or failure of a given negotiation may be related to the way the actors perceive the issues under discussion, on the one hand, and the adversaries on the other side of the negotiating table, on the other.

PERCEPTIONS OF ISSUES

Any bargaining situation is characterized by the coincidence of cooperative and conflictual elements: "Without common interest there is nothing to negotiate for, without conflict nothing to negotiate about" (Iklé, 1964:2). If the conflictual elements predominate at the expense of the cooperative ones in the perceptions of the negotiating parties, agreement becomes a remote possibility (see Cristal, "Camp David, 2000," in this book). For instance, the earliest disarmament negotiations after World War II were ideological shouting matches between the United States and the Soviet Union. It was only after both nuclear superpowers realized that they had a common interest in halting or slowing down the arms race, which entailed mutual losses both in terms of economy and international goodwill, and in preventing the spread of nuclear weapons, which threatened their duopoly, that arms control negotiations began in earnest.

Similarly, experimental psychologists have identified the fixed-pie bias, the tendency to see negotiations as distributive, fixed-sum games in which one's own interests are directly opposed to those of the other, as a major contributing factor to persistent failures to reach mutually beneficial agreements (Bazerman, 1983; Bazerman and Neale, 1983). This bias may be the result of either faulty or incomplete information or errors in information processing (Pinkley, Griffith, and Northcraft, 1995).

The predominance of the conflictual elements may also be associated with a phenomenon labeled punctuation, which refers to differing perceptions concerning what is stimulus and what is response in a sequence (Sillars, 1981:280). The term "punctuation" is used in analogy with writing symbols that mark beginnings and endings, thus giving structure to otherwise fluid processes. First, negotiating parties frequently have divergent perceptions of the cause-effect patterns that created the bargaining situation. "You started it," is a common assessment of mutual conflict. Second, during the negotiating process, punctuation often manifests itself as misinterpretations of the effect of one's own action on the opponent. There is a tendency, on the one hand, to overestimate the extent to which one's own actions have elicited concessions by the other side, and on the other hand, to underestimate the extent to which one's own behavior has caused intransigence or retractions by the other side (cf. Kelley, 1971:19; Sillars, 1981:285).

Paradoxically, an overemphasis on cooperation may also aggravate negotiations. As World War II was drawing to an end, the Swedish diplomat Staffan Söderblom was stationed in Moscow with instructions to improve relations with the Soviet Union, which had been strained as a result of Swedish concessions to Germany during the war. When Soviet deputy foreign minister Vladimir Dekanozov delivered a note to the Swedish embassy on January 16, 1945, to the effect that Raoul Wallenberg had been found by Soviet troops in Budapest and was in Soviet custody, Söderblom failed to refer explicitly to this important information in subsequent diplomatic communications with his Soviet counterparts. This may well have been interpreted in Moscow as a lack of interest in the Wallenberg case. Moreover, on several occasions, when Wallenberg was discussed, Soviet diplomats demanded that a number of Soviet citizens in Sweden be extradited, which may have signaled a willingness to arrange an exchange. Most likely, the lack of Swedish reactions to these hints, along with Söderblom's "personal" guess that Wallenberg had died in an accident, was interpreted in the Kremlin as Swedish attempts to sweep the whole issue under the carpet and to provide an excuse for the Soviets to shirk their responsibility. In any event, the initial eagerness to avoid conflict seriously hampered subsequent Swedish efforts to hold the Soviet Union accountable for Wallenberg's fate and to negotiate his release from Soviet captivity (see SOU, 2003:18). This case indicates that exaggerated emphasis on cooperation at the outset may hamper subsequent negotiations.

Perceptions of the issues under negotiation go beyond the cooperation-conflict dimension. More generally, cognitive psychology teaches us that judgments are often rendered according to certain heuristics, or rules of thumb, which may distort assessments of the frequency and likelihood of certain outcomes and thereby limit the range of perceived alternative solutions in negotiations. Three judgmental heuristics that have been extensively documented in experiments — representativeness, availability, and anchoring — can affect judgment of options in predictable ways.

The representativeness heuristic involves using resemblance or similarity rather than the base rate, that is, frequencies and probabilities, in assessing the likelihood of an alternative. The frequent use of historical analogies by diplomats and negotiators is a case in point. One obvious example, where the representativeness heuristic limited the range of perceived options, concerns the negotiations in the wake of Egyptian president Gamal Abdel Nasser's nationalization of the Suez Canal Company in 1956. British and French decision-makers relied on the Munich analogy and perceived parallels between Nasser's nationalization and Hitler's remilitarization of the Rhineland in 1936. In the same way that the occupation of the Rhineland was followed by successive acts of aggression, the seizure of the Suez Canal was, in British premier Anthony Eden's words, "the opening gambit in a planned campaign designed by Nasser to expel all Western influence and interests from Arab countries" (quoted in Jönsson, 1990:106). This made British and French decision-makers exclude any option that smelled of "appeasement." In U.S. judgments, on the other hand, in particular those of Secretary of State John Foster Dulles, the situation was representative of East–West confrontations during the Cold War. Nasser was then reduced to a pawn in a larger game where the main enemy was international communism. The Soviet-Egyptian arms deal in 1955 and Nasser's recognition of Communist China confirmed U.S. beliefs that the Middle East was an arena of East–West confrontation. The reliance on different historical analogies thus contributed to miscommunication between allies in the unsuccessful efforts to find a negotiated solution to the crisis (cf. Jönsson, 1990:91–121; Jönsson, 1991).

The availability heuristic means that categorizations and assessments of likelihood are based on events or outcomes that are readily "available" in memory. Salient and traumatic events hold greater impact than pallid, abstract, or statistical information; recent or repeated events are likely to be more available in memory; and events that have already occurred are much easier to imagine than those that have never occurred. Before September 11, 2001, few could imagine the possibility of using commercial aircraft as high-speed missiles; after the attack on the World Trade Center, suspicious behavior at and around airports is easily interpreted in that light. The experience of the AIDS pandemic influenced the perceptions of, and responses to, the outbreak of local or regional epidemics, such as SARS and the bird flu, among decision makers around the world. As for the initial response to AIDS, once decision makers realized that the epidemic affected less developed countries in particular, development assistance emerged as the most available solution. Whenever an issue is categorized in terms of underdevelopment, aid comes most easily to mind as a remedy at the exclusion of other, perhaps more effective, measures. The other side of the coin is that events or outcomes that are less available in

memory are not considered as options or alternative interpretations in negotiations. For example, the prevalent association of environmental protection
measures with slower economic growth and diminished competitive strength
among policy makers in less developed countries has precluded categorization
of climate change as a development issue.

Anchoring, finally, refers to the tendency to base predictions about likelihood on initial values (anchors) and to adjust these insufficiently to reach new
estimates. One central feature of negotiations is that the parties initially ask for
more than they expect to get. These initial, extreme positions provide anchors
from which negotiators will adjust, considering moderate positions in between
these extremes to be reasonable and probable, while possibly overlooking possibilities that are not anchored in the initial bids (see Wanis-St. John, "Nuclear
Negotiations," in this book). For example, the earliest negotiations on a nuclear test ban, 1958–63, for many years were bogged down in haggling about
the number of control posts and on-site inspections needed to verify a test
ban. The Soviet Union considered national systems of control to be sufficient
but was willing to allow fifteen posts in the USSR, whereas the United States
initially demanded twenty-one posts on Soviet territory. There was a similar
gap between the initial U.S. call for twelve to twenty on-site inspections an-
nually and the Soviet proposal for a maximum of three inspections per year.
The two superpowers continuously exchanged proposals and counterpropos-
als anchored in these initial demands, while not considering alternative safeguards and methods of verification. When such an alternative was suggested
by Western scientists at a Pugwash Conference in 1962 in the form of so-called
black boxes, sealed automatic stations, it made a short appearance in the negotiations and led to a new "numbers game." Yet in the final Moscow talks,
the whole controversy about control was discreetly put aside, and the word
"control" is not even mentioned in the partial test ban treaty of 1963 (Jönsson,
1975:124–38).

PERCEPTIONS OF ACTORS

Categorization is basic to human thought, perception, and action. Without the
ability to categorize things and people we would not function in our physical
and social environment: "We impose structure on the phenomenal field by
organizing features of the environment into meaningful clusters or categories"
(Wilder and Cooper, 1981:248). Social stereotypes constitute one important

type of categorization. As in the categorization of physical objects, social categorization may be functional, allowing us to reduce complexity and deal efficiently with large amounts of information. Moreover, stereotyped perceptions of "the other" constitute a key element of national identity, along with mythical perceptions of one's own nation's past and unique features (see Saner, "The Cyprus Conflict," and Goodwin, "Two Hostage Negotiations," in this volume). However, national stereotypes may turn international negotiations into encounters between "ingroups" and "outgroups," where greater homogeneity is attributed to the outgroup relative to the ingroup, and information is preferred that enhances the dissimilarity of the outgroup (Wilder and Cooper, 1981:260–65).

Thus, one may speak of a "reputation effect" among actors that are engaged in continuous bargaining relationships. The reputations of the negotiating parties precede their interactions. Reputations provide information about a counterpart that is based on either prior interaction or credible information from external sources. A counterpart's reputation evokes a stereotype of that counterpart (cf. Tinsley, O'Connor, and Sullivan, 2002).

Examples of the harmful effect of national stereotypes and reputations of intransigence in international negotiations are not difficult to find. U.S.-Soviet negotiations during the Cold War are cases in point, as are negotiation encounters between Israelis and Palestinians or Arabs, between ethnic groups in the Balkans, and between China and Japan. Incidentally, the voluminous literature on national negotiating styles has tended to produce and reproduce stereotypes, which may ultimately serve as self-fulfilling prophecies. National consistency and coherence are emphasized, and the authors seldom allow for variation in styles and behavior depending on who the opponent is, what issue is negotiated, or other contextual factors. By amplifying the conflictual elements of negotiations, national stereotypes may give rise to vicious circles of self-fulfilling prophecies:

> When the other party is viewed within the framework of an "inherent bad faith" model the image of the enemy is clearly self-perpetuating, for the model itself denies the existence of data that would disconfirm it. At the interpersonal level such behavior is characterized as abnormal — paranoia. Different standards seem to apply at the international level; inherent-bad-faith models are not considered abnormal, and even their underlying assumptions often escape serious questioning. (Holsti, 1968:17)

Contemporary actors seldom admit to their reliance on national stereotypes. An unusually clear-cut example dates from the 1919 Paris Peace Conference. In an exchange with Georges Clemenceau, Woodrow Wilson recommended that moderation be shown toward Germany, arguing that excessive demands would provide Germany with reasons for seeking revenge and sow the seeds of a future war. In his reply, Clemenceau referred to the "German spirit," which, in his view, entailed a desire to impose force on others and unwavering aggression. Only by imposing sanctions on Germany could aggression be avoided. Clemenceau recalled the historical inheritance of his country. "Unfortunately," he said, "we have come, to our cost, to know the Germans, and we are aware that as a nation they submit to force in order that they themselves may impose force on the world." Clemenceau also claimed personal knowledge of the Germans: "Since 1871 I have forced myself, almost every year, to visit Germany; I wanted to know the Germans and, at various times, I hoped a means could be found to bring our two peoples together" (quoted in Bonham et al., 1987:11–12).

Attribution theory, which deals primarily with human perception of causality, especially the causal inferences that people make about social behavior, has identified dynamics through which stereotyped enemy images may persist even in the face of conciliatory behavior by the adversary. Actors in international negotiations are constantly faced with the problem of looking beyond manifest signals and trying to draw inferences about their adversaries. Why did they make this concession? Was it meant as a genuinely conciliatory measure or merely as a trap to make us lower our guard? Did they make that hostile move to intimidate us, or were they compelled to take a tough stance in order to satisfy a vociferous public opinion and powerful pressure groups? To interpret signals, the actors have to search for causes and motives. Only by assessing the motives underlying the adversary's proposal can the actor judge whether it represents a concession or a retraction and decide upon his response. Negotiation, in short, inevitably entails attribution.

First, attribution theorists have pointed to a common tendency to overemphasize dispositional factors (stable personal traits) when explaining and interpreting the behavior of others, while stressing situational factors to account for one's own behavior. This double standard is commonly labeled "the fundamental error of attribution" (even if "bias" is a more appropriate label than "error"). The dispositional-situational distinction does not really represent a dichotomous classification. Rather, we can observe tendencies and weightings of the relative importance of each. Thus, situational attributions are those explanations that state or imply no dispositions on the part of the actor beyond those typical of all or most actors; whereas dispositional attributions are those explanations that state or imply something unique and distinguishing about the actor (Heradstveit and Bonham, 1986:347; Lee Ross, 1977:176–77).

To some extent, this double standard reflects the difference between actors, attributing their actions to situational requirements, and observers, attributing the same action to stable personal dispositions (Jones and Nisbett, 1971:80). This kind of bias is not confined to passive observers, but is even amplified when the observer is also an actor tied into mutually contingent interaction with the observed actor, as in international negotiations (88).

A related bias is the tendency to attribute behavior that is consistent with our image of the adversary to dispositional causes, but behavior that is discrepant with our image to situational causes (Pruitt and Rubin, 1986:116–17). In general, "the good behavior of a liked person and the bad of a disliked one are attributed to personal factors whereas inconsistent behavior is attributed to situational factors" (Kelley and Michela, 1980:469). Translated to international negotiations: "We tend to believe that countries we like do things we like, support goals we favor, and oppose countries we oppose. We tend to think that countries that are our enemies make proposals that would harm us, work against the interests of our friends, and aid our opponents" (Jervis, 1976:117–18; see also Cristal, "Camp David, 2000").

The actor-observer and consistency biases are often reinforced by a self-serving bias — the tendency to take credit for success and deny responsibility for failure, to attribute positive outcomes of one's actions to personal qualities while attributing negative ones to external factors beyond one's responsibility or control (cf. Ross and Ward, 1995:276; Stein, 1988:227). In sum, these documented biases combine to reinforce stereotyped images by producing attributions along the lines of "my country is essentially good but is occasionally forced by circumstances to behave badly, whereas your country is bad but is occasionally forced by circumstances to behave well."

These attributional biases are often coupled with, and reinforced by, a common tendency to see the behavior of the adversary as more centralized, planned, and coordinated than it actually is (Jervis, 1976:319–42). In the same way that mutual sensitivity to the other side's internal bargaining processes may contribute to an agreement, insensitivity to this "two-level game" (Putnam, 1988) aspect of international negotiations may contribute to failure.

The "win-set" in any international negotiation is determined not only by the negotiating parties' strategies at the international level, but also by the interplay of various preferences, coalitions, and institutions at the national level. Thus, if you treat adversaries as monoliths, you fail to identify all possible solutions and miss the opportunity to feed into their internal bargaining.

Moreover, the fact that positive actions tend to be more ambiguous than negative ones adds to these attributional biases in perpetuating negative images. As beneficial actions may serve ulterior, manipulative purposes, concessions are often interpreted as tactical tricks, designed to divert one's attention (cf. Jones and Davis, 1965:259; Larson, 1988:286–87). Social psychologists speak of the "reactive devaluation" of concessions. The tendency to characterize concessions by the adversary as relatively advantageous to them and relatively disadvantageous to us is commonplace and can, of course, be seen as a tactical ploy. Yet psychological experiments indicate that such devaluation occurs in the negotiating parties' private evaluations as well. Recipients of offered concessions are apt to believe that the adversary has given up nothing of real value and, therefore, to resist the suggestion that something of real value should be offered in return (see Ross and Stillinger, 1991:394–95; Ross and Ward, 1995:270–75).

It is easy to dismiss such biases and uncharitable interpretations as tactical posturing, but the application of different yardsticks to their own and their adversaries' behavior seems to go beyond self-serving rhetoric and manipulative intentions. Social psychologists who have worked with seasoned negotiators testify to this:

> First, the negotiators we've encountered seem to hold the conviction that other people engage in more frequent and elaborate strategic ploys than they themselves do. Others, they feel, make completely unrealistic offers and demands, whereas they merely leave themselves a little negotiating room; others exaggerate grossly the difficulty of making the concessions that obviously will be required to consummate a deal, whereas they themselves exaggerate only slightly. Others, they maintain, frequently resort to empty threats, or feign interest in reaching agreement when their main goal is obstruction and delay; whereas they themselves rarely resort to such tactics, and are guilty only of "fighting fire with fire" or showing appropriate caution in the face of the other side's penchant for less than scrupulous negotiation behavior. More importantly, they insist that the other side's protestations and expressions of disappointment or frustration are

insincere, whereas their own are genuine. To some extent, of course, such claims may be self-serving and manipulative, but we suspect there is something deeper going on. We suspect that, frequently, both sides in the negotiation may be over-estimating the other side's penchant for devious tactics and strategies, and un-derestimating their sincerity, precisely because they do not recognize the extent to which the other side's assessments (and their own as well) have psychological rather than strategic bases. (Ross and Ward, 1995:275–76; see Goodwin, "Two Hostage Negotiations," in this volume, especially the Waco case)

In recent research on differential perceptions of self and others the focus of analysis has shifted from judgments about traits to judgment about biases (see Pronin, Gilovich, and Ross, 2004). For instance, studies have shown that people overestimate the extent to which they themselves are influenced by "objective" concerns and/or overestimate the extent to which others are in-fluenced by "self-serving" concerns. In other words, they detect self-serving biases in others' judgments and behaviors while being unaware of the influ-ence of similar processes on their own judgments and behaviors. Moreover, we tend to view people with whom we disagree as more biased than people whose views approximate our own. This "bias blindness" has to do with the so-called introspection illusion: although people can reconstruct accurately the contents of their thoughts and deliberations, the psychological processes determining their behavior are often inaccessible to introspection.

Lee Ross and his collaborators suggest that these differences in construal reflect a more general worldview or lay epistemology that they have character-ized as "naïve realism" (cf. Ross and Ward, 1995:278–84; and Pronin, Gilovich, and Ross, 2004). Its defining features are (1) I perceive and respond to the world objectively, or "as it is"; (2) other rational actors, exposed to the same stimuli and information, will share my perspectives and responses; (3) other actors' differing views and responses reflect either exposure to different infor-mation, irrationality, or biases that distort reality. In international bargaining situations and conflicts, the conviction that one's own side has a monopoly on objectivity and that it is only the other side that fails to see the situation as it really is, can have serious consequences.

The convictions of naïve realism can make parties feel that the other side is ir-rational or too biased to be reasoned with (rather than merely subject to the same cognitive and motivational biases that afflict all human beings — including oneself and one's ideological and political allies). Moreover, when the parties do air their grievances, they may conclude that the other side is being "strategic" and doesn't really believe what it is saying. Or perhaps worse, the conclusion reached may be that the other side really does believe what it is saying and that a rational, interest-based negotiation will thus prove fruitless. (Pronin, Gilovich, and Ross, 2004:796)

Decision Making

Judgmental heuristics and biases can, as we have seen, erect barriers to agreement in international negotiations by providing an inadequate basis for decision making: "Intersubjective differences in construal not only can lead parties to reject particular settlement proposals, they can also promote misunderstandings and misattributions that escalate conflict between the bargainers" (Ross and Ward, 1995:278). Yet even if the negotiating parties manage to steer reasonably clear of attributional biases and strive to approximate the utility maximization of rational choice theory, the decision-making process itself may entail additional psychological barriers. I will address two sources of limited rationality in decision-making situations: framing effects and group processes.

Framing

Prospect theory, developed by psychologists Daniel Kahneman and Amos Tversky (1979), posits that the way people frame a problem affects their choices. A psychological theory of decision making under conditions of risk, prospect theory has proved influential in political science and political psychology. Specifically, it claims that people overvalue losses relative to gains of equal magnitude (loss aversion) and that they tend to be risk-averse with respect to gains and risk-acceptant with respect to losses. Decision makers tend to risk large but uncertain losses rather than accepting smaller but certain ones: translated to negotiations, loss aversion implies that both sides have a tendency to treat their own concessions as losses and those of the other side as gains, thus overvaluing their own concessions relative to those of their adversaries (Stein, 1993; Levy, 1996).

Rose McDermott notes, "Concession aversion, whereby different evaluations are made depending on whether a concession is offered or received, is common. Negotiators do not treat what the other side offers to give up as being as important as what they have offered to give up. . . . Making concessions feels worse than gaining benefits. Thus, for these structural reasons alone, both sides end up risk averse to concessions" (2004:139; also see Cristal, "Camp David, 2000").

The broader lesson of prospect theory — that framing makes a difference — resonates well with other branches of cognitive science as well as negotiation theory. Cognitive scientists have shown the contingent character of categorization, which is basic to human thought generally and constitutes an important aspect of the framing of problems. Categories do not exist "in the world," independently of who does the categorization (Lakoff, 1987). The way a specific issue is framed affects not only possible solutions but also which participants will be relevant. For example, whether an issue is characterized as an environmental or an economic problem empowers one set of actors while it disempowers others. Similarly, the initial, most available categorization of the AIDS issue as a medical problem entailed the selection of the World Health Organization as the principal arena of international negotiations about measures to halt the spread of the pandemic, at the same time as it tended to exclude alternative categorizations in terms of human rights or socioeconomic development.

The significance of framing is recognized in the negotiation literature as well, most explicitly in the notion of a formula, "a shared perception or definition of the conflict that establishes terms of trade, the cognitive structure of reference for a solution, or an applicable criterion of justice" (Zartman and Berman, 1982:95). In the same way that an agreed formula may facilitate negotiations, the absence of a formula may contribute to negotiation failures.

Group Processes

Since many individual decisions affecting international negotiations are shaped by small groups, such as cabinets, committees, commissions, or informal networks, the dynamics of these groups and group-level interactions may have a profound impact on the process and outcome of policy making. While several group processes germane to the formulation of each party's negotiating position may be identified (see, for example, Hart, Stern, and Sundelius, 1997; McDermott, 2004:239–60), groupthink refers to a distortion or pathology of special relevance to negotiation failure. Irving Janis (1972) formulated his notion of groupthink in a study of a number of historical fiascoes in U.S. foreign policy and later developed his initial hypotheses into a more fully articulated theory (Janis, 1982).

Janis argues that groups tend to develop strong in-group pressures toward conformity and cohesiveness. Groupthink refers to a tendency toward premature and extreme concurrence-seeking within policy-making groups under stress. Group members are keen to preserve the prevailing mood of optimism and presumed agreement, they become increasingly isolated from the outside world, and the desire to minimize controversy compromises the quality of the deliberations: crucial information is ignored or misinterpreted, alternatives to the group's preferred course of action are not considered or taken seriously, and the group tends to persist in its original policy choice even when confronted with feedback indicating that it is inadequate or risky.

If decision making in one or several of the negotiating parties is distorted by groupthink, deadlock rather than mutual concession is the likely outcome. Terrence Hopmann describes the consequences of groupthink for international negotiations thus: "All of these factors are likely to translate into an approach to bargaining that resists the exploration of multiple options, brainstorming, and other techniques that may be necessary for successful problem solving within negotiations. They may make it harder for the negotiators, who have direct and personal contact with the other party, [to have] much of an impact on the decision, either because their input may be largely disregarded or because they may feel themselves under subtle pressure to tell their superiors back home what they believe their superiors want to hear" (1996:215).

Emotion

Psychologists started out stressing the importance of emotion for behavior, but have since moved in the direction of emphasizing purely cognitive processes. As political scientists have borrowed from prevailing psychological theories, emotions have largely been assumed away in models of decision making and negotiation. Yet there are good reasons to reconsider that conscious or unconscious choice: "Few people examining their own lives would reject the power and prominence of emotion in daily life. Yet a great deal of scholarship, including predominant models in political science, does just that" (McDermott, 2004:153).

In fact, modern neuropsychology indicates that rational decision-making is dependent on prior emotional processing and suggests that emotion rather than cognition may eventually prove dominant in decision-making models. For instance, recent studies indicate that trust is as much an emotional as a cognitive dynamic (McDermott, 2004:169). And lack of trust figures prominently in game theory as one major factor explaining why actors fail to abandon lose–lose solutions in favor of win–win solutions in bargaining situations of the Prisoners' Dilemma type. At the same time, social identity theory points to the relationship between trust and identity. Social identity rests on trust within the ingroup while entailing hate and mistrust of outgroups. In short, mistrust, whether defined cognitively or emotionally, is commonly seen as a factor impeding success in negotiations.

Recent psychological research has paid increasing attention to the interplay between thoughts and feeling, between cognitive and emotional factors. This interaction can be studied more systematically than was possible before advances in the neurosciences in the past decade (McDermott, 2004:183). Perceptions of actors often have a strong emotional component, which contributes to the self-reinforcement of mutually consistent images (be they positive or negative) in an interactive setting such as negotiation (Kumar, 1997:86). For example, studies carried out in the Middle East indicate that feelings of threat, which represent emotional rather than logical or rational responses, correlate very strongly with policy choices. The more threatened actors feel, the more likely their policy choices will intensify the conflict (McDermott, 2004:185–86; see also Cristal, "Camp David, 2000," in this book).

Negative emotions also influence judgments about issues. If negative emotions lead negotiators to define ambiguous bargaining situations as distributive rather than integrative, the ability to find a positive solution is compromised (Kumar, 1997:92–93). "Decision affect theory" contends that unexpected outcomes exert a greater impact on emotional reactions than expected ones (McDermott, 2004:164). This means that unpleasant surprises may have a disproportionately negative impact on negotiations because of the emotional reaction they elicit. "Mood-dependent retrieval" refers to the recall of a previous emotional event at a time when the actor is in a similar mood. It is simply easier to remember sad events and harder to remember happy events when you are sad (McDermott, 2004:168–69). Similarly, negotiating actors under international pressure or in the midst of an acute crisis are likely to recall previous humiliations and conflicts. At the other end of the emotional spectrum, the phenomenon of wishful thinking, which often leads negotiators astray, operates through both emotional and cognitive mechanisms. Emotionally, desire impels actors to hold certain beliefs; cognitively, distorted expectations disrupt information processing (McDermott, 2004:170).

In sum, much can be learned from the renewed interest in emotions in the psychological literature. Thus far, students of political psychology and international relations have tended to discard emotions as irrational, unpredictable, or impossible to study in a systematic way. Yet the impact of emotions on politics in general and international negotiations in particular remains important and deserves to be studied more seriously, not least in the context of negotiation failure.

CONCLUSION

The most common reason why international negotiations fail to produce successful outcomes is probably the lack of common interests among the negotiating parties. In situations of pure conflict, negotiations can achieve little. Yet observers often have overconfidence in the potential of negotiations. "Why can't they just sit down and negotiate?" is a common reaction to many international conflicts. Psychological factors enter as possible explanations of failure when common interests exist in addition to conflictual ones (in other words, when a true bargaining situation prevails), and yet no agreement can be reached. Then a combination of overemphasis on the conflictual aspects and cognitive and emotional biases may contribute to an explanation, such as this one of the failure of the adversaries to negotiate a solution to the Cyprus issue: "In their adversarial stance, they talk almost solely about the *what* of the conflict, in we-they terms, and bring forward their opposing solutions in the context of positional bargaining. Antagonism is expressed, but is not used as a springboard for reflective reframing, invention or action planning. The parties are caught in self-defeating processes of antagonism, including blaming the other side, attributing negative qualities to them, and polarizing one's own side against them" (Ronald Fisher, 2001:321–22).

This chapter has introduced a suggestive, but by no means exhaustive, list of relevant psychological mechanisms. These have to be weighed against other explanatory factors in each individual case of negotiation failure, and their impact will no doubt vary from case to case. My claim is simply that they should not be disregarded out of hand.

Culture and International Negotiation Failure

CATHERINE H. TINSLEY, MASAKO TAYLOR, AND WENDI ADAIR

International negotiations are exchanges that involve parties who come from different nation-states. When these negotiations fail, culture is an oft-cited culprit. A search (in January 2012) on Google.com using the keywords "negotiation," "failure," and "culture" produced over ten million hits. One link on the first page is generally representative as it discusses how "no situation presents greater risks to strategy execution and bottom line than a cross-cultural negotiation."[1] Moreover, a contemporaneous Google search on the keywords "why international negotiations fail" and "culture" produced over sixty million hits. The content of the hits similarly implies that intercultural competency is a challenge to these negotiations. One, for example, asserts, "Research shows that around 70 percent of intercultural negotiations fail not simply due to technical difficulties — such as the lack of adequate preparation and planning, participants' involvement, etc. — but rather by culturally-conditioned factors."[2]

The sheer number of Google hits for these keywords is testimony to the fact that common wisdom assigns culture a major role in accounting for difficulties and failures in international negotiations. And the specific examples illustrate that culture appears to hamper both international negotiations in the political and diplomatic realm as well as in the area of economics and commerce. So just what is it about culture that makes it such a threat to international negotiations? And why should we question some of our common wisdom about how culture can be an obstacle?

In this chapter, we begin with a brief explanation of culture and the components of culture that we investigate in the international negotiations process. We briefly review past research and wisdom as to how culture threatens the success of international negotiations. We then highlight some of our recent research that offers a picture that somewhat contradicts common wisdom about the threats and obstacles of culture. We then propose some practical applications of our research findings. This includes the notion that the myriad "cultural sensitivity" trainings may not help negotiators to overcome culture's obstacles, but rather that a focus on Dynamic Awareness Adjustment (DAA), or the ability to refocus negotiation goals and behaviors on the fly in response to cues from the counterpart, may be more beneficial.

CULTURE

Culture has been described as the unique social identity of a group that can be broken down into a set of interrelated patterns or dimensions, which describe the nature of a culture's values, beliefs, or organizing structures (Hofstede, 1980; Schwartz, 1992). That culture has an influence on negotiation is common wisdom that we see supported in the tales and data of researchers, theorists, diplomats, and managers alike. Culture embodies systems of meaning, symbols, and artifacts that can constrain negotiators' behavioral repertoires and guide their interpretation of others' behavior (Tinsley and Pillutla, 1998). Culture is reflected in language, categorization, and labeling of objects (Faure, 2002; Faure and Rubin, 1993). Culture influences how negotiators think and the underlying logic they use to make sense of the situation. Hence, culture affects not only the goals negotiators set but also how behavior is organized and action is taken. Michele Gelfand and Jeanne Brett's recent book (2004) synthesizes culture and negotiation research into three broad areas: basic psychological processes or the influence of culture on negotiator cognition, emotion, and motivation; social processes or the role of culture in negotiation process and conflict management; and context, or how culture affects social context, third parties, justice, and technology in negotiation. Similarly, Faure's (2002) recent chapter on international negotiation notes that culture affects negotiation actors, structure, strategy, process, and outcome. Clearly, culture is understood to influence a broad range of social psychological processes related to negotiation and nearly every component of the negotiation process.

Another way to synthesize prior work on culture and negotiation is to consider single-country, versus comparative, versus intercultural studies. Single-country and comparative-culture studies describe negotiator values, norms, and strategies in different national cultures with the goal of promoting cross-cultural awareness. For example, single-country studies on China (e.g., Chen, 1999; Kirkbride, Tang, and Westwood, 1991) or Japan (Graham, 1993) provide an in-depth country-specific analysis of culturally derived negotiation norms and practices.

Comparative studies investigate how norms and practices are similar or different in two or more nations (Adair et al., 2004; Nancy Adler, Braham, and Graham, 1992; Druckman et al., 1976; Gelfand and McCusker, 2002; Gelfand et al., 2001). For example, Brett and colleagues (1998) found that U.S. American and Japanese negotiators held very different values for collectivism and hierarchy but shared similar norms for the importance of information sharing in negotiation. This was in contrast to Russian and Hong Kong Chinese negotiators whose value profiles were similar to the Japanese but who did not espouse information-sharing norms in negotiation. Other empirical studies include Natlandsmyr and Rognes (1995), who found that Mexican negotiators make more single-issue offers and Norwegian negotiators make more multi-issue offers. Hall and Hall (1990) take an anthropological approach to describing differences in German, French, and U.S. American negotiations. In a similar vein, Faure (2003) offers a selection of essays and cases illustrating how people (and animals) negotiate in different cultures.

In contrast, research on intercultural negotiation addresses the dynamics of negotiation when people from two different national cultures meet (Elgström, 1992; Faure and Rubin, 1993; Graham and Sano, 1989). Raymond Cohen uses cultural differences in low context, explicit communication in individualist societies and high context, implicit communication in collectivist societies to explain and analyze cultural dissonance or culture-related misunderstandings in diplomatic international negotiations over the course of a half century. He notes that "cultural factors may hinder relations in general, and on occasion complicate, prolong, and even frustrate particular negotiations where there otherwise exists an identifiable basis for cooperation" (1991:8). Adair, Okumura, and Brett (2001) show that cross-cultural Japanese negotiators tend to adapt their indirect behavior styles to more direct U.S. American styles, albeit without the expected benefits to negotiation outcome. Our research falls within this category as we address how U.S. American and Japanese negotiators adjust and adapt their goal and process norms when they negotiate interculturally.

CULTURE AS THREAT TO INTERNATIONAL NEGOTIATION SUCCESS?

Culture is a set of values and norms unique to a group of people that is fundamental to their individual and social identity. Thus, when negotiators come from different cultural traditions, espousing different values and norms, irreconcilability in these differences could lead to negotiation breakdown. Tinsley and Pillutla (1998), for example, found that U.S. and Chinese negotiators espoused different cultural values and preferred different negotiation approaches (loosely labeled as "maximize equality of gain" in China and "maximize joint gain" in the United States). Hence, cross-cultural disparities in what negotiators want (goals) as well as how they go about getting what they want (behaviors) introduce tensions into the international negotiations process, which could lead to negotiation breakdown.[3]

Popular explanations for the breakdown of international negotiations are differences in either what negotiators are trying to accomplish (the negotiation goal), and/or how they are trying to accomplish it (the specific negotiation behaviors).

DIFFERING NEGOTIATOR GOALS ACROSS CULTURES

Negotiation goals are the general orientation that a negotiator has toward the negotiation. The dual-concern typology describing a negotiator's general approach toward conflict management can be applied here (Pruitt and Rubin, 1986). In this typology, a negotiator can have one of five orientations or goals. A negotiator may try to maximize his or her own gain, maximize joint gain, maximize the other party's gain, minimize the difference in parties' outcomes (compromise), or minimize the effort invested (avoidance).

Note that these negotiation goals differ from what economic trade theorists call preferences. Preferences are about specific terms of the negotiation at hand — such as a preference for minimizing risk or a preference for timely delivery, which can be a tradeoff to promote joint gain. A negotiation goal, on the other hand, reflects a broader assumption about the purpose of a negotiation in general — such as to maximize joint gain or maximize equality of gain. These generally require some agreement in order for negotiations to move forward. Of course, if one party has the goal of maximizing their own outcome and the other party has the goal of maximizing that other party's outcome, there is compatibility. But generally, negotiators espouse goals such as maximizing joint gain or minimizing differences in gain, which although not mutually exclusive in theory are fairly incompatible in practice. If one party is trying to compromise while the other is trying to grow the joint value, they are likely to become frustrated with each other, leading to negotiation breakdown. Hence, differences in broad negotiation goals are one viable threat to international negotiations.

DIFFERING NEGOTIATOR BEHAVIORS ACROSS CULTURES

The other viable threat to international negotiations is that negotiators from different cultures either espouse different negotiation behaviors and/or attach different meanings to a particular behavior. Examples of these behavioral differences abound. In prior research, we found that Japanese prefer to negotiate based on appeals to social status; Germans prefer to negotiate based on the interpretation of regulations; and Americans prefer to discuss interests (Tinsley, 1998 and 2001). Others have found that Americans tend to move from discussing details to general principles or conclusions, while Chinese prefer to attend to the larger picture first and then work out smaller issues. Swedes tend toward formal negotiation relationships and dislike haggling, whereas Italians express themselves with considerable gesticulation and emotional expression and enjoy haggling over prices.

If negotiation is a verbal dance, imagine the frustrations when one partner is doing a waltz and the other partner a tango (Adair and Brett, 2005). Behavioral differences imply that parties in international negotiations may not be able to get in step, effectively communicate their preferences, or establish any rapport with the other side. This increasing frustration over the quality of the communication and the quality of the relationship will decrease parties' motivation to coordinate and negotiate, which could lead to uncompleted negotiations.

Behavioral differences among negotiators from different cultures may stem from cultural differences in the meanings attached to specific behaviors. For example, in the hierarchical Japanese culture, the party with lesser status may avert his or her eyes during the negotiation, to convey respect for the other party's superior status. However, in the relatively egalitarian U.S. culture, eye averting tends to connote caginess or deception. Hence, the meaning of any specific negotiation behavior can change as it crosses the cultural boundary between one party and another in international negotiations. The problems here are obvious. First, as mentioned above, parties engaged in different negotiation behaviors have less probability of being able to coordinate their exchange. Second, one party's attempts to be deferential or to build the relationship may be interpreted in a very different (and negative) light by the other party. This misattribution will decrease rapport and trust, and could eventually lead to negotiation breakdown. Hence, the behavioral differences among negotiators in an international negotiation might either confuse the other party or be misinterpreted by the other party, leading to negotiation failure.

DIFFERING NEGOTIATOR SCHEMA ACROSS CULTURES

In recent research we synthesized these findings that negotiation goals and the behavioral repertoires for achieving these goals differed across cultures to argue that negotiators from different cultures will espouse different negotiation schema. A schema is a cognitive representation of knowledge about a stimulus domain that guides perception and behavior (Fiske and Taylor, 1991). Schemas store descriptive information such as traits, roles, and behaviors, as well as rules and procedures that are used for making inferences. We define a negotiation schema as a mental representation of the goals and behaviors a negotiator associates with the negotiation process.

Negotiation is a goal-directed interdependent decision-making process. For example, we engage in negotiation because we have a specific objective, such as a home purchase or contractual business relationship, that we cannot achieve independently. Moreover, we enter into any negotiation with an idea of the sort of give-and-take exchange of behaviors that will result in our desired outcome. Hence, negotiator schemas (as the set of a negotiator's goals and behaviors for achieving those goals) encompass the critical components of the negotiation process.

Given the above mentioned research specifying that cultural values influence negotiators' goals and that negotiators' behaviors will differ across cultures, it is clear that negotiators' schema will differ across cultures. Moreover, if differences in negotiator goals can lead to negotiation incompatibilities and differences in negotiator behaviors can lead to confusion and misattribution, it seems evident that failure in international negotiations can be attributed in part to differences in negotiator schemas across cultures. Yet, a more detailed look at negotiation schemas suggests that it is not the schema differences per se but how negotiators respond and adjust to schema differences that may be a major source of negotiation failure. Schemas are quite adaptable knowledge structures and are highly influenced by situational cues. This means that negotiator differences across cultures (for example, the French negotiate with one another intraculturally differently than U.S. Americans negotiate with one another) do not necessarily translate into intercultural negotiation difficulties (that when U.S. Americans and French negotiate with each other, interculturally, failure is more likely). Prior research that catalogues negotiator differences across cultures tends to discount the fact that negotiators themselves may make a distinction between an intracultural setting (negotiating domestically) and an intercultural setting (negotiating internationally), and that negotiators may adjust themselves to this intercultural environment. Schema theory helps explain why this adjustment occurs and how, more specifically, negotiators will adjust their negotiation schema.

INTERCULTURAL SCHEMA ADJUSTMENT
IN INTERNATIONAL NEGOTIATIONS

Our minds house multiple schemas within any single domain (such as the domain of negotiation). That is, there may be a schema for negotiation in general and then "sub-schemas" for negotiating with the French or negotiating with the Japanese. In real life situations, these sub-schemas are evoked more easily than a general schema. This means an American negotiator initially thinks in terms of a "French negotiator" rather than simply "counterpart" when confronting a French counterpart. Hence, negotiators should distinguish between intra- and intercultural negotiations.

Situational cues are an important catalyst for schema activation. In international negotiations, a counterpart's social category (such as nationality) is an especially influential situational cue for schema activation. In experimental settings, negotiators have been found to alter their intracultural negotiation behaviors to be different in an intercultural negotiation. Because schemas guide behaviors, we argue that it is the shift in schema that facilitates the changes in their behaviors. Thus, we propose that negotiators shift their negotiation goals and negotiation behaviors in systematic ways when entering into an intercultural setting, as they activate an intercultural negotiation schema that differs from their intracultural one.

Otherwise said, negotiators will adjust their schema to the international context in which they find themselves. How they specifically adjust their schema should depend on the other national cultures present in the international setting and the negotiator's knowledge of these other cultures. We propose that a negotiator's schema for intercultural negotiation will be based primarily on stereotypic information and knowledge of the counterpart's culturally derived negotiation goals and strategies.

Negotiations are marked by uncertainty because neither party has full information about the other party's goals and intentions. This uncertainty motivates people to look for a reliable base of information about the other party to anchor their behaviors, especially during the preparation stage. In the absence of information about a specific negotiating party, negotiators may use information related to the social group to which he or she is a member — that is, a stereotype.

A stereotype is "a cognitive structure containing the perceiver's knowledge and beliefs about a social group and its members" (Hamilton, Sherman, and Ruvolo, 1990). A stereotype is a person-schema consisting of acquired, generalized information about a social group of which an individual is a member. In interpersonal encounters, the first schema that is called to one's mind relates to diffuse categories such as the others' social membership (i.e., national culture) in a process called categorization. Negotiators categorize others as a general "first cut" of information about that other party (given what is known about the social group to which the party is a member). Categorization is thought to be a primary automatic process useful in preserving cognitive energy for other tasks. This categorization process anchors the initial intercultural negotiation schema, providing a set of negotiation goals and behaviors based on stereotypic knowledge of the counterparts' culture. As such, we find that negotiators' intercultural negotiation schema closely mirror their perceptions of the negotiation goals and behaviors characteristically normative in the counterparts' culture. Thus, negotiators adjust their intercultural negotiation schema to reflect their stereotypes of the counterparts' negotiation schema.

Negotiators' adaptation of their schema to the intercultural setting, by moving toward the schema of the other party, suggests that intercultural negotiations could flow fairly smoothly. As each party is moving toward the other party's schema, they should meet somewhere in the middle and enjoy an efficient (if not effective) negotiation. What we found in our research, however, is that while parties successfully adjust their own schemas to the international context, they fail to recognize that the other party is adjusting as well. Rather, negotiators' stereotypic knowledge of the counterpart's cultural negotiation schema anchors their own intercultural schema. Because of this anchoring, negotiators' intercultural schema look like their counterparts' intracultural schema rather than their counterparts' intercultural schema. What results is a schema mismatch, but this mismatch does not come from being anchored on one's own intracultural schema, but rather being anchored on the other party's intracultural schema.

A TALE OF OVERADJUSTMENT IN NEGOTIATION SCHEMA

In a recent project, we surveyed one hundred business managers from the United States and Japan who had confirmed that they had experience negotiating with a business person from the other culture (Adair, Taylor, and Tinsley, 2008). We asked them questions designed to elicit: (1) the schema (goals and behaviors) they used when negotiating with someone from their own culture; (2) their perceptions of the other culture's negotiation schema; and (3) the schema they used when negotiating with someone from the other culture. What we found was that negotiators' own intracultural negotiation schema looked significantly different from their own intercultural negotiation schema, both in terms of the negotiation goals and the negotiation behaviors. Of the nine different schema elements that we studied (three goals and six behaviors), all nine elements were significantly different depending on whether it was contained in a negotiator's intracultural schema or intercultural schema.

As well, we found a context-by-nationality interaction effect on negotiator schemas, where context was either intracultural or intercultural setting, and nationality was either U.S. American or Japanese respondent. What this interaction term indicates is that the U.S. American negotiators were adjusting their schema elements in ways that were different from how the Japanese negotiators were adjusting their schema elements. This would be consistent with our theory that U.S. American negotiators are adjusting their schema toward the Japanese, while the Japanese negotiators are adjusting theirs toward the U.S. Americans.

Moreover, we found that each party's intercultural negotiation schema almost perfectly matched their stereotype of the other culture's negotiation schema. That is, U.S. American negotiators' intercultural schema matched almost perfectly to their perceptions of how Japanese negotiate. Similarly, Japanese negotiators' intercultural schema matched almost perfectly to their perceptions of how U.S. Americans negotiate. As a result of being anchored on their stereotypes of the other party, U.S. and Japanese intercultural negotiation schema were largely mismatched. And ironically, this mismatch occurred because of what might be termed an overadjustment to each other. Both parties were anchored on the intracultural schema of their counterpart, failing to notice that their counterpart had made his or her own adjustments to the international context!

WHY DO NEGOTIATORS OVERADJUST THEIR SCHEMA?

Thus, international negotiation failure may actually arise from an overadjustment by both sides, rather than simply because each side starts out with a different schema. Why might this overadjustment process occur? Why cannot the negotiation process itself facilitate the emergence of a shared negotiation schema?

In theory, negotiators' information about their counterparts (whether through experience, formal training, or some combination of the two) should give them some understanding of how their counterparts' schema differs from their own. Then, as negotiators gather new information and engage in the social process of sense making, they should see how their counterpart is adjusting to the intercultural setting. Negotiators should then update their own schemas accordingly so that their intercultural negotiation schemas become more similar. In reality, however, the strength of stereotype information as an anchor and the prevalence of confirmation bias make this process more challenging than it sounds.

The confirmation bias is the tendency to selectively notice or look for information that supports what we already know while ignoring conflicting information (see, e.g., Jonas et al., 2001). Affected by confirmation bias, negotiators may seek information that confirms their stereotype-based perception of the other party while ignoring information that is inconsistent with it. A schema is like a filter that tends to retain only schema-consistent new information. For example, once a U.S. negotiator thinks of a Japanese counterpart in terms of a

Japanese stereotype (i.e., reserved and relationship-oriented), it is difficult for the U.S. negotiator to accept that the Japanese counterpart is very fact-oriented and assertive. For this reason, stereotype information may get in the way of developing a set of shared goals and behaviors at the international negotiation table. If the stereotype-based schema is persistent, the stereotype is reinforced while little is discerned about the other party's actual goals and behaviors.

Moreover, the powerful anchor created by this stereotypic information may make negotiators less likely to see that their counterparts might, themselves, be adjusting their negotiation goals and processes to the intercultural setting. Prior research documents how negotiators tend toward an egocentric memory of concession making in that they ignore or discount the concessions of their counterparts (Thompson and Lowenstein, 1991). Similarly, in an intercultural setting, negotiators might ignore the adjustments of their counterparts. One reason they may ignore the adjustments of their counterparts is that they are less predisposed to seeing how situational circumstances influence the counterpart. Attribution research shows that people make internal attributions for the actions of others, ignoring how others' behavior is shaped by their situational circumstances. This suggests that negotiators should be less attuned to how the international context is influencing the other negotiator and inducing a shift in that other negotiator's schema. If negotiators ignore the impact of the intercultural setting on their counterpart or cannot see that their counterpart is actually making adjustments, then negotiators' own intercultural negotiation schema is not likely to deviate much from their stereotypic perceptions of their counterparts' schemas.

One caveat we should add, is that when we split our sample in terms of negotiation experience, those highly experienced negotiators' intercultural schema did match better to each other than those with less negotiation experience. That is, experienced U.S. Americans and Japanese negotiators seemed to have some awareness that their counterparts will have an intercultural negotiation schema that would be different from their intracultural negotiation schema.

IMPROVING INTERNATIONAL NEGOTIATION SUCCESS RATE

In our recent project, we found that respondents from both the United States and Japan were remarkably similar in how they perceived the differences between U.S. versus Japanese negotiation schema. For example, respondents from both cultures agreed that U.S. schema had goals that were higher on maximizing self-interest and lower on maximizing equality than Japanese schema, and that U.S. behaviors were marked by more information sharing and information persuasion and less hierarchical persuasion than Japanese behaviors. This suggests that these negotiators had strikingly accurate stereotypes for what the other culture's negotiation schema might be, assuming negotiators from their own culture are accurate about what their own intracultural negotiation schema is.

Moreover, these differences echo what has been documented in prior literature on cross-cultural differences. Individualistic U.S. Americans are generally thought to be self-interested and to rely heavily on information exchange, whereas collective Japanese are generally thought to make sure all parties have an adequate outcome and rely on social status as a basis for legitimate persuasion. That our respondents accurately reflected the U.S. versus Japanese negotiation discrepancies signals that our sample had learned about cross-cultural differences in negotiators' schema — whether through their own experience, stories of their colleagues, or formal training on cross-cultural differences. Fortunately, negotiators appear to begin an intercultural exchange with a fairly accurate idea of how their counterpart's culturally derived negotiation schema differs from their own.

Yet, while negotiators do carry accurate stereotypes for how the other culture negotiates, this is only half of the challenge of intercultural negotiations. The second half is for negotiators to take into account that the other party is adjusting his or her culturally derived negotiation schema to the intercultural situation. Because negotiators' intercultural schema are so fundamentally anchored in their stereotypes of the other party, they appear unable to process individuating information, specifically that this intercultural setting is unique and its influences on the counterpart need to be acknowledged. We found, instead, that negotiators appear not to process this context-specific information that could offer them important signals about how their counterparts are making schema adjustments.

This suggests that cultural sensitivity training addressing how people from other cultures negotiate has been fairly successful but also has perhaps been fully exploited. Programs abound that purport to teach negotiators about various cultural differences (particularly in behaviors — do not make gifts of clocks in China because clocks are associated with death; be prepared to spend plenty of time building the relationship in Latin America;

haggle hard in the Middle East). Yet, it appears that most negotiators who have any experience negotiating with counterparts from another culture know these culturally derived schema differences. In fact, what our research shows is that negotiators anchor too heavily on these stereotypic schema differences.

Perhaps, then, training international negotiators should highlight the importance of Dynamic Awareness Adjustment (DAA), or the ability to process cues from the counterpart to adapt and update, spontaneously, one's negotiation schema. This would require flexible planning and active information search in intercultural negotiations. Negotiators should use cultural profiles as a guideline but be instructed to actively search for disconfirming information. This should help negotiators see the counterpart as a unique individual rather than simply a member of a social category with stereotypic goals and behaviors. Another idea is to have negotiators chart out precisely how they, themselves, change when moving from an intracultural setting to an intercultural setting. Ask negotiators why they change their schema, and whether they then suppose that their counterparts behave in a similar fashion. That is, by highlighting the adjustment process for negotiators and the fact that their counterpart is in the exact same situation (of moving from intra- to intercultural setting), these negotiators should better be able to reason that their counterpart is similarly adjusting.

TOWARD A BROADER APPLICATION

In this chapter, we have argued that negotiation failure may arise from negotiators' inability to see their counterpart as an individual influenced by the situational contexts, and rather see him or her as a cultural stereotype. As a result, negotiators overadjust their goals and behaviors because they are firmly anchored on the other cultures' stereotypes. While our discussion focused exclusively on intercultural encounters, the basic argument can be broadly applied to other negotiation settings. Indeed, in the cases presented in this book, we find evidence that negotiation partners are anchored on the stereotypic perceptions that they have derived about the counterpart, exaggerating or misleading their negotiation goals and behaviors. Although we cannot fathom from the cases whether the negotiation partners overadjusted their schemas or not, it is clear that the inability to create a shared understanding of appropriate goals and strategies led to negotiation failures.

In the case of Waco negotiations that Goodwin discusses ("Two Hostage Negotiations"), there was a substantial difference in the framing of situations between the Branch Davidians and the FBI. The Davidians perceived the situation as a "state to state" or "citizen to government" encounter, while the FBI viewed the same situation as a "state to individual/hostage taker" encounter. As a consequence, the FBI acted toward Koresh, the leader, anchored on the stereotypes of a "hostage taker" who was threatening and manipulating the followers. Thus the FBI negotiation goal was to capture Koresh and free the hostages. Meanwhile, the Davidians saw themselves as a group of citizens with firm religious beliefs who were negotiating with representatives of a government that was opposed to their beliefs. Accordingly, their goal was to convince the government of the righteousness of their beliefs, leading Koresh to repeatedly preach his beliefs to "convert" the FBI/government officials. The resulting failure in the Waco negotiations may be partly attributed to this mismatch between the Davidians' goals to "convert" the FBI and the FBI's goals to save the "hostages" from immediate threat.

Similarly, the negotiation at the Munich Olympics may be interpreted as a failure based on their anchoring on the opponents' negative stereotypes. While the authorities were anchored on the stereotype of terrorists as "hostage takers," the terrorists were anchored on the stereotype of authorities as a "state." Neither the terrorists nor the authorities expected the other to deviate from their stereotypic behaviors. In reality, however, in facing the authorities, the terrorists adjusted their strategies to be more characteristic of a group with some political demands. Likewise, in encountering the hostage takers, the authorities representing the "state" accentuated their position as authorities. As a consequence, we see a major disconnect between the terrorists who view the situation as a "group versus state" encounter, and the authorities who view the situation as an "authorities versus hostage taker" encounter.

At a societal level, Saner, in "The Cyprus Conflict," illustrates in the case study the complexities of the conflicts between Southern and Northern Cyprus. The complexities involve not only the political intentions of two mother countries, Greece and Turkey, but also the interference from external stakeholders such as the United States, the EU, the UN, and the UK. At the root of the negotiation failure, which is explained in terms of the elaborate network of conflict relationships between Greece and Turkey and the political powers surrounding the two, is the mismatch of perceptions about the conflict situation. Greeks viewed the conflict in terms of "intervention" by Northern Cyprus and

Turkey, while Turkey viewed the conflict as "invasion" by Southern Cyprus and Greece. These differing interpretations of behavior, which stem from each party's negative stereotypes of the other, is likely a root cause of continued negotiation failure.

Finally, the Security Council negotiation on Iraq (Marschik, "The UN Security Council and Iraq") details how parties had very different perceptions about Iraq and about each other and how this led to differing negotiation goals, hindering settlement. Throughout the negotiation, the United States espoused a firm belief that Iraqis stored weapons of mass destruction, and that Iraq was somehow related to the September 11 attacks. These stereotypes manifested in goals to apply sanctions, and disarmament, and they eventually proceeded with military action against Iraq. Other countries, especially France, were anchored on the notion that the United States was trying to get even with Iraq after the September 11 attacks, a stereotype that manifested in goals of inspections rather than disarmament and trying to prevent the UN resolution from becoming a trigger for military enforcement. Thus, we see that both the United States and France, with their allies, formulate their negotiation goals and strategies based on their anchoring in stereotypes. Had the two parties openly discussed and agreed on the goal of the negotiation, we might have seen a different phase in the history. Of course, such openness and agreement are increasingly difficult to achieve for political reasons.

CONCLUSION

Much common wisdom on the failure of international negotiations blames culture, specifically cultural differences in negotiators' goals and behaviors (or schema). Yet, is culture really the culprit? Perhaps, but not in the ways we generally accept — that is, because unawareness of cultural differences leads directly to confusion and misattribution. Rather, the problem appears to stem from negotiators' anchoring too heavily on these cultural differences. By anchoring on their stereotypic knowledge of the counterparts' culturally derived negotiation schema, negotiators fail to see the counterparts as individuals influenced by the international context. Thus, negotiators fail to see that their counterpart is adjusting to an intercultural schema. With both negotiators overcompensating in their intercultural schema, these schemas are again misaligned, which could produce failure. Yet, the mutual goal of reaching agreement and natural processes of schema adjustment suggest international negotiators might develop a shared intercultural negotiation schema, representing shared goals and behaviors, that could facilitate communication and generate efficient solutions. To achieve this, we suggest less focus on cultural differences training and more focus on Dynamic Awareness Adjustment.

NOTES

1. Lothar Katz, "International Negotiation: How Do I Get Ready?" at Leadership Crossroads website, 2004, http://leadershipcrossroads.com/arti_inn.htm.

2. Elena Groznaya, "East Meets West: Negotiating Interculturally," *TCWorld* October 2008, http://82.165.192.89/initial/index.php?id=87 (accessed January 2012).

3. Of course, classic trade theory argues that differences in tastes or preferences can lead to negotiation optimization as nations trade low-preference goods for high-preference goods (cf. Pareto, 1971; Wicksteed, 1950). Below we argue our negotiator goals are different than these tradable preferences.

PART FOUR

Structures as a Cause for Failure

Structural Dimensions of Failure in Negotiation

ANTHONY WANIS-ST. JOHN AND CHRISTOPHE DUPONT

> Structuring, or creating order out of complexity is the prime
> activity of the negotiator, as it should be of the analyst.
>
> —I. WILLIAM ZARTMAN

To what extent might the failure of a negotiation be due to structural factors? This chapter attempts to shed some light on the role of negotiation "structure" on international negotiations that do not end in agreement. To some degree the analysis extends to negotiations that resulted in an agreement but failed when it came time to implement. We argue that the inherent structure of international negotiations indeed is related to the failure to reach agreement. However, we note at the outset that "structure" is also a verb: negotiators structure a negotiation by their actions and omissions. The set of contextual variables present at the onset of a negotiation is often very fluid, amenable to skillful manipulation by negotiators who are intuitively or consciously aware of the structural nexus to success and failure. Our findings are grounded in theoretical analysis and empirical observations of failed international negotiations, and we organize our chapter around three salient expressions of negotiation structure: parties, issues, and power.

NEGOTIATION ANALYSIS AND STRUCTURE: DEFINING NEGOTIATION STRUCTURE

Structure is an aspect of negotiation analysis that was previously limited to discussions of power asymmetry among the parties. But structure, as an analytical framework, can at least be broadened to include analysis regarding the parties involved and the issues being negotiated. Party structure, issue structure, and power structure help add complexity to theoretical analysis of negotiation and better reflect the multiparty, multi-issue, and fluidly asymmetrical nature of international negotiations. The list can be extended to other elements of a contextual nature, some of them purely or mainly physical — location, timing, and procedures — but also communication channels and linkages to the past or to simultaneous events that have an impact on the interaction from its inception to the endgame. Several chapters in this volume address some of these complementary aspects of negotiation structure, including Axel Marschik's review of the 2002–3 UN Security Council negotiations in the run-up to the Iraq war.

One standard analysis of negotiation (Kremenyuk, 2002) proposes five major components (or "levels") present in any negotiation: actors, process, structure, strategy, and outcome. These components or levels of analysis are seen as part of a negotiation "system." Some authors argue that of these five components, "the structural approach to negotiation analysis is the simplest approach and at the same time the most comprehensive" (Zartman, 2002:72). "Analysis is structural when it relates the explanation of outcomes to the distribution or disposition of key elements — initially the numbers and powers of the parties — and examines resulting concepts from their implications" (72). "Systems, processes, strategies, and outcomes flow from their structural underpinnings," argued Zartman, who, in contrast with Kremenyuk, traces all competing explanations for success or failure to a negotiation's inherent structure (84).

The most basic structural "sketch" of a negotiation is that of a simple one-issue, two-party interaction in which the parties attempt to achieve a jointly agreed solution by reciprocal bargaining and have at least a rough symmetry in terms of their relative ability to reach an agreement more favorable to their position. Both sides also display this fundamental and theoretical symmetry through their respective ability to veto any potential solution (Zartman, 2002:72). Obviously real international negotiations present significantly more complex structural characteristics in terms of the sheer number of parties; the linked negotiations with internal parties, constituencies, and bureaucratic actors; the kinds and numbers of issues at each table; the shifting interests underlying the various issues; and the asymmetrical possibilities in terms of perceived or objective sources of leverage or power that can be brought to bear at the main negotiation table. Negotiation analytical literature, particularly research on international negotiations, has, over the past several decades, progressively come to reflect the complex and asymmetrical conditions of reality.

With structure at the core of other attributes of negotiation, it is not surprising that structural defects — or defective structuring by negotiators — may help explain why certain international negotiations do not end in agreement. With the exception of cases characterized by bad faith or hidden agendas, in which negotiators deliberately seek to derail agreement because of perceived partisan gain derived from the blockage of an agreement, negotiators enter the negotiation process with the intention of finding a jointly agreed solution acceptable at least to them, and perhaps others as well. When negotiators fail to reach agreement, practitioners and theorists legitimately may ask what structure has to do with the outcome. The remainder of this chapter examines party, issue, and power dimensions of structure in more depth and is illustrated with contemporary cases of international negotiation. Several linkages among the three dimensions are noted as well.

PARTY STRUCTURE

A first structural dimension of failure concerns the party element of structure. Party structure can be problematic in terms of the sheer quantity of parties, and multiparty negotiations are widely understood to pose more problems to negotiators than two-party negotiations. But quantity is not the only party-related problem, as will be seen below.

Somewhat paradoxically, the number of parties may be too large or too small. If the sheer number of negotiating parties is too large, a constructive negotiation process tends to be more difficult to develop as communication problems multiply. These include diluted decision-making authority of negotiators, conflicting messages from within delegations, shifting coalitions among parties, and increasing chances of spoilers being present among the parties included. Brook Boyer takes note of the institutional crowding that characterizes multilateral negotiations within institutional frameworks (see Boyer's chapter, "Institutions as a Cause for Incomplete Negotiations," in this volume). Additionally, as the number of parties goes up there may be a variant of the free rider problem that manifests itself as a dilution of party commitment to the process (as parties seek to shift responsibility for concession-making to others). This will often be accompanied by analytical difficulties in discovering the zone of possible agreement due to informational challenges inherent in constructing proposals that approach optimality — the negotiating maxim that prescribes solutions that cannot be improved for any party without worsening the payoffs of others. This analytical problem ties together the numbers of parties and the issue aspect of structure. It is exacerbated by the well-understood problem of strategic misrepresentation. If even a handful of parties "misrepresent" their preferences in an attempt to maximize their own distributive gains in a large multilateral negotiation, the likelihood of creating a shared vision of optimal solutions may be significantly decreased, and the likelihood of a no-agreement outcome increased. The successive rounds of the World Trade Organization demonstrate that failure to reach agreement can result from the emergence and dynamics of coalitions among various member states (Odell, 2005).

In many contemporary cases of international conflict resolution, even the number of mediators can begin to multiply in the absence of any barriers to entry and the lack of coordination mechanisms for third-party intervenors (Ould-Abdallah, 2000; Touval, 2002).[1]

Before the 1995 Dayton conference that helped end the Bosnia war, progress was hindered by the intransigence of the parties, the escalatory dynamic of the military conflict, the large number of conflict parties unable to create enduring coalitions among themselves, and the large number of intervening parties (O'Brien, 2005:89–112). Until the United States took a leadership role that had a direct impact on the structural dynamics involved, much of the pre-Dayton diplomacy can be regarded as having failed to stop the wars, even though such diplomacy did lay the foundation for the later Dayton Accords (Touval, 1996). An example of the subordination strategy mentioned above was the shift in negotiation structure that took place during the war, in 1995, when Yugoslav president Slobodan Milosevic forced the Bosnian Serbian leaders to "formally sign a document empowering him to negotiate on their behalf" (556). This structural simplification is believed to have been instrumental in reducing the negotiation intransigence of the both the Bosnian Serb leadership and of Milosevic — at least at Dayton (the Bosnian Serbs' role in the implementation of the accords was less than ideal, but the scope of this chapter is on agreements). An additional structural modification created by the United States at Dayton was the sidelining of the European mediators who had played a central role in the pre-Dayton diplomacy (first through the Steering Committee of the International Conference on the Former Yugoslavia, and its successor, the Contact Group) (Holbrooke, 1998). These structural changes, although not without their own problems, were critical in transforming the painful record of diplomatic failure regarding Yugoslavia's wars toward at least partial success in peacemaking.

Progress toward agreement at large multilateral conferences may be achieved by the creation of coalitions that reduce the effective number of negotiators and positions from hundreds to tens (Koh, 1990). A caveat to coalition formation is in order, however: while coalitions help make complex party structures more compact, they can also become problematic with the emergence of a hegemonic dominant coalition, or the emergence of one or more blocking coalitions composed of less powerful parties whose members' influence might have been diluted had it not been for the strength of their coalition. The impasse at the 2003 WTO ministerial meeting at Cancun, Mexico, is attributed to the successful coalition formation among a group of developing countries known as the G20, who banded together against the interests of the developed countries (Narlikar and Tussie, 2004). While the G20 possibly felt that they had succeeded in avoiding being "railroaded" by the G8, the end result did not produce an agreement, even one that favored the G20.

Agreements involving large numbers of parties can be conceptualized as an attempt to create a coalition of the whole. Beyond all of the structural obstacles to agreement noted above, it is also possible that there is no single all-party solution that satisfies the interests of the parties more efficiently than smaller, exclusionary arrangements. Such negotiation problems are said to have a "hollow core"; the zone of possible agreement for an all-party agreement is elusive or nonexistent, because agreements among a subset of the parties can always distribute more value to at least some of the included parties than any agreement that included all of the parties (Raiffa, Richardson, and Metcalfe, 2004:436). Axel Marschik explains in his chapter in the present volume ("The UN Security Council and Iraq") that at least one of the factors contributing to the failure of the 2002–3 negotiations on a UN Security Council resolution on Iraq's purported weapons of mass destruction programs was the lack of overlap between the U.S./UK/Spain position and the preferences of all other Security Council members; in other words, a "hollow core" that resulted in the U.S.-led unilateral war. This aspect of party structure is obviously tied to issue structure since preferences link parties to issues and help define any space (or lack thereof) for agreement.

In contrast to the overabundance of parties, negotiators, and mediators, the absence of key parties and negotiators may also be a cause for failure. In the EU-Iran negotiations that began in 2003 and are analyzed by one of the present authors (Wanis-St. John) elsewhere in this volume, negotiations failed in part because major actors with a stake in the outcome — the United States in particular — were never present at the table, and instead tried to influence them (mostly by exerting pressure on the Europeans and issuing threats against the Iranians) from the outside. Thus it is not only that the right parties are not talking to each other, but what they do away from the table that affects the outcome. The outside pressure has been mostly unconstructive, focusing on maximal demands that the European negotiators could not extract and that the Iranians could not concede (see Wanis-St. John's chapter, "Nuclear Negotiations," on the Iran-E3/EU negotiations in this volume). Impeded by the U.S. refusal to establish diplomatic contact — except for a momentarily encouraging offer of conditional talks by the U.S. secretary of state, the parties that most need to negotiate cannot talk to each other publicly. Deborah Goodwin, elsewhere in this volume ("Two Hostage Negotiations"), notes the destructive influence of absent decision makers and parties who contributed to the catastrophic outcome of the Munich hostage and Waco siege crisis negotiations.

A critical component of party structure concerns how negotiators address the possibility of spoilers (parties opposed to an agreement) and extremists. Negotiators are faced with a dilemma: exclusion of extreme parties tends to facilitate the reaching of agreements, but this must be weighed against the consequences of their exclusion. Distanced from any agreement that has been signed, excluded spoilers can become politically mobilized and seek to not only derail the implementation of an accord, but return to violence or other obstructionist methods for attaining their preferred outcomes, unless provision has been made to deal with them by inclusion, co-optation, or defeat. The Arusha Peace Accord of 1993, while it constituted an agreement among the conflict factions in Rwanda, appears to have contained the seeds of its own failures and the genocide that followed it the next year, in part due to deficiencies regarding this aspect of party structure (Daley, 2006).

The 1999 Rambouillet talks between Serbia and Kosovo were mediated by a multinational delegation led by the United States, Russia, and France, among others, and yet failed to achieve a negotiated autonomy for Kosovo. Instead, the talks resulted in deadlock. NATO implemented a long-threatened bombing campaign against Serbia, resulting in civilian deaths among Serbs and

Kosovars, a massive displacement of Kosovar Albanian refugees, and continuing ambiguity in the international legal status of Kosovo despite putting an end to Serbian killings of Kosovars.

At Rambouillet, the party structure was not conducive to progress. Key decision-makers were missing from the talks or remained on the sidelines from both the Serb and Kosovar delegations. The locus of real decision-making authority within a party's negotiating delegation is an essential question: in the case of the Serb delegation at the 1999 talks, it became clear during and after the talks that they lacked substantial authority to sign any agreement while they were in France, and that president Slobodan Milosevic — absent from the talks — was the only person who had any real negotiating authority (Weller, 1999).

While the conflict parties' delegations lacked authority (Serbia) and unity (Kosovo), the oversupply of interested mediators created its own challenges. More problematic from a structural standpoint was the friction among the mediators. While the United States seemed to lend support to the Kosovars, Russia was an open partisan of the Serbs. "Russia's contribution to the process was ambiguous. Its particular relationship with Serbia enabled crucial diplomatic steps but its rigid commitment to veto any enforcement action was the major factor forcing NATO into an action without mandate" (Independent International Commission, 2000). Peace negotiations in Burundi, while they eventually resulted in agreement, were delayed and complicated by the multiplicity of mediators — thirteen, according to the UN's special envoy — Ambassador Ould-Abdallah, as well as some eighty non-governmental organizations seeking a role (Ould Abdallah, 2000; Sollom and Kew, 1996).

In addition to number of parties and intervenors, the organizational dynamics within a party's negotiation team can manifest as structural contributions to failure. Defective working arrangements within a delegation — such as leadership deficits; hostility among delegates; internal or external pressures, including a poor relationship between negotiators and constituencies, between lead negotiators and their teams, or between agents and principals — can all make reaching agreements more difficult. After the failure of the February 1999 Rambouillet negotiations, the government of Slovenia secretly engineered the resignation of Kosovar hard-liner Adem Demaci in the hopes that this would avoid further bloodshed and facilitate an agreement between the Serbs and Kosovars when talks were to resume in Paris the next month (Petric, 2006).

The simple existence of an inflexible internal constituency is often the driver of negotiation intransigence. There is abundant research describing the linkage between internal (domestic) and external (international) negotiations (Putnam, 1988). This linkage may in fact be a significant obstacle to agreement when the preferences at one table (domestic) reduce the zone of agreement at the other (international) table. The inability of negotiators to create possible solutions that were not only acceptable to other countries and coalitions of countries, but also palatable to internal constituencies has dogged the successive WTO negotiating rounds of recent years. The suspension of global trade talks in July 2006 was a stark reminder of the difficulties of complex multilateral negotiations regarding the distribution of the benefits and costs of global trade. Just prior to the suspension, WTO director general Pascal Lamy upbraided the major economic powers: "I am aware of your domestic political problems. However, I ask you to ponder, in the decisions you make, the risk of a failure, which is considerable — and indeed every bit as political" (Lamy, 2006). Of course, the two-level game concept brings together party and issue structure, and thus we continue the discussion of issue structure in the following subsection.

ISSUE STRUCTURE

While conducted by parties, negotiations are undertaken to resolve disagreements on issues — whether they are about general principles or specific details. Parties negotiate on the assumption that they can create a jointly agreeable outcome better than the status quo with regard to those issues. Negotiations end in agreement when negotiators are able to overcome the gaps between their respective stakes, values, interests, and positions or the perceptions of a gap among them. But the issues themselves may in fact be (or at least perceived to be) intractable (Kesner and Shapiro, 1991). In general, issues per se have been increasingly neglected in negotiation analysis and uncritically accepted. After all, negotiations are about issues. But some analysts have proposed that certain types of issues do not lend themselves to negotiation, especially if negotiation is framed as a game of concessions (see P. Terrence Hopmann's chapter, "Issue Content and Incomplete Negotiation," in this volume, and especially his subsection on inherently intractable issues). People, groups, and states are reluctant to negotiate over elements of their identity, and over basic human needs, such as security. We also tend to be somewhat skeptical about the need to negotiate over issues that involve entitlements or rights and other "indivisibles" (see Wanis's chapter, "Nuclear Negotiations," on Iran-EU negotiations). Such obstacles have often been resolved by shifting the frame around negotiations so that zero-sum perceptions are set aside in favor of discussion concerning the modality on the satisfaction of a human need or the implementation of a human right (see Cristal's chapter, "Camp David, 2000").

But intractability may be also due to a defective assessment of the existence of an "objective" zone of possible agreement (ZOPA). In the EU/Iran negotiations of 2003–6 the ambiguity in the framing of the negotiation masked an extraordinarily narrow zone of possible agreement that only began to show signs of slight widening after three years. The Kosovo-Serbia conflict is a clear example of how intractable the issues really are when both parties have from the start completely opposing views that are not simple strategic misrepresentations of their preferences but real, substantive disagreements over which compromise is seen to be highly problematic. The Serbs in the past negotiations genuinely appeared to oppose not just secession but even meaningful autonomy and may not have perceived a negotiated autonomy preferable to an armed conflict — even one in which they lost control of Kosovo. But this line of inquiry continues in our discussion of power below.

The complexity of issues may also be a factor that helps us explain negotiation failure. Whereas adding to the issue complexity by increasing the number of issues to be resolved has sometimes been recommended as a strategy to facilitate trade-offs necessary to reach agreement, the sheer presence of issue complexity — if not managed appropriately — may also prevent negotiators from advancing toward a positive-sum outcome for all parties involved (Watkins, 2003:164–65). When issues are highly complex (for example, issues that involve "nonnegotiable" principles, values, symbols, or matters of a highly specialized nature, such as nuclear nonproliferation purposes, political self-determination, or an aggregation of substantive and symbolic issues) the consequence may be that negotiators who advance on one issue are blocked on another. Dean Pruitt early on cautioned negotiation analysts that "human intellectual capacity severely limits the number of issues that can be considered simultaneously [but] . . . the alternative of dealing with issues one by one has its limitations because the issues are often highly interrelated" (Pruitt, 1981:14).

Complexity requires a shared vision of the end game in order to move beyond an issue-specific impasse. Issue structure has a direct impact on what is discussed and when it is discussed, as well as what is not discussed: in short,

the negotiation agenda. Although examination of the negotiation agenda begins to take us in the direction of negotiation process, it must be said that issue
structure can lead to highly significant choices regarding what we consider
to be a further structural sub-element: whether the negotiations are pursued
in incremental fashion or comprehensively. Incremental negotiations — those
that start with principles and smaller issues and only later address more contentious substantive issues — have an embedded risk because if the parties
commit mistakes or fail to implement early commitments, their confidence in
each other is eroded instead of built up, and the more critical issues that were
reserved for the future may never get addressed.

The interim peace negotiations between the Palestinians and Israelis after 1993 were predicated mainly on Palestinian security cooperation with the
Israelis in exchange for gradual withdrawals of Israeli troops and administrative structures from the West Bank and Gaza. The troop withdrawals, however,
were always constrained by the Israeli reluctance to redeploy away from Israeli
settlements. But negotiations on the withdrawal of the settlements were excluded from interim talks and reserved for the thornier permanent settlement
talks. The parties' decision to negotiate separately over issues that were op-
erationally linked has contributed to the faulty implementation of the interim
accords as well as the failure to date to agree on a permanent status accord
(Wanis-St. John, 2006).

Another aspect of issue structure that may contribute to failure involves
the very manner by which issues are negotiated. The failed bilateral Egyptian-
Israeli talks of 1978 were characterized by clashing approaches to structuring
the issues in dispute. In brief, the Egyptian delegation pushed for an agreement on overarching principles in advance of discussions on details, while the
Israeli negotiators sought to bargain over the individual issues without any
prior "formula." Zartman and Berman (1982:89–91) called this a choice between inductive (details first, to culminate in a general agreement) and deductive (general formula first, followed by details) approaches to negotiation. It
was not until U.S. president Jimmy Carter reconciled these two approaches by
proposing a jointly accepted formula and by proactively integrating principles
and details into a single text that agreement became possible at Camp David
the following year (Carter, 1982; Quandt, 1993).

While the negotiation process is a separate domain that addresses what negotiators do at the table with the structural aspects that confront them, process

choices are tightly linked to issue structure, and in ongoing negotiations, process may become part of the issue structure. We argue that negotiator choices need to fit the parties, context, and possibilities. The inability of the negotiators to find an agreed formula for a general framework, their disagreement on the need for an initial formula, and the recourse to unilateral drafting instead of a single negotiating text are examples of process choices that can ruin the chances of success if not appropriate to the dispute. In the 1999 Kosovo-Serbia negotiations it was the mediators who maintained jealous control of drafting, hoping to short-circuit the problems inherent when conflict parties submit competing drafts to each other and to maintain the momentum of prior shuttle diplomacy. However, this appears to have dangerously minimized the input of the parties into the proposed Rambouillet Accord as it evolved. The EU/E3 side of the EU/Iran negotiations also seems to have maintained a monopoly on drafting of possible agreements, with the result that the drafters' interests predominate in the draft final framework agreement, at least from the Iranian perspective.

The gaps that negotiation is supposed to overcome with respect to the discrepancies between the parties on the issues on the table may become unsolvable if flexibility and creativity are lacking for one or more of the parties. Issues may have to be reconfigured or recast as subsets of superordinate goals. In the absence of flexibility or creativity, impasse looms larger and may give way to collapse. The prescriptive literature on negotiation offers different ways to deal with such situations, including facilitated brainstorming and other value-expanding actions that defer commitment to negotiating positions while the parties explore the frontiers of possible solutions (Fisher, 1996).

While it is believed that careful advance preparation helps ensure that value-creating proposals can be found to reduce or eliminate the gaps among the parties with respect to their most contentious issues (Koh, 1990), there are systematic ways that parties undermine their own success in negotiation, and some of these are reflected in attitudinal or belief domains (Bazerman and Neale, 1992; Rubin and Brown, 1975). Even when a powerful, skilled, and well-prepared mediator (or set of mediators) is present to maximize the parties' ability to overcome issue structure problems, the parties may be unable to come to agreement, in part, due to their own intolerance for political accommodation, overconfidence, or zero-sum beliefs and frames (see Cristal's chapter, "Camp David, 2000").

POWER STRUCTURE

Power has long been thought to be one of the most "powerful" explanatory variables for negotiations. Power in classic approaches to negotiation was considered a direct determinant of outcomes; the more powerful the party, the more likely it could impose its will on parties of lesser power, but from whom agreement was desirable, expedient, or indispensable. In international negotiations, the classic characteristics of power have tended to include military might, economic resources, territory, and technological advantage (Iklé, 1964). And yet these must be seen as only partial aspects of power. Power in international negotiation in the classic sense need not be determinative of success for the party that wields it. Nuclear weapons and overwhelming wealth sometimes have little or no impact at the negotiation table. Elsewhere in this volume, Cecilia Albin ("Explaining Failed Negotiations") discusses the relational dimensions of power as being correlated to value-creating negotiation strategies and to positive outcomes, contrasting this with the value-claiming strategies that she argues flow from classic power formulations, and that are correlated with negotiation failure and stalemate. Habeeb had earlier defined negotiation power as if it were strategy ("the way actor A uses its resources in a process with actor B so as to bring about changes that cause preferred outcomes in its relationship with B" [Habeeb, 1988:15]). Zartman and Berman long ago noted several dimensions along which a party can "structure" its delegation and the tactics available to them under the condition of power asymmetry (1982:203–29). Legality, moral legitimacy, a sense of unwavering commitment, and the ability to build alliances can be and often are leveraged by so-called weaker parties, and clearly contribute to the power equation at the negotiation table (Zartman and Rubin, 2000). In terms of contributions to negotiation failure, international negotiators' perceptions of their own power can have an impact on the strategies they choose and may encourage them to take steps that lead to impasse (see Cristal's chapter, "Camp David, 2000"). History repeats itself with the Taba talks, where an acute sense of an imbalanced power relation on the Palestinian side added to the difficulties.

It is sometimes posited that power symmetry in negotiations is a precondition for a successful negotiation to take place. However parties of equal power may on the contrary find negotiations more difficult (Zartman and Rubin, 2000:273–74). Equal power may induce negotiators to continue to vie for superiority in the bargaining relationship. Recent research suggests that a more balanced approach is in order: power asymmetry may also be conducive to successful negotiation outcomes and help explain why "weak" parties do not always "lose" in their negotiations with strong parties. In their comparison of experimental studies on the psychology of negotiation with international negotiation case studies, Zartman and Rubin (2000) concluded that the mere perception of symmetry could be an obstacle to reaching agreement.

Power is a thus a problematic structural element in negotiation. The relationship between power and outcome is not straightforward, and it presents difficulties due to its perceptual, subjective quality. It is difficult to agree on what in the end constitutes power at the negotiation table. A party's perceptions concerning its own power and its perceptions of other parties' power may be just as or more important than any "objective" reckoning.

Power asymmetry, if poorly managed, can also be destructive for a negotiation. The Rambouillet negotiations between the Kosovars and Serbs, with the third party assistance of the Contact Group in February and March 1999, demonstrated the nonlinear relationship between power asymmetry and negotiation outcome. The Serbs may have been thought to be the more powerful party in the classic sense and should have been able to impose their views on the Kosovars, under the threat of continued ethnic cleansing. In the strict bilateral dimension, they were able to inflict costs on the Kosovars and escalate violence against them before, during, and after the Rambouillet negotiations. But the Kosovars were balanced against the Serbs by the Contact Group and NATO. These interested third parties altered the power equation considerably. To measure the real power balance one has to look at the implicit coalition of the Contact Group and NATO with the weaker power, the Kosovars.

And yet one may question whether or not this "rebalancing" of the prior power asymmetry went too far. The Rambouillet negotiations did not, after all, succeed in either attaining a negotiated autonomy arrangement or preventing further war and ethnic cleansing.

In general, while enjoying the benefits of a "strong" position, the more powerful negotiator runs the risk of turning this asset into a cause of negotiation failure. This strong party may be tempted to take advantage of its favorable bargaining position to forcefully extract concessions from the other party that exceed the bounds of equity or the political limits for that party. Seen in this light, the Contact Group's desire to impose a solution on the Serbs under the threat of force may have backfired, since the Serbs seemed willing to risk the use of force rather than make concessions to the Kosovars in the shadow of the greater power of the Contact Group and NATO. The Kosovars too ignored NATO and UN Security Council warnings to have the KLA stand down. Perhaps parties that see themselves as "stronger" seek to act upon the maxim that the "winner takes all." But "winning" a negotiation in such circumstances may paradoxically lead to failure in the short term, when there is need to formalize agreement, or in the long term, during implementation. Taking too much for granted, lacking empathy, frustrating the weaker opponent, having recourse to certain adversarial tactics (such as excessive threats, false promises, creating "facts on the ground," etc.) may well result in a desire for revenge or reprisal tactics that undermine the immediate and long-term success of negotiation, especially in cases where negotiations continue over time (Salacuse, 2000:268). The constructed power "symmetry" created by the Western alliance with the Kosovars contributed to the failure to reach agreement because it either created a new power asymmetry that only provoked Serbian defiance, or it simply provided the Serb leadership with a lethally convenient excuse for relinquishing its hold on Kosovo: a NATO attack, or both.

The weak-power negotiator (according to the party's own construal of its power) may thus be in a dilemma in which yielding to the stronger party at the negotiation table is contrasted with negative consequences that the stronger party may try to impose in the absence of agreed concessions. If there is a suitable alternate course that can be pursued instead of seeking agreement with the stronger party, the weaker party may exit the negotiation altogether or put its bets on continued intransigence or even violence, according to the context. Furthermore, less powerful parties are able to exercise a veto over the decisions and tactics of the "more powerful" party by reason of their very "helplessness": by appealing to a lack of authority, they can credibly act as if the locus of decision making were elsewhere and thus try to reduce the scope of their unilateral concessions. Of course, such behavior may be at least partially strategic, and parties in any negotiation can be tempted to narrow the zone of possible agreement while seeking to claim as much as possible in distributive bargaining.

Mediators and parties thus frequently use strategies and behaviors intended to level the playing field and reduce perceived or real asymmetries. Their efforts may not always be helpful, and they may simply reverse the direction of the asymmetry and provide a previously "strong" party with the weapons of the weak. The complex power structures in Kosovo, Iran, and numerous other locations of international negotiation also point to the difficulties encountered when power imbalances are intertwined with other structural dimensions such as party and issue.

STRUCTURE, NEGOTIATION, AND . . . FAILURE?

Three subcomponents of negotiation structure (parties, issues, and power) have been examined here and illustrated with examples from international negotiations discussed above. A theory-oriented analysis points to the importance of the structural elements of a negotiation as influential or even causal factors of negotiation failures. However, we recognize that international negotiations are not static. Negotiations that initially fail can and sometimes do eventually succeed. This begs one of the definitional questions motivating this entire volume and the research projects it has generated: what really constitutes a negotiation failure? If time lapses between negotiation encounters between the same parties on essentially the same issues, is their early failure or later success more worthy of analysis? And as Brook Boyer argues in the next chapter of this volume: "a failed (or incomplete) negotiation is not necessarily one that has not reached agreement, but rather one in which the integrative potential of the issues has not been maximized."

A future project that complements this analysis could address three further concerns: how to best prevent structural aspects from contributing to negotiation failure, how to achieve a breakthrough in a follow-up negotiation after initial negotiations have been deemed a failure, and how to modify disadvantageous structural elements wherever possible in order to facilitate not only agreement, but effective implementation, a topic that we have hinted at but that exceeds the scope of our research.

Our outlook is not deterministic. Rather, we are optimistic that negotiators can learn from mistakes and make better choices in the future. We are cognizant of an issue raised by other analysts: to what extent has a failed negotiation really failed (see, for example, Kesner and Shapiro, 1991)? Or to reframe the question in a somewhat more provocative way: Can a failed negotiation later turn out to have been a necessary development on the long road to successful agreement? Much turns on the analytical and behavioral skills of the international negotiators at the table. It is our hope to contribute to their future success with this analysis of negotiation structure and its role in negotiation outcome. Furthermore, while this chapter has offered insights and glimpses from numerous international negotiations, we believe that negotiation structure, like negotiation itself, is dynamic: negotiators can and do modify structural elements to both facilitate and complicate agreements.

On the prescriptive side of negotiation analysis we believe that better initial analysis is needed in order to maximize negotiators' chances of success when structural elements are problematic. It is entirely possible (though not, perhaps, very probable) that negotiations taking place at the time of publication for the future of Kosovo's political status may succeed where the 1999 negotiations failed. And it is also possible that a future set of negotiations concerning Iran's nuclear fuel cycle can benefit from the failures to date. Future peace talks regarding the conflicts in Darfur, Kashmir, Nepal, and Uganda may similarly benefit from past failures to reach or implement agreements and make them meaningful for those most affected by these conflicts. Future WTO negotiations may similarly succeed at reaching adequate compromises among the developed and developing countries while simultaneously safeguarding the economic interests of the most vulnerable groups and other constituencies within each member state.

Finally, it is important to note the interlinkages among the three structural elements discussed here. While it is convenient to discuss each separately, we have occasionally noted their interrelationships in order to affirm that each affects the other. Parties have preferences on issues and differ in how they construe relative power at the negotiation table. While we believe in a correlation between the structural elements and negotiation failure, there are numerous other nonstructural dimensions of negotiation that are separate from — and yet interact with — structure as we discuss it. For example, psychological aspects of negotiation, such as those discussed by Christer Jönsson in this volume ("Psychological Causes of Incomplete Negotiations"), play a critical role in process choices and behaviors at the international negotiation table. Various manifestations of negotiation uncertainty — that vexing conditional variable under which nearly all critical negotiations take place — can even result in structure and process choices (Wanis-St. John, 2006 and 2011). Structural analyses can contribute only some portion of a more holistic understanding of international negotiation success and failure. While the desire of the practitioner is to harness all aspects of negotiation cumulatively, the complementary duty of the researcher is to more clearly delineate the various elements involved, and to describe their function, impact, and interactivity, in order to better prescribe courses of action.

NOTES

We are indebted to the PIN Project, as well as Darren Kew, I. William Zartman, G. Olivier Faure, Franz Cede, and two anonymous reviewers for their critique and insightful commentary on the prior drafts. Any errors or omissions are ours.

1. See Saner's chapter, "The Cyprus Conflict," in this volume for a rich analysis of the many levels at which party structure and conflicts among outside intervenors contributed to the failure of the reunification negotiations for Cyprus. Also see Goodwin's chapter, "Two Hostage Negotiations," on failed hostage/siege negotiations with a multiplicity of mediators (Munich Olympics) and negotiators (Waco, Texas).

Institutions as a Cause for Incomplete Negotiations

BROOK BOYER

Optimism and pessimism aside, the reality is that many negotiations do not end; many negotiations do not end on schedule; and, if and when negotiations do end, the outcome may be less than optimal, or worse, unsatisfactory for one or more of the parties. Cases of incomplete or unsuccessful negotiations are certainly just as commonplace as successful ones. Yet, as the editors of this volume point out, few studies have systematically examined this phenomenon from analytical and practical angles. Extending William Zartman's (1992) fitting description of the division of labor between these two perspectives, the practitioner's job is to avoid not getting it done (or not getting it done on time), and the analyst's is to explain why it didn't get done right (or on time).

Many observers are quick to conclude that a negotiation that does not end with an agreement, or end with an agreement when scheduled, signifies failure. Indeed, expressions such as "high-level negotiations failed to result in agreement," "the final plenary session failed to adopt the draft text," or "the committee is unable to make a recommendation to the conference" are all too common. But evaluating success and failure, just as determining if a negotiation is complete or incomplete, is highly subjective. A negotiated agreement could be reached on a number of important substantive issues, yet one could arguably characterize the process leading to the outcome as incomplete or worse, a failure.[1] A conference adopts a decision, which may enjoy a certain degree of success, but the negotiation process of the decision and its relationship to having any practical effect on the ground may be far from complete. In December 1997, the Third Session of the Conference of the Parties (COP3) to the United Nations Framework Convention on Climate Change (UNFCCC) adopted the Kyoto Protocol, which was hailed by many as an important step forward in combating climate change. Although the protocol represents a concrete outcome to more than two years of negotiations, the incomplete nature of the negotiation process of that outcome required parties to resume negotiations for several years on the instrument's implementation mechanisms.[2] Without the subsequent negotiations, it's unlikely that the protocol would be in force today. This illustration underlines the need to distinguish between outcomes — whatever their form — and the negotiation process of the outcome.

This leads to a second observation: does an incomplete negotiation represent an end state, a point of no return, or is it a temporary, and indeed natural if not necessary, phenomenon in the context of an unfinished or curtailed strategic or consensual decision-making exercise? In other words, could failure to reach agreement be part of the process, and could failure — as momentary or enduring as it may be — be turned into a positive dynamic in order to move forward toward a satisfactory negotiated outcome?[3] As the British foreign secretary Jack Straw said at the June 2005 European Council Summit in reference to the stalemate over the EU budget, failure could prove to be a "turning point." Many negotiations get bogged down to the point of extinction, only to be rekindled hours, days, or months later in extraordinary sessions, a good number of which result in a satisfactory agreement.

The third and perhaps most important observation draws on Arild Underdal's understanding of the meaning of failure. He argues that the definition must extend beyond the simple notion of nonagreement (and, we could add, incompleteness) and incorporate concepts of gross benefits and transaction costs (Underdal, 1983:184). Thus, a failed (or incomplete) negotiation is not necessarily one that has not reached agreement, but rather one in which the integrative potential of the issues has not been maximized.

Having briefly reviewed some defining elements of the outcome variable of this study, why then do some negotiation processes fail to end, or at least not end when expected or scheduled? At first glance, one could easily posit on the basis of the antithesis of conditions necessary for success, but arguing solely along these lines may leave uncovered important explanatory factors. This paper puts forward a series of propositions that together form the basis of an argument that institutions provide much insight as to why negotiations may not end on schedule, may not end at all, or may visibly not meet their integrative potential.

Institutions are pervasive and omnipresent features of society, and their existence and development are widely viewed as beneficial. International institutions, for example, have helped promote cooperation among states in an anarchic world and mitigate problems of collective action. Although research on institutions has grown rapidly over the past two decades, it has focused for the most part on explanations that give rise to institutions or on identifying factors responsible for their development and evolution. With some exceptions, only recently has analysis begun to investigate implications that institutions may have on negotiation dynamics (Bjurulf and Elgström, 2004; Putnam, 1988; Spector and Zartman, 2003; Young, 1992). Most institutions are created through some process of negotiation, and institutions, once established, shape behavior and create both positive and negative negotiation dynamics (Zartman, 2003b). As Bjurulf and Elgström (2004:250) argue, "a focus on institutional arrangements enhances our understanding of negotiation processes and the final negotiated outcomes." Examining institutions and their components as an independent variable for analysis of incomplete negotiations is thus very appealing.

This paper argues that institutions, despite their many positive attributes, may also be responsible for incomplete negotiations. Discussion is broken down into three sections and examines international, domestic, and micro-level institutions, respectively.[4] Before concluding, a fourth section of the paper briefly addresses the question of institutional adaptation or change in light of incomplete negotiations. In each section, I summarize existing analytical claims and put forth either new or existing propositions that together contribute to an explanation for incomplete negotiation processes and outcomes. Each proposition is accompanied by several short illustrations taken from intergovernmental negotiations.

INTERNATIONAL INSTITUTIONS

Since the early 1980s, literature has characterized international institutions or arrangements as regimes, with the widely accepted definition being "a set of implicit or explicit principles, norms, rules and decision-making procedures around which expectations converge" (Krasner, 1983:1).[5] Any institutional explanation of incomplete or failed negotiations must therefore look at regime components and question how their nature, or how actors use or manipulate them, can cause negotiation processes to drag on, fold, or break down for good.

Zartman observes that, as is the case with virtually any negotiation, regime building "is marked by periodic confrontations between proponents and opponents as the former seek to advance the process and the latter to retard, evade, or undo it" (2003b:22). "Parties seek to maintain, gain, or regain through negotiations what was gained, not gained or lost in the past" (27). And as Spector and Zartman (2003) conclude, this post-agreement negotiation process, in the context of existing institutions, can be just as contentious (I would add more) than the initial regime negotiations.[6]

In developing an initial series of propositions, we assume, obviously, that international regimes or their meta-regime components must already exist in order to influence first, their own self-development and post-agreement process, and second, the conception, development, and evolution of other international institutions.

> PROPOSITION 1: Uncertain or questionable institutional components may have a
> constraining effect on post-agreement negotiation processes, particularly when
> the objective is to make adjustments requiring new or renewed action to re-
> spond to exogenous or situational changes.

Just as principles, norms, rules, and decision-making procedures may lead to regime stability and evolution, they may also be the source of instability and constrain post-agreement negotiations. As Gunnar Sjöstedt argues, "normative support may push an implementation process forward, but contradictions between the norms and the rules included in the same regime may produce counterforces hindering rule implementation" (2003:101–2).

Although norms and principles enshrined in some regimes may have deep roots and enjoy universal or near universal acceptance or legitimacy (e.g., the principles of most-favored nation and reciprocity in the GATT/WTO), other norms or principles, particularly those that are in their early stages of development, may be defined ambiguously and lack widespread acceptance. This ambiguity may negatively affect the post-agreement negotiation process, either in terms of defining or refining the norms, principles, or rules of the institution, or in terms of negotiating the modalities for implementation and compliance or other post-agreement processes. This can lead a negotiation to stall — or worse, collapse — if negotiators anchor or frame their positions on the basis of more attractive precedents. Although Iklé (1964:28) discusses the positive effects a previous agreement may have on the negotiation of extension agreements (e.g., by limiting the area of dispute, introducing weighty precedents, etc.), the opposite may also be true, particularly when the extension of existing agreements involves new measures that may be valued differently by the parties concerned. As Elgström explains, "actors . . . defend vigorously the values they hold dear — negotiations are thus likely to be conflictual to the extent that a new norm is seen as challenging existing ones" (2000:462).

Several examples from contemporary intergovernmental negotiations are worth citing besides the Biological Weapons Convention (see Littlewood's chapter, "The Biological Weapons Convention," in this volume). In the European Council negotiations on the EU budget for the period 2007 to 2013, Prime Minister Tony Blair anchored the UK position in the previously agreed norm of the UK rebate, which Prime Minister Margaret Thatcher had successfully secured in 1984, and then he linked negotiations on abandoning the contentious rebate to reform of the long-disputed Common Agricultural Policy, a move that was immediately rejected by France. As a result, the European Council failed to break deadlock by the end of the mid-June 2005 summit, spinning the EU into deeper political crisis following the French and Dutch rejections of the European Constitution Treaty.

In the context of the UNFCCC, the norm/principle of "common but differentiated responsibilities and respective capabilities" has encountered varying degrees of interpretations, particularly concerning what rule actions are required under the Climate Change Convention to meet the specific needs of developing country parties listed in different subgroupings (e.g., small island developing states, low-lying coastal states, countries whose economies are highly dependent on fossil fuels and energy intensive products, etc.).[7] These different interpretations bogged down the negotiations on the impacts of climate change and of response measures on developing countries and on the least developed countries at COP6 in The Hague. After two weeks of negotiations, parties agreed to suspend the meeting and reconvene six months later in Bonn for part 2 of COP, where an agreement was eventually reached on a number of important issues of the Buenos Aires Plan of Action, including decisions on capacity building and technology transfer for developing countries.

Another example from the same regime illustrates how the nature of a decision to adjust rules frames the ensuing negotiation process and outcome. The

Berlin Mandate, adopted as a decision in 1995 at the conclusion of COP1 of the UNFCCC, calls on parties to take "appropriate action for the period beyond 2000, including the strengthening of the commitments of the Parties included in Annex I to the Convention." Among other guidelines, the mandate instructs parties to set "quantified limitation and reduction objectives with specific time-frames" and excludes additional commitments for non-Annex 1 Parties.[8] The mandate rules out options (e.g., voluntary commitments for certain developing country parties) that would have arguably provided more space for the creation of joint gains, particularly in light of the domestic constraints faced by the United States. In the final leg of the Kyoto Protocol negotiations, certain Annex 1 parties attempted to reintroduce the issue of voluntary commitments into the negotiations, although developing countries succeeded in defeating this proposal on the spot. Kyoto ended on schedule and with an agreement, but one could easily argue that even in light of the protocol entering into force in 2005 (some seven years after adoption!), the negotiation of the instrument failed to maximize joint gains. At the time of entry-into-force in February 2005, two important Annex 1 parties — the United States and Australia — were not on board.[9] Moreover, while Kyoto ended successfully with an agreement, the negotiation process was incomplete and required an additional four years of negotiations on the protocol's implementation mechanisms before the required number of parties would ratify the instrument.

The negotiations on the draft resolution in the Security Council prior to the breakout in hostilities in Iraq in early March 2003 provide yet another illustration. A likely reason for the incomplete and unsuccessful negotiations on the draft resolution tabled by Spain, the United Kingdom, and the United States may have been the intentional ambiguities in resolution 1441, which the council adopted in November 2002. As Byers (2004) describes, the resolution provides grounds for both pro and anti use-of-force arguments, and the Permanent Five used this ambiguity to further their respective interests — intrinsic, instrumental, or both. As with all Security Council resolutions, 1441 was binding and became part of the collective security regime's rules. Spain, the United Kingdom, and the United States latched on to language in 1441 arguing that it provided grounds for military intervention. France, Germany, and Russia, and then China, argued that 1441 provided no element of "automaticity" and eventually reverted to the institutional tools provided by the charter (Glennon, 2003). Once the word "veto" was uttered in late February 2003, the negotiation process ended abruptly.

HORIZONTAL INTERPLAY:
WHEN "TWO" BECOMES A CROWD

Zartman (1994c) appropriately uses the proverb "two's company, more's a crowd" to characterize the numerical and social complexity of multilateral negotiation. Since the late 1980s, the proliferation of regimes has created a "crowding effect," to the point where "two" is no longer "company" and may well be a crowd. The phenomenon of institutional crowding has required policy makers to examine regime relationships more closely in view of avoiding overlap, preventing contradiction, and enhancing mutual supportiveness (Boyer, Valasquez, and Piest, 2003; Kimball, 1999; Young, 2002; Zartman, 2003b). Zartman captures this challenge aptly: "As regimes grow, they run up against other growing regimes and the two, like two meeting streams, become involved in the complex and contradictory processes of maintaining their own separate integrity and taking each other's jurisdiction into account" (2003b:30). The questions that need to be asked, of course, are how negotiators respond to institutional interplay, what effect it will have on the negotiation process and outcome, and how this affects the evolution of the regime(s).

> PROPOSITION 2: When a negotiation or post-agreement process relates to more than one institution, parties anchor positions in institution(s) where their power base is most secure.

> PROPOSITION 2.1: Incomplete negotiations are likely to result from complex dynamics at play when more than one institution has a stake in post-agreement negotiations.

In the absence of appropriate management and coordination mechanisms, institutional crowding may lead to institutional collision as parties embrace and anchor positions in institutions where their power base is most secure.[10] The effect that such an institutional collision has on the negotiation process is either deadlock or, at best, a slowly moving or incomplete negotiation process.[11]

Several recent and ongoing intergovernmental processes illustrate this anchoring phenomenon and its effect on post-agreement negotiations. In February 1999, the final session of the CBD Biosafety Protocol negotiations in Cartagena, Colombia, collapsed when the Miami Group, consisting of Argentina, Australia, Canada, Chile, the United States, and Uruguay, refused to accept the draft negotiated text, arguing that its provisions restricting the movement of living modified organisms and, particularly, genetically engineered crops, were fundamentally against international trade rules. Although the strong domestic agribusiness interests were clearly behind Miami Group's intransigence, the complaint that the United States logged in the WTO against EU regulations on genetically modified organisms seemed to play a pivotal role in turning the final stages of Cartagena negotiations into a trade — and not environmental — debate. The U.S.-led coalition anchored their position in the rules of the free-trade regime for intrinsic and/or instrumental reasons, and this contributed to framing their intransigent positions vis-à-vis the other parties. Despite the convening of an immediate, two-day Extraordinary Conference of the Parties (ExCOP), the negotiations collapsed without a Biosafety Protocol.

A similar anchoring effect can be observed in the context of the WTO negotiations on paragraph 6 of the Doha Declaration on the Trade-related Aspects of Intellectual Property Rights (TRIPS) Agreement and Public Health. While there is unquestionably universal interest in fighting global health pandemics such as HIV/AIDS, WTO member countries failed to meet the deadline to find an "expeditious solution" to address the declaration's concerns that developing countries with insufficient or no manufacturing capacity are unable to make use of the flexibility mechanisms (e.g., compulsory licensing) in the TRIPS Agreement. Developing countries latched on to the global health and human rights regimes, arguing that principles such as "Health for All in the 21st Century" put forth by the World Health Assembly several years earlier should be upheld at the expense of intellectual property rights (IPR). This was in stark contrast to the U.S. position, which was firmly anchored in upholding the integrity of the TRIPS regime. As was seen with the collapse of the Cartagena Protocol negotiations, the WTO TRIPS Council negotiations polarized, resulted in a stalemate, and did not result in agreement prior to the 2002 year-end deadline imposed by the 4th Ministerial Conference to address paragraph 6 concerns.[12] As this and the previous example illustrate, institutional crowding and collision can easily produce structural cleavages in negotiations, the result of which is often polarization, positioning, distribution, and deadlock (Boyer, 1996; Hopmann, 1996).

In another example, efforts to follow up on the CBD and give more meaning to the convention's objective to provide access to genetic resources and equitable sharing of benefits (access and benefit sharing, or ABS) were initiated in 1995. Following several years of debate and discussion by a panel of experts, the Parties to the convention established in October 2001 an Ad Hoc

Open-ended ABS Working Group, which was mandated in 2002 to negotiate an international regime. The eight years of ABS negotiations that eventually produced the Nagoya Protocol in December 2010 were marked (in part) by the complexities of institutional overlap among the objectives laid down in the CBD, and the objectives, principles, and rules of other agreements, including the TRIPS Agreement, which entered into force for many of the WTO member countries in 1996; the FAO's International Treaty on Plant and Genetic Resources for Food and Agriculture (ITPGR), which entered into force in 2004; and WIPO's Patent Cooperation Treaty and Committee on Intellectual Property and Genetic Resources. During the course of the negotiations, countries anchored positions on a number of elements in the rules of the regimes and regime components where their power base was most secure. While the negotiations produced an agreement, the process is considered by many as incomplete, and the outcome ambiguous and likely to produce disagreement in implementation. Efforts to negotiate an international arrangement on forests encountered similar challenges, given the sixty legally and nonlegally binding agreements related to forests embedded in thirty-three organizational structures![13]

DOMESTIC INSTITUTIONS: VERTICAL INTERPLAY

As with horizontal interplay, domestic institutional structures may also inhibit effective negotiation processes. As a follow-up to earlier studies and research attempting to link domestic and international politics (e.g., Rosenau, 1969), Robert Putnam (1988) captured an important and inescapable element of vertical interplay between systemic and domestic levels of decision-making and bargaining, or between chief negotiators (so-called level I negotiators) and their domestic constituencies. Putnam posits that agreement "is possible only if those [level I and II] win-sets overlap; the larger each win-set, the more likely they are to overlap" (Putnam, 1988:438). He further suggests that the size of the win-set depends on level II political institutions, such as the voting formulas for ratifying treaties.

> PROPOSITION 3: Incomplete and/or unsuccessful negotiations will result when domestic "win-sets" do not overlap. (Putnam, 1988)

The conclusion of the work of the Convention on the Future of Europe and the Intergovernmental Conference, as well as adoption in 2004 of the Treaty

Establishing a Constitution for Europe, were hailed as great successes, only to be now brought into question with the unequivocal "non" and "nee" in the French and Dutch referenda in May and June of 2005, respectively. We had a similar rationale at work with the Biological Weapons Convention (see Littlewood's chapter, "The Biological Weapons Convention," in this volume).

In another example, the adoption of the Byrd-Hagel Resolution by the U.S. Senate in July 1997 — five months before the eighth and final session of the Ad Hoc Group on the Berlin Mandate and COP3 — sent a powerful message to U.S. negotiators. The resolution, which was adopted 95–0 and stated that the United States should not sign any post-UNFCCC agreement on climate change that may do harm to the American economy and that does not also require commitments from developing countries, created a very small "win-set." Although this gave U.S. negotiators bargaining leverage, which may have contributed to the United States' succeeding in ensuring that market-based approaches such as emissions trading were included in the agreement, it was not sufficient to enable the United States or its like-minded negotiating group partners (Japan, Canada, Australia, and New Zealand) to extract additional commitments or even promises from non–Annex 1 parties to consider including the possibility of negotiating commitments for non–Annex 1 parties down the road. The introduction by New Zealand of the "Next Steps" proposal on voluntary commitments in the late stages of the Kyoto negotiations could well be viewed as an attempt to obtain a side payment to increase the size of the level II win-set in the hopes that it would satisfy domestic political constituencies.[14]

Putnam's two-level game metaphor is just one dimension of vertical interplay, however. In addition to domestic political institutions, legal, legislative, and administrative arrangements at the country level may also constrain negotiators and negotiations (Zartman, 2003b). As highlighted above, the TRIPS Council failed to meet the 2002 year-end deadline to find an expeditious solution to problems raised in the Declaration on the TRIPS Agreement and Public Health. Part of the reason for initial failure stemmed from horizontal institutional interplay phenomenon, the way in which WTO member countries latched on to these regimes, and how this latching-on phenomenon framed positions. Closely connected with this, however, were vertical links in the form of legislative constraints. Although domestic political institutions, industries, and nongovernmental organizations were involved in lobbying level I negotiators, the legal complexity involved in amending Article 31 of the TRIPS Agreement, as proposed by many developing member countries, combined with the complexity and lengthy process of amending national IPR legislation, made an alternative position (i.e., a moratorium on dispute settlement) much more appealing in view of finding an expeditious solution to paragraph 6 concerns. While there was merit to the U.S. preference to pursue the moratorium approach, many developing countries dismissed this as simply a "value-claiming" or delaying tactic. The result, as discussed earlier, was a polarized negotiation that failed to reach agreement before the end of 2002 as instructed by the Doha Ministerial Conference.[15]

Differences in legal systems may also create conditions for negotiations to falter. The negotiations between Switzerland and the United States from 1969 to 1973 on bank secrecy dragged on and almost broke down not because of incompatibility of objectives (e.g., fighting money laundering and white collar criminals), but because of the importance of bank secrecy as an institution in Swiss law and society, and the different legal systems and methods used in the two countries (civil versus common law systems).[16] This gives rise to a corollary:

> PROPOSITION 3.1: Incomplete and/or failed negotiations are likely to result when domestic institutions bring different conceptual frameworks to the table. (Eichengreen and Uzan, 1993)

Eichengreen and Uzan (1993) argue that the 1933 World Economic Conference failed to agree on a coordinated response to the economic crisis of the 1930s as a result of incompatible conceptual frameworks, which emerged from the countries' respective historical experiences and which were embraced by their respective domestic government institutions.

INSTITUTIONAL CONSIDERATIONS AT THE MICRO LEVEL

Regimes and their negotiations require the existence of micro-level institutions to function effectively. Micro-level institutions are often embedded in organizational systems and include structures such as assemblies, bureaus, councils, committees, secretariats, subsidiary bodies, and working groups; organizational persona such as chairpersons and other presiding officers, facilitators, and staff; and procedures, including explicit or implicit rules for decision making within the structures.[17] Taken together, these institutions often assume lives of their own either by inheriting, becoming, or contributing to the effective functioning of full-fledged organizations.[18] For example, as a follow-up to the 1992 United Nations Conference on Environment and Development, the Economic and Social Council created the Commission on Sustainable Development as one of its functional commissions, which was given the task of monitoring progress in the implementation of Agenda 21 and, more generally, the regime on sustainable development. The CSD is an intergovernmental body with objectives and explicit functions, members, sessions, procedures, elected leadership, and a secretariat.

Conference secretariats perform important support services for regimes and negotiations. The functions may be of a proactive or passive nature (Sanford, 1992). Passive functions include the preparation and follow-up of the sessions of the conferences of the parties and subsidiary body meetings, including logistics, accreditation, registration, and reporting. In addition to the servicing role, some secretariats are instructed to provide more proactive roles, such as facilitation or negotiation support. The Secretariat of the Convention on International Trade of Endangered Species of Wild Flora and Fauna (CITES), for instance, coordinates the consultation process of proposals to amend the appendices of the convention; the FCCC Secretariat servicing the climate change regime provides support to the parties in their negotiation on specific issues (Yamin and Depledge, 2005). Secretariats also perform important functions related to the implementation of the regime, such as providing advice and recommendations on the application of decisions, organizing training and capacity-building activities, or providing other forms of technical assistance to assist parties to comply with rules.

In addition to these structural components, presidents, chairpersons, and other presiding officers are also instrumental for effective and successful negotiation. These actors are more than just organizational personalities; they represent an institutional response to collective action and are thus fundamentally important to the effective functioning of regimes (Tallberg, 2002). Chairpersons and presiding officers perform a number of formal or explicit functions clearly enumerated in the rules of procedure, such as setting the agenda in collaboration with the secretariat; managing debate; ruling on points of order; determining if consensus exists or, if the rules allow, suggesting that a decision be put to a vote; and announcing decisions. Presiding officers also perform a number of implicit functions, such as facilitating and even mediating (e.g., proposing compromise language). For the most part, these functions are performed in the informal context of negotiations. The former director-general of the GATT and chairman of the Uruguay Round negotiations, Arthur Dunkel, initiated the so-called green room process in which he invited a select group of chief negotiators of the major trade blocs to private, off-the-record meetings and, eventually, to private dinners with the aim of seeking to identify creative solutions to impasses.[19]

Taken together, secretariats and chairpersons are important facilitators who can assist parties in searching for more integrative potential in negotiation by modifying the way in which coalitions are aligned (e.g., through structural interventions) or intervening as neutral intermediaries in the negotiation process (Boyer, 1996; Sanford, 1992; Sjöstedt, Spector, and Zartman, 1996; Wagner, 1999). Zartman (2003b) describes how parties in a multilateral negotiation attempt to manage or reduce complexity by taking a conceptual scan of the process through simplification, structuring, and direction processes.[20] Secretariats and chairpersons, either individually or together, perform similar tasks, particularly in view of streamlining texts and giving direction in view of forging consensus.

The absence of experienced and effective chairpersons (and secretariats) can lead to agenda instability, where the combination of multiple parties, preferences, and issues can create incompatible and uncompromising positions. Tallberg (2002) suggests that the vesting of agenda control in presiding officers provides a functional solution to the problem, although explicit procedures or implicit custom for electing conference presidents and chairpersons based on geographic rotation or host country status can prevent effective and instrumental chairpersons from holding office (Wagner, 1999). The Cancun Ministerial, as is the case with virtually every multilateral negotiation, experienced agenda instability especially with the development of the so-called new issues. Hernandez (2003) questions the procedures for selecting conference presidents and observes that in the case of Cancun (as with so many other conferences) the chairman of the conference was a senior government minister who did not necessarily have the trade negotiation experience or substantive knowledge in the run-up to the ministerial. In such cases, managing issue instability may not be effective, and, as a consequence, the negotiation processes may fail to produce an outcome.[21]

> PROPOSITION 4: Post-agreement negotiations may fail if the regime lacks micro-level institutional features that meet the requirements of the regime and have not achieved legitimacy among the regime's members.

PROPOSITION 4.1: The more complex multilateral negotiations are in terms of the issues, parties, and expectations, the more elaborate the micro-level institution will have to be to service the regime and promote constructive negotiation processes.

Proposition 4 suggests that absence of such micro-level institutions will lead to inefficient and ineffective negotiation processes. The 5th Review Conference of the Biological Weapons Convention (BWC) may have failed due to the absence of such institutions. Nicolas Sims argues that this "institutional deficit" is partly to blame for the breakdown in the negotiations: "The BWC has no annual assembly, no governing council, no standing committees or advisory panels, not even a permanent secretariat. . . . Instead, the BWC relies upon Review Conferences at five-year intervals, with no institutions mandated systematically to follow up decisions or recommendations, and with no chance to get the states parties together more regularly to steer its treaty regime or even commission work in the common interest" (2003). Sims's observations are supported by those of Patrick McCarthy: "multilateral disarmament diplomacy on nuclear or biological weapons . . . is characterized by brief bouts of intensive negotiations separated by long periods during which the multilateral process does not advance" (2005:60). The consequence of this lapse is that negotiators lack a forum for informal negotiations, as opposed to other forums, such as the climate or biodiversity negotiation processes that include subsidiary bodies meeting regularly between sessions. Because of the presence of these micro-level institutions in climate change governance, negotiators succeeded in turning the lack of agreement at COP6 in The Hague into agreement in Bonn some six months later.[22]

The failure of the WTO third and fifth Ministerial Conferences resulted partly in the changing nature of the free-trade regime, the requirements to address new issues, and the emergence of powerful developing countries in the trading system. In reference to the failed third Ministerial Conference in Seattle, the former EU Commissioner for Trade, Pascal Lamy, remarked that the "WTO's procedures have proved to be ill-suited to the need to encompass both new players, that is to say, the increasing number of developing countries seeking a place at the table, and new topics going beyond the usual matters of trade, such as environmental and social standards" (1999).

Similarly, the failure of the Security Council to reach agreement on a second resolution prior to the outbreak of hostilities in Iraq can be attributed (at least partly) to major geopolitical changes taking place at the systemic level of international peace and security, and the inability of the council as an institution servicing the regime on global collective security to keep pace with these realities (see Marschik's chapter, "The UN Security Council and Iraq," in this book). Oran Young's reference to the council is also a case in point: "When systems of ideas collapse . . . regimes built on the old construct may quickly lose their effectiveness whether or not some new cognitive construct is waiting in the wings to fill the vacuum left by the collapse of the old construct" (1992:192).

INSTITUTIONAL ADAPTATION AS A RESPONSE TO INCOMPLETE NEGOTIATION

Just as international institutions must adapt to changing circumstances, micro-level institutional features of organizations must also follow this evolutionary course. One very good example of institutional adaptation is the deepening and widening phenomenon observed in the European Community and European Union, and how the structure and procedures of European institutions have evolved over time to keep pace with enlargement and the overarching goals of European integration (Pfetsch, 1999).

> PROPOSITION 5: Incomplete or unsuccessful negotiations are drivers for institutional change — formally or informally.

Incomplete or failed negotiations are drivers for change and reform either from within or from outside institutions. A good example of institutional adaptation is the 1994 restructuring of the Global Environment Facility's (GEF) operating policies and procedures, which facilitated consensus-building and, as a result, increased legitimacy in the GEF and enabled it to become a permanent financing mechanism under major global environmental regimes. Several years earlier, discussions on financial issues failed to make headway in the context of the UNFCCC and CBD negotiations, and at one point, the proposal to include the GEF in the agreement virtually derailed the final session of the CBD negotiations.

Sjöstedt, Spector, and Zartman describe the new consensus-building procedural elements of the restructured GEF, which would be "carried out not as ad hoc activities, but as prescribed tasks. . . . The redesign of the GEF's decision-making structure in response to North-South debates at UNCED was just a small step toward institutionalizing mediation-based consensus building mechanisms into the operation of an important international environmental regime" (1994:245). In addition to revised decision-making procedures, new organizational structures of the institution were added, such as the creation of the Scientific and Technical Advisory Panel (STAP). Since the 1994 restructuring, the GEF has expanded its scope to cover not only the climate and biodiversity conventions but to also cover the UN Convention to Combat Desertification (UNCCD) and the Stockholm Convention on Persistent Organic Pollutants. In 2002, the World Summit on Sustainable Development recommended reform of the CSD to ensure more effective implementation of sustainable development and, as a consequence, discussion of policy issues is organized around thematic clusters.

In the mid 1970s, the negotiations on the Third United Nations Convention on the Law of the Sea had come to a virtual stalemate, and it was only after the president of the conference proposed that the chairpersons of the three main committees be mandated to produce informal single negotiating texts that the conference regained momentum and eventually produced an agreement (Buzan, 1981). More recently, the failure to reach agreement on a second Security Council resolution in February 2003 prior to the breakout of hostilities in Iraq was one of the motivations or drivers for the secretary-general to appoint a High-level Panel on Threats, Challenges and Change, the mandate of which included making proposals for reform in view of strengthening the regime on collective security. As a follow-up to the panel's findings, the secretary-general has elaborated proposals for strengthening the United Nations, which include reform proposals of the Security Council, in his report entitled "In Larger Freedom: Towards Development, Security and Human Rights for All."[23]

Incomplete or stalled negotiations may also drive actors to change the institutional context in which negotiations are taking place. Thus, reconvening the collapsed ExCOP biosafety negotiations in Cartagena some six months later in Vienna in the context of informal consultations among spokespersons for the major groups eventually paved the way to adopting the protocol in Montreal in January 2000. Or, as shown by Underdal, "the fading away of the 1974 Geneva Conference on the Middle East was a consequence of the fact that at least three major negotiating parties found that more progress could be made through another channel, viz. the shuttle diplomacy of the American envoy, Henry Kissinger" (1983:185).

One could also argue that the disarmament regime, which is embedded in the Conference on Disarmament structure, has not adapted to the evolving nature and changing circumstances of the present international security environment (Borrie and Randin, 2005), and that this institutional failure has spilled over and hindered the progress of various arms control negotiations, including the breakdown of the fifth Review Conference of the Biological Weapons Convention (BWC) in November 2002 (see Littlewood's chapter, "The Biological Weapons Convention," in this volume).

CONCLUSION

This paper reviewed an institutional perspective for incomplete negotiation and developed a series of propositions explaining why institutions may constitute a constraint to successful negotiation processes and outcomes. In attempting to show the important role that institutions have on negotiation, the paper examined institutional factors at three levels of analysis: international regime, domestic, and the micro-organizational level.

At the international level, the ambiguous nature of some institutions, particularly the meta-regime elements of norms and principles, may lead to incomplete or unsuccessful negotiations if parties anchor or frame positions in attractive precedents or parallel negotiations. The negotiations that ended abruptly in the Security Council in early March 2003 and the stalemate in June 2005 over the EU budget are but two illustrations of actors anchoring positions in contradictory norms or institutional precedents. This anchoring effect is accentuated in post-agreement negotiations in cases where more than one international institution has a stake in a negotiation process and outcome. As witnessed in the very slow response to find a solution to paragraph 6 concerns of the Doha Declaration on TRIPS and Public Health, or the collapse of the biosafety protocol negotiations in Cartagena, actors clearly anchored positions in institutions where their power base was most secure. Institutional crowding easily creates structural cleavages among parties, producing "we-they" or "us–them" relationships, which tend to condition negotiation processes and outcomes of a distributive, value-claiming nature (Boyer, 1996; Hopmann, 1996).

At the domestic level, political and legal institutions, both in metaphorical (e.g., two-level games) and practical (e.g., institutional-administrative constraints) terms also constitute important factors possibly giving rise to incomplete or unsuccessful negotiations. Months before the final Kyoto Protocol negotiations took place, the U.S. Senate sent an unequivocal message that the United States would not be party to an instrument that did not also require commitments from developing countries. The TRIPS Council negotiations dragged on, and member countries missed the 2002 year-end deadline to find a solution to paragraph 6 concerns not only because parties had different institutional "frames" of the outcome, but also because of the legal and administrative complexity involved in amending national IPR legislation.

Finally, the absence of effective micro-level institutions (from committees to secretariats to chairpersons) that support the effective functioning of international conferences (and regimes) can hinder negotiation processes and outcomes, and contribute to an incomplete or unsuccessful negotiation. As discussed earlier, the lack of such institutions appeared to play a role in the breakdown of the BWC negotiations.

Although institutions provide a convincing explanation for incomplete or unsuccessful negotiation, particularly for those cases presented in this chapter, the explanation is only partial. Other factors, such as the characteristics of the issue under negotiation, information, strategies, timing and process, are perhaps equally important. What's most interesting, however, is that connections can be easily drawn between or among analytical approaches. Without policy issues shaping institutions, for example, it is difficult to posit that actors will anchor positions in institutions where their power base is most secure, or that this anchoring phenomenon may create structural cleavages, which in turn condition strategic responses of negotiators, which then lead to incomplete outcomes. The challenge for practitioners, of course, is not explaining negotiations that do not end in agreement, but responding effectively and efficiently to cases of incomplete or unsuccessful negotiations so that processes and outcomes are, in the end, rendered as completely and successfully as possible.

NOTES

The opinions expressed in this paper are those of the author and do not necessarily reflect the views of the United Nations Institute for Training and Research or of the United Nations. The author is grateful to Hyun-Binn Cho and Arun Seetulsingh for providing research assistance. The author is also grateful to the editor of this volume,

Guy Olivier Faure, to my UNITAR colleague Trisha Riedy, and to the participants of the 2007 IIASA Workshop on Incomplete Negotiations for their many helpful comments.

1. Of course, the opposite is also true: namely, that process may not actually result in an agreement, but one could characterize the process as being very successful.

2. Only once negotiations on the protocol's implementation mechanisms were successfully concluded did most parties ratify the instrument.

3. Hernandez (2003) raises a similar question in connection to the failure (or incompleteness) of the WTO Cancun Ministerial Conference.

4. Institutions mean different things to different people. This paper acknowledges that differences exist and will likely persist between and within academic and practitioner circles.

5. Young (1989, 1992, and 1993). This paper will use the terms institution, arrangement, and regime interchangeably.

6. Spector defines post-agreement negotiation as the "dynamic and cooperative processes, systems, procedures, and structures that are institutionalized to sustain dialogue on issues that cannot, by their very nature, be resolved by a single agreement" (2003:55).

7. See Article 4 and 4.8 of the United Nations Framework Convention on Climate Change.

8. See text of the Berlin Mandate, Decision 1/CP.1, FCCC/CP/1995/7/Add.1.

9. Australia subsequently ratified the protocol in December 2007.

10. The anchoring effect here is similar to the first proposition, the difference being one of competing regimes and not competing elements (e.g., varying interpretations of norms) within the same regime.

11. In many respects, this argument for negotiation failure is similar to the competing conceptual frameworks argument of Eichengreen and Uzan (1993).

12. WTO Members eventually addressed paragraph 6 concerns — almost a year later — in a decision adopted on August 30, 2003. See Implementation of paragraph 6 of the Doha Declaration on the TRIPS Agreement and public health, Decision of the General Council of August 20, 2003, WT/L/540.

13. For an overview of the developments of forest-related instruments, see Report of the Ad hoc Expert Group, "Consideration with a View to Recommending the Parameters of a Mandate for Developing a Legal Framework on All Types of Forests," E/CN.18/2005/2 and Background Paper 2, "Recent Development in Existing Forest-Related Instruments, Agreements, and Processes," working draft, United Nations Forum on Forests, Ad hoc expert group on Consideration with a View to Recommending the Parameters of a Mandate for Developing a Legal Framework on All Types of Forests, New York, September 7–10, 2004.

14. The United States and Australia are the only two Annex 1 parties to the UNFCCC who are not party to the Kyoto Protocol.

15. It is interesting to note that the wto Decision of August 30, 2003, takes the form of an interim waiver and shall remain in effect until member countries are able to amend the agreement.

16. The two countries arrived at an agreement in 1973 with the Mutual Legal Assistance Treaty.

17. Here procedures may be considered either an integral part of, or exogenous to, the regime.

18. This is, of course, the principal reason why confusion exists between international institutions (e.g., regimes) and organizations. See discussions in Young (1989, 1992, and 1993).

19. For a detailed account of chairing tactics in the wto negotiations, see Odell (2005).

20. Also see discussion in Winham (1977).

21. The president of cop3 in Kyoto certainly experienced the negative effects of agenda instability in the final moments of the next to last plenary, particularly when New Zealand tabled the Next Steps proposal on voluntary commitments.

22. The Bonn Agreements on the Implementation of the Buenos Aires Plan of Action were adopted in July 2001 at the resumed session of cop6 (Part II).

23. See "In Larger Freedom: Towards Development, Security and Human Rights for All," Report of the Secretary-General, a/59/2005.

Issue Content and Incomplete Negotiations

P. TERRENCE HOPMANN

Negotiations that encounter significant obstacles in reaching agreement may be referred to as "incomplete negotiations" in that they may either continue on at great length with little or no evident progress or may be suspended, whether or not the parties intend to renew the process at some indefinite time in the future when conditions appear "ripe." The premise of this chapter is that in at least some portion of these cases the content of the issues under negotiation may be partly responsible for the inability to bring these negotiations to a successful conclusion.

However, at best the relationship between issue content and negotiation outcome is problematic. That is, there is no such thing as issues that are absolutely and inevitably intractable, nor are there issues that are absolutely guaranteed of success. Even the easiest issues may end in stalemate or collapse for many reasons, including poor negotiation technique and changes in the international or domestic environment that undermine negotiations; "spoilers" may appear to break up agreements that seemed to have been achieved on almost any issue (Stedman, 1997:5–53). Similarly, even the seemingly most intractable issues may reach successful agreements if the parties learn to reframe the issue to enhance negotiability, or if external conditions change for one reason or another to make the context for the negotiations "ripe"; under such conditions integrative or "resolving" formulas may appear that bridge the differences between the parties on the central issues under negotiation by either overcoming "mutually hurting stalemates" or creating "mutually enticing opportunities" (Zartman, 2008:232–44). Therefore, the focus of this paper is to identify how the content of issues under negotiation may affect the likelihood of a successful outcome versus an "incomplete" outcome "ceteris paribus."

At the most general level, basic theories of bargaining tend to assume that negotiations are more likely to succeed if the issues are essentially non-zero sum, that is where there exist common interests or common aversions even in the midst of conflicting interests or preferences. By contrast, zero-sum issues are more likely to result in failure, as in this situation a gain for one party by definition means that the other must lose in roughly equal proportion. But the issue here usually is dependent not so much on the "objective" character of the issues as on how they are "constructed" or "framed" by the participants, that is, whether or not they are framed as being essentially intractable or whether the construction of the issue by the parties includes the possibility of mutually beneficial outcomes (Hopmann, 2001:445–68). Therefore, the interesting question here is not so much one of categorizing issues as it is trying to understand why issues are so often framed as being zero sum by participants in negotiations, making them appear to be intractable, whether or not they are inherently so.

Furthermore, the fact that issues are initially framed as zero sum does not necessarily make them nonnegotiable. In cases of clear differences in power between the parties, the stronger may effectively pressure the weaker to concede, although one may question whether this in reality constitutes negotiation or simply coercion operating in the guise of negotiation. However, zero-sum issues are less likely to be resolved through negotiated agreement to the extent that the parties are more or less equal in power; in most such cases, however, some kind of reframing will be necessary in order to break through a long-term pattern of failed negotiations, and the introduction of a third party as mediator may be helpful in this task.

Conversely, it is generally assumed that non-zero-sum issues are more likely to offer either opportunities to obtain mutual benefits, to avoid joint losses, or both. Thus incentives of common interests and of averting common losses may militate in favor of agreement. But even most non-zero-sum negotiations are mixed motive in nature, and as much of the literature on negotiation emphasizes, the pressures of the competitive aspects of mixed-motive games may drive out efforts to realize joint benefits or to avoid common aversions. This situation, often referred to as the paradox produced by the "negotiator's dilemma" (Sebenius, 2002:241–42) or the "toughness dilemma" (Zartman,

2008:5), is one in which both parties recognize a potential common interest that could lead to a cooperative outcome, but in the absence of mutual trust each party fears that the other may seek unilateral advantage by defection and thus decides to defect itself, producing a suboptimal outcome for both parties.

Therefore, in this chapter I try to identify some of the classes of issues that seem most likely to lead to stalemate or breakoff of negotiations, to leave the negotiations incomplete in the sense that no resolution presents itself over long periods of time. There is little systematic empirical data of a quantitative nature available to examine empirically the relationship between issue definition and negotiation outcome, with one notable exception. Jacob Bercovitch, although he focused solely on mediated disputes, compiled data on international mediation from 1945 through 1990. He found a significant difference between the general nature of the negotiation issues and the probability of a mediated agreement. Security issues were most often stalemated (59.3 percent failed to reach any agreement), followed by sovereignty issues (55.3 percent failed to settle), ethnicity disputes (33.3 percent failed altogether), and lastly resource disputes (failed only 30 percent of the time) (Bercovitch, 1996:24–25). I shall return to these findings later, but again, these are only data from mediated international disputes, and issues are defined quite broadly.

Given these limitations on existing large-n data, this chapter will largely have to rely on case studies by way of illustration. Since so many negotiation case studies are defined by their successful outcome, however, even the number of cases that were never completed remains smaller than the set of successful cases, at least in the published case-study literature. Nonetheless, there are sufficient cases to at least illustrate the various categories of issues that seem to be prone to negotiation failure, and to generate hypotheses about how issues influence the likelihood of incomplete negotiations. I will also conclude by suggesting that this question is one, however, that ought to be readily susceptible to systematic, even quantitative investigation.

NEGOTIATIONS INTENDED TO FAIL:
NEGOTIATIONS FOR "SIDE EFFECTS"

In perhaps the first systematic text on international negotiations, Fred Charles Iklé in "How Nations Negotiate" introduced the concept of "negotiating for side effects" that has not received much attention over the past forty years (Iklé, 1964:43–58). Yet clearly many negotiations are undertaken specifically with the intent of being "incomplete" in the sense that at least one of the parties, if not all, has no intention of ever reaching an agreement. Side effects, according to Iklé, may include maintaining contact without seeking agreement, gathering intelligence from an opponent, deceiving another party or one's own public, or propaganda intended to influence domestic or international public opinion. Most often "negotiating for side effects" occurs because a party that seeks to avoid resolving a conflict, or even seeks to justify escalating a conflict, must first satisfy some important domestic and/or international constituency that they have tried unsuccessfully to negotiate a resolution of the conflict without any real intent of doing so. In short, generally the "side effect" of such negotiations is some kind of public relations ploy to justify the party's (or parties') doing what they really wanted to do anyway, which is often something other than reaching a negotiated settlement of the conflict. This is similar in many ways to Ned Lebow's concept of a "justification of hostility crisis" (Lebow, 1981:23–40), in which parties to a conflict initiate a crisis in order to justify their escalation to war, while trying to put the blame for escalation on the opponent. However, in the case of negotiations, with a longer time frame, parties may initiate negotiations with an enemy while preparing for war, perhaps in part to buy time while making war preparations, but also to convince domestic and international public opinion that the resort to force constituted a "last resort" after all efforts to achieve a negotiated settlement had failed. Of course, in some cases such negotiations may really be intended to reach agreement, but in others they may simply be a ruse. One indicator of the difference may be when the party seeking to justify escalation laces its negotiation proposals with "jokers" that are clearly intended to be unacceptable to the other party and thus guarantee their rejection.

One illustrative case of this is the Rambouillet negotiations that preceded the outbreak of the Kosovo war in 1999. Under the government of Federal Yugoslavia, Kosovo was granted a status in 1974 of an "autonomous region" within the Republic of Serbia, one of the six constituent republics of Federal Yugoslavia. In 1987 Serbia proposed taking away Kosovo's autonomous status, and the centrality of Kosovo to Serbian identity was stressed in a 1989 speech by Serbian president Slobodan Milosevic at Kosovo Polje, site of an historic battle between Serbs and the conquering Ottoman Empire exactly six hundred years earlier. As Yugoslavia began to break apart after 1990, tensions grew between Kosovo's majority ethnic Albanian population and Serbia. Defying Belgrade's rule, the Kosovar Albanians elected Ibrahim Rugova, leader of the League for a Democratic Kosovo (LDK) and a proponent of nonviolence, as president of the self-proclaimed republic of Kosovo. Tensions continued to escalate between the government of Serbia and Kosovo, and after 1997 the Kosovar population became increasingly radicalized; it also became armed following the looting of munitions depots in neighboring Albania and the disarmament that took place in Bosnia-Herzegovina following the Dayton Accords; in the latter case, some portion of the arms destined to be decommissioned found their way across the border into Kosovo. As the situation continued to deteriorate and violence increased, the Organization for Security and Cooperation in Europe (OSCE) deployed an unarmed team of monitors to Kosovo in the fall of 1998 called the Kosovo Verification Mission (KVM). Although scheduled to reach two thousand monitors, the mission was removed before it reached full strength because of the escalating violence, which made an unarmed verification mission inadequate to keep the peace (Hopmann, 1999:22–24).

In January 1999, NATO threatened military action to protect Kosovar Albanian civilians from the escalating violence. Having until that time largely ignored the rising tide of violence in Kosovo, the United States and some of its NATO allies suddenly became concerned that there was a serious risk of Serbian actions against the Albanian population under what was known as Operation Horseshow that might eventually constitute genocide; at minimum, there was growing evidence of massacres of Albanian civilians by Serb police and internal security forces. So NATO began to prepare for war, directed primarily against Serbia. At the same time, in order to try to gain international support for this war, especially within NATO but also within the United Nations and the OSCE, the United States, in cooperation with the Contact Group, consisting of the other major international powers, organized a conference at Rambouillet Chateau near Paris between the Kosovar Albanian leaders and Serbian leaders in February 1999.[1]

Billed as an effort to negotiate a settlement over the status of Kosovo in relationship to Serbia, it called upon the parties to disarm and to accept a NATO-led occupation force, similar to the one deployed in Bosnia-Herzegovina, during a transition period. The real "joker," however, hidden away in Annex B of a lengthy proposal drafted by the U.S. government, was the provision that the NATO occupation force would not only have access and complete immunity throughout Kosovo, but throughout all of Serbia-Montenegro as well (Judah, 2002:210). In other words, this "joker" would have effectively permitted NATO occupation of the entire territory of Serbia-Montenegro, in effect making the Milosevic government powerless on its own country. This provision was likely inserted in the U.S.-drafted proposal for purposes of guaranteeing Serb rejection. However, the Rambouillet negotiators were surprised when the ethnic Albanian leaders of Kosovo also rejected the draft agreement, leaving the United States without any clear party to blame for the failure of the negotiations. After a recess of some two weeks, the United States persuaded the Kosovar Albanians to sign the proposed agreement, while assuring them privately that they would not have to implement it since it would surely be rejected by the Serbs anyway. This time their calculation proved correct, and when the negotiations resumed, the Kosovo side agreed to sign, while the Serbs continued in their opposition, thus effectively enabling the international community to blame them for failing to reach a negotiated settlement on the eve of open military hostilities (221–24).

Thus, the Rambouillet negotiation achieved its intended result, namely to show the world that Serbia had rejected all efforts to negotiate a peaceful resolution of the crisis, thereby justifying the air campaign launched by NATO in April 1999. The point of this illustration is not to make an argument one way or the other about the ultimate justification for NATO's behavior in Kosovo, but to suggest that the abortive negotiations at Rambouillet were intended by most, if not all participants to fail from the beginning, in order to provide a justification for NATO's escalation of the conflict after the breakdown of the negotiations. A side effect, however, was that Russia, a member of the Contact Group, strongly opposed this outcome, threatened to veto authorization of the war by the UN or the OSCE, and assumed a position of hostility to the interests of Kosovar Albanians thereafter.

A similar situation occurred in the negotiations on Intermediate Nuclear Forces in Europe that began in 1981 and were broken off in late 1983, only to be resumed several years later under much more favorable conditions, eventually producing the Intermediate-Range Nuclear Forces (INF) Treaty of 1987. However, the first phase of the negotiations provides another illustration of a negotiation intended to fail. Confronted with a modernization of the already substantial Soviet force of missiles capable of striking Western Europe, but not the United States, the North Atlantic Council decided in December 1979 on INF deployments in Western Europe, known as the "dual track" decision, representing a compromise among alliance members. Some believed that deployment of a new generation of intermediate-range missiles (with ranges between six hundred and five thousand kilometers) was essential to counter similar deployments on the Soviet side, whereas others feared that this would lead to another escalatory round in the nuclear arms race within the context of the Cold War. The compromise consisted of a commitment by the United States to deploy 562 new weapons, including 464 Ground-Launched Cruise Missiles (GLCMs) and 108 Pershing II missiles replacing its older generation Pershing I missiles, in five West European countries. Within the compromise on "dual tracks" adopted by NATO, deployments along the first track were scheduled to begin in late 1983, by which time the sites and the weapons would be ready for deployment, but in the interim an effort would be made to make the deployment unnecessary through the second track: U.S.-Soviet negotiations to reduce Soviet intermediate nuclear missiles targeted at Western Europe. The clear understanding among the NATO partners in Brussels in late 1979 was that the "track 1" deployment would take place only if the "track 2" negotiations failed, a position to which the U.S. administration of President Jimmy Carter seemed clearly committed.

Shortly after this agreement, Ronald Reagan was elected president of the United States, replacing Jimmy Carter, and his advisers advocated moving ahead with the INF deployment as rapidly as possible without wasting time in what they believed to be "fruitless" negotiations, arguing that the new administration was not bound by Carter's "dual track" agreement with the NATO allies (Nolan, 1993:956). Most Western European members of NATO, however, insisted that both tracks of the "dual track" decision had to be honored and that negotiations should be initiated. After being persuaded that they had to go through at least the pretense of negotiating, the U.S. administration came up with a proposal evidently initiated by Assistant Secretary of Defense Richard Perle that would appeal to Western European public opinion, while also guaranteeing a Soviet rejection. The so-called zero option would have required the United States to give up its plans to deploy new INF missiles, while the Soviet Union would have to withdraw some 464 SS-4 and SS-5 missiles as well as to cease the deployment of any newer generation SS-20s and to remove those that had already been put in place. Thus the proposal appealed to the European political left because it called for complete elimination of this category of weapons, while guaranteeing Soviet rejection because it would require them to dismantle a large number of their existing weapons. At the same time, the United States would only have to dismantle a small number of deployed weapons and to cancel plans for a deployment that had not even begun, while also allowing the United Kingdom and France to maintain their intermediate-range nuclear forces.

Not surprisingly, the Soviet Union rejected this proposal immediately upon its introduction into the Geneva negotiating forum; they replied with a proposal to reduce Eurostrategic weapons on both sides, but they sought to include British and French nuclear delivery vehicles and U.S. medium-range bombers, both excluded from the U.S. proposal. The United States had approached the negotiation as a bilateral effort to reduce U.S. and Soviet intermediate-range missiles, whereas the Soviets contended that an agreement had to reflect the potential forces that could be targeted against either side in the European region (Nolan, 1993:957). True to form, the negotiations went nowhere, in spite of several abortive attempts to break out of the impasse. Most importantly, a personal and apparently unauthorized agreement struck during a "walk in the woods" near Geneva in July 1982 between U.S. ambassador Paul Nitze and Soviet ambassador Yuri Kivitsinsky would have reduced the number of new U.S. deployments from 464 to 300 Cruise missiles and canceled the scheduled deployment of 108 Pershing II missiles, in exchange for Soviet limitations of their new generation ss-20 missiles to 75. Apparently Ambassador Nitze, an experienced negotiator, had failed to get the message that he was supposed to be negotiating for "side effects," namely to justify deployment in the eyes of the European allies, rather than to reach an agreement that would somehow compromise the second track of full-scale deployment of U.S. missiles. From this point, overall U.S.-Soviet relations continued to deteriorate, as did the INF negotiations, until they were finally broken off in late 1983 and the deployment began (see Talbot, 1985: esp. chap. 6). The ultimate irony of this case was that, after a break of almost two years, the Soviet government, then under Mikhail Gorbachev, accepted the idea of the zero option, much to the consternation of its proponents; indeed, Richard Perle ultimately resigned when, contrary to his advice, President Reagan agreed to accept the United States' own proposal.

The result was that the INF Treaty was signed by Reagan and Gorbachev in 1987, marking one of the most significant steps in winding down the Cold War; however, agreement in this case would have been unlikely had it not been for the substantial improvement in U.S.-Soviet relations following Gorbachev's ascent to power. In short, within a changed domestic and international environment, conflicts previously perceived as fundamentally zero sum in nature and thus apparently doomed to failure may be reframed as positive sum, making an eventual breakthrough in negotiations possible (Hopmann, 1991:54–55).

NEGOTIATING "FROZEN CONFLICTS"

The two cases examined so far, the Rambouillet negotiations on Kosovo and the INF negotiations, involved cases that broke down largely because the parties entered the process with no clear desire to achieve an agreement, but primarily for "side effects," that is, to gain international support for decisions that they wanted to take unilaterally but felt obliged to achieve broader international acquiescence in those actions. A somewhat different situation applies to many so-called frozen conflicts, where the issues that originally created an incentive to negotiate largely become irrelevant, but the conflict itself turns out to be sufficiently "profitable" for one or both parties that they resist agreement even after the basis for conflict has largely disappeared. In other words, these include conflicts where the issues under dispute were initially the source of significant tensions, often turning violent, but where the negotiations remain stalemated long after the issues that led to the conflict initially changed or even disappeared altogether. Typically in these situations a residue of the experience of violence itself hangs on as the major obstacle to agreement long after the issues that led to violence in the first place have been modified. Alternatively, key individual actors or groups may gain a stake in the stalemate and thus may perpetuate it even after the issues themselves have been transformed. As Rubin, Pruitt, and Kim note: "People in the throes of escalating conflict often lose site of the issues with which they began their struggle. They experience a lack of creativity and imagination that deprives them of the opportunity to work their way out of the hole they have dug for themselves" (1994:207–8).

The case of negotiations between the Republic of Moldova and the breakaway region of Transdniestria illustrates very well this type of negotiation of a frozen conflict, negotiations that remained incomplete some twenty years after their initiation.[2] Moldova was one of the fifteen Union Republics of the Soviet Union that achieved its independence in late 1991 when the Soviet Union collapsed. The region west of the Dniestr River is populated by people who are primarily ethnically Romanian, and their native language (often called Moldovan) is essentially a very close dialect to that of the larger state of Romania to their immediate west. As the Soviet Union was falling apart, many among the majority sought unification with Romania, a movement strongly supported by nationalistic populations in Romania as well. However, a long strip of territory between the Dniestr River and Ukraine (Transdniestria or Pridnestrovskaya) is populated by roughly one-third Russian speakers, one-third speakers of

Ukrainian, and one-third Moldovans (but largely Russified). Their political loyalties lay to the east, and they were fearful of being incorporated into a greater Romania and being forced to speak the Moldovan dialect. These fears were exacerbated when the government tried to convert the written Moldovan language from the Cyrillic to the Roman alphabet. Transdniestria, also the site of a large base for the Soviet 14th Army at the time of the breakup, declared its continuing loyalty to the Soviet Union even after it had ceased to exist (Kirilov, 1995:55–65).

After a period of negotiations, the Moldovan government attempted to assert its authority over the territory on the left bank of the Dniestr by force, which the citizens of Transdniestria, evidently with some support of the Russian forces stationed there, successfully resisted in fighting that killed eight hundred to a thousand people in 1992. A cease-fire was brokered by Moscow, which installed peacekeeping forces along the line of division more or less following the river. Negotiations on the political status of the region in relation to the Republic of Moldova began in early 1993, with the Organization for Security and Cooperation as the primary mediator, later assisted by the Russian Federation and Ukraine, and joined in 2005 by the United States and the European Union in a format known as "5 + 2."

These negotiations made considerable progress at the formal level, actually finding solutions to most of the issues nominally dividing the parties. The Moldovans essentially wanted to create a unitary state with some degree of autonomy for Transdniestria, including a right for Transdniestria to secede if Moldova ever united formally with Romania; by contrast, the Transdniestrians preferred complete independence and sovereignty. Regular meetings at a technical level, mediated by the osce, resolved numerous specific issues in dispute and agreed upon some confidence-building measures, while leaving the basic formula unresolved (Hopmann, 2001:129–34).

In 2002 the osce embarked upon a more active attempt to create a formula on the central issue of the status of Transdniestria. They proposed a federal solution, with a power-sharing arrangement in which considerable agreement was achieved regarding the division of powers between central and regional authorities within the overall framework of a Moldovan state. The language issue that had been so important at the outset was largely settled through agreement to allow multiple official languages for business and instruction in schools. In 2003 the government of Moldova also proposed that the federal state would be demilitarized, with the region of Gagauzia as well as Transdniestria having full autonomy. The mediation efforts by the OSCE and other parties thus had the curious effect of producing several draft agreements that appeared to be acceptable to both sides, but when submitted to the highest level officials, they were consistently rejected with little or no explanation, especially by the authorities in Tiraspol.

Russia further entered the scene in 2003, when an aide to President Vladimir Putin, Dmitry Kozak, also put forward a plan for a symmetric federation, rather than the loose confederation originally advocated by Transdniestria. In this instance, Transdniestrian president Igor Smirnov accepted the Kozak proposal, which in turn was rejected by the government of President Vladimir Voronin of Moldova. Ukraine also proposed a seven-point peace plan in 2005 to integrate the two regions into a loose federal structure; this proposal was welcomed by both sides, but neither was prepared to negotiate on details. In 2008 Presidents Smirnov and Voronin met for the first time in seven years and agreed on several concrete measures, but Voronin did not accept Smirnov's proposal of a "Treaty of Friendship between Moldova and Transdniestria" that would have treated the two parties as equal and sovereign; this proposal also would have required Moldova to accept a permanent status for Russian military forces in Transdniestria. The two leaders met again in Moscow with Russian president Dmitry Medvedev in March 2009, and committed themselves once again to finding a solution, while still failing to agree on the central status issue that divided them. Nonetheless, the differences between them seem to be largely based on terminology rather than substance; confederalism versus federalism versus deep autonomy are abstract concepts that would likely disappear in the face of an agreement on the specific content of the competences granted to the authorities in Transdniestria, irrespective of the label given to it by the two parties.

What became apparent was that most specific issues of conflict could be or already had been resolved or had become irrelevant, but the conflict remained frozen nonetheless. With Romania's entry into NATO and the EU, talk of creating a "greater Romania" that would incorporate Moldova all but disappeared except among a small cadre of Romanian nationalists in Moldova. President Voronin established closer ties with Russia than his predecessors, meaning that his government no longer had an incentive to quash pro-Russian feelings among the population of Transdniestria. And the issues of language, education, and many other specific issues were effectively resolved. The obstacles to agreement on the status of Transdniestria within some kind of Moldovan state certainly included the loss of mutual confidence that resulted from the violent episode of 1992. But more importantly, both sides had built up entrenched interests among the most powerful members of the elite, who saw the continued division of Moldova as profitable for their own private interests, which may include trafficking in human beings and illicit goods, and other illegal activities that are aided by the fact that Transdniestria has no international status and is thus not subject to any external political pressure to control illegal activity in its territory. As these individuals were in a position to block formal agreement, they kept the conflict frozen to serve their own interests at the expense of the interests of their citizens.

In cases such as this, the interests on both sides in avoiding a settlement of the conflict worked together to modify the issues over time; as issues are resolved, new issues need to be created to preserve the stalemate, and issues are manipulated by political elites for their own political and economic interests. Thus the conflicts remain frozen, even though the issues that produced the conflict in the first place have been (or at least can readily be) resolved. Similar problems seem to have reinforced other "frozen conflicts" on former Soviet space, such as the conflict between Azerbaijan and Armenia over Nagorno-Karabakh and, before 2008, between Georgia and its breakaway regions of Abkhazia and South Ossetia. In all of these cases of "frozen conflicts," while there still are substantive issues over which the parties disagree, I conclude that the issues are in principle negotiable; where negotiations remained unfinished or without agreement, however, the stalemate is largely because of the effort by one or more parties to manipulate the issues to prevent agreement.

IDENTITY CONFLICTS AND INTRACTABLE ISSUES

The preceding cases illustrate a situation in which the issues themselves are not the primary obstacle to agreement, but where the issues are constructed with the apparent intent to prevent a successful outcome. In this section, I turn to the heart of the matter, where the issues themselves, especially the way in which they are constructed, are intrinsically the primary obstacles to negotiations. The most relevant distinction here is between issues that can be divided into discrete parts, displayed along a continuum or series of continua, and thus aggregated and disaggregated in all sorts of ways. The fact that issues can be disaggregated and reaggregated into new packages provides opportunities for building tradeoffs and inventing new combinations that are amenable to agreement. The multiple dimensions of such issues permit actors to lose on some issues and gain on others, and agreement is possible as long as the net value for all actors is positive. Building positive-sum solutions and avoiding negative-sum outcomes is thus facilitated by the multiple opportunities to construct, deconstruct, and reconstruct issues in different ways until one package is finally acceptable to all parties. With these kinds of issues, given enough time, patience, and creativity, parties can frequently define an appropriate compromise or even an integrative solution that serves their joint interests, so that the probability of agreement is high (Hopmann, 1996:chap. 6).

The exact opposite situation applies, however, when the central issue in dispute involves an absolute value that is by definition indivisible, where the issue is holistic rather than multidimensional, and generally where it is highly abstract and intangible as opposed to concrete and tangible. Generally, these conflicts are based on abstract and often absolute values rather than interests, whether defined in absolute or relative terms. Here the usual bargaining tactics traditionally employed in negotiations are virtually useless. Bargaining by definition requires making concessions and compromises, which are possible only when one can speak of continuous dimensions along which positions may move toward one party and away from another. It also requires making tradeoffs across issues, or creating new packages of issues that reaggregate divergent issues so that in the net they produce at least some benefit for all parties. In such situations, even if the actors are concerned primarily about relative rather than absolute gains, there still may be opportunities for agreement, even if diminished in frequency and in the ease with which they can be discovered. This is impossible, however, when the issues constitute a single, absolute whole that is not readily divisible and thus where a bridging formula is virtually impossible to identify. To the parties engaged in such a conflict, it appears to be an absolute contest in which the winner takes all and the loser gets nothing. When constructed in this way, these sorts of conflicts at least appear to be zero sum, with no possibilities for compromise or integrative outcomes.

It is my contention that most of the distinctions between issues that are likely to produce agreements versus those that are more likely to result in incomplete or failed negotiations are picked up by this underlying theoretical dimension. Thus the data reported previously by Bercovitch seem to be consistent with this underlying distinction, with abstract identity conflicts being the most difficult to resolve, followed by security issues where survival or at least continuation of the state (or sub-state identity group) may be at stake, whereas conflicts over resources and other more tangible issues tended to be most amenable to mediated settlement (Bercovitch, 1996:24–25).

Perhaps the classic form of such a conflict is the "identity" conflict. Jay Rothman defines identity conflicts as "relatively intangible and deeply rooted in the more abstract and interpretive dynamics of history, psychology, culture, values, and beliefs of identity groups. . . . [T]hey derive from existential and underlying psychological concerns that are perceived as threatened or frustrated as a result of, or resulting in, intransigent conflict. These disputes are usually, at their source, very complex, relatively intangible, and often hard to define clearly" (Rothman, 1997:11). Identity conflicts are most likely to be serious when one group literally fears that its identity as such is threatened with extinction. For example, the Abkhaz, who now rule in a breakaway region of the former Soviet Republic of Georgia, claim that Georgia's postindependence nationalism threatened to extinguish the unique identity of their people after depriving the region of the autonomy that it had experienced in Soviet times; they frequently expressed the fear that Abkhaz identity would suffer the same fate as the Circassians, another ethnic group of the Caucasus that was submerged during the Soviet period, with the primary trace remaining only in the name "Circassian chicken," a dish popular throughout the region. This logic, however, provided the Abkhaz people, who constituted only 18 percent of the population of the region called Abkhazia when the Soviet Union collapsed, with the justification for declaring their independence from Georgia. In the civil war that followed, they drove the population of ethnic Georgians, Migralians, and others from the land that they then claimed as their own. After twenty years and extensive mediation by the United Nations, no visible progress has been detected by most observers of these "incomplete" negotiations, and a resolution of the conflict was made even more difficult by the Russian intervention in the other Georgian breakaway region of South Ossetia in 2008. Following the war between Russia and Georgia, Russia increased its troop strength in Abkhazia and recognized Abkhazia as an independent state, a move supported only by Nicaragua at the time.

Identity conflicts may also manifest themselves in more concrete ways, as for example when two identity groups clash over the same territory. This can be most serious when each claims a primordial identity with and rights over the land, often a right believed to have been granted by God. These identity conflicts based in different religious beliefs, or in primordial origin myths, are among the most difficult to resolve through negotiations. Thus, for example, Serbs believe that the roots of their culture and history spring from Kosovo, the site of the most holy relics of the Serbian Orthodox Church. It was also the site of the infamous battle of Kosovo Polje in 1389, when Serbian land was taken from them by the invading armies of the Ottoman Empire, to be occupied by Muslims ever since, first Turks and then Albanians. These "myths" of national origin and identity, partly based on real historical events but glorified through their retelling over generations, lay at the root of the conflict over the political status of Kosovo. The land is of little material value to Serbs, and indeed Kosovo was generally a drain on the Serbian economy; the attachment of Serbs to Kosovo is one of cultural and religious identity, not of economic or political interest. Therefore, proposals to redraw the borders of the former Yugoslavia more along contemporary ethnic lines had no appeal; only a small minority of Serbs might have lived in Kosovo, but it was believed to be the very foundation of the Serbian nation and church.

Of course, the most widely analyzed, discussed, and seemingly intractable international conflict of modern times, that between Israel and Palestine, also has its roots in a similar identity conflict. Many Jews see Zion as the Promised Land given them by God, from which many were driven away, but to which they were destined to return and to live as God's people on their holy ground. Palestinians, on the other hand, have lived in the lands of the Levant for well over a millennium, land that came under Muslim domination from the early days of the foundation of Islam, and for centuries they had to defend it against Christian crusaders from Europe who sought to reclaim the land for Christianity. Furthermore, many of their holy sites are located on the same piece of land, where they largely lived in peace with those Jews who had remained in their original homeland after the dispersal of the Jewish people throughout Europe and beyond. The situation was undoubtedly aggravated by the long history of discrimination against Jews in many regions of Europe, culminating in the great horror of the Holocaust where the existence of the Jewish people as such was clearly threatened by the genocidal policies of the Nazis and their collaborators. Therefore, the possibility of returning to their homeland in Zion seemed not only to fulfill a long-held religious prophecy, but to offer hope of safety in a Jewish nation-state in which they would no longer be persecuted as a minority and threatened with extermination as had so often been the case when they lived in the nations of Europe.

Therefore, the identity conflict between Palestinians, who believe that the lands of Palestine had been ceded to them by history and long occupation under various overlords, including primarily the Ottoman Empire and the United Kingdom, and the returning Jews, who sought refuge from the genocidal campaigns in a nation of their own, founded in the land of Zion that God gave to the Jewish people millennia ago, represents a situation where intractable conflict seemed to be virtually inevitable, with no easy and obvious outcome. This is not primarily a conflict about land as such, although borders, settlements, and walls (or "fences") are all concrete manifestations of that conflict. Above all it is a conflict about an abstract and absolute value, a covenant between God (Yahweh or Allah) and God's people about their rightful land and their right to identity as a people to live in the land that their supreme deity "gave" them in ancient times. No amount of argument, no extensive evidence is likely to persuade one or the other of the rightness of the other side. Perceived as an absolute, god-given right, it seems unlikely that creative ways can be found to divide the goods, trade off interests, or package arrangements that will come close to satisfying the abstract, yet absolute belief of each party in the correctness and even the righteousness of its own cause. Thus, after more than sixty years, negotiation of this conflict has remained "incomplete."

This Israeli-Palestinian conflict may be the best-known identity conflict of this type, but there are undoubtedly many others like it around the world that pose similar challenges for negotiations and that are likely to be as difficult to resolve despite extensive efforts on all sides. Of course, some issues between Israel and Palestine have been successfully negotiated, but these generally involve specific, concrete differences. Where the conflict remains apparently intractable, however, it involves the abstract and fundamentally absolute divisions over issues such as the status of Jerusalem and its holy sites for Jews, Muslims, and Christians. The identity and even the survival of the Jewish people in a hostile world have been wrapped by most Jews into the issues involving the survival and expansion of the state of Israel. The identity of the Palestinian people, who do not wish to be thrown into a large pot of Arabs (or even worse, integrated into a Jordanian state), as Israeli leaders have often been inclined to do — their desire not to become the Circassians of the Middle East and simply disappear from the face of the earth as a distinct people — is wrapped up in their effort to create a Palestinian state out of the limited remaining territory where their people once lived. Thus the Palestinian-Israeli conflict remains at its core an identity conflict, whose bloody and difficult history of failed and partially successful negotiations has made it the prime example of an intractable conflict where negotiations remain incomplete after more than sixty years of failed attempts.

As Jay Rothman points out, premature efforts to push negotiations toward a solution in identity conflicts may actually backfire (1997). If parties are forced by outsiders, such as by powerful mediators, to seek compromises that they believe essentially represent a betrayal of their fundamental values, then the compromises at one stage might well become obstacles to further progress down the line (16). Before engaging in any concession–convergence bargaining, there clearly must be an agreement about some kind of an "identity formula" that embraces rather than divides the values held as absolute and indivisible by the parties. Such an identity formula must provide a shared legitimacy to the negotiations before the parties engage in bargaining over details and concrete interests that are at best superficial representations of the underlying conflicts (Zartman, 1998:318).

This issue is well illustrated by the long-term, ongoing negotiations to resolve the division of Cyprus, which has produced a long series of incomplete and at times seemingly failed negotiations. Cyprus achieved independence from the United Kingdom in 1960, based on a series of treaties, especially the Treaty of Guarantee, negotiated among the UK, Greece, and Turkey, the "guarantor powers." This included a complex power-sharing arrangement in which the Turkish Cypriot minority, constituting approximately 20 percent of the population of the island, was granted representation in the governance that exceeded its overall proportion of the population, including the right of mutual veto held by both parties over certain basic legislation. This arrangement fell apart in 1963, when the Turkish Cypriots withdrew from the government, leaving the Greek Cypriots to govern the entire island for the subsequent eleven years. During this period frequent acts of violence took place between both communities, prompting the United Nations to deploy its peacekeeping force, the United Nations Force in Cyprus (UNFICYP) in 1964. During the period of the military dictatorship in Greece after 1967, pressure in support of *enosis* (unification) between Greece and Cyprus grew in both entities. In 1974, the Greek military junta staged a coup d'état in Nicosia, in which they overthrew Archbishop Makarios, President of Cyprus and head of the Greek Orthodox Church on the island. Seeing this as the forerunner of enosis, the Turkish army intervened massively and occupied approximately 35 percent of the island's territory in the North; the UN established a buffer zone between the two sides of the island, effectively separating Greek and Turkish Cypriots. The fighting was also followed by massive population redistribution, as most Greek Cypriots moved south while their Turkish counterparts moved north. This UN buffer still divides the island, with two separate governments operating on each side of the "green line," with the government in the North recognized only by Turkey, in contrast to the government of the Republic of Cyprus in the South that is broadly recognized and belongs to most international organizations, including the UN and the EU. However, both sides viewed the partition as temporary, and efforts to negotiate a reunification of Cyprus began in 1974 and are still going on at the time of this writing in 2012. However, the history of these negotiations is one of numerous failures, in spite of the high level intervention of some of the world's leading mediators, of the UN, and major state actors.

These negotiations have sought to develop various formulas to respond to the major issues that ostensibly underlie the conflict. These include arrangements for power sharing that would assure Turkish Cypriots of the preservation of their rights and identity as Cypriots, and therefore considerably more extensive privileges than the usual formulation of "minority rights," since the Turkish population considers itself to be a constituent people of Cyprus and not a minority. Other issues result primarily from the legacy of the 1974 war, including the withdrawal of Turkish troops stationed in the North since 1974, rights of return and restitution on both sides of property abandoned during the fighting, locating and identifying the "missing persons" whose remains have not yet been located or identified following the war, the right to remain on Cyprus of Turkish "settlers" who have emigrated from Turkey since 1974, and finally the role of international guarantees that might supersede the 1960 Treaty of Guarantee. All of these issues are in principle negotiable, and indeed various agreements have been reached between the parties on most of these issues in the series of negotiations between 1974 and the failure of the "Annan Plan" in 2004 (see Saner, "The Cyprus Conflict," in this volume). Yet, in spite of agreement on many concrete issues, a final settlement has eluded the parties for almost forty years. I would suggest that the reason behind the continued series of incomplete and failed negotiations is not the difficulty in finding agreement on these concrete issues, but rather the failure of the two parties to come to an agreement about the central, underlying issue of identity. The fundamental question remains whether or not a Cypriot identity emerges in the consciousness of the island's people that in any way transcends or supplants their identity as Greek or Turkish. Indeed, these different identities have led the two parties consistently to frame the origins of the conflict in ways that ignore or delegitimize the narrative of the other. These divergent narratives make it difficult to accept a common formula for agreement in negotiations because there is no underlying "identity formula" upon which to build (Hopmann, 2009:413–26). Thus, seemingly complete agreement on substantive issues still regularly leads to rejection because these underlying differences of identity have not been addressed.

The divergent narratives extend back into classical times, especially since Greek Cypriots view the island as essentially based on Hellenic civilization, culture, and values. This divergence became more salient with the period of the Crusades, pitting European Christendom against Islam. Similarly, the Ottoman conquest implanted an Islamic rule on top of Byzantine culture in Cyprus. These events from long ago continue to influence popular memory, due in part to the presence throughout the island of artifacts dating from those earlier periods. It is these backward-looking and highly selective narratives of victimization at the hands of the "other" that, more than anything, have framed the dialogue between the two Cypriot communities and have reinforced the development of two distinct "identities" on Cyprus.

Most people in the world hold multiple identities — some are tied to family, tribe, religion, ethnicity, region, nationality, or even civilization. When these identities are crosscutting, so that issues that emanate from them fall along different lines of division, there are opportunities to identify trade-offs, to develop new formulas, and thus for negotiations to lead successfully to agreement. Alternatively, conflict with an "other" may lead to a consolidation of identities into a single, strongly held identity, in which differences on the issues reinforce one another; in this case, these absolute identities make compromise with the "other" virtually impossible and prevent a negotiated solution. The divergent historical narratives of the two Cypriot communities have done just that, thereby framing the negotiating positions of the two sides for the last half century. The specific differences in contemporary negotiating positions, therefore, emerged from the opposing narratives of the period since Cyprus achieved its independence from the United Kingdom in 1960. Although the following summaries of these narratives may be excessively sharp and may overlook the nuanced views of many individuals on both sides, their general contours have become so pervasive that they exert an overwhelming influence on the way the Cyprus problem is framed and thus make the development of a mutually acceptable solution to the immediate political and economic issues difficult to realize.

Prior to independence, Greek Cypriots led the struggle against British colonialism, initially seeking not so much independence as enosis with Greece. They associate the Turkish Cypriots with the British efforts to grant independence to a binational Cyprus. Greek histories largely emphasize the belief that the 1959 Zurich Agreement and the 1960 constitution were imposed on Cyprus by the guarantor powers, especially by the departing British. They contend that the attempt to create a government in which power was shared significantly "over represented" the Turkish "minority" in the governance of the newly independent state. From the beginning this power-sharing arrangement was criticized by the Greek Cypriot majority, which justified the effort in 1963 by President (and Archbishop) Makarios to propose thirteen amendments to the 1960 constitution that would have effectively changed the status of the Turkish Cypriots to that of a protected minority within a unitary state. Turkish Cypriots then walked out of the government, thereby justifying the domination of the Republic of Cyprus by Greek Cypriot officials.

Greek narratives are relatively silent about the ensuing eleven years of civil strife between the two communities. They acknowledge that the coup d'état against the government of Archbishop Makarios by the Greek military junta in 1974 represented a challenge to the independence of Cyprus, but they emphasize that the coup was not only successfully defeated on Cyprus, but it set off a chain of events that led to the overthrow of the military junta in Athens and the restoration of the previous political order on Cyprus. The attempt by the coup's leaders to change the balance of political forces on the island is dismissed in contemporary official documents of the Republic of Cyprus as a mere "pretext" for the Turkish invasion of 1974, which they condemn as an illegal military intervention in their internal affairs by an outside power.

In the Greek Cypriot narrative, therefore, all subsequent problems and obstacles to negotiation have been caused by the Turkish army's "occupation" in northern Cyprus since 1974 and by the alleged domination of the unrecognized Turkish Republic of Northern Cyprus by the Turkish government in Ankara. This narrative emphasizes the destruction promulgated by the Turkish invasion in 1974, their subsequent military occupation of the northern third of the island, displacement of many Greek Cypriots from their property, and the destruction by Turks of historical and religious artifacts; they also contend that the Turkish army has frustrated efforts to locate and identify the remains of numerous "missing persons" who disappeared during the fighting. Greek Cypriots also focus attention on "illegal" settlers who subsequently arrived from Turkey and thus reinforced the "occupation" of the northern portions of the island by changing the demographic composition of the country. Above all, it stresses the insecurity for Greek Cypriots created by the presence of 21,000 Turkish soldiers on a small island.[3]

Whatever the justification for the intervention, Greek Cypriots fail to see any rationale for the continued presence after nearly forty years of a large contingent of Turkish troops, especially considering the proximity of Cyprus to the Turkish mainland (a distance of about sixty kilometers), the relative absence of violence on the island since 1974, and the presence of UNFICYP peacekeepers. They view the presence of the Turkish army as a serious threat to their security, and in the most extreme versions possibly even as the basis for a future effort by Turkey to seize the entire island. Finally, the Greek Cypriot narrative notes that Turkish Cypriot leaders have advocated *tacsim* (partition) or even unification of the northern part of the island with Turkey, both of which are forbidden by the 1960 Treaty of Guarantee.[4] Thus the desire of Turkish Cypriots to create a federation composed of two sovereign states is widely perceived as a political arrangement that could be rapidly transformed into full-scale partition of the island or even into the annexation of the northern region by Turkey. In short, the Greek Cypriot narrative, almost uniformly taken for granted by citizens of the South, generally assigns blame for the conflict to the Turkish side and absolves themselves of responsibility.

However, a different narrative dominates in the North. The Turkish Cypriot account frames the conflict as stemming from the danger for a minority community, constituting about 20 percent of the island's population, of being dominated by the majority in a unified Cyprus. To guard against this danger, the 1960 constitution created a power-sharing regime that guaranteed the Turkish Cypriot community disproportional representation in governance of the island, a necessary provision from their perspective to preserve their distinctive identity. However, within three years of independence, Archbishop Makarios, president of the Republic of Cyprus, cited the "overrepresentation" of the

Turkish community in the federal structures to justify unilaterally amending the constitution to effectively reduce the Turkish community to the status of a "protected minority" within a unitary Cyprus. The Turkish community felt that these "protections" would be insufficient to preserve the rights and property of Turkish citizens, especially since attacks against Turkish Cypriots became widespread. Therefore, they contend that they were "forced out" of the government and deprived of their positions in the power structures, thereby becoming unprotected victims of a Greek Cypriot government that failed to respect their rights.

When the Greek military junta in Athens staged a coup d'état against the Greek Cypriot regime in 1974 in an effort to achieve enosis with Greece, Turkish Cypriots believed that a massive Turkish intervention on the island was justified under the Treaty of Guarantee of August 16, 1960, which granted any of the three guarantor powers "the right to take action with the sole aim of re-establishing the state of affairs created by the present Treaty." Although the treaty did not specify the nature of the "action" that may be taken, it did not rule out the use of military force if necessary to reestablish the status quo ante.[5] Contrary to the assertion by Greek Cypriots that "constitutional order" was restored following the defeat of the attempted coup on Cyprus and the overthrow of the Greek junta, the Turkish Cypriot narrative notes that the "constitutional" order established after 1974 in the Republic of Cyprus consisted of a unitary state dominated by Greek Cypriots.

Furthermore, they believe that the island's division into two separate zones, and the presence in the northern zone of the Turkish army, is not only justified, but provides their only security guarantee against a hostile Greek Cypriot government and an indifferent and at times hostile international community. Confronted with a series of UN Security Council resolutions that refused to acknowledge the legitimacy of their position,[6] policies of the European Union that were perceived as driven by the desire of Greece to bring the Republic of Cyprus into the EU as a unitary state dominated by the Greek Cypriot majority, and what might be described as "benign neglect" on the part of the U.S. government throughout this period, they see dependence on Turkey and the presence of the Turkish army on their territory as the only guarantee of their safety.

In short, these different narratives of the history of the island, especially of the conflict of the past half-century, created what are often referred to as "mutual enemy images." In such a classic conflict, both parties perceive themselves as victims of the hostile behavior of the "other," and each believes that it bears no responsibility for the conflict. As the perceived victim of the other's aggressive actions, neither party believes that it has a responsibility to initiate efforts to respond to the fears and insecurities of the other. Not only are the narratives different, but each largely denies the legitimacy of the other's claims and refuses to acknowledge its own role in creating the feelings of insecurity. Since each believes in its own self-righteousness, each contends that any agreement that accommodates the needs of the other amounts to acquiescence in the injustice it perceives that the other has perpetrated against it. Both sides fear losing their own self-identity in the face of the alien "other." As psychologist Ralph K. White argues: "Selective inattention is the chief means of sustaining both sides of the black-and-white picture, and absence of empathy is the most dangerous, war-producing form of selective inattention" (White, 1970:242).

As this diagnosis suggests, selective inattention and absence of empathy are both widespread in Cyprus. In a deadlock of images and identities, normal negotiation processes face serious challenges for creating mutually acceptable agreements to resolve the Cyprus problem. In a situation where a popular vote is required to approve any agreement or to ratify a new constitution, these "inverted mirror image perceptions" on the part of the two populations must be confronted in order to find a lasting formula for agreement. Even politicians such as Demetris Christofias and Mehmet Ali Talat, who opened bilateral negotiations in 2008 and appeared to share a sincere desire to reach a negotiated settlement, had to frame their negotiating positions in ways that did not deviate too far from the views held by the constituencies they represented.[7] In this context, negotiating a viable solution to the Cyprus problem remains a formidable task, not primarily because of the concrete issues in dispute but because of the underlying images and beliefs of the opposing parties in which each constructs its identity in opposition to the alien "other." Thus each party finds it hard to agree with the other even if negotiations produce tangible, mutual benefits that would clearly leave both parties better off in material terms (see Saner, "The Cyprus Conflict," in this book).

Therefore, as the Cyprus conflict illustrates, discovering identity formulas in the midst of deep-rooted conflicts over identity is often a very difficult and time-consuming process that requires a great deal of patience, a focus on looking for openings when changes appear either in the domestic or the international environment, and seeking to work with the parties to improve confidence and trust and to identify potentially viable integrative formulas. The difficulties of doing this provide a clear explanation of why identity conflicts so often seem to produce long, "incomplete" negotiations.

CONCLUSION

In this paper I have hypothesized that the content of issues in a conflict between two or more parties may lead to incomplete negotiations, either in the form of continued unproductive negotiations or stalemate and the breaking-off of negotiations, for several reasons:

1. One or more of the parties may have no interest in finding a solution to the issues, pursuing negotiations primarily for the "side effects" of those negotiations.

2. Negotiations may become frozen, even when agreement on the issues in principle seems within reach. This may be a consequence of the impact of "spoilers" or of key parties in participating states that oppose compromise on the central issues and therefore engage in behaviors that prevent negotiations from reaching fruition. It may also be due to the intense animosity generated by the history of violence that eclipses the specific issues and makes negotiated solutions to even tractable issues virtually impossible to achieve.

3. The issues themselves may be framed by the parties as intractable, because they are perceived to be absolute values such as identity that cannot be divided, traded in search of compensation on other issues, or in any way compromised; in this case, the zero-sum framing of the issues is perceived to pose an insuperable obstacle to finding formulas to resolve or bridge conflicts that may serve as a framework for reaching agreement.

Each of these explanations has been illustrated with relevant case studies of negotiations that have eluded resolution over long periods of time and thus remained "incomplete." These case studies reinforce the plausibility of each of these hypothesized explanations of how the content of issues affects negotiations. Future research, however, could supplement these case studies with a systematic, quantitative analysis of the impact of issues on negotiation outcomes. In this task, Bercovitch's (1996) study of the relationship between, inter alia, issues and the effectiveness of mediation points the way, but needs to be expanded in the following ways:

1. The data should be extended to include all available cases of inter-state negotiations, not just those where a mediator was involved.

2. The data set should also be updated to bring it well past the 1990 time frame, especially, therefore, to include post–Cold War negotiations.

3. Issues need to be defined and operationalized more specifically beyond the general categories of security, sovereignty, ethnicity, and resources in order to provide a more fine-grained analysis of how issue content impacts negotiation outcomes.

This is clearly a major undertaking that would require considerable resources to implement in a proper way. But given the huge costs of so many conflicts in the world that remain unresolved, with negotiations that are "incomplete," this would be a project well worth undertaking.

In conclusion, it is important to emphasize that an "incomplete" negotiation is not necessarily a permanently failed negotiation, just one that has not completed an agreement to resolve the underlying differences on the issues among the parties. With additional research we may be in a better position to identify the sources of "incompleteness," thereby finding clues to strategies that may assist negotiators to overcome the obstacles and to find new ways of identifying formulas that may eventually lead incomplete negotiations to successful resolution. Therefore, even in the face of seemingly intractable negotiations, we need to search for ways in which incomplete negotiations may eventually be completed successfully and produce results that will be viewed by the parties as being worth all of the effort, hard work, and patience entailed in the process of conducting such protracted negotiations. Creating formulas that bridge differences on the concrete issues without undermining the essential "identities" of the parties is thus an extremely challenging, but not necessarily an impossible task. The challenge to the research community is thus to provide better theory and data about the sources of these obstacles to success to aid negotiators in the task of finding new, creative solutions to long-stalemated and incomplete negotiations.

NOTES

1. For a more detailed summary of these negotiations, see Judah, 2002:199–224.

2. Interestingly, the name itself suggests an important difference in framing. In the West the region is referred to as Transdniestria (across the Dniestr River), reflecting its location to the east of the Dniestr; in Russian the name is Pridnestrovskaya or "next to the Dniestr," as viewed from Moscow or other points to the east. Hence the self-proclaimed entity adopted the Russian name of the Pridnestrovskaya Moldavskaya Respublika.

3. Most Greek Cypriot accounts report somewhat larger troop deployments in northern Cyprus. This figure is the estimate by UNFICYP of the number of Turkish troops on Cyprus in 2009.

4. In Article 2, the Treaty of Guarantee prohibits "all activity having the object of promoting directly or indirectly either the union of the Republic of Cyprus with any other state, or the partition of the island."

5. The argument that the initial Turkish military involvement could be legally justified has received support from impartial legal scholars. See, for example, Hoffmeister, 2006:47. This same conclusion, however, does not provide a legal basis for their long-term stationing on the island.

6. Although most Turkish Cypriots have not insisted on formal diplomatic recognition for the TRNC except by Turkey, they do believe that its status as an identifiable community should be acknowledged by the international community; frequently Turkish Cypriots cite a parallel between their international status and that of the Palestinian Liberation Organization (PLO) or, more recently, the Palestinian Authority.

7. Indeed, Talat lost the presidency in Turkish Cyprus in 2010 in part because he was perceived by the electorate as too willing to compromise Turkish Cypriot interests in order to negotiate a settlement with the government of the Republic of Cyprus.

PART FIVE

Strategies as a Cause for Failure

Explaining Failed Negotiations

Strategic Causes

CECILIA ALBIN

> It's settled then. . . . We've agreed to agree to an agreement to talk
> about more talks when we talk.
>
> — Former Secretary of State Madeleine Albright in a cartoon
> of American-mediated talks between Israel and the PLO,
> *Rocky Mountain News*, October 8, 1997.

Many international negotiations fail to result in an effective agreement. It usually takes many parties to make them succeed, but a single party alone can make them fail. Yet research in the field, both theoretical and applied, has focused almost entirely on explaining successful results. In international negotiations, as elsewhere, there should be at least as much to learn from failure as from success.

This chapter discusses how strategy affects the outcome of negotiations, and particularly how it can contribute to failure in the sense of failure to reach agreement. Of course, this is not the only aspect, because many other things can, and do, go wrong. An agreement reached may be deficient in some way — for instance, ineffective (not resolving the core problem), unjust, wasteful, or untimely. One or more parties may not implement the agreement, or may backtrack later on commitments made, and yet other actors may spoil and undermine it. Sometimes it is unclear, or disputed, whether an agreement was in fact reached. Moreover, so-called agreements may be mere "agreements to disagree" and to break off the talks or to continue negotiations now or later. Such ambiguity of what exactly constitutes an agreement — and "successful negotiation" in this sense — is often found in large-scale multilateral talks. As recognized in this volume, however, the absence of any agreement at all remains a hallmark of failed negotiations.

The concern here is with a party's choice of negotiation strategy, its interaction with that of other parties ("strategic interaction"), and the result. The term "strategy" refers to an overarching set of planned behaviors and actions, designed to achieve a specified goal. "Tactics" are the moves intended to implement the strategy in particular situations. Drawing on the research literature, this chapter argues that most negotiation strategies contain both "claiming" (distributive) and "creative" (integrative) behaviors. Both are usually needed for negotiations to result in satisfactory agreements. At the same time there are inherent contradictions and tensions between claiming and creative strategies to be managed. This means that the two types of strategy need to be balanced. Failure to reach agreement in negotiations is often the result of excessive claiming. Moreover, various contextual factors influence what type of strategy, or combination of strategies, will lead to agreement or failure.

CHARTING THE FIELD: TYPES, CHOICES, AND EFFECTS OF STRATEGY

The most significant contribution to the systematic study of strategy as such came early on from game theory (Nash, 1950; Neumann and Morgenstern, 1947). As a theory of interactive decision-making, it explains the outcome of an encounter in terms of the players' preferences and strategic options. The most frequently cited game, the Prisoners' Dilemma, captures a basic reason for which cooperation, and indeed negotiation, so often fail: the contradiction between what is or appears to be the most profitable strategy for the individual party (to act selfishly, "defect"), and what is required to achieve optimal joint gains at the collective level (to cooperate). Work on repeated Prisoners' Dilemma games introduced a longer time horizon — the concept of a relationship involving future cooperation and some interdependence — and the well-known strategy of matching, or tit for tat (Axelrod, 1984). Game theory clearly has wide applicability in the study of conflict and politics. But it is absent in large parts of the research literature on international negotiation (see Avenhaus, 2002), one reason undoubtedly the need for other conceptual tools to capture the intricacies of the bargaining process in that context.

What then does the literature on negotiation strategy do, and what are its main findings? Roughly speaking it delineates different *types* of strategies with associated tactics, conditions, and factors that affect the *choice* of strategy, and its impact on the negotiation process. Studies specifically concerned with the *effects* of strategic choice and bargaining dynamics on the outcome are few, and focus on the nature of the agreement reached rather than the likelihood of an agreement being reached per se (e.g., Wagner, 2008). The common assumption is a bilateral or small-scale context.[1] Pruitt (1991 and 2002; Pruitt and Rubin, 1986) distinguishes five basic negotiation strategies: contending, problem solving, yielding, inaction, and withdrawal. Fisher and Ury (1981) delineate three: competitive bargaining, integrative negotiation, and their own favored "principled" negotiation. Others discuss a list of well-known rules and tactics for how to carry out the principled negotiation strategy: that is, to separate people from the problem, to focus on interests and not positions, and to invent options for mutual gain (Fisher, Ury, and Patton, 1992; Ury, 1990). By and large, these are tactics of integrative negotiation.

The negotiation literature thus confirms and develops what Walton and McKersie (1965) established some forty years ago: there are two basic approaches to negotiation, integrative and distributive, each of which involves a distinct type of strategy. Most other strategies mentioned are either variations or combinations of these two types, or in fact integral features of all negotiations (such as yielding or concession making). In the *integrative* approach, parties see negotiation as an opportunity to resolve a shared problem. They work together to locate a mutually gainful agreement that avoids the costs of heavy compromises and continued conflict. Used are *value-creating* strategies, also called problem-solving or simply integrative, to generate new alternative solutions based on two pillars: an exploration of essential interests and needs underlying formal positions in the conflict or negotiations, and exploitation of any "differences among parties — in what they have and under what conditions they have it, in what they want and when they want it, in what they think is likely and unlikely, in what they are capable of doing, and so forth" (Lax and Sebenius, 1986). Brainstorming, resource expansion, linkage of issues, compensation, and cost cutting are examples of tools involving such trading and analyses of central concerns. In the *distributive* approach, negotiation serves to allocate a fixed number of items (resources or burdens) between parties with opposing interests. Any agreement is reached through the exchange of concessions based on stated positions rather than analysis and integration of underlying concerns, and typically necessitates considerable compromising. Strategies of distribution take many forms and are not always heavily competitive. Under the given circumstances, however, they are often *value-claiming* strategies aimed at maximizing a party's own gains at the expense of (or at least without regard for) the other's. They are implemented through tactics that pressure the other side to make concessions or otherwise move in a particular direction — for example, the use of threats, warnings, promises, deadlines, and strategic misrepresentation of genuine interests (Raiffa, 1982).

Put briefly, value-claiming strategies draw and depend mostly on "structural" power while value-creating strategies depend mostly on "relational" power (Albin, 2005). Structural power refers to resources (e.g., military and economic assets, access to information) that enable a party to unilaterally pressure another to do something that will gain advantage for itself. Relational power refers to more intangible resources (e.g., diplomatic and social skills) acquired and exercised in interaction with others that enable a party to persuade another to do something willingly that will gain advantage for them both. Relational power is dynamic and targets the other's will and perceptions of its interests, while structural power more or less bypasses these.

In practice, the two types of strategy may of course be hard to distinguish. Claiming strategies and tactics can be used deceptively, for instance, and appear cooperative and mutually beneficial on the surface. The literature provides no single measuring rod for how the two types are ultimately to be told apart in observing actual negotiations. One criterion suggested is important but hard to apply: the nature of the negotiators' aims (Pruitt, 2002). Nonetheless, value claiming and value creating, as strategies used in isolation and as strategies combined within the same negotiation, have been much analyzed. Problem-solving behavior has been found to be more common in the early stages of negotiation, and claiming strategies in the latter stages, including in international settings (Lax and Sebenius, 1986; Wagner, 2008; Zartman and Berman, 1982).

What Makes a Party Choose One Type of Strategy over Another?

There is a body of knowledge in this area, drawing on research in interpersonal and business-related conflicts. Value claiming has been found to result from a win–lose orientation and a lack of concern about the other party, a fixed-sum payoff structure, high stakes, and a lack of problem-solving skills, among many factors (Pruitt, 1991; Walton and McKersie, 1965). Value-creating negotiation then results from a win–win orientation, concern about one's own interests as well as those of the other party, a positive-sum payoff structure, and the presence of problem-solving skills and information about genuine needs required to use them.

Conditions and factors behind strategic choice in international negotiation are much less explored. In a study of international economic negotiations, three major factors are found to influence strategic choice and outcomes: changing market conditions, negotiators' beliefs, and domestic politics (Odell, 2000). Many actual cases suggest that domestic politics is a dominant factor — and more influential than individual negotiators' beliefs. The American political system of checks and balances, and domestic politics, go a long way to explain why both U.S. presidents Bill Clinton and George W. Bush pursued similar tough claiming strategies with regard to a number of important agreements concerned with, for example, climate change (the Kyoto Protocol), a ban on land mines, and the International Criminal Court. With more scope to act based on their own beliefs, their strategies would probably have shown more variation along the value-claiming/value-creating axis (see further Busby and Ochs, 2004).

A number of studies stress how value-claiming situations can be transformed into value-creative ones to enhance the prospects of successful negotiations, including in the international arena. Methods and tactics drawing on concepts of exchange, resource expansion, and confidence building are described to demonstrate how attitudes can be changed and issues redefined as necessary to make such transformations possible, including with the help of a third party (Fisher and Ury, 1981; Susskind and Cruikshank, 1987; Touval and Zartman, 1985). A basic message is that conflict situations tend to carry far more integrative potential than may be immediately apparent or commonly assumed. This is particularly true for international negotiations involving a large number of issues.

How Does Strategic Choice Affect the Outcome?

Research on international negotiation has not examined systematically the effect that choice of strategy has on the likelihood of success or failure, in the sense of any agreement being reached per se. It has, however, examined the effect of strategic choice on the type of agreement reached in "successful" cases. Integrative strategies are shown to lead to integrative outcomes, and distributive strategies to compromise outcomes (Wagner, 2008). Studies of interpersonal bargaining, particularly from social psychologists, shed more light on the conditions under which value-creating strategies are most likely to result in an agreement of high joint gains: highly valued issues or resources are involved that cannot be compromised or distributed easily; the conflict is long lived and deeply rooted; each party maintains high aspirations (moderately high security points) regarding its essential interests; time costs are relatively low; the will and skill to use problem-solving tools exist (including a preparedness to reveal truthful information about interests and priorities); and parties expect to depend on each other or to cooperate in the future (e.g., Pruitt and Lewis, 1975). Conversely, the use of claiming strategies is regarded as more likely to lead negotiations to fail, or to result in an agreement based on costly compromises, especially under one or more of the above-mentioned circumstances.

When negotiation is seen as necessarily encompassing both value-creating and value-claiming methods, the path to a successful outcome becomes to manage the so-called Negotiator's Dilemma — the inevitable tension between the two. Good management means that value-creating behaviors are strengthened over value-claiming ones; for example, through the development of good working relationships. It also entails knowing how to use tactics associated with both in the same negotiation, so as to enhance the chances of reaching an agreement (Pruitt, 2002). Among the pieces of advice are to use claiming and creating tactics in sequence, in separate fora, and for different issues; that is, claiming for basic interests and creative flexibility for ways to achieve them. Axelrod's strategy of matching, or tit for tat, is also endorsed as an effective means to promote cooperation based on reciprocity, while minimizing the risks of being subjected to excessive claiming and exploitation (Lax and Sebenius, 1986).

STRATEGIC CAUSES OF FAILURE:
THE INTERNATIONAL NEGOTIATOR'S DILEMMA

The value-claiming/value-creating paradigm captures basic strategic choices and dilemmas to be tackled in international negotiations, if agreement is to result. A core dilemma is indeed the tension between the need for cooperative efforts to create value (increase joint gains or "expand the pie" by working toward shared goals), and the inclination to compete to claim value (secure maximum gains or "divide the pie" as favorably as possible for oneself). Put differently, it is a tension between the need to serve larger public goals (the stated overall objectives of the negotiations) and the concern to protect or further one's own more immediate interests. Left unmanaged, the contradictions between them will contribute to failure in negotiations. Value claiming, like value creation, can take place from the earliest phase when the agenda is set and in later stages when agreements are interpreted and implemented, or even renegotiated.

How then are value-claiming and value-creating behaviors to be defined and distinguished, independently of the outcome? The actual intentions and/or perceptions of parties, for example, can constitute a valuable dimension: a strategy with apparent value-creating features could be perceived as or exploited for claiming. The focus here, however, is on distinguishing strategies by their overt features. A detailed study of strategy in ten major cases of economic negotiations provides some indicators (Odell, 2000). It distinguishes between *offensive* claiming tactics whereby one party seeks to take value from another, and *defensive* claiming tactics used by a party to prevent another from taking value from itself. A third type is added here: *obstructive* claiming tactics, whereby a party purposefully seeks to cause negotiations to fail. Among numerous examples, the president of the European Council explained the failure of the negotiations on a new European Union budget in June 2005 with reference to such tactics: "Those who, just before concluding, were calling for a full review of Europe's budgetary structures, were well aware that it was impossible for the 25 countries to agree on a complete restructuring, disregarding all the agreements we reached in the past. Those calling for such a solution were seeking failure."[2]

The following broadly valid indicators can be distinguished, drawing partly on Odell (2000):

INDICATORS OF VALUE-CLAIMING STRATEGY:

- Engages in positional bargaining. Commits (publicly) to and reiterates a particular position and outcome, and shares little or no information about central or genuine concerns, priorities, and objectives.

- Exhibits distinct partiality. For example, no (genuine) expression of concern about others' interests or about creating mutually beneficial agreement. No responsibility assumed for the problem, only agenda issues of own interest advanced, only information and alternatives for a solution favorable to oneself presented. Parties that may counteract own interests are excluded or marginalized.

- Makes no or very few concessions, even when other side concedes considerably, or backtracks (cancels) concessions or commitments made and agreed earlier.

- Demands one-sided (unilateral) concessions, followed by competitive steps to secure them. Threats are made, ultimatums delivered, or other actions taken to undermine the other party's alternative to a negotiated agreement (offensive).

- Advances last-minute high demands unexpectedly, which are known to be (nearly) impossible to meet (obstructive).

INDICATORS OF VALUE-CREATING STRATEGY:

- Manifests problem-solving behavior through sharing truthful information about core concerns and priorities, and inviting other party to do likewise. Shows willingness to move from official positions (at least in informal, confidential setting) to explore new alternative, mutually beneficial solutions.

- Displays impartiality and enlightened self-interest. Assumes responsibility for problem, presents information, and engages in discussions in an evenhanded manner. Focuses on agenda issues and objectives of shared interest. Includes all key parties and takes account of their interests, even when opposed to own interests. Expresses concerns about fairness and mutual gains.

- Reciprocates concessions, when demanded. They are secured through relational power (as defined above) and made willingly.

More so than commonly recognized, some concerns about value claiming and distribution are necessary and desirable in negotiations: parties must firmly uphold and protect their own vital interests if mutually satisfactory agreements are to result. Yet, at a certain point or in some forms, value claiming begins to conflict and interfere with value creation and to undermine the shared fruits to be reaped from cooperation. When states become too concerned with securing for themselves as large a slice of the pie as possible, the pie available for division shrinks and may even disappear. Tactics meant to improve a state's own position may end up leaving it, along with everyone else, worse off than they would have been in a state of cooperation.

In many cases, value-claiming strategies as exemplified above have contributed visibly to the breakdown of international negotiations. Following the American failure in March 1975 to secure a second disengagement agreement in the Sinai Peninsula, U.S. president Gerald Ford explained: "As the talks dragged on, [Israeli prime minister Yitzhak] Rabin became less flexible. . . . He didn't seem to understand that only by giving do you get something in return. — The Israelis kept stalling. Their tactics frustrated the Egyptians and made me mad as hell. Both Henry [Kissinger, U.S. secretary of state] and I had received firm assurances from Rabin . . . [b]ut Rabin now . . . would — or could not — deliver on commitments he had made" (qtd. in Saunders and Albin, 1993:62).

Parties themselves often have conflicting perceptions of events and causes and may blame each other for stalemate or failure; and available accounts and records may point in different directions regarding the reasons. An example is the U.S.-facilitated Camp David talks between Israel and the PLO in July 2000, which to date lack an independent record (see Cristal, "Camp David, 2000," in this book). Israeli officials have described the outcome as the result of the continuing Palestinian refusal to accept the Jewish state's very right to exist. Palestinian officials for their part have argued that the negotiations failed because Israel, with U.S. backing, tried to impose a one-sided solution without regard for Palestinian concerns (see Bar-Siman-Tov et al., 2005).

While inherent in all negotiations, the argument here is that *the tension between claiming and creating value is particularly sharp in international negotiations and frequently explains their failure or poor results.* One reason, most obvious in large-scale multilateral negotiations over global resources, is that the immediate incentives to claim value are often very high. The need to create value is at the same time great and very difficult to satisfy. This is a basic problem in numerous international talks concerned with cooperation over global public goods, which are vital to human welfare and security worldwide (Albin, 2003).[3] Negotiations concerned with the international trade regime, the global climate, and nuclear nonproliferation are cases in point. The benefits of such goods are nonrival in consumption, and can rarely be denied those who choose to "free ride" on the contributions of others. At the same time there is a shared dependence on cooperation to ensure the adequate provision and management of global public goods.

Another common reason for the high tension between claiming and creating value in international negotiation is sharp inequalities between parties; for example, in power, resources, and responsibility for the problem being discussed. In the negotiation process itself, value claiming often plays a role in disagreements over whether or how privileges, duties, benefits, and cost burdens under cooperative agreements ought to reflect differences in parties' resources, contributions to the problem being negotiated, and historical or other circumstances. This is a common barrier to cooperation that all too often undermines the capacity of negotiation to produce effective agreements. It has been a persistent feature of nuclear nonproliferation talks and environmental negotiations concerned with climate change and acid rain, among other cases (see, e.g., Albin, 2001). Global climate change, for example, threatens many countries with devastation primarily due to the actions of other states. Negotiations in this area keep stumbling over disagreements over who should have to reduce their greenhouse gas emissions and who should pay for it, given the primary responsibility of the industrialized world for the problem to date and the development needs of poor Third World countries.

MANAGING THE VALUE-CLAIMING/VALUE-CREATING TENSION: THE IMPORTANCE OF CONTEXTUAL FACTORS

Successful international negotiation will thus usually depend in part on good management of the tension between claiming and creating value in the process. Conversely, poor management of that tension will frequently contribute to failure to reach an agreement. What then is good management and how is it achieved? What is a good balance between claiming and creating value?

As for balance, the literature on claiming and creating value refers to processes and outcomes that ensure mutual (reciprocal) gains. "Good management" ensures that value creation is allowed to progress to the full, which can maximize joint gains, and that claiming plays a role when they are divided up. "Poor management," by contrast, entails that value is claimed in ways that interfere with the creation of mutual gains and thereby undermine an agreement (Lax and Sebenius, 1986). The concrete management advice and tools discussed pertain mostly to small-scale domestic settings (e.g., interpersonal or business-related) and are not developed specifically for international negotiations. Evidence demonstrates that parties in international negotiations also take justice and fairness into account (see Wanis-St. John, "Nuclear

Negotiations," in this book) when assessing the acceptability (or not) of procedures and outcomes, and that these concepts go beyond mutual gains (Albin, 2001). In other words, balance requires that claiming respects both mutual gains and fairness.

Furthermore, a vital and much neglected aspect is contextual factors, which will greatly influence what strategy, or combination of strategies, will result in agreement or failure. Strategic choices need to be made with sufficient regard for how the context will influence their likelihood of success. A series of contextual factors will indicate when a predominantly integrative approach is more promising than a distributive one, and vice versa, and what the best balance between the two is likely to be.

Some important contextual factors are as follows:

1. *Multilateral or bilateral negotiations*: The format of the negotiations when it comes to number of parties and issues will definitely affect how a strategy or combination of strategies will work. Whether a predominantly integrative or distributive package of strategies is used in this context — and which is more likely to lead to agreement — is disputed. A greater number of issues certainly means greater integrative potential (for highly beneficial agreements), but also greater complexity in terms of interests to balance and reconcile. The multilateral context is further discussed below.

2. *Nature of the issues*: Are they indivisible or divisible? Highly valued (absolutes, irreplaceable) or not? Integrative strategies tend to be far more promising for indivisible or highly valued goods (e.g., Albin, 1991), yet parties tend not to choose such strategies for very important issues (Wagner, 2008).

3. *Availability of information*: Is information about the issues at stake, party interests, and the implications of alternative solutions plentiful (sufficient) or poor? Integrative strategies have far greater requirements in this respect.

4. *Relationship between and problem-solving capacity of parties*: If these are not particularly good, distributive strategies are more likely to lead to an agreement. Of course, working relations will be influenced by the environment (institution, surrounding political climate) in which the talks take place. During the Cold War, many international negotiations

were conducted in a predominantly distributive mode and perhaps necessarily so: the East–West political divisions instilled mistrust that often made any kind of close cooperation extremely difficult, even in areas such as the environment. By contrast, strong institutional norms and regimes in some areas of international affairs today favor problem solving.

5. *Distribution of power between parties*: This too will affect how well a particular type of strategy will work. In a situation of great power inequality, the stronger party may be more tempted to claim value through distributive tactics. Integrative strategies definitely proceed from a notion of basic equality between parties and their essential concerns, which may be hard to sell in such a context. However, some empirical case study research has found integrative behaviors more commonly associated with asymmetrical parties (Wagner, 2008).

6. *Public or private forum*: Integrative strategies will by nature have a lesser chance to succeed in a public forum.

7. *Time frame*: Integrative strategies usually require more time to produce a successful outcome. If time is short, relatively simple distributive approaches are more likely to produce an agreement.

On the international stage, multilateral talks have surpassed bilateral encounters in scope and significance. Existing studies illuminate how much more complex the dynamics of multilateral negotiations are, and how they challenge traditional negotiation analysis based on two or a few parties and issues (Zartman, 1994 and 2003a). The presence of a large number of actors and issues, and the importance of leadership roles and coalition building, are among the factors that create a very different landscape.

Value claiming and creating, and good management of the tension between them, will obviously take different forms in this context. It has been argued that a multilateral forum encourages value-creating behaviors over value-claiming ones: The greater number of parties and issues present mean that problem solving is needed to arrive at an agreement (Touval, 1991). The interests and dividing lines among these multiple parties usually differ across the range of issues on the agenda. Such "crosscutting cleavages" — the fact that a party has both an enemy and a friend in another party across the various issues — supposedly mute conflict, create interdependence, and make integrative negotiation most preferable (Hopmann, 1996). Empirical examinations of actual cases, particularly large-scale multilateral negotiations, yield a more ambiguous picture of the real possibilities and practices in such complex contexts. While the potential and gains to be had from integrative negotiation certainly tend to be greater, multilateral negotiators often still bargain predominantly in a distributive mode (e.g., Wagner, 2008).

In the absence of findings from any more systematic and comprehensive study on the subject, some tentative conclusions can be drawn from concepts and actual cases of multilateral negotiation. An individual negotiator's choice of strategy toward another party will generally be less influential than the strategic choices made by the chair of the talks, by entire coalitions or steering groups, and by major states toward draft agreements that often coordinate concession making in multilateral fora. The chair or another lead party will nearly always need to direct the process firmly toward a balanced outcome, and thus will do most of the management of the value-claiming-/value-creating tension. One method used is for the chair first to draft and facilitate the adoption by parties of an agreement on guiding principles for the negotiations. Once they are under way and parties engage in excessive claiming or other obstructive behavior, the principles aid the chair to "bring back needed structure and order to the negotiating process" (Björkbom, 2001). Multilateral negotiations, being complex, can result in failure for many different reasons. But a common reason is clearly the absence of a strong chair or leader, able and willing to steer a chaotic and competitive process toward a balanced package agreement with benefits for all. The chair played exactly such a role in the 1995 Review and Extension Conference of the Nuclear Non-Proliferation Treaty (NPT). The conference became a vitally important and conflict-laden encounter between the nuclear haves and the nuclear have-nots, which eventually ended rather sensationally in a consensus agreement. The chair, Jayantha Dhanapala, led the efforts to work out a balanced package agreement acceptable to all, and eventually all 175 participating states adopted the NPT extension decision by consensus (Dhanapala, 1998).

CONCLUDING NOTE

Most negotiation strategies contain both "claiming" (distributive) and "creative" (integrative) behaviors. Both are usually needed for negotiations to result in satisfactory agreements. At the same time there are inherent contradictions and tensions between claiming and creative strategies, which are particularly challenging in international negotiations. That tension needs to be managed by balancing the two types of strategy. Failure to reach agreement in negotiations is often the result of excessive claiming. Moreover, various contextual factors influence what type of strategy, or combination of strategies, will lead to agreement or failure. "Good management" entails, among other matters, choosing a strategy or designing a package of strategies on the basis of contextual factors. These include the nature of the issues, the availability of relevant information, relationship(s) between or among parties, and the nature of the forum, among others.

The value-claiming/value-creating lens is a powerful tool in the analysis of international negotiation, which needs to be further developed and better operationalized. Three important areas have been identified and discussed here, all calling for more detailed empirical research across many issue areas of international negotiation. An important one is improving understanding of the multiple factors behind excessive value claiming, and the interplay between them. Such knowledge would contribute to more practical and effective methods for avoiding failure in international negotiation.

NOTES

1. Notable exceptions are Hopmann (1996) and Wagner (2008), further discussed below.

2. Jean-Claude Juncker, Prime Minister of Luxembourg and President of the European Council, quoted in "No Agreement on Financial Perspectives at European Council," Press Release, European Council, General Affairs and External Relations, June 18, 2005.

3. "Global public goods" are goods (tangible and intangible) that do not have exclusive owners and whose benefits may cross national boundaries, population groups, and even generations. Their benefits are widespread, nonrival in consumption (one party's use or gains from the good do not limit others' use or benefits from the same good), and often also nonexcludable (i.e., they cannot be reserved for certain parties, even if only certain parties have paid for or contributed to their supply). The benefits of "pure" or perfectly global public goods are at once universal (universally accessible or beneficial), nonrival in consumption, and nonexcludable.

A Failure to Communicate

Uncertainty, Information,
and Unsuccessful Negotiations

ANDREW KYDD

Uncertainty is one of the most important causes of bargaining failure. If diplomats had complete information about one another's preferences and bargaining power they would usually be able to craft deals that spare their countries the costs of conflict. Paul Wolfowitz, one of the architects of the 2003 U.S. invasion of Iraq, acknowledged that if the United States had known that Saddam Hussein did not possess weapons of mass destruction, it would not have invaded. Saddam did not want to reveal his lack of such weapons for fear of looking weak before domestic and regional actors. Given that uncertainty — a lack of information — causes negotiation failure, it follows that the provision of information should lead to negotiation success. Indeed, the degree to which the process of negotiation produces new information and resolves uncertainty is a key determinant of whether negotiation will be successful or not. If negotiation did not generate or communicate new information, there would be no point in engaging in it.

Three types of uncertainty may bedevil negotiations and prevent agreement. These are private information about the parties' bargaining leverage, mistrust between the parties, and uncertainty about the state of the world. Uncertainty about bargaining power can lead to negotiation failure by encouraging each side to hold out in the hope that the other side will make greater concessions. For instance, a trade war could arise because each side thinks the other will be hurt more by the interruption of trade and so demands more favorable terms than the other will accept. Mistrust can cause negotiations to fail because each side suspects that the other is bargaining in bad faith and will ultimately cheat on whatever deal is reached. In peace talks during a civil war, for instance, each side may fear that the other side will use the cease-fire to secretly prepare its forces for a renewed offensive. Finally, uncertainty about the state of the world can cause bargaining failure by causing a doubt about which is the right policy to pursue. For instance, if one state does not believe that industrial emissions contribute to climate change, it will be uninterested in negotiations aimed at curbing those pollutants.

In this chapter, I discuss each of these problems in turn. I outline the problem, discuss why the uncertainty might arise or be difficult to resolve, and then discuss steps that can be taken by the players and by third parties to overcome the problem by providing credible information. I conclude with some brief reflections on whether it is possible to have too much information in the bargaining context. I adopt a rationalist approach to bargaining and information, informed by the game theoretic literature on the topic. By focusing on rational choice theories, this chapter is complementary to Christer Jönsson's chapter ("Psychological Causes of Incomplete Negotiations") on psychological causes of bargaining failure.

PRIVATE INFORMATION ABOUT BARGAINING LEVERAGE

The most common form of uncertainty that can cause negotiations to break down is private information about bargaining leverage. The historian Geoffrey Blainey famously argued, "Wars usually end when the fighting nations agree on their relative strength, and wars usually begin when fighting nations disagree on their relative strength" (1988:122). This insight has become the basis of many analyses of bargaining and war initiation in political science, and it applies more generally even if the outcome of negotiation failure is not literally war (for a review, see Powell, 2002).

To see how the logic works, consider the July Crisis of 1914 that preceded the First World War (see Albertini, 1952; Fischer, 1975). The assassination of the Austrian Archduke Franz Ferdinand in Sarajevo precipitated a month of negotiations conducted mostly by telegraph that ultimately failed to craft a mutually acceptable resolution, with catastrophic results. The dispute pitted the Central Powers — Germany and Austria-Hungary — against the Dual

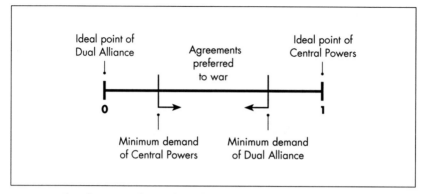

FIGURE 3. The July Crisis with complete information.

Alliance: France and Russia, with Britain loosely tied to France and Russia in the Triple Entente. The two sides had opposing preferences on a number of issues. Russia wished to extend its influence in the Balkans at Austria's expense, and France wished to regain Alsace and Lorraine, lost in the Franco-Prussian war of 1870. Germany wished to establish continental hegemony and overthrow British hegemony at sea. These issues can be bundled together and represented graphically as a continuum between zero and 1, illustrated in figure 3. The Central Powers' ideal point is located at 1 while the Dual Alliance most prefers 0. Looming in the background of the negotiations is the possibility that war will break out. Each side had its own evaluation of how well it was likely to do in a war, and these war payoffs implied the minimum demand a player would accept from the negotiations, for no side could be forced to live with a deal that it liked less than war. If these minimum demands were compatible, as illustrated in figure 3, there would be a range of deals that both sides preferred to war, so negotiations should have ended successfully.

Under fairly general assumptions, if parties face no uncertainty there will be deals that both sides prefer to conflict (Fearon, 1995).[1] As Blainey implied, if the parties split the difference in proportion to their relative power, they will both be better off than if they choose to fight. The stronger one side is, the more the range of mutually acceptable deals shifts in its favor. For instance, if the Central Powers' strength increases, the range of mutually acceptable deals shifts to the right, which benefits the Central Powers.

Unfortunately, uncertainty about relative power can potentially eliminate this range of mutually acceptable deals. Uncertainty about relative power was a

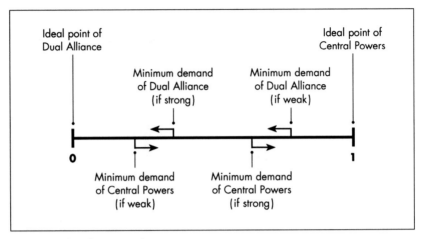

FIGURE 4. The July Crisis with uncertainty.

key problem during the July Crisis. One source of this uncertainty was the difficulty in predicting British behavior. Germany hoped Britain would sit out the war, and France and Russia hoped Britain would fight alongside her entente partners. Other sources of uncertainty had to do with the quality of secret war plans, military production capacity, and the fighting spirit of the troops. With uncertainty about relative power, the two sides' evaluation of war was a function both of their beliefs about their own power and of their belief about how likely the other side was to be strong (see Cristal, "Camp David, 2000," in this book). The alliances would have a higher payoff for war and hence a higher minimum demand in the negotiations if they viewed themselves as strong than if they thought themselves weak. The situation with uncertainty is illustrated in figure 4.[2]

The key difference from figure 3 is that there is no longer a range of deals that both sides definitely prefer to war. In particular, if both sides think they are strong, each side will demand more than its opposite number will accept, so negotiation will fail and war will result. These irreconcilable demands are a product of uncertainty, not just the fact that both sides are strong. If both were strong and this was common knowledge between them, then any deal reflecting their balance of power would be mutually acceptable. The problem is that strong types on each side think that the other side may be weak, so that they overestimate their own relative power and therefore bargaining strength. This simultaneous over-optimism is the cause of bargaining failure. Each side thinks that the other side may be weak, and therefore the other side should make a bigger concession. If both sides persist in this opinion, the bargaining will fail. In July of 1914, both sides believed the war would be short and victorious; this made their minimum demands incompatible, which made war inevitable (Van Evera, 1984).

This uncertainty about relative power, or bargaining leverage more generally, may be difficult to overcome through ordinary communication. Imagine Germany sending France and Russia a telegram during the July crisis saying that since Germany was very strong and likely to win any war that might arise, France and Russia should allow Austria a free hand against Serbia. A strong Germany would like to send such a message and have it believed, because it would help achieve its goals without war. The problem is a weak Germany would also want to send such a message, since it too would want Austria to prevail. With both strong and weak types claiming to be strong, ordinary communication or "cheap talk" on this topic will be uninformative (Farrell and Rabin, 1996).[3]

Instead, the negotiators may attempt to communicate through "costly signals." Costly signals are actions that are costly to the party taking them, and serve to separate one type from another (Riley, 2001). In the bargaining context, they are actions that a type with strong bargaining leverage would find acceptable, but a type with weak bargaining leverage would find too costly. The most widespread costly signal is simple delay; by being in no rush to get an agreement, one signals that one's payoff for no agreement is not so bad, so that any deal needs to be quite favorable to be acceptable. Another mechanism of costly signaling is the generation of "audience costs" by making public demands that would be costly to retreat from later because of the potential that domestic audiences will punish a leader for failing on the international stage (Fearon, 1994; Schultz, 1998). For instance, in the July Crisis, the Austrian ultimatum to Serbia set forth demands in such a manner that to retreat from them later would be humiliating. The analysis of bargaining as a process of costly signaling is perhaps the dominant perspective on the topic in international relations theory today. The bottom line is that costly signaling provides a noisy and inefficient means that can sometimes provide the required information to avoid conflict, but does not always do so. Bargaining with incomplete information is necessarily costly and prone to breakdown.

Given the difficulties of costly signaling, it would be convenient if third parties could provide the required information. Unfortunately, similar problems dog third parties when they attempt to communicate about bargaining leverage. They cannot simply act as conduits of information, because if the parties have incentives to lie to each other, they have incentives to lie to a mediator who is talking to the other side as well (Myerson, 1991). If a mediator has an independent source of information on the relative power or bargaining leverage of the parties, the mediator may be able to communicate that information, however. To do so credibly, the mediator must be biased toward the side it is communicating with (Kydd, 2003). If a mediator just wants to avoid conflict, he or she would have an incentive to say whatever made agreement more likely, namely that the other side is strong, so that each side should make more concessions. Only a mediator who is biased toward one side, such that she or he would not urge a concession unless it was considered truly necessary, will be trusted when he or she does urge a concession.

Uncertainty about bargaining leverage is widely held to be the most common cause of bargaining failure. In the security issue area, war itself may ultimately provide the information that is lacking, as Blainey argued (see also Goemans, 2000). In other areas, prolonged delay and costly strikes or demonstrations of one form or another may be required before the parties agree on the balance of leverage, and can come to an agreement.

MISTRUST

A second source of uncertainty that can cause bargaining failure is mistrust. Mistrust has been blamed for conflict since Thomas Hobbes (1968:184) argued that life under anarchy amounts to a war of all against all in which individuals, motivated by a desire for security, attempt to preserve themselves by destroying others. The argument rests on mistrust, since if everyone was benignly motivated and knew this to be the case, there would be no need to lash out. As a result, latter-day Hobbesians such as John Mearsheimer (2001:31) make uncertainty and mistrust a bedrock assumption. Psychological and game theoretic treatments of trust and mistrust offer more nuanced hypotheses of how these factors affect the possibilities for cooperation and the likelihood of conflict (Jervis, 1976; Kydd, 2005). The central problem is, when can actors who are themselves trustworthy cooperate in the face of at least some fear that the other side may not be trustworthy? (See Goodwin, "Two Hostage Negotiations," in this volume.)

SOVIET UNION

		Implement	Cheat
UNITED STATES	Implement	1, 1	-1, e_2
	Cheat	e_i, -1	0, 0

FIGURE 5. The Arms Control Treaty Game.

Consider the nuclear weapons negotiations of the early 1980s between the United States and the Soviet Union (Talbott, 1985). The two sides had negotiated the Strategic Arms Limitation Treaties (SALT) of 1972 and 1979 placing limits on their arsenals. The United States began to suspect that the Soviets were cheating, however, and a debate arose as to whether the United States should continue abiding by the limits of the treaties. This erosion of trust frustrated negotiations on strategic and intermediate range weapons in the early 1980s, leading to a breakdown in relations in 1983.

In any arms reduction treaty, each side is vulnerable to exploitation by the other side. If one side fulfills the treaty and the other side cheats, the side implementing the deal will regret doing so. For both sides, the worst outcome is to fulfill the treaty while the other side cheats. Next worst is if both sides cheat: then there was no point in negotiating the treaty. A better outcome is if the treaty is implemented by both sides. This dilemma is represented in the matrix in figure 5. If both sides implement the deal, they receive a payoff of 1. If both sides cheat, they receive a payoff of 0. Finally, if one side cheats and the other side implements the deal, the cheater gets "e_i" (for exploitation) and the other side gets −1.

Two types of player can be identified in the Arms Control Treaty Game. If the payoff for unilaterally cheating is lower than the payoff for mutually implementing the deal, $e_i < 1$, then the player is said to be "trustworthy," because he or she prefers mutual cooperation to cheating while the other side cooperates. If a trustworthy player believes that the other side will cooperate, therefore, that player wants to cooperate and implement the deal as well. If both players are trustworthy and this is common knowledge, there is no reason they cannot cooperate.[4]

If, on the other hand, exploiting the other side is preferred to implementing the deal, $e_i > 1$, then the player is "untrustworthy," in that she or he would prefer to have the other side cooperate and then cheat so as to exploit that player. Untrustworthy players want to cheat regardless of what the other side does.[5] Even if only one of the players is known to be untrustworthy, then both sides will cheat. A trustworthy player would have to cheat because he or she would know that the other player, being untrustworthy, would cheat, leaving the trustworthy player with −1 if she or he were to attempt to implement the deal (see Cristal, "Camp David, 2000," in this book).

If it were obvious who is trustworthy and who is not, trust would not be an interesting problem. Trustworthy actors would simply avoid the untrustworthy and cooperate only with each other, and no one would ever be taken advantage of. In reality, however, it is not always obvious whether the other side is trustworthy, and uncertainty over who is trustworthy and who is not, that is, mistrust, can impede cooperation.[6] In the U.S.–Soviet nuclear case, there was tremendous debate on the American side about whether Soviet actions such as the construction of the Krasnoyarsk radar were violations of SALT II, and therefore indicators that the Soviets were untrustworthy and should not be negotiated with.

Cooperation is possible in the face of mistrust if the level of trust exceeds a certain "minimum trust threshold." We can think of the level of trust that the United States has for the Soviet Union as the probability the United States thinks the Soviets are trustworthy. The higher this probability, the more likely the United States thinks it is that the Soviets would prefer not to cheat if they thought the United States would implement the treaty. This probability that the other side is trustworthy must exceed a minimum trust threshold for each side. If the likelihood that the Soviets are trustworthy falls too low, the United States will not find it worth negotiating further arms control treaties, because the risk of exploitation is too great.[7]

What affects the minimum trust threshold? Three factors are important. The better the deal is, the lower the minimum trust threshold is. The better the deal, the more willing one is to bear the risk of exploitation in order to have a chance at realizing it. This offers some scope for adjusting the deal to accommodate differing levels of trust. Second, the greater the cost of being cheated, the higher the minimum trust threshold. If it is bad to have one's trust betrayed, then one will have to be very trusting to be willing to cooperate. Finally, the higher the payoff for exploiting the other side, the higher the minimum trust threshold, making cooperation harder to achieve. If trustworthy players find exploiting the other side to be almost as good as implementing the deal, they will have to be very trusting in order to cooperate.

What strategies can be employed to overcome mistrust? Unfortunately, simple communication may be insufficient. In matters of trust there are incentives to misrepresent one's type, just as there are in communication about bargaining leverage. Soviet diplomats hotly contested the charge that they had violated the SALT agreements and were untrustworthy, until the Yeltsin era when they admitted that the Krasnoyarsk radar was a violation. The problem is that untrustworthy types would also want to convince the other side that they are trustworthy, because that would convince the trustworthy party to cooperate, which would give the untrustworthy type a chance to exploit them. Trustworthy and untrustworthy types share a desire to get the other side to cooperate, and so both claim to be trustworthy. This means that ordinary communication or cheap talk is uninformative in the context of mistrust.

Where cheap talk fails, costly signals once again can succeed (Kydd, 2005). In the mistrust context, costly signals can take on the form of carving up the deal into stages, so that cooperation on the early stages can serve as a costly signal of trustworthy preferences that enables cooperation on later, more important stages. After Gorbachev became leader of the Soviet Union, for instance, nuclear negotiations began to make headway. The Intermediate-range Nuclear Forces (INF) treaty of 1987 is a perfect example of a costly signal of reassurance. The treaty eliminated a class of weapons of middling importance; not the highest-level strategic weapons, but a step in that direction. The implementation of the deal enabled the parties to build trust and move toward more cooperative negotiations in the future both on conventional weapons and on strategic nuclear forces. The deal favored the United States, in that the Soviets destroyed 1,846 missiles while the United States eliminated 848. This was in part because the United States was more suspicious at this point, so the deal needed to be more attractive to lower the U.S. minimum trust threshold.

Third parties may also be able to build trust between the parties. As before, third parties cannot directly convey messages about trustworthiness; if a player has an incentive to lie to the other player, the first player will have an incentive to lie to a mediator who is in communication with the other player. However, if the mediator has independent information about the trustworthiness of the players, the mediator can sometimes communicate this information to the players and foster trust. During one of his famous rounds of shuttle diplomacy, for instance, U.S. secretary of state Henry Kissinger said to his Israeli hosts, "I have to tell you honestly: my judgment is that Egypt is genuinely willing to make peace with Israel" (Kissinger, 1982:964). This was an effort to build trust, to overcome suspicion that the other side was bargaining in bad faith. In a mistrust game with mediation, the mediator needs to have moderate preferences to be credible to the two sides about the trustworthiness of the other player (Kydd, 2006). Mediators who are too biased toward one side will not be viewed as credible or trustworthy by the other side, preventing mutual reassurance. To be a credible trust builder, a mediator must be seen as averse to either side being exploited.

UNCERTAINTY ABOUT THE STATE OF THE WORLD

The third type of uncertainty that can cause negotiations to fail is uncertainty about the state of the world, sometimes called "analytic uncertainty" (Iida, 1993). Here the uncertainty is not about the power or trustworthiness of the other side, but a shared uncertainty as to whether there are joint gains to be had from cooperation in the first place, and if so which policy is the best one. This type of uncertainty has been less studied in political science than the previous two. In conflict studies, for instance, it is generally assumed that the costs of war guarantee that there are joint gains from a negotiated settlement. Every war must end, after all, and if one could simply implement the outcome without suffering the costs along the way, both sides would be better off. However, in issues where there is considerable scientific or economic uncertainty about the consequences of various actions the parties may take, there may be great uncertainty about whether certain courses of cooperation will pay off or not. A free-trade area might lead to great increases in mutual trade, or it might stagnate because the economies have little to offer each other. A joint venture like Airbus might become competitive and make profits, or it might remain dependent on subsidies from the sponsoring countries.

Consider the issue of climate change negotiations and the Kyoto treaty, which resulted in a U.S. decision not to participate. In the climate change debate, the central uncertainties have been whether the climate is changing, whether this is caused by human activity, and whether actions can be taken to mitigate the problem without causing tremendous privation from reduced

UNITED STATES \ EUROPE	Tough Agreement	Loose Agreement
Tough Agreement	$pV-1, pV+1$	0, 0
Loose Agreement	0, 0	$(1-p)V+1, (1-p)V-1$

FIGURE 6. The Climate Change Game.

energy usage. Other debates concern what is the best policy for dealing with the problem. Some advocate a tough agreement on the argument that the problem is serious and the remedies not too costly. Others favor a looser agreement in the belief that tougher measures would be too damaging to the economy.

A very stylized representation of the dilemma is shown in figure 6. There are two possible agreements under consideration, tough and loose. There is uncertainty about which policy is best. With probability p, a tough agreement is the way to go and will produce a benefit of value V, but with probability $1-p$, a loose agreement would be the way to obtain the benefit. The United States and Europe negotiate over whether to sign a tight or loose agreement. If they agree, the deal is implemented, and the world learns if that was the right policy to pursue. If they disagree, the status quo remains in place with payoffs of zero for both sides. Finally, the two sides are biased toward certain policies. The United States generally likes loose agreements and Europe likes tighter ones, reflecting different attitudes toward international law and constraints on sovereignty. If a loose agreement is signed, the United States receives a payoff of 1 and Europe suffers a cost of -1. If a tight agreement is implemented, the roles are reversed and the United States pays the cost -1 and Europe receives 1. This sets up a conflict of interest over which policy is best.

How would negotiations proceed in such a dilemma? The United States would be happy to sign a loose agreement provided that the Europeans would agree, and similarly, the Europeans would be happy to sign a tight one. The key question is, when will one side be willing to go along with the version it does not prefer; when will the United States support a tight agreement or Europe support a loose one? Basically, each side will support the treaty version it is biased against, provided that it is likely enough to be the one that produces the most value in the long run, and if the value it produces is sufficiently great.[8]

There are three possibilities. First, if the value of the treaty is expected to be too low, then neither party will ever be willing to support its less preferred version, no matter how likely it is to be the right policy.[9] The only outcome in the game is for the United States to favor a loose treaty and Europe to favor a tight one, and for negotiations to fail. This is because the potential value of cooperation is not enough to outweigh the costs for each party of the form of cooperation it does not prefer. No amount of learning about which option is best will help in this case. Second, if the potential value of the treaty falls in a middling range, each side would be willing to support the other side's favored version, but only if it was likely enough to be better than the alternative.[10] If the policy uncertainty is very high, such that it is unclear which policy is best, the two sides will revert to supporting only their favored version. Information about which policy is best could make the difference between cooperation and noncooperation in this case. Finally, if the benefits from cooperation are very great, then the players will be willing to coordinate on one policy regardless of the level of uncertainty about which one is best.[11] If a tight agreement looks better, then the United States will support it; if a loose agreement looks better, then the Europeans will be willing to go along with it. In this case the value of coordination is so great that it overwhelms the sides' individual biases toward particular policies. The failure to secure U.S. participation in Kyoto can be loosely interpreted as an illustration of the second case, where policy uncertainty, at least in the minds of decision makers, does not justify supporting a mechanism against which one is biased.

This game illustrates opportunities for information provision to identify the potential gains from negotiations. Unlike in the case of private information about bargaining leverage and mistrust, direct communication between the parties can sometimes be helpful in overcoming shared uncertainty about the state of the world. James Morrow (1994) has analyzed a more complex version of the Climate Change Game in which the parties have an opportunity to share information about the quality of the two options before deciding what to do. The main results are that if the distributional conflict between the parties is not too great, the parties can credibly share their information, and coordinate on the option that emerges as the one more likely to be better. If the conflict of interest is too great, however, communication breaks down because each party has an incentive to recommend its ex-ante favored position regardless of what information it has, so the parties will be unable to trust each other's arguments about the merits of the two options. For example, militarized crises over territory will experience little information-sharing about the merits of various options, as compared with negotiations over establishing a customs union or environmental treaty, because in the former case interests are clearly defined and sharply opposed.

As in the mistrust problem, agreements can be structured over time to overcome problems posed by uncertainty about the state of the world. Barbara Koremenos (2001) studies this problem in a model of how agreements are designed. She argues that if the benefits of agreement are subject to random shocks that may realign the distribution of benefits, agreements will tend to be designed with provisions for renegotiation. She analyzes the Nuclear Non-Proliferation Treaty as a case in point. The parties were uncertain about the economic and scientific consequences of forgoing nuclear weapons programs, so regular five-year review conferences were scheduled, culminating in a conference in the twenty-fifth year to decide on whether to end, renew, or make the treaty permanent. As time went by, the parties confirmed that economic growth and technological progress were fully compatible with nonnuclear status, and hence the treaty was made permanent in 1995.

The role of third parties is obviously important in the provision of information about the benefits of cooperation. Peter Haas has argued for the importance of epistemic communities, "network[s] of professionals with recognized expertise and competence in a particular domain and an authoritative claim to policy relevant knowledge within that domain" (1997a:3). The archetypal epistemic community is a network of scientists, such as the atomic scientists who pioneered deterrence theory and arms control and the atmospheric scientists who placed the ozone hole and climate change on the international agenda. Ideally, their scientifically grounded knowledge enables them to identify problems and craft solutions to problems that are difficult to recognize or grapple with for policy makers without scientific training. Adler (1997) argues that the development of modern arms control theory in the 1960s and its implementation in treaties in the 1970s and 1980s is a case of an epistemic community in action. Peter Haas analyzes the banning of ozone-depleting chemicals in the Montreal Protocol as a similar triumph for scientifically informed international negotiations (1997b).

The influence of epistemic communities may be limited by two factors, however. First, divergent policy preferences may still prevent policy makers from adopting the recommendations of an epistemic community even if they believe the community's data and analyses are sound. For instance, an oil company executive could believe that global climate models and historical data do point to a human-made warming of the atmosphere, but face overwhelming financial incentives to persist with the status quo regardless.

Furthermore, in part because of such differences, and in part because of genuine scientific uncertainty, for every epistemic community there is often a countercommunity making opposite claims. The arms control community that developed in the 1960s spawned an anti–arms control community that became deeply entrenched in the neoconservative movement and the U.S. Republican Party, and it is this anti–arms control community that currently exercises the most influence on U.S. policy on weapons of mass destruction (Gray, 1992). In the arms control issue area the emergence of countercommunities is particularly understandable, since the issue is one of international relations and of human behavior on which scientific consensus is elusive. Yet even in climate change, where scientific opinion is much more united, a relatively small dissenting minority is presented in the political realm as deserving an equal hearing. In areas of even more settled science, evolutionary biology and epidemiology, proponents of "intelligent design" are gaining ground in U.S. high school biology classrooms, and the leader of South Africa has denied the link between HIV and AIDS, despite the fact that the proportion of actual scientists advocating these positions probably falls below 1 percent.

Uncertainty about preferences can even lead to self-censorship. Stephen Morris (2001) presents an interesting model in which a policy maker receives advice from an adviser who is suspected of being biased toward one particular outcome. If the adviser wishes to overcome this suspicion, he has an incentive to recommend the policy against which he is suspected of being biased, even if he has information in favor of his supposed favorite policy. In this case, information is not transmitted because of suspicion and a desire not to be seen as biased. Sometimes, policy makers will undervalue the potential contributions of objective scientific inquiry and reduce contentious debates to questions of loyalty and identity; those on our side can be trusted and conferred with, while those on the opposing side must be undermined and discredited. In a partisan environment, third parties attempting to provide expertise must be seen as "on one's side" if they are to be believed.

TOO MUCH INFORMATION?

I have argued that lack of information is a key cause of negotiation failure and that the key task in achieving a successful outcome is to credibly provide information, either from one party to another or from a third party to the bargainers. The difficulty in credibly providing information is the main obstacle to a successful settlement of the dispute.

But can there be such a thing as too much information? Bernard Finel and Kristin Lord (2002:144) argue that international transparency can be harmful. In their view, transparency can overwhelm signals with "noise" and provide more ammunition to actors with preexisting beliefs and prejudices, and that the news media tends to over-report hostile behavior rather than reassuring behavior. These arguments are not supported by rationalist models of information. For rational actors, the more data available, the easier it is to extract the signal from the noise, the faster preexisting incorrect beliefs will be replaced by correct beliefs, and the easier any bias in the press can be adjusted for. However, these arguments highlight the need for research on the interaction of cognitive limitation, psychological bias, and information processing in international negotiations (see Jönsson, "Psychological Causes of Incomplete Negotiations," in this volume).

Jarque, Ponsatí, and Sákovics (2003) develop a model in which information transmission is limited. In their setup, a mediator listens to both sides as time goes by and as they make concessions, but the mediator tells the parties nothing at all except that an agreement has not yet been reached. When the two sides' positions become reconcilable, the mediator announces that an agreement has been reached. In this way, each side learns from the passage of time that their previous offer was not accepted, but not what the other side's previous offer was. This can produce faster concessions because it makes the other side look more resolute than it might be if its concessions were reported. While the model is an interesting theoretical exercise, it is not clear that real-life mediators could get away with such a silent negotiating strategy. In fact mediators tend to play up the other side's previous concessions in an effort to extract a reciprocal one, rather than keep them quiet. Kissinger noted that he "almost invariably transmitted any proposal about which either side felt strongly" unless he felt deadlock was imminent in which case he would suggest compromises of his own (1982:814). However, on occasion he would hold a concession that one side had made in reserve while talking to the other, in order to be able to trade it in at an opportune moment (833). Concealing positions regularly, however, will weaken the credibility of the mediator. Kissinger himself was burned in this fashion when he held some Israeli concessions to Syria in reserve during negotiations over the 1974 disengagement of forces, only to have the Israeli position leak to the press in Israel, revealing the concessions and Kissinger's deception (1071).

A final related issue is to what extent information from the negotiations should be made public. There is general agreement in the mediation literature that publicity is a bad thing, that information about what is going on in the negotiations should be kept private. In practice, this seems to be adhered to at many high profile mediation efforts, such as the Camp David negotiations and the Dayton negotiations (Holbrooke, 1998:236). Several logics may be involved. Negotiators may be accused of selling out if they make concessions that are made public, particularly if the concessions fail to generate reciprocal concessions and the negotiations fail. Domestic groups whose interests are compromised by a concession will be given additional time to mobilize against the agreement the earlier the concession is made known (Koremenos, 2002). It is worth pointing out, however, that the literature on democracy, audience costs, and transparency suggests that open societies are better able to make and keep commitments internationally, and if relevant political forces in the legislature are not consulted in the negotiation process, the likelihood of ratification can be greatly reduced (Martin, 2000).

CONCLUSION

Uncertainty and information are central aspects of any negotiation. Before a negotiation, it is not known what the two sides will be willing to agree to and afterward, if the negotiation is successful, this will have become known. The provision of information is therefore a vital aspect of promoting agreement, and obstacles to the provision of credible information are key explanations of bargaining failure. The central obstacle to the provision of credible information is the conflict of interests inherent in bargaining situations. If the two sides disagree on their relative power or bargaining leverage, they cannot simply clear this up with a quiet discussion, because each side has an incentive to claim to be stronger than it is, in order to get a better deal. A third party could be trusted to provide such information provided that it was viewed to be on one's side, and so would not say the adversary was strong unless it really was. Similarly, if mistrust is preventing agreement, the two parties cannot simply say, "I'm trustworthy" and clear up any misconceptions, because untrustworthy actors claim to be trustworthy too. Here, third parties who do not want to see either side exploited can be of use if they have information about the prior behavior or trustworthiness of the parties. Third parties have the biggest role, perhaps, in providing information about the state of the world. Objective scientific knowledge can identify common problems and feasible solutions. However, in politicized contexts or with political actors with only a weak commitment to science, epistemic communities will proliferate and political actors will simply cite the groups that support their preferred policy position, however small and lacking in credentials.

To sum up, lack of information is indeed the key problem in many bargaining situations, and communication is indeed the answer. However, the obstacles to credible communication are many and profound, and they are not easily overcome by the parties themselves or by third-party mediators or advisers. Bargaining with uncertainty is inherently inefficient and prone to breakdown; social science can hope to minimize the costs of this uncertainty but not to eliminate them.

NOTES

1. For instance, let player 1's payoff for a deal be x, and player 2's be $1 - x$. Let each side have a stock of military resources, m_i, and a player's chance of winning a war be its relative power, $m_i / (m_i + m_j)$. If war is winner-take-all and costs c, a player's value for war will be

$$w_i = m_i / (m_i + m_j) - c.$$

This implies that any deal between

$$m_1 / (m_1 + m_2) - c$$

and

$$m_1 / (m_1 + m_2) + c$$

will be preferred to war by both parties.

2. Formally, let each side have a likelihood s_i of being strong, with power M_i, and a $1 - s_i$ chance of being weak, with power $m_i < M_i$. The minimum demands for the two types are

$$W_i = s_j \, (M_i \,/\, M_i + M_j) + (1 - s_j) \, (M_i \,/\, M_i + m_j) - c,$$

and

$$w_i = s_j \, (m_i \,/\, m_i + M_j) + (1 - s_j) \, (m_i \,/\, m_i + m_j) - c.$$

3. For an interesting exception, see Sartori, 2002. She analyzes a model with repeated disputes in which players sometimes wish to preserve a reputation for honesty and so can signal leverage with cheap talk.

4. Trustworthy players have Stag Hunt or Assurance Game payoffs.

5. Untrustworthy players have Prisoners' Dilemma payoffs.

6. A related form of uncertainty is over whether the other side is capable of cooperating, as opposed to being willing to cooperate. This can have similar effects.

7. Formally, the likelihood that player j is trustworthy, t_j, must exceed $1 \,/\, (2 - e_i)$ for player i to cooperate.

8. Formally, each side will support the nonfavored version if $p > 1 \,/\, V$.

9. This holds for $V < 1$.

10. For V between 1 and 2, if $p > 1 \,/\, V$, both can support a tight agreement, and if $p < 1 - 1 \,/\, V$, both can support a loose one.

11. For V greater than 2, the two sides can always find a version to support.

PART SIX

Process as a Cause of Failure

Process Reasons for Failure

I. WILLIAM ZARTMAN

There is more debate these days about the reasons for the durability of some negotiated settlements than there is about the success or failure of the negotiations in the first place. It is generally noted that negotiated settlements are usually failures at bringing an end to internal wars (the most frequent kind of wars at the moment), one-sided victory being more common, and that even negotiated settlements are not very durable (Collier et al., 2003). Similar findings occur on interstate wars (Pillar, 1983; Stedman, 1991; Wallensteen and Sollenberg, 2000). International war data for the 1946–97 half-century show twenty-four cease-fires, of which only ten lasted and only two (the Bangladeshi independence war in 1971 and the Yom Kippur War between Egypt and Israel in 1973) could by any stretch of imagination be called a resolution; few of the others made any attempt to look for a resolving formula (Singer 1979; Fortna, 2004). A growing literature looks at incentives and implementation as a reason why negotiated settlements succeed or fail (Berdal and Wennmann, 2010; Gartner and Melin, 2009; Hampson, 1996; Stedman, Rothchild, and Cousens, 2002; Toft, 2010), but not as a reason why negotiations fail to reach settlements. Procedural and substantive grievances tend to have been downplayed or not even measured in many explanations of durability (Bueno de Mesquita and Lalman, 1992; Collier et al., 2003; Mason, Weingarten, and Fett, 1999; Walter, 2002; Werner, 1999). Although Werner (1999) looked at settlement terms as a source of durability, she found the evidence ambiguous. There is even less attention given to reasons why cooperation negotiations succeed or fail, in the sense of reaching an agreement (Hampson, 1996).

This study proposes a process explanation for negotiation failure, not replacing others but equally consistent with the facts. It does so in a complex way, by looking at process in both its procedural and its substantive forms. The first adopts the standard staged understanding of the negotiation process, running through the diagnosis, formulation, and specification (detail) phases, hypothesizing that negotiations fail when they do not accomplish these stages properly. It then examines the content of process, in terms of the necessary if not sufficient conditions for its opening, or ripeness, and for its conclusion, with an analysis of the elements involved in reaching that objective. It will examine two hypotheses:

1. In order to be successful, negotiations have to accomplish the three stages in the process of producing a mutually agreeable outcome, and their failure to do so will result in their failure as negotiations (within the meaning defined in the initial chapter); and

2. In order to be successful, negotiations have to maintain the effects of a Mutually Hurting Stalemate (MHS) and devise a Mutually Enticing Opportunity (MEO) that contains a resolving formula for the conflict and a project for future cooperation (Ohlson, 1998; Zartman, 2000 and 2006; Zartman and Kremenyuk, 2005), and their failure to do so will result in their failure as negotiations (within the meaning defined in the introduction). MEO represents the pull factor that draws negotiations to a successful conclusion, corresponding to the push factor supplied by a MHS, the necessary (but not sufficient) factor that impels the parties into negotiations.

This study shows that negotiations fail to lead to a durable settlement when they do not build a process leading to normal politics or normal diplomacy (Thuderoz, 2003). Negotiations fail when the parties — alone or with the help of a mediator — cannot find an MEO to pull themselves out of their conflict or noncooperation, that is, when they cannot find a formula for a multi/bilateral solution to their situation that is preferable to a unilateral solution or the status quo.

To avoid a tautological explanation — agreements are achievable only when they are achieved — this explanation looks into the negotiation process itself, between initiation and agreement, for the reasons for success and failure (Pillar, 1983; Wagner, 1999). The explanation must focus on the reasons why

MEOS are adopted or not, so it must begin with "how" to explain success, and then turn to "why not" to explain failure. It will be found that the terms of a resolving formula, among others, are generally present from the beginning of the negotiations, but they are seized as an MEO only when they constitute a single salient solution (as opposed to double salient solutions) and address the post-agreement interests of the parties, beyond resolution of the conflict.

Conflict here refers to its basic meaning of dispute, whether violent or not. This chapter will begin with a discussion of the MEO process in cases of violent conflict, because the argument is clearer, and then turn to cases of cooperation, with appropriate rectifications. Along the way, some important distinctions beyond the two types will be brought to light. The analysis then proceeds into an examination of why intuitively evident resolving formulas do not reach agreement.

PROCEDURAL ANALYSIS

It is useful to spell out the negotiation process before developing the conceptual components. After their pre-negotiation or diagnosis phase, negotiations face the challenge of elaborating a formula — a common understanding of the conflict/problem and its solution, a common sense of justice, and/or a set of terms of trade — and then applying that formula to resolve the details of the conflict and the agreement (Hopmann, 1996; Zartman, 1978; Zartman and Berman, 1982). The basis of the conceptualization is to identify what parties do when they do it well, and hence what they omit when they do fail.

In the so-called pre-negotiation phase — actually the important first phase of negotiations — the parties ask themselves such important questions as "What am I really after?" separating interests from positions (Fisher and Ury, 1982); "What is this conflict like?" providing comparisons for difficulties and solutions; and "What precedents are there for resolving conflicts like this?" offering guidelines for resolution. The same questions need then to be considered in the perception of the other party. Parties also need to address the functions of pre-negotiation, including establishment of costs and risks, so that parties know what they are getting into; agenda, so that the parties know what aspects of the conflict can be subjects of negotiation and agreement, and what can/must be avoided; participants, so that parties know with whom they are making a deal and who can/must be excluded; support, so that parties know they are speaking for a client group and can deliver their engagements; and bridges, so that parties will not be meeting for the first time and have already established some contacts and experience between themselves (Stein, 1989). Diplomats have indicated that 75 percent of their time in negotiation is spent, optimally, in such diagnosis, and that if the pre-negotiation functions are not established before negotiations open formally, they must be established during the negotiations, wasting time and momentum in the process.

In the formulation phase, parties turn first, explicitly or implicitly, to establish the formula that will govern the ultimate distributions of costs and benefits, variously defined as a common definition of the problem and its solution, a common sense of justice, and/or agreed terms of trade (Zartman and Berman, 1982; Zartman et al., 1996). The formula can take one of two forms: a minimal agreeing formula to end or lessen hostilities or constraints, as symptoms of the problem, or a resolving formula to address the cause of the conflict or constraint itself (with much grey area in the real world between the two types). An agreeing formula is a conflict management measure, the minimum that the parties can agree to, a cease-fire to end or suspend violence or the effects of the problem, but not its resolution. A resolving formula is a conflict resolution agreement, dealing with the issues of the conflict, an enticing opportunity that the parties perceive as a way out of their problem. In other basic terms, an agreeing formula is a procedural agreement; a resolving formula is a substantive agreement. The contents of the formula are discussed below, in the exploration of substantive aspects of process. Failure to find a formula leads to an incoherent outcome, if an outcome at all, and slows the process.

Only when a formula is understood can parties turn to the final phase of specification, applying the general framework for a solution to the settlement of the details under contention. During this phase, parties check the formula to see if it applies and guides satisfactorily; if not, they return to revise the formula (just as they can continually return to the diagnosis phase whenever they need more information and preliminary stage-setting).

Although this is a condensed presentation of the necessary phases of negotiation, it enables an understanding of the successive (and repetitive, if necessary) tasks that are required to reach a mutually satisfactory agreement, understanding process as procedure. Using the cases as examples, one can note instances where failure can be ascribed to incomplete accomplishment of the necessary phases. Not only did the selected cases stumble on the formula phase, but they locked in their failure by proceeding to the specification phase without an agreement on the overarching principles governing the allocation of the details. The parties at Waco did not even agree that they were talking about hostages. The parties on Cyprus did not achieve a meeting of the minds on the meaning that lay underneath the term "federalism," but nevertheless proceeded to implement the concept with unacceptable specifications. The parties at the UN Security Council were unable to establish whether they were authorizing an invasion or not, yet attempted to set the conditions for the unagreed goal. The parties at Camp David II busily set to work on the details before establishing a formula, and the mediator did a paltry job on diagnosis compared with the rich preparatory work that went into Camp David I (Quandt, 1986). In the historic case of nineteenth-century Belgium, King William of the Netherlands saw the negotiations as a means to recover his lost provinces, whereas the other parties were looking at a larger picture of a stable configuration in Europe. In general, the salient causes for failure were a lack of attention to diagnosis, and a rush to specification without a formula as a basis.

There is also a substantive sense of process, indicating the content of the negotiation encounter and its components that must be handled if the negotiations are not to fail. The opening of negotiations responds to a condition of ripeness, defined as the existence of an MHS and a Way Out (WO), both existing only subjectively as perceptions although related to objective elements. The completion of negotiations requires the translation of the WO into an MEO that meets the parties' perceived needs and interests better than the status quo. Obviously, the two are related, since the acceptability of the status quo is governed by the MHS, and the WO has to be developed to the point where it becomes an MEO. As discussed in the Belgian case by Daniella Fridl ("The Negotiations on the Status of Belgium," in this book), at the London conference in 1830 there was never a point at which both parties felt they were hurting and instead they found themselves in an S5 situation, a soft, stable, self-serving stalemate, even though the term was not current at the time.

Discussion of the negotiation process begins with the assumption that an MHS, as a perception, is already present to motivate the parties to seek a plurilateral (i.e., bi- or multilateral) solution to their conflict or problem. If the parties were not stalemated and pained, they would simply continue to live with the problem or wage the war. However, while it is insufficient to pull the negotiations to a successful conclusion, that perception needs to continue throughout the negotiations, lest the parties reevaluate their positions and drop out, in the revived hope of being able to find a unilateral solution through escalation. An MHS also needs to be kept alive and present in the negotiators' minds as the basis of their security points, the value of the outcome to be obtained in the absence of negotiations. If the hurt or the prospects of it fades during negotiations, an agreement becomes less pressing, and the party will adopt a tougher position, raising its demands and becoming less interested in a successful outcome. It is therefore important that constraints or "pain" imposed by the unresolved problem continue to be present and felt, and most likely that the problem occasionally remind the parties of its presence or in internal conflicts the rebels brandish a little violence from time to time, to keep the "supply side" credible. For the most part, the supply of pain is perceived, latent and contingent (as is the other side's supply of concessions, as in any negotiation, until the deal is closed), as a threat to be used if negotiations break down (Schelling, 1960). However, exogenous inputs such as unexpected catastrophes and new information have been noted to spark negotiations and by extension promote progress in negotiations already under way, as they heighten the sense of an MHS (Sjöstedt, 1993; Spector and Zartman, 2003).

Thus the payoff from continued conflict or nonagreement, either as active violence, as a hurting stalemate, or simply as a nonsolution, is the continual point of comparison determining the value of the proposed solution. The status quo often appears in the form of an S5 Situation, a condition not conducive to solution (Arnson and Zartman, 2005; Zartman, 1995b). However, in potentially cooperative cases, it is the normal condition, and this again is why attempts at cooperative agreement so often fail. Unless a nonsolution is actually painful, it may constitute a viable situation that leaves the future open, creates no pressure for a search for a solution, and requires no risky decision. The decision to seize a negotiating opportunity and turn it into a search for a solution depends not merely on a judgment of how well that or any solution meets the parties' needs and interests or objectively resolves the conflict, but an estimation of how its uncertainty compares with the better known value of the status quo (Zartman, 2000). Thus, the value of the status quo can serve as an effective pressure point for mediators, as the basis of their security point, as already noted. These calculations will be determinant in deciding whether any proposed resolving formula will or can constitute an MEO. Thus an MEO is a resolving formula that is seen by the parties as meeting their needs better than the status quo.

The second substantive element in the negotiating process is the search for an MEO to pull the parties out of the problem or conflict and into an agreement. Like the MHS, the MEO is a figment of perception, a subjective appreciation of objective elements, but unlike the MHS, it is an invention of the parties (and their mediator) internal to the negotiation process, not a result of an objective external situation. It must be produced by the parties, using their analysis of the conflict and its causes, their appreciation of their interests and needs, and their creativity in crafting a mutually attractive solution, all compared to the status quo discussed above. A negotiated end to a conflict contains forward-looking provisions to deal with the basic dispute, with un-resolved leftovers of the conflict and its possible reemergence, and with new relations of interdependence between the conflicting parties. In judging the attractiveness of any posited formula, or in proposing one, conflicting par-ties compare the value of the proposed solution to two other images: their own needs and interests, and the value of the status quo (their security point or reservation price) (Raiffa, Richardson, and Metcalfe, 2002). One could say that the mutually hurting stalemate occurred in both failed hostage situations analyzed by Deborah Goodwin ("Two Hostage Negotiations," in this book), but they produced no search for an MEO.

Three types of conflict or problem situations exist, each posing different types of challenges to the search for an MEO. The typology is based on the nature or presence of a salient solution, that is, an existing, prominent idea for a solution that predominates in the discourse about the conflict. The types are conflicts with a single salient solution, conflicts with two (or more) salient solutions, and those with no salient solutions.

Curiously, conflicts with a single salient solution are frequent, if not the most frequent type. In many conflicts, the solution is generally agreed on by the parties and analyst, and the problem is getting there. It is not to say that there are not other conceivable and even publicly mooted ideas, but they have generally been rejected, for practical or logical reasons; they may even reemerge at another time, but for the moment, general opinion on both sides regards them as the idea to attain or the idea to beat. Arriving at a salient solution involves trust, in a distrustful atmosphere. The challenge to negotia-tors seeking an MEO is to establish mechanisms of trust, allocation of costs and benefits, terms of trade, and a shared sense of justice — common elements in a formula. Single-solution conflicts take the familiar form of a Prisoners' Dilemma Game (PDG), where mistrust of the other side prevents both par-ties from achieving the solution of common benefit (even if not total satisfac-tion) — a Nash point — leaving them in a mutually hurting stalemate — a Nash solution or equilibrium — and posing a cooperation problem:

PRISONERS' DILEMMA GAME (PDG)

COLUMN

		Negotiate	Do not Negotiate
ROW	Negotiate	3/3	1/4
	Do not Negotiate	4/1	2/2

The Israeli-Palestine conflict has long — but not always — been a conflict with a single salient solution, in this case, a two-state outcome. The split-the-territory, two-state formula has been the dominant solution from the beginning, posing in UNGA resolution 181 in 1947, although from time to time it has slipped in a two-solution conflict, described below. The mechanics of this failure during a specific round are analyzed by Moty Cristal ("Camp David, 2000," in this volume). For an illustration from cases not covered here, Macedonia's internal ethnic conflict has had a single salient solution since independence in 1991, that is, resolution of ethnic relations through a democratic, not a territorial, solution, and that formula was reaffirmed after the violent second Macedonian crisis of 2001. In Sudan, federation/autonomy has been the single salient solution, discredited through its misused application in 1972–83, and then replaced by the single solution of secession.

Studies of successful negotiations show that the elements of the resolving formula that eventually become an MEO are present from the beginning of the negotiations, "proposed" by the nature of the conflict itself and the demands of the situation, whether they are salient as a solution or not (Zartman, 2005a). This in no way diminishes the skill and perseverance required by the negotiators, and in their absence by the mediators, to put the elements into an attractive form with appropriate details. Potentially resolving elements are present for the picking and assembling; the challenge to negotiators is often to pull the solution out of the conflict and make it salient. Cases completed later, such as the Belgian situation and hostage negotiations, and cases likely to be completed later, such as Cyprus and Palestine, show resolving elements of a single salient solution to be present from the beginning, even if at the moment of the negotiations they were not more attractive than the status quo, because of their risks and uncertainties compared with the risks and uncertainties of the current situation. The raw material is present for the shaping from the outset and that therefore focuses attention on a double question: is failure explained by the absence of resolving elements from the beginning, or are they present but unenticing for some other reason?

Conflicts with two (or more, even if difficult to portray in a two-dimensional space) salient solutions are those where each party holds out for its own preferred outcome, finding no potential attractiveness in any proposed solution. Although the outcome is the same as in a PDG, as the parties are locked in a stalemate, they prefer it to any conceivable joint outcome, leaving the situation in what Snyder and Diesing (1977:45) have appropriately termed Deadlock Game (DLG), where the Nash point is the Nash solution:

DEADLOCK GAME (DLG)

	COLUMN	
	Negotiate	Do not Negotiate
ROW Negotiate	2/2	1/4
Do not Negotiate	4/1	3/3

In a two-solution situation, negotiators seeking a joint outcome — and hence also mediators — have a complex and difficult challenge. They must reduce the attractiveness of a deadlock by increasing its pain, turning it into an MHS, and they must devise a potential joint outcome that is both salient and attractive enough to constitute an MEO — all while both parties are exerting their utmost to make their preferred solution prevail.

Such situations abound, notably in Nagorno-Karabagh, Kosovo, Western Sahara, and Kashmir. The examples suffice to show that other and even potentially attractive solutions are not absent in a two-solution conflict; they simply are not salient: that is, they have not grabbed the stage. The illustrations all show that although single salient solutions may have existed in the past, they have been overshadowed by double solutions because they have been worn out, tried and failed, or otherwise been discredited or delegitimized. Autonomy might be the single solution for Nagorno-Karabagh, but it was discredited by misuse under the Soviets (even though an MHS existed in 1994 enough to bring the parties to a durable cease-fire, but not to a solution). A somewhat similar situation existed in Kosovo, where there is simply no conceivable intermediate solution between independence and domination by Serbia, and where the middle solution of autonomy has been tried and abused in the past. Again, in the case of Cyprus, the existence of two Nash equilibria at a Greek state (as in the republic of Cyprus) or a separate Turkish state (as in the Turkish Republic of Northern Cyprus) prevent any acceptable formulation of a conceivable solution in a bi-communitarian state, as seen in the case study by Raymond Saner ("The Cyprus Conflict," in this book). Similarly, the crest of sovereignty divides any Indian and Pakistani and any Moroccan and Algerian solution to Kashmir and the Sahara, respectively, whatever the details of the arrangement, although the latter conflict has found a logically combined solution in an autonomy status under Moroccan sovereignty ("Morocco gets the outside of the box, all Sahrawis get the inside of the box"), currently still rejected by Algeria.

The two sets of examples also show that single salient solutions, if discredited or unpursued, can give way to the dual solution problem. The autonomy solution in Sudan was abused and discredited in 1972–83, leaving the parties — particularly the South — wary of it ever again. Hence the 2005 agreements provide autonomy/federation as a trial period, not a final solution. Again, in Palestine, after the failure to implement the 1993 Oslo Accords, with their inherent promise of a two-state solution, public opinion in both parties began to fall back on the two salient solutions previously held — an all-Israeli versus an all-Arab Palestine.

The third situation is one where there is no salient solution, but only a blank where there should be ideas for ending the conflict, amid no strong proposals from the parties themselves. (Such a situation, though common, is hard to matricize.) Typically, the status quo is an S5 situation, unattractive to either side but not impellingly painful. No-solution situations are challenging for negotiators and mediators, although perhaps not as strongly as dual-solution situations. Like the dual-solution situations, they require creative ideas for a positive outcome, along with pressure to turn the status quo into an MHS, either by providing the objective ingredients or by sharpening the subjective perception. They do not need to combat salient positions on the part of the parties, however.

Situations with no salient solution abound, although they are often marked by characteristic ambiguity. The aftermath of the Framework Convention of Climate Change (FCCC) before and even after the Kyoto Protocol is an example; no outcome, not even the protocol, was a very satisfactory or meaningful solution to the problem, and the opponents of Kyoto, notably the United States, had no countersolution to propose. Similarly, the situation in the UN Security Council constituted a typical S5 situation, where progress was blocked but no one (except the Iraqi people) was hurting; no solution was envisaged, just continuity, until the United States and UK pressed for action. The situation of the Biological Weapons Convention can also be considered an example. In fact, on a more proximate level than that of "final solutions," many conflicts that appear to contain dual solutions are really no-solution situations; the two share the absence of an MHS and of a clearly indicated joint outcome. Thus, while Cyprus and Palestine are marked by two clear and opposing solutions held by the parties — Greek unity versus Turkish division, and a one-state Israeli versus Palestine solution, respectively — the current status has long been one of a stable, self-serving situation made bearable by comparison to the threat of the other's demands, in both cases. There was no single salient solution in the hostage case, but worse yet, no one sought one. Formulas could have been devised since such do exist in negotiations with terrorists, but the two sides did not agree on the subject of their bargaining, nor did they try to find any Enticing Opportunities for a solution (Faure and Zartman, 2010). In such cases, the problem is not how to get there, as in the case of the single salient solution, but where to get, and how to make the current stalemate less soft, stable, and self-serving, and more mutually painful.

Therefore negotiations, and especially mediation, work on both sides of the equation, keeping the supply of violence and other elements in the MHS under control in internal conflicts on one side and seeking to tailor demands to meet the amount of concessions acceptable to constitute an MEO on the other side, and in keeping the pressure on all parties of the problem to be resolved as part of the MHS in cooperative conflicts compared with the costs and benefits unequally available to all to make for an MEO. As in any negotiation, there is no telling where the lines will cross; parties and mediators alike make their estimates of the firmness and softness of demands and supplies on either side (Bueno de Mesquita and Lalman, 1992; Mason, Weingarten, and Fett, 1999; Raiffa, Richardson, and Metcalfe, 2002). If the mediators can show how continued or renewed violence would lose a party international respect and support, the violence can be kept at the threat level in case of failure rather than at the actual level during negotiations. Similarly, if the parties in cooperative negotiations can show how continued resort to unilateral measures would offend the other without resolving the problem, single-shooting (the opposite of free riding) can be kept at the threat level in the negotiations. If parties start out with already less than total demands as initial positions — total replacement of the government, total disbanding of the rebels, secession and independence, total state unity and integration, total solution to the problem, total acceptance of a regime or resolution as written, and so forth — it is easier to effectuate further softening than if demands are absolute, as the Cyprus, Camp David, and hostage cases illustrate (Pillar, 1983; Stedman, 2000). The preexistence of bargaining zones is not a requirement for negotiations, as the cases show; the job of negotiators is to create a zone of agreement where none exists, and then to draw the parties within the zone to a resolving and enticing outcome.

This challenge is generally beyond the grasp of mere bargaining or concession–convergence behavior, constituting zero-sum reductions of demands on a single item until a midpoint agreement is reached. Of the three types of negotiation, it takes at least compensation, the introduction of additional items of trade, and construction, the reframing of issues to meet both sides' needs, to produce the positive-sum outcome that constitutes an MEO. As usual, in line with prospect theory (Farnham, 1994), promises of inducements work less well than threats of losses, as the Cyprus, Israeli, bioweapons, and hostage cases unfortunately show. It was this inequation that was the basis of the failure in proposed trade-offs between the EU and Iran, as shown in the chapter in this book by Anthony Wanis-St. John ("Nuclear Negotiations"). Where development was part of the original formula, even though unattained, it may be used as an enticing prospect, since dropping it would mean a loss, but in general, aid packages and other inducements come into the negotiations only in adjunct with negative pressures and are not as widely used or effective as sanctions (including their threat). The tension between the effectiveness of implied losses and the need for positive compensations and constructions to produce an MEO underscores the narrow field of play open to those who would prepare an attractive resolving formula, and deserves further investigation.

REASONS FOR FAILURE

If the ingredients of a resolving formula and an MEO, and the process by which they are obtained are identified, we can surmise why they were not achieved in cases of failure. The present cases show both internal and external reasons that are evident only when the process itself is examined: failure of the parties to be receptive to a resolving formula that would entice the parties to agreement, failure of the parties to be able to make a decision, and failure of third parties within or outside the protagonist group to pursue their efforts.

One reason is that the parties may not have pursued the process through its necessary stages together. They may have failed to diagnose thoroughly, not only leaving unexplored their own positions and precedents, separating interests from positions, but also failing to understand the interests and precedents of the other side. As a result, they may have failed to establish and identify a zone of possible agreement (ZOPA) out of the competing demands, tailored to overlap. They may have neglected even to search for a joint formula for agreement, identified as a common definition of the problem and its solution, a shared sense of justice to cover results, or agreed terms of trade. They may have sought to win back on the details what they gave up in the formula, to the negation of the formula on which they had agreed. All of these apply, in various pieces, to the cases in the first part of this book.

Another cause is that the MHS that brought the parties into negotiation may not have been sustained throughout the negotiations. The MHS may have been weakly perceived at the beginning; a party may indeed estimate that a unilateral solution is attainable, that is, it feels no MHS that impels it even to engage sincerely in negotiation, taking part only because — for some reason of international politics such as pressure or prestige — it has to. This was the case among several parties in regard to Belgium in the 1830s or Cyprus in 2003, and in a broader, softer situation, in regard to the Biological Weapons Convention negotiations where the weapon is now little used and the status quo is comfortable. Or the initial MHS may weaken during negotiations. This was clearly the case in Cyprus in 2005, when the Republic (of southern Cyprus) was admitted to the EU. An MHS, it must be remembered, is a perceptional condition, and the perceptions can grow cloudy, especially if the parties are not reminded to keep their perceptions clear. But threats and coercion, through necessary reminders, can have the opposite effect. In addition, in many such cases, external support kept the status quo alive, enabling the holdouts to continue the conflict and not feel the pain in doing so.

Third, the negotiation process may fail when parties are resistant to any efforts to find an MEO or resolving formula, again for several reasons. In situations where a single salient solution is already available, they may not have found adequate mechanisms to overcome their characteristic distrust or devised ways to reach the visible but elusive promised land, as in the

Israel-Palestine dispute. In situations where salient solutions are either dual or absent, the negotiators or mediator may have lacked the creativity to devise a solution out of the already available elements of the problem that could become salient, as in the hostage or Iran cases. Or the parties may be unenticeable into a resolving formula; each may feel a priori that its own unilateral solution is the only acceptable one. Such a solution need not be attainable. Rebels and governments alike can be spoilers, interested only in winning but unable to escalate to victory, or they may be principled negotiators holding out for justice over peace (Zartman and Kremenyuk, 2005).

Spoilers or not, negotiators may fail to agree because they faced no formula that constituted an MEO in comparison to the status quo (the other side of the previous reason for failure). For some, the status quo of conflict is always preferable to the terms offered or conceivable, and the stalemate in which they found themselves is an S5 situation, without any pain that they could not absorb. In Israel/Palestine in 2000, comfort in the status quo led one or both parties to reject the given formula (or its details); as in many — perhaps all — cases this perception was not one of finding eventual victory but fear of eventual defeat through the terms offered. Even before they could get to the delicate details, objectively good and fair formulas for resolution, such as federation/ autonomy in Cyprus, were rejected by one of the parties in favor of continued conflict that did not hurt the leadership too badly (although it hurt the population mightily).

A fourth reason is that parties may fail because failure is anticipated and so they prepare for it, making it a self-proving hypothesis. Up to some point, negotiators naturally keep two tracks of action alive, hedge their bets, and prepare for failure and the resumption of conflict. Only when the proposed formulas begin to look like they might constitute an MEO do they gradually drop alternative plans and fully commit to the joint solution (Zartman, 1989). Some negotiating encounters are "organized to fail," in the phrase addressed to the Rambouillet conference on Kosovo in 1999, and also applicable to Camp David II the same year and the UN Iraq negotiations in 2003. The experiment must be tried, against all hope and expectations, and the parties are so concerned about being blamed for its failure that they take all measures to prepare for it.

An entirely different element that prevents perception of a resolving formula, let alone an MEO, is the absence of a coherent organization with a sense of goals and an ability to achieve consensus and make decisions about them within the parties — the absence of a Valid Spokesman that is often associated with ripeness (Zartman, 1989). This problem can take several related forms. In some instances, a party is merely a congeries of bandits and marauders with no clear idea of their political goals and no central organization to pursue them. This was the case of Mozambique up to 1989 (Msabaha, 1995). In others, the closer negotiations get to an agreement, the more they pose a challenge to individual leaders to break away from the main group, form their own organizations, and sprint to capture a piece of the goal on their own. Similarly, a government or a multiparty coalition is often so weak and fractured that it cannot perceive and seize an enticing opportunity, as in Cyprus.

Finally, external to the parties but crucial to the process, the mediation efforts are often insufficient. Too frequently, mediators lack persistence, are satisfied (and exhausted) with superficial agreements and merely agreeing formulas, neglect substantive demands and fail to pursue procedural details, and are loath to provide incentives and sanctions to keep the parties on track, and make the status quo uncomfortable and the temptation to return to violence unattractive. Such insufficiencies are easy to understand, even if not to approve; after all, it's not their conflict, whatever their interests in a positive outcome, and their ministrations are not particularly welcomed by the parties. Cyprus and Camp David were examples of flabby mediation, compared with the firm efforts expended elsewhere.

MHSs and MEOs make for successful and durable agreements because they resolve problems and start parties on the road of cooperation. The elements of resolving formulas and enticing opportunities are generally present at the beginning of negotiations, although they need tinkering and tailoring, and persistence and pressure, to constitute the salient solution for a final agreement. They also need to be supported by external incentives to stay on track and external constraints not to stray off track in comparison with the status quo of the conflict or problem. These are process elements that are visible only through an examination of the course of interaction between the parties and among the parties and mediators. When they are not present — that is, not provided by the negotiators and mediators — the negotiations fail.

Prolonged Peace Negotiations

The Spoiler's Game

KARIN AGGESTAM

In recent years, we have witnessed several peace negotiations collapsing and peace processes being stalled. The odds of such negotiations failing are especially high in cases of internal conflict. The peace that follows an agreement is often unsatisfactory and marked by continuation of interethnic tensions, lack of order, and eruption of violence. The lack of sustainable peace is illuminated in the body of literature, which conceptualizes peace as temporary and contested, using such terms as "fragile," and "unstable," which reflect the acute problem of durability.

The notion of liberal democratic peace has been widely promoted by the international community and is based on peaceful conflict resolution, protection of human rights and minority rights, political representation, good governance, and rule of law. Hence, many negotiators and mediators have adopted the influential idea of liberal democratic peace as the ultimate goal for peace talks. At the same time, most peace negotiations are highly divisive and uncertain in their outcomes.

Several contemporary conflicts are identity based and draw heavily on historic enmity, hatred, and insecurity, which may trigger basic existential fears of group survival. Peace negotiations tend to be surrounded by a wall of suspicion about the intentions of the adversary. Hence, the negotiation process is frequently framed as a zero-sum game and major risk-taking endeavor since concession making involves existential questions. Furthermore, the role of religion as part of identity construction and justification of violence exacerbates the difficulties of conducting peace negotiations based on compromise, as religion is about absolute and particularistic values. Hence, political goals become less visible, and incentives to compromise are limited at best and nonexistent at worst (Kaldor, 2006). Such an existential framing of negotiation combined with an uncertainty about the direction of a peace process feeds mistrust and fear. Moreover, belief perseverance is strengthened if there is a continuation of violence. It proves that the other side has not changed and consequently confirms firmly held images of the enemy. A negotiation process by itself may therefore challenge the adversaries' sense of understanding "self" and "other." As Richmond (2006a:59) rightly points out, a compromise solution to conflict is not necessarily viewed by the adversaries as the optimal rational outcome of a peace process. Compromise may be very difficult to achieve, and there is an overwhelming risk that the negotiations will end in failure. At the same time, parties may continue their participation in a peace process because of certain resources that the process may generate, even though they do not share the sort of outcome that the international community or third parties visualize. This is one of several reasons why many of the contemporary peace processes become prolonged and extended over time. Peace negotiations become a continuation of the conflict by other means while avoiding the costs of warfare (Richmond, 2006a:59, 72).

This chapter highlights some of the contextual dynamics of contemporary conflicts, which make compromises and negotiated settlement difficult to achieve. First, what are the major challenges and obstacles of getting to the negotiating table? Second, how are we to understand devious objectives during peace negotiations? Third, what is the likelihood of spoiling activities during peace negotiations and in the post-agreement phase? As we have seen, many peace negotiations are frequently accompanied by violence and spoiling activities since the negotiations tend to challenge well-established assumptions of who is a patriot and who is a traitor. Spoiling may also be triggered by the fact that some groups have been excluded from the negotiation process. In recent years, the notion of spoiling has received increasing attention as several peace processes have collapsed. Stephen Stedman (1997) introduced the notion of spoilers, but in academia it is still a relatively unexplored area (Newman and Richmond, 2006; Darby, 2001; Mac Ginty, 2006b). Spoiling activities may be defined either in a more narrow understanding by focusing on spoiler groups outside the peace process who actively and with violent means attempt to derail a peace process. Spoiling may also be understood

more broadly by including actors inside as well as outside the peace negotiations who attempt to spoil peace negotiations. However, as Robert Mac Ginty
(2006a) underlines, there may be times when spoiling is a by-product of other
activities and not necessarily violence. Yet, the outcome may thwart or complicate the negotiations. This chapter will primarily focus on an insider perspective, that is, the objectives and behavior of the negotiating parties. These
objectives are context-dependent and thus primarily framed and guided by
situational rationality. Hence, empirical examples, particularly drawing on the
Middle East peace process, will be used to illustrate the theoretical argumen-
tation. The chapter concludes by identifying and elaborating on areas where
more research is required.

THE PROBLEM OF GETTING TO THE TABLE

As mentioned above, many contemporary conflicts are identity based and involve internal conflicts. One major barrier for constructive peace negotiations
relates to the asymmetry between the disputants, which has consequences
concerning power relations, status, inclusion, and the diplomatic rules of diplomacy and negotiation. Moreover, these aspects have repercussions for the
willingness and motivation to negotiate in good faith as well as for the potential likelihood of spoiling activities.

Persistence of Unilateral Strategies

William Zartman's seminal work (1989) on ripeness in conflict has been an
important contribution and inspiration for other scholars to enhance negotiation theory (Aggestam, 2006; Hampson, 1996; Pruitt, 1997b). Zartman (1995a)
labels such a ripe moment as a mutually hurting stalemate in which the parties
are trapped in a painful situation while not being able to unilaterally move
away from destructive and escalating circumstances. Yet, as he points out, such
a moment is less likely to arise in internal conflicts due to gross power inequalities among the disputants in economic, political, and military spheres.
The power asymmetry makes unilateral actions more probable, as the stronger
parties most often have other alternatives to a negotiating process. Hence, the
incentives to compromise are lower and spoiling activities, which may undermine the negotiations, are more probable since some parties may have a strong
Best Alternative to a Negotiated Agreement (BATNA). For example, one of the

major hurdles to overcome since the outbreak of the al-Aqsa intifada is Israel's preferred strategy of unilateralism and disengagement from the Palestinians, such as the territorial withdrawal from the Gaza Strip in 2005 and the military actions taken against the Hamas regime since 2007. Most Israeli governments have not been inclined to view the Palestinian Authority as a fully fledged and reliable negotiating partner.

Increasing symmetrical relations that enhance interdependence may therefore create windows of opportunity for negotiations. The start of the Sri Lankan peace process in the mid-1990s is a case in point. The Liberation Tigers of Tamil Eelam (LTTE) had at that time transformed from a relatively small guerrilla group to a powerful actor who now firmly held military, political, and administrative control over the northern parts of Sri Lanka. With widespread war weariness among the general public, a People's Alliance (PA) was formed, which won the parliamentary elections in 1994 on a platform that included a promise to negotiate peace with the LTTE. Another crucial factor for the success in initiating peace negotiations was the inclusive nature of the PA. Political parties that represented the minorities of Sri Lanka also supported the alliance. As a consequence, Sinhalese extremists were to a large extent marginalized (Höglund, 2004:156–57).

Struggle for Recognition

Many conflicts involve state and non–state actors, which demonstrates the problem of legal asymmetry and the importance attached to international legitimacy. Stronger parties, such as states, draw upon authority, legitimacy, sovereignty, and institutionalized alliances, whereas weaker and rebellious groups lack these large-scale resources. Their power and mobilization derive from ethnic, ideological, and nationalist sources combined with strongly held commitment to resist domination, exclusion, and dispossession of land (Zartman, 1995a:10). Hence, peace negotiations may be stalled because recognition needs to be resolved before any meaningful progress can be made in the negotiation process. As Oliver Richmond (2006a:68) underlines, non–state actors fight for their lack of recognized status while governments reject claims for proto-political status. Moreover, the question of leadership — that is, who is to be considered a valid spokesperson and a legitimate leader of a non–state actor — is frequently difficult to resolve. King emphasizes that "[o]vercoming the asymmetry of status is often a major goal of insurgent groups and can represent an important step on the road to a negotiated settlement" (1997:48). Yet, one side withholds recognition either as a way to undermine the other side's position or simply because it does not benefit its own long-term interests. These kinds of dynamics frequently trigger spoiling behavior. In the Israeli-Palestinian case, this was one critical factor for the constant deadlocks that characterized the start of the peace process in the early 1990s. The Palestine Liberation Organization (PLO) struggled for many years to gain international recognition as the legitimate representatives of the Palestinian people. Initially and officially, however, it was not part of the process since the Israeli government viewed the PLO as a terrorist organization and tried to locate an alternative Palestinian leadership. Hence, the greatest achievement for the Palestinians of the secret negotiations in Oslo 1993 was the mutual recognition between the PLO and the Israeli government.

Dynamics of Inclusion and Exclusion

Linked to the struggle for recognition and international legitimacy is the setup of the parameters of the negotiation process. As peace negotiations often revolve around thorny issues of security, territory, sovereignty, and self-determination, they are inclined to be elite based. There are several good reasons to limit the number of negotiating partners and why it may be necessary to resort to more discreet negotiations as a way to avoid negative side effects of media exposure (Aggestam, 2004). A complex transition from conflict to cooperation requires a fine balancing act of politics and negotiation. It is not an easy task for political leaders to transform their rhetoric of war to one of negotiation and compromise. As a consequence, many political leaders are often accused of cowardice and treachery when they change paths from war to peace. This is the reason why secret peace negotiations may be sought at times to avoid arousing public anxiety, despite the fact that secrecy is seen as democratically offensive. Out of fear, political leaders may talk peace in private but advocate war in public (Stedman, 1996:350). For instance, Yasir Arafat was frequently accused while negotiating with Israel of speaking with two tongues, one in Arabic calling for Jihad (interpreted by the Israeli government as terrorism), and one in English calling for "peace of the brave" (referring to peace with Israel).

The sheer fact of being excluded from the negotiations may generate opposition. If the negotiations are framed among a wider public as elitist, exclusive, and unjust, the negotiation process may be exposed to spoiling behavior and thus jeopardize concession making. Hence, limiting the number of parties to the process involves difficult trade-offs in public support and mobilization for peace, which may have consequences for the implementation of a peace agreement. Hence, there is a growing recognition of the necessity to have most of the warring parties represented at the negotiation table (Hampson, 1996). John Darby (2001:118, 119) argues for a "sufficient inclusion," which includes those with the power to bring the peace process down by violence, such as militant organizations. The principle of "sufficient consensus" was, for instance, adopted in South Africa as a way to promote efficient negotiations and to avoid a situation in which all participants had veto power. Also, in the Northern Ireland peace process, the intentional inclusion of veto holders was adopted. It was recognized that one important reason why all previous peace initiatives had failed was precisely the exclusion of powerful veto holders. Hence, "opportunities for spoiling activities were drastically reduced" (Mac Ginty, 2006a:153).

Disputed Parameters of Negotiation

Another consequence of asymmetrical conflicts among state and non–state actors are the contested rules about de-escalation and negotiation. The diplomatic rules tend to be vague, imprecise, and at times nonexistent. Moreover, the power asymmetry by itself often prevents the development of a just negotiation process. Spoiling behavior may therefore be a way of expressing resistance to what is assumed to be an unjust negotiation process. Theoretically, justice is implemented when the parties comply freely and rationally with the contents of an agreement (Albin, 1999:255–67). Yet, in asymmetrical negotiations the stronger party is inclined to stipulate the rules of the negotiations and impose conditions of an agreement. As a result, there will always be some groups who may continue with violent opposition and attempt to prevent a negotiation process from starting. In the Middle East peace process, this has precisely been the case where various Palestinian groups constantly have complained that Israel, with support from the United States, dictates the principles and rules of engagement. After the failure of the Camp David summit in July 2000, the Palestinian side complained that the Israeli negotiators had not shown enough sincerity by refusing to establish shared basic parameters of a permanent status agreement. A strategy of the weaker party may therefore be to withhold an agreement that is desired by the stronger party as a way of balancing the asymmetry of power (Habeeb, 1988). This may for instance be one of several reasons why PLO chair Yasir Arafat refused to accept the Israeli prime minister's proposal on how to "end the conflict" during the Camp David summit.

DEVIOUS OBJECTIVES AND THE PROBLEM OF
GOOD FAITH PEACE NEGOTIATIONS

Many peace negotiations are initiated after heavy international pressures are exerted on the disputants. A major challenge is therefore how to establish good faith negotiations, which are based on the commitment, good intentions, and willingness of the parties to reach a mutually satisfying agreement that will be honored. Even though the phrase "negotiating in good faith" is frequently mentioned, it is difficult to distinguish any specific definition of the term. It is often equated with the notion of trust and willingness to negotiate, which are essential prerequisites in any working relationship between negotiators. For instance, the constructive working relationship between the British and Irish governments in the early 1990s was based on a shared interest to facilitate a settlement that would attract support from the majority in each community. This was critical for the success of the peace process as well as a way to delegitimize political violence (Mac Ginty, 2006a:155).

According to Pruitt (1997b:239), cooperative behavior is motivated by a desire to achieve mutual cooperation as well as optimism about the other parties' willingness to reciprocate positively. It is closely associated with the basic assumptions held in a problem-solving and integrative approach to negotiation. Such an approach focuses on a readiness and flexibility to make concessions as well as a willingness to enroll in a joint search for a formula that will facilitate long-term exchange between the parties. In short, willingness to negotiate in good faith expresses an intention as well as an expectation that the other side will reciprocate to do "what is right" (Hoffman, 2002:379).

Competitive Negotiations

Terrence Hopmann has written, "the dilemma of traditional [competitive] bargaining is that the contradiction between cooperative and conflictual tactics may make the negotiation process somewhat schizophrenic, alternating between cooperative moves and conflictual ones. Deceit and manipulative behaviour may serve one's short-term or individual interest, but it often detracts from the long-run collective interest in reaching an agreement" (1996:72).

Competitive negotiations are the prevailing mode of negotiation in peace processes involving reluctant parties. Furthermore, the dynamics of competitive negotiations may increase the likelihood of spoiling activities. The key component in competitive negotiations is power, where persuasion, compromise, and the threat of force are combined. The dynamics of such a strategy lies in escalation and negotiation. So-called red lines are drawn to signal a resistance point where an agreement becomes unacceptable as well as to signal that no further concessions will be possible (Schelling, 1960). By the use of manipulation, using either sticks (punishment and threat of force) or carrots (rewards), one side may try to change the payoff structure of the negotiations and the preferences of the opponent in order to get desired concessions and move toward an agreement.

> It is the *threat* of damage, or of more damage to come, that can make someone yield or comply. It is *latent* violence that can influence someone's choice — violence that can still be withheld or inflicted, or that a victim believes can be withheld or inflicted. (Schelling, 1966:3)

A competitive strategy emphasizes self-interest, autonomy, and strategic choice in a negotiation process, and the main focus is on the advancement of one side's interests relative to those of the opponent. Accordingly, goals and interests are frequently framed as incompatible, which may result in distrust and obstruct candor and flexibility about preferences and interests (Hopmann, 1995).

The use of threats and escalation is a high-risk strategy. The parties may keep on escalating in the hope that the other side will give in. At the same time, they may find themselves unable to escape escalation. As a consequence, they are likely to end up in a "competitive irrationality" in terms of possible outcomes, such as war (Zartman and Faure, 2005a:10). For instance, the recent outbreak of hostilities in the Middle East has invariably been accompanied by feverish diplomatic activity. Since the breakdown of the Camp David summit in the summer of 2000 and subsequently the peace process, Israelis and Palestinians have been locked in a dangerous violent escalation in which each party tries to get the other side to yield and back down.

Devious Objectives and Side Effects

What characterizes many peace negotiations is precisely the lack of trust, motivation, and optimism that is the essence of good faith negotiations. The parties may instead hold devious objectives and accept negotiations for reasons other than reaching a peace agreement (Richmond, 1998). Fred Iklé (1964) underlined in his seminal work on how nations negotiate the fact that parties frequently negotiate for side effects rather than trying to reach an agreement. Paul Pillar (1983), in his study on war termination, also stresses that peace negotiations frequently are used for a variety of reasons other than successfully concluding a peace accord. A negotiation process might open up new opportunities for improving relations with third parties, acquiring intelligence, or gaining international prestige, publicity, and attention. As Pillar (1983:51–52) underscores, a negotiation process might be a way of extending combat in a nonviolent form by bringing some of the rules of combat into the negotiations, such as attrition of the enemy's strength and sapping of its morale. A temporary pause in the war by the conduct of negotiations may provide time to rearm, alter the balance of strength by new alliances, and boost domestic as well as international support for the preparation for the use of force. For instance, a common Israeli version and explanation to the outbreak of the al-Aqsa intifada in the autumn of 2000 is that the Palestinians simply used the peace process as a way to gain time to rearm and mobilize for a continuation of the conflict. Arafat, by his actions and nonactions during the Camp David summit and his reluctance to confront terror groups such as Hamas and Islamic Jihad, according to this Israeli narrative, revealed the Palestinian leader's "true" intention, which was not to negotiate in good faith but to continue the armed struggle indefinitely. In contrast, a Palestinian version often emphasizes how the Israeli government used the negotiations as a way to consolidate and expand its power and hegemony in the region as well as its control over Jerusalem and the occupied territories by the expansion of Jewish settlements.

As mentioned above, many peace negotiations may potentially turn into new battlegrounds and sites for contestation, aiming to achieve recognition and international legitimacy rather than compromise and conflict resolution. Hence, the parties may value peace negotiations for certain resources whereas "the assumption of a compromise is so often of only secondary concern" (Richmond, 2006a:66). In such circumstances, international mediation may, for example, be used as a strategy to legitimize the parties' negotiation positions and status. Again, the Israeli-Palestinian negotiations in the 1990s may be used as an empirical illustration of how a peace process may be prolonged by active mediation despite the increasing mistrust between the negotiating parties. To keep the negotiations on track, the American mediators acted as bridge builders by resorting to the diplomatic practice of "constructive ambiguity." Deadlocks were thus temporarily resolved by postponing detailed interpretations until the implementation phase. The underlying rationale was that the parties would become committed to a signed agreement following the diplomatic principle of *pacta sunt servanda*. However, as this case illustrates, these unresolved ambiguities reappeared later in the negotiation process, when the agreement should be interpreted and implemented. Consequently, the parties became trapped in an endless game of negotiations concerning interpreting previous agreements, starting with the Declaration of Principles in 1993 followed by another four agreements and ending with the Sharm Al-Sheikh Agreement in 1999. International mediation might also be accepted as a way of preventing any breakthrough in the negotiations and to avoid costly concessions. For example, Yitzhak Shamir, the Israeli prime minister, who accepted the invitation of the United States to attend the Madrid peace conference in 1991, admitted after having lost the elections in 1992 that his decision to accept the invitation was primarily made to avoid American pressure while resisting any compromise. His intention was to prolong the negotiation process indefinitely while settling "half a million [Jewish] people in Judea and Samaria [the West Bank]" (Zittrain and Caplan, 1998:81). This misuse of mediation is why Stephen Stedman warns that intervention "should not be offered like buses that come along every fifteen minutes" (1996:363).

In sum, devious objectives and competitive negotiations increase the likelihood of prolonged negotiations and risk ending up in failure as insecurity, fear of deception, and mistrust become recurrent characteristics of the negotiation process. At the same time it is difficult to determine beforehand what are calculated efforts to torpedo the negotiation process from consequential action emanating from competitive strategies. One person might view him- or herself as a tough negotiator but with honest intentions while the other side perceives the actions of the opponent as intentional deception. This is what is commonly referred to in international negotiation as the "problem of credibility" (Jönsson, 1990:79–87).

THE PROBLEM WITH SUSTAINABLE
PEACE AGREEMENT

Anthony Wanis-St. John has noted, "Peace negotiations, even when they result in agreement, may not definitively resolve the underlying conflict issues and, worse still, they may not mark an end to the violence. The outcome of a peace process therefore is not necessarily peace, even if the principal parties sign a peace agreement before applauding global leaders and gratified mediators. Despite all our knowledge and experience with structuring the substance and process of peace negotiations, they resist predictability" (2008:1).

The challenges of implementing a sustainable peace are manifold. The statistical records are also discouraging when it comes to the adherence to signed peace agreements, as alternations between negotiations and violence frequently continue (Stedman, Rothchild, and Cousens, 2002). Hence, several peace processes are prolonged, at times indefinitely, such as in Bosnia-Herzegovina, and resisted because peace agreements have in some cases been imposed. In other cases the negotiating parties have held devious objectives. The precarious transition from war to peace and the immense problem of implementing peace agreements have triggered a number of interesting academic studies in recent years (Mac Ginty, 2006a; Richmond, 2006a; Stedman, 2003).

Uncertainty about the End Game

The transition from war to peace is full of risks and uncertainties. It entails a transition of turning warriors into peacemakers and transforming a culture of violence to one of negotiation. Insecurity usually continues to be a major concern among the parties in the post-agreement phase as well, and becomes particularly troublesome if it is accompanied with violence. As John Darby (2001:52–53) underlines, any violence during peace negotiations may be interpreted as a confirmation that the transition has failed. This is further exacerbated if the political leaders hold devious objectives and are evasive in public about the direction and endgame of the peace process. This is one of the major criticisms of the Middle East peace process in the 1990s and the reason why the Quartet launched the "road map" for peace between Israelis and Palestinians based on the notion of a two-state solution in 2001.

Veto Holders

As Andrew Kydd and Barbara Walter underline, "extremists are surprisingly successful in bringing down peace processes if they so desire" (2002:264). For instance, only 25 percent of signed peace accords in civil wars between 1988 and 1998 were implemented, due to violence taking place during negotiations. Without any violence, 60 percent of the peace agreements were implemented (Kydd and Walter, 2002:264). As a consequence, these groups who attempt to spoil the peace process become veto holders (Darby, 2001:118). Their power also increases when political leaders with dubious objectives publicly declare they will not negotiate and make concessions under fire. As discussed above, in competitive negotiations, pursuing peace talks while violence continues signals weakness to the other side. Yet, in practice the negotiating parties become hostages to these groups who use violence to determine the pace and direction of the peace process. This is well illustrated in a comparison between the different negotiation styles of the Israeli leaders Yitzhak Rabin and Ariel Sharon. Early on, the peace process in the 1990s was beleaguered by terrorist attacks, and yet Rabin declared after every attack in Israel by Hamas and Islamic Jihad that to stop the peace process would be to give in to terror and extremism. Sharon, on the other hand, argued consistently as a prime minister that he refused to deal with the Palestinian leadership as long as the violence continued, which partly explains why every attempt at de-escalation failed.

Hence, a major challenge is how to manage spoiler groups, which is an expanding area of research, particularly concerning the role and contribution of international custodians (Stedman, 2003). As Marie-Joëlle Zahar (2006:41) underlines, peace implementation is a highly political act and not simply a technical matter. The development of loyalty and a genuine commitment by the parties to the peace process is critical for achieving a sustainable peace. If that is lacking, there is a need for international custodians. Custodians are international actors overseeing implementation of negotiated peace agreements and have been used in many instances, such as in Cambodia by the United Nations and in the Northern Ireland peace process by the United Kingdom and Ireland acting as internal custodians. In the latter process, an Independent Monitoring Commission was set up to adjudicate breaches and recommend appropriate penalties (Mac Ginty, 2006a:167). At the same time, the presence of international custodians, such as the European Union in the Western Balkans, is one reason why peace processes may go on indefinitely. More research is therefore needed to elaborate on the problem of exit by international actors in peace processes.

Detached Peace Constituencies

The presence and engagement of peace constituencies is critically important to any sustainable peace agreement. However, as Wanis-St. John (2008:3) underlines, we need much more systematic studies of peace processes that focus on the interrelationship between elites conducting negotiations, parties sidelined by those negotiations, and civil society, as well as the dynamic engagement of the international community. Moreover, depending on how active or passive war and peace constituencies are, they will determine the effects of spoiling activities.

Peace negotiations are, as mentioned above, frequently envisaged within a so-called liberal peace framework, and labeling a particular group as a spoiler may thus indicate a political agenda and an extension of the conflict itself (Newman and Richmond, 2006:4–5). Violence under such circumstances may spread fear and uncertainties among a general public about the direction of a negotiation process. Opposition groups may convincingly argue that compromise does not lead to peace, but rather to more violence (rewarding and giving in to violence), which inhibits implementation. Consequently, the negotiation process may run high risk of ending in deadlock or collapse.

CONCLUSION

This chapter has elaborated upon some reasons why peace negotiations may lead to failure and why peace processes are prolonged despite the existence of peace agreements and post-negotiations. Devious objectives and spoiling activities have been discussed in a broad sense and analyzed both as products of the characteristics of contemporary conflicts as well as outcomes of the negotiation dynamics.

Asymmetrical conflict in particular poses a challenge. Three critical barriers to peace negotiations have been identified: persistence of unilateral actions; struggle for recognition and international legitimacy; and contested rules of diplomacy and de-escalation. Despite the fact that the disputants are persuaded to commence peace negotiations, these barriers may continue to plague the peace process if they are unattended. It may be that the parties view the negotiation process as a continuation of the conflict by other means. By being present at the negotiation table, non–state actors gain international legitimacy and recognition. At the same time, the likelihood for deadlocks and a breakdown of negotiations looms large. The fact that parties may seek negotiations primarily for side effects rather than to reach an agreement indicates the presence of devious objectives and the ways these may interact with spoiling behavior. For instance, a party may accept and use a negotiation process primarily as a way to gain time to rearm. Yet, it is difficult to identify the presence of devious objectives beforehand. The dynamics of competitive negotiations, which contain manipulation of power and escalation of threats, may result in competitive irrationality and accidental spoiling behavior (Zartman and Faure, 2005a).

Still, we need to recognize that there may be times when negotiations are not the most conducive form or the appropriate tool for conflict resolution. There tends to be an exaggerated optimism in the international community about the extent to which negotiations may resolve intractable and internal conflicts. Endless negotiations indicate in many cases an unwillingness or lack of support to make the concessions necessary for compromise, as it is not viewed as an optimal outcome by the disputants. Hence, there are times when other alternatives to negotiations ought to be sought in order to de-escalate conflict. As Edward Newman and Oliver Richmond rightly point out: "An important proviso is that it is wrong to assume that all — or even most — conflict situations can be resolved by accommodation or that a peace process is about finding consensus among parties that basically all seek peace" (2006:6).

Furthermore, research is also needed to explore the links between peace negotiations and the implementation phase in order to improve our knowledge about the durability of peace agreements. As we have seen in several peace processes, conflicts are prolonged and continue in the precarious post-agreement phase. Hence, the lack of implementation produces a situation of no war–no peace. There is a need to recognize that peace agreements are often a result of urgency and pragmatism and thus need to be revisited and adapted to the transformed realities in the post-agreement phase. Moreover, the interplay between the existence of insecurity among the general public and the presence of active or passive war and peace constituencies depends to a large extent on how the peace process is perceived and if it includes a sufficient majority of the people.

In sum, the discussion above illuminates how important pre-negotiations are to resolving and clarifying basic issues of recognition, inclusion, and the rules of engagement. Moreover, the objectives and motivation of political leaders are crucial for the success of negotiations and the mobilization for peace. A certain degree of political will and optimism about reaching a negotiated settlement is necessary, as well as readiness to lead such a precarious transition from war to peace. The turbulent and yet so astonishing transition of South Africa illustrates well the importance of combining leadership and political willingness when pursuing conflict resolution. F. W. de Klerk surprised the world by announcing the release of Nelson Mandela and his intention to negotiate in good faith the end of apartheid. Mandela responded with courage by calling for national reconciliation and embracing white leaders with no sign of bitterness (Sisk, 2001:107). Finally, the failure to implement indicates the need of enforcement mechanisms and custodian monitoring of compliance as a way to provide space to revisit and adapt peace agreements. This may decrease fear and insecurity about the overall direction of a peace process and thus prevent its collapse.

Managing Complexity

LAURENT MERMET

Let a researcher open the file of a negotiation that did not lead to agreement and interview participants in that negotiation, and he is likely to be offered too many explanations for comfort rather than too few: interpersonal relations were unusually bad; the politics were intractable; party x or y was just unamenable to reason; small procedural incidents had major effects; the difficulties in the science and the technicalities of the topic being negotiated were too complicated or controversial; and so forth. Each such explanation seems sufficient alone to explain the absence of agreement. Paradoxically, however, since each one seems to do so as well as the next one, the researcher soon gets the impression he has opened Pandora's box and let out a web of complications that expands as he goes on with his interviews. Was the situation, then, or were the issues, just too complex to negotiate? What is the place of complexity in understanding the negotiation processes that did not lead to agreement? The aim of this chapter is to examine this question.

To avoid misunderstandings it is important to note at the outset that complexity per se should not be considered a cause of negotiation failure. Every day, at all scales, many very complex situations are negotiated successfully, whereas many simple situations are not. Of course, part of this chapter will discuss this issue more in depth, but it will then mostly focus on another, more important, connection between complexity and the interpretation of negotiations without agreement. Complexity is a major challenge for the analyst, the researcher, the commentator, who embarks on the task of analyzing a complex negotiation process, as she must find ways to orient herself in a multitude of aspects, factors, and moments, and as she must choose ways to access, select, simplify, and organize information that will necessarily remain partial relative to the complexity of most negotiations. The main argument of the chapter, thus, is twofold. First, when a negotiation reaches agreement, the agreement itself and the process leading to it provide markers and organizers that are essential (even if often implicitly) for the analyst's work. Such markers fail in the case of negotiations that did not lead to agreement. As a result, in the latter, the challenge to the analyst of dealing with the complexity inherent to most negotiations is different, usually more difficult, and has to be taken up on a very different basis. Second, in interpreting complex negotiations, analysts rely heavily (again, partly implicitly) on the activities whereby the negotiators themselves already simplify and order issues, values, possible trade-offs, and so forth, in complex negotiation situations. When a negotiation leads to an agreement, this reliance of the analyst on much of the negotiators' ordering of the situation is much less problematic than when it does not. As will be seen, in the latter case the ordering of the situation by the negotiators themselves has led to an impasse, and it is difficult to decide whether the problem lies in the way the negotiators have ordered the situation (defined issues, laid out values, characterized possible outcomes, etc.) or in the situation itself. As a result, the analyst can only, to a much lesser extent than in successful negotiations, take as the basis for his work the markers of the negotiations that he otherwise freely shares with the negotiators.

So the question of complexity in negotiations that did not lead to an agreement is not one of complexity causing failure but of complexity deeply affecting the analysis of negotiation, the relations between the analyst and the negotiators, and their respective interpretations of the negotiation's process and outcomes.

The question of complexity is important in negotiation research because both practitioners and analysts know that complexity is an intrinsic and fundamental dimension of international, especially multilateral negotiation. As writes I. W. Zartman in the concluding lines of an earlier volume of the PIN series, "if the basic analytical question for any negotiation analysis is How to explain outcomes?, the question is answered for multilateral negotiations in the form of another question: How did/do the parties manage the characteristic complexity of their encounter in order to produce outcomes?" (1994a). The relevance of examining this question afresh in the context of the current volume stems from the fact that it calls for quite a different treatment in the analysis of negotiations that respectively did, and did not, lead to an agreement.

We will start by taking a closer look at the theme of complexity, underscoring that it is a major feature of most negotiations and recalling that negotiations that lead to agreement do often successfully cope with very high levels of complexity indeed. It will clearly appear that negotiation, as a conflict resolution process, rests on specific ways to reduce complex situations to tractable proportions. In the second part of the chapter, we will turn to complexity in the analysis of negotiations that have led to agreement (NLAS). We will try to show that in such cases, the main task of the analyst is to reconnect the comparatively simple outcome of the negotiation with its more complex backgrounds, both by showing how complex issues and situations have gradually been brought to tractability, and by pointing to the potential for difficulties when the agreement will be implemented concretely in situations that the negotiation will probably not have entirely relieved of their complexity. In the third and main part of the chapter, we will then use the insights gained and examine if NANs (no agreement negotiations) raise specific issues in management of complexity by the parties, and in the treatment of such complexity management by the analyst. We will see that complexity per se cannot be considered the cause for a negotiation to fail in not reaching agreement. However, since the analyst cannot use the agreement reached as a central reference for organizing his analysis, he is placed in a very different situation relative to the negotiators, to the issues at stake, and to what is to be explained. As will become clear, there is no easy symmetry between explaining the existence and content of an agreement, and interpreting the absence of an agreement. We will try to show some of the very specific choices that are open for the analyst and the practitioner when debriefing a complex negotiation that did not lead to agreement.

COMPLEXITY: AN IMPORTANT ATTRIBUTE
OF MOST INTERNATIONAL NEGOTIATIONS

In his analysis of complexity in international negotiations, Gilbert Winham (1977) rests first on a definition of complexity as a synonym for complication. In his approach, he follows Simon's analysis of complexity as presenting "a challenge to comprehension because it consists of a large number of parts that interact in a non-simple way" (1969). In this perspective, international negotiations must be regarded as complex because the number of issues and relations involved are such that they exceed the capacity of the participants to compute the consequences of a given move, to clearly understand the strategies of their counterparts, or to precisely assess the value of a given proposal that is put on the table. In Winham's approach, complexity is a psychosocial variable of negotiation: the degree to which the negotiator's computing abilities are challenged. At first glance, one might think that the higher the complexity, the more difficult the task for the negotiators, because it impedes their ability to analyze situations and to make rational decisions. However, based on a study of the Kennedy round of the GATT negotiations, both through interviews of negotiators and a role-playing simulation game, Winham shows that this is not necessarily the case, for three reasons. First, in the middle of so much uncertainty, the negotiators tend to adopt a bias in favor of settlement, for psycho-sociological reasons (group momentum) and to avoid the failure of nonagreement. In Winham's words, "complexity works in favor of reaching agreement because the inherent lack of precision in the material makes it difficult to argue effectively against an agreement" (1977). Second, the complexity at the negotiation scene strengthens the position of the negotiator back home, vis-à-vis the constituents he is representing: because the issues are so intricate, and the negotiator has a better grasp of them, it is more difficult for them not to rely on him. A third effect of complexity shown by Winham is that it pushes parties to adopt simplified logics and goals that may, in some cases (and that did, in the case of the Kennedy round), create a momentum for collective action.

This first approach to complexity, which equates it with complication, puts at the center of the analysis a gap in computing capabilities. Complexity bridges two worlds. In the world of the analyst, consequences of moves can be computed, and rationality as it is understood in decision analysis, or in experimental designs, reigns supreme. The world of the practitioner, on the other end of the bridge, submitted to time constraints, to limited cognitive capabilities, and to the passions of action, is ruled by "limited rationality" (March and Simon, 1958), threatened by "cognitive bias." It could seem then that the analyst would be in a position to give the practitioner rationality lessons. But the limited rationality approach of the 1960s and 1970s ends up turning the tables. Beyond a certain level of complication, the analyst's computing capability is itself overwhelmed. In the case of international negotiations, no analyst possesses a template that could substitute a complete, encompassing rational perspective to the rationalities of the actors of the negotiation themselves. Actors and analyst are both engaged in an exercise of limited rationality. In the developments in negotiation research of the 1980s and 1990s, this is made still more manifest by clearly staging each theoretical approach of negotiation, each research design, as one limited (but hopefully, enlightening) attempt at grasping some aspect, or dimension, of what is at work in negotiations (the books in the PIN series this volume belongs to illustrate quite well this approach).

In this renewed context, complexity appears as a crucial concept, which both legitimates the limited character of any approach of an international negotiation, and still allows grasping its unity. "There is . . . a single activity of multilateral negotiation, and its name is managing complexity. Each analytical approach is a particular answer to the essential question of multilateral analysis and practice alike: How is complexity to be managed?" (Zartman, 1994a:218). Henceforth, however, complexity is no more equated with complication. It is used as the central concept in the important corpus on systems theory (Le Moigne, 1990), complexity (Atlan, 1979; Morin, 2005), chaos (Prigogine, 1984), paradox (Bateson, 2000; Watzlawick, 1994), and soft systems methodology (Checkland, 1989) that had a major impact on the evolution of ideas in the early 1980s.[1] In this perspective, complication is the characteristic of a situation (or system) with numerous heterogeneous elements, connected by numerous relations. It takes large (human or machine) computing capabilities to be tractable. By contrast, a complex situation or system is one that has additional features of ambiguity, incomplete knowledge, controversy, instability, or partially unpredictable behavior: even with large computing capabilities, one cannot reach an unequivocal reading of the situation, and the best actors and analysts can do is propose, discuss, and act on various interpretations.

As soon as one gets beyond the simplest textbook examples of negotiation, such complexity becomes an obvious feature of all real negotiations. In international negotiations, both complication and complexity are usually very high. Taking environmental negotiations as an example, it is often noted that the number and heterogeneity of actors involved, the complications, controversies, uncertainties and instabilities in the science involved, the often inextricable economic consequences of decisions, and so forth confront negotiators with remarkably complex files and situations (Sjöstedt, 1993).

All the more striking is the ability of international negotiation fora to deal with such complex issues as climate change, biodiversity, world trade, and other matters. In examining how they do so, it soon appears that the format of multilateral negotiations provides a combination of resources to bring complexities of all sorts into tractable forms.

- Huge, complex, heterogeneous sets and networks of actors are brought to be represented by a few dozens, a hundred, at most a thousand, people participating in the meetings of parties, subsidiary bodies, and side events of a multilateral convention.

- The immensely complex economic, political, and geographic structures associated with an agenda such as climate change become translated into lists of issues and associated groupings of positions that become the structure of the negotiation itself.

- Negotiation mandates and strategies provide Ariadne threads that, even if complicated at first sight, still remain strikingly simple in view of the labyrinths that they can guide the negotiators through.

- Through negotiation procedures, techniques, and practical know-how, vague, profuse, and contradictory clusters of preoccupations get gradually transformed into the cleanly numbered, ordered, and hierarchized language of texts that may become agreements.

- And if there is agreement, a comparatively simple text — a convention, a protocol — becomes a reference that may then develop its ramifications into the complex contexts of its implementation.

On the whole, negotiation can usefully be viewed, in this discussion, as based on capabilities to format, or translate, complex situations into agreeable language.[2] Examining a multilateral negotiation forum quickly reveals the variety and extent of these capabilities: institutionalized procedures, procedural techniques (drafting parties, negotiation text formats, etc.), and specific expertise of the participants (secretariat staff, delegates, experts, etc.) all contribute to this translation process. It should be noted however, lest one would be considered really too naïve, that the eschewing of the too-difficult, the too-complicated, or the too-controversial, the retaining only of the (sometimes small) potentially negotiable part in the complex mass of the realities under negotiation, is a major and multifaceted part of this capability to deal with the complex!

To summarize, negotiation is the art of translating complex situations into agreeable language. If this is so, complexity per se is no more useful an explanation for the failure to reach agreement than the excessive quantity of rock in a quarry could be considered an explanation for not being able to extract stone from it.

What contribution to the analysis of a negotiation can then be expected from a consideration of its complexity? Let us consider first negotiations that did reach an agreement, and then negotiations that did not.

ANALYZING SUCCESSFUL NEGOTIATION: RE-ROOTING AGREEMENT IN ITS COMPLEX BACKGROUNDS

When negotiations result in an agreement, this demonstrates the tractability of their complex objects and contexts. This practical tractability actually provides the underpinnings for their analytical treatment. In the analysis of a given complex negotiation and its outcome, the challenge facing the analyst overlaps to a certain extent with the challenge that has already been successfully met by the negotiators. Both have to order the potentially innumerable, disconnected, contradictory, badly known factors in the situation: they identify, they list, they word, they choose, they hierarchize. The negotiators turn them into agreeable language. The analyst's aim is to turn her own selection into enlightening language. The links between the two exercises are strong and numerous. Much of the analyst's task is to describe and explain how the negotiators have translated complexity into agreeability; much of the data comes from the narratives volunteered by the negotiators, and thus, on their own ordering and sequencing; the agreement itself, as well as the positions of the negotiators in various phases of the process (and thus, the phases of their ordering), are both the products of practice and major components of the analysis. Of course, lest it be just a paraphrase of the negotiators' narratives, the analysis also has to differ from them in significant ways, in its selection of the factors it considers relevant, in the way it organizes them, and especially in the formalities of the ways it treats them. The various ways to conceive and achieve such a result are the bases for the various disciplines and approaches of negotiation research. But beyond this diversity, there are deep connections between the treatment of complexity by the negotiators and by the analyst. It may be worth noticing, for instance, that major analytical approaches of negotiation tend to correspond to clearly identifiable aspects of the practitioner's experience: organizing her priorities (decision theory), identifying her opponents' priorities and the resulting combinations (game theory), pondering on the resources and constraints offered by the organization hosting or servicing the negotiation (organization theory), grasping the psychological interactions in the negotiation room and corridors (small group theory), trying to find allies for coalitions (coalition theory), and so on.

So in various forms, the work of analysts proposes to extend or to complement the experience and reflection of the negotiator. Apart from the purely scholarly rewards, what added value of research is apt to go beyond the avenues that the negotiators have already opened themselves? In the case of a negotiation that has led to agreement, we would like to propose the following answer: in various forms, the essential contribution of analysis is to bridge the relative simplicity of the agreement and the complexities of the situation before the agreement, and also of the situations in which the agreement is going to be implemented. The importance of such a contribution stems from the risk, underlined by Faure and Zartman in their introduction to this volume, that in successful negotiations, the agreement reached becomes self-explanatory and self-legitimizing to such an extent that it becomes disconnected from the complex realities from which it has emerged, and into which it should develop its effects. We suggest here that it is an essential role of the analyst to reconnect the agreement to those complex realities in relevant and specific ways: (1) Showing how the agreement has emerged from, and is rooted in, the complex, controversial, preexisting situation; (2) recalling some of the aspects of the situation that have been set aside to reach agreement but may be met again in implementation or in further controversies and negotiations; (3) helping people who have not been involved in the negotiation to gain an understanding of the mind-set that has become shared by the negotiators and may, in the context of implementation, provide the bases of a shareable culture of the problem; (4) identifying, by comparing the structure of the problems/situations on the one hand, and the agreement on the other hand, specific difficulties that may be encountered in implementation. Those are just four examples of the roles that analysis may play by re-rooting agreement to its complex backgrounds in ways that are complementary to the reflections of the negotiators themselves.

So we agree with the idea put forward by Faure and Zartman, that the agreement reached polarizes the analysis of a negotiation. But this circularity between the results of practice and the orientation of analysis is not just a negative bias. It is also a fundamental feature of meaningful analysis of a successful negotiation and maybe even, we will venture, of the meaningfulness of negotiation analysis.

This raises, however, major questions for the analysis of negotiations that did not reach agreement, to which we will now turn.

ANALYZING THE ABSENCE OF AGREEMENT: REROUTING INTERPRETATION

Explaining the Absence of Agreement: Complexity Strikes Back

In the absence of agreement, as we suggested in the chapter introduction, explanations tend to proliferate, as if complex aspects of the situation, having failed to be ordered into an agreement, were also challenging the effort of the analyst to order them. The absence of agreement creates a situation that lacks the kind of closure provided by agreement. And since, as we proposed earlier, precisely this closure provides so much leverage for analysis, its absence creates an essential challenge in the analysis of NANs. Notions from gestalt theory can be useful to outline the problem. In psychological and, by extension, social, terms, the absence of agreement creates a situation of "unfinished business" (Perls, 1977 and 1981). In cognitive terms, it characterizes a situation with no clear figure/background differentiation (Guillaume, 1937) to start from for (analytical or practical) post-agreement interpretations. Instead of one gestalt becoming the reference through agreement, we are stuck with multiple gestalts: each negotiator's framings, perceptions, and business; and competing proposals and aborted agreements. As a result the analyst — instead of being able to use the framing and leverage provided by the gestalt underpinning the agreement to actively probe the background for complex aspects to re-root the agreement into, as in NLAS — is confronted with the task of choosing among the innumerable aspects of the complex situation that blur the multiple, imperfect, unfinished figures of unagreed demands and packages. In the case of negotiations without agreement, complexity is no more to be reconstructed at will by the analyst. It is pervasive and has to be handled in a situation that differs profoundly from that created by a NLA.

Faced with overwhelming complexity, the analyst of a NAN has "to find rough ways of 'decomplexifying' to the point where complexity becomes manageable" (Zartman, 1994a:219). In the absence of one agreed gestalt as a structuring reference, he will have to take responsibility himself for the choice of one gestalt that will organize his approach, both in terms of cognitive structuring and in terms of committing itself, de facto, to a certain point of view. Here we touch a major theme of complexity: it dissolves the line between cognition and action and redefines analysis as "an active cognitive experience" (Le Moigne, 1984). Choosing one way to decomplexify is positing an organizing gestalt, both cognitively (to organize the analysis), and in terms of action, making one point of view the analyst's "business," to use Perl's notion, with all the additional connotations it may carry. We will examine here four alternative choices that are available to the analyst of a NAN:

- Analyzing it as a quasi agreement (we will show that this is usually a poor choice),

- Identifying another interaction process (conflict, avoidance, etc.) the overarching logics of which may, in the case under study, block or override the emergence of a negotiated gestalt,

- Analytically expanding on the point of view of one of the protagonists in the negotiation situation,

- Choosing one dimension of the situation (for instance, geopolitical, economic, cultural, etc.) to broaden the scope far beyond the negotiation situation itself.

ALMOST AN AGREEMENT IS NO AGREEMENT

Let us deal first with situations where the analyst tries to treat a NAN as a "quasi agreement" (almost agreeable language), that is, treating it as he would treat an agreement, only introducing little differences: the ones that blocked agreement. The temptation to use this approach is easily understood: it seems to lead the analyst straight back to the case of a negotiation that reached agreement and, furthermore, to point clearly to fairly simple causes for the lack of agreement: those points of difference that were on the table when the negotiation process stopped short of agreement. This hope, however, can be very misleading.

In French trade-union language, a situation where a package proposed by management is deemed not to be acceptable is referred to by the phrase "the sum total is not there" (*le compte n'y est pas*). But exactly which aspect of the package can be pointed to as the cause for the absence of agreement? Imagine a student fails a series of exams by a small margin: two points more in one of the ten disciplines involved would have meant an average grade sufficient to pass. Which discipline can be deemed responsible for the failure? The one in the last exam? The one with the lowest grade? The one where the student has studied least seriously? The one where the exam was hardest? Or where the grades given to all students averaged lowest? In this situation, as in a negotiation where packages proposed do not lead to agreement, two aspects can be pointed out. First, all factors in the situation (all exams in our metaphor) are together responsible for the absence of agreement (for not passing, in our metaphor). Even if the actors themselves point to one factor as explaining the absence of success, the analyst probably ought to consider all the factors taken together. Second, each explanation that privileges one or two factors is paramount to recommending a given course of action or attribution of responsibility (the student should study more the topic examined last, she should focus on topics where grading is most severe, he should have been more serious in all topics, etc.). It leads us straight back to the complexity of the situation: choosing one explanation is adhering to one point of view.

So the choice of this point of view is the main point in the analyst's moves, not identifying the apparent failures of the fallacious quasi agreement. Practitioners and analysts of international negotiation know from experience and observation that a common stratagem in negotiations is to present them as very far from agreement to increase pressure in favor of compromise. In reverse, presenting a situation as very close to agreement is a favorite stratagem for a party that has hidden strategic reasons to wish the negotiations to fail, but does not want to show it.

The absence of agreement characterizes a situation as a whole. Even if the negotiators have preferred to conclude that they were almost agreed, and to point to one chosen difference as being decisive, taking this at face value may lead to missing important factors in the overall situation, and to serious misinterpretation. An "almost agreed on" package provides a very fragile reference for analysis indeed. The analyst does better to consider a "quasi agreement" as no agreement at all, and seeing the situation as calling for a new negotiation: a negotiation that should not start from the point where the previous one failed, lest it stumbles again on the same blocks.

What analysis can provide here is a fresh start in reading the complex backgrounds and fragmented figures of the negotiation as a first step of (re) ordering that may lead to other translations into language that may be more agreeable — and, if not agreeable, provide an important step in the interpretation of the difficulty in finding agreement. The file, as it were, has to be reopened. But given the volume of the file involved by any serious international negotiation and its inextricable complexity, the analyst would be ill-advised to try to empty all its contents helter-skelter on the autopsy table for NANs. He ought to consider options to guide his reconsideration; we now propose to examine three of them.

LOOKING FOR ORDERING AND SIMPLIFICATIONS IN OTHER MODES OF INTERACTION

In the absence of agreement, the negotiation itself fails to provide a framework that the analyst can use and start from. But negotiation is but one of several leading modalities of interaction that may be at work between the parties. While they negotiate, parties may be engaging also in confrontation (as in battle, in unilateral actions), in litigation (or other forms of delegation of decision-making power to a third party), in avoidance (for instance, in economic competition without coordination, or tactical avoidance of social or diplomatic interaction), or even in cooperation (such as in a case where one party has tried, and failed, to obtain a modification in an existing pattern of cooperation, and falls back on the cooperation as it functioned before the attempt). Each of these modes of interaction has its own specific ways of bringing order into complex situations that are tackled through interaction between parties, be it in terms of actors, structure, strategies, process, or outcomes. In the terms we have adopted above, it rests on its own figure/background differentiation process, its own "decomplexifying" moves.

Let us just consider one example: confrontation. The simplification regarding the actors is brought about by the polarization process that, in confrontation, transforms complex networks into binary opposed sides. The structure is also brought in line with the polarization. It is simplified by the fact that with each side reacting to the other, they together create a "front" that orders the complex situation. The choices of strategies are limited by the necessity to react to the other side's actions. The process becomes organized by the succession and the logics of the steps and events in the confrontation. The outcome brings increased simplicity through victory (the winning side reorganizes the situation as he chooses), or through a switch of mode, such as to negotiation, and the specific ways that negotiations introduce to treat the complex situation at hand.

In a similar way, one could show that decision by a third party, avoidance, or cooperation have their own very different ways of ordering (and, to a certain extent, simplifying) complex situations. The important point here is that failure to reach agreement in a negotiation does not necessarily lead to a complex situation with no ordering process being under way. It may bring the leading interaction mode back to confrontation, or to a situation (or phase) where avoidance (or cooperation, or litigation) prevails. This is of major importance for analysis. Just as we have shown for NLAs that the analyst can organize his analysis around the agreement and the specific ordering that has concretely been provided by the negotiation, in the case of many NANs, the concrete ordering provided by confrontation (or litigation, or avoidance, etc.) can underpin the framing of the analysis. If the analyst makes such a choice, his selection of one mode as the leading key to explanation and ordering of the process, his selection of one theoretical understanding of the workings of that mode, become crucial interpretive moves.

Such interpretations may amount to stating that a situation is too complex to be adequately accounted for if viewed as a negotiation, but that its complexities can be ordered and captured clearly enough, if it is viewed mainly as a confrontation (or a third-party decision, or avoidance situation, etc.).

THE ANALYST ACTING AS COMPANION TO A PARTY

Another, different option for the analyst to orient his reopening the file of a NAN is to guide his work on proximity, on sharing of purpose, on similar worldviews, between the analyst and one of the parties (or one group of parties). Since in the absence of agreement there is no reference that all parties share, the analyst has to choose one coherent, even if partial, point of view on the situation. The action logic of one party, what this party was trying to accomplish through the failed negotiation, what it may still be trying to accomplish more generally, may well provide such an Ariadne thread in the complexity of the situation, an ongoing reference for his work in interpreting the situation, the process, the outcome, the strategies.

To give an example in principle, let us imagine a negotiation about the creation of a marine sanctuary for the protection of a population of whales in waters between three countries. The negotiation fails. An analyst may choose to reconsider the situation, based on the more general concern for protection of this whale population. The NAN is reframed into the wider context of all interactions relevant to the success or failure of the protection of those whales, beyond the particular instance of the marine sanctuary project. This framing puts the analyst in a position of proximity, of sharing of purpose and world-view with one group of parties in the negotiation: those that pushed in favor of the sanctuary, those that are dedicated to conservation of the whale popula-tion that is at stake in the failed negotiation. As is often remarked, this group of parties may not correspond to one of the three countries in the negotiation, but to a network, an advocacy coalition (Sabatier and Jenkins-Smith, 1993) cutting across those countries. It may be organized in a loosely structured way. But it certainly provides one firm thread for the interpretation of the situa-tion, whatever its complexity (and environmental situations are, routinely, very complex). In the same case, another analyst may well choose as the leading thread the long-term strategy of one of the countries involved to defend its sovereignty in the ongoing confrontation with its two neighbors. And still an-other analyst might posit the viability of the fishing industry, also defended by a strong network of actors in the negotiation, as the beacon of his analysis.

Choosing such an option amounts to considering the negotiation that failed not mainly as an interaction between countries, but as one step in the evolu-tion and management over time of an ongoing issue (in our example, the pro-tection of whales, sovereignty of country x, or the development of a regional fishing industry, respectively). It may provide very useful insights into the causes of the absence of agreement; for instance, a failed international negotia-tion for the creation of a marine sanctuary may be a major success in the over-all strategy of the regional fishing industry to avoid constraints being imposed on its access to resources. It may also provide insights into new options for practical action; for instance, the failed negotiation for the marine sanctuary may well reveal the potential for a more powerful coalition to advocate for the whales, by recruiting allies who were not in favor of the sanctuary itself but who may well be instrumental in pushing for alternative solutions.

Choosing such an option to analyze a NAN may be criticized as too nar-row: would it not be even more enlightening to consider the action logics and the concerns of all parties to the negotiation, and thus obtain a more com-plete picture? The problem is that if the analyst follows this appeal, she ends up right in the place she was trying to eschew: analyzing the whole package of the NAN, structured (badly, in view of the absence of agreement) by the negotiation itself. For instance: where is she to stop the list of all those actors, whose action logics ought to be analyzed? If they are the main protagonists of the NAN, major but discrete power players may be overlooked, and the analysis may reinstitute one of the causes for failure of the negotiation instead of shedding light on it. And if they are all relevant actors in the field, the analyst is led back to the intractability of trying to exhaust a complex situation in a complete picture. He will, as the French phrase goes, embrace a lot, and hardly hold anything.

Another critique against such an option for guiding the analysis is that it leads to a biased reading of the situation. Here, we would like to object: biased in reference to what? Since there is no agreement, there is simply no shared reference. Both the negotiators and the analysts of the negotiation are operating in a space where all points of view are partial. No one can claim to have an overview, and the only reasonable claim the analyst can make is to offer one point of view to enter into dialogue with other points of view, other interpretations. The best one analyst can do is to offer one coherent, explicitly structured, carefully researched point of view, and accept (and hope) that other analysts will produce other equally well developed points of view. In the same way that the analyst of an NLA can rest on the common reference the negotiators created with the agreement, the analyst of a NAN must share the predicament of the negotiators themselves, and accept that the point of view he bases his work on (even if only implicitly) is but one point of view among several that did not manage to rearticulate themselves around one agreed overview. It is discussion between the negotiating parties, and between analysts espousing different stands, that will be crucial to continuing fruitful exchanges, beyond a situation of no-agreement.

SCREENING THE BACKGROUND FOR ALTERNATIVE FIGURES TO GUIDE ANALYSIS OF NANS

In the previous two options, the analyst starts afresh based on one aspect of the dynamics of the negotiation. She finds the organizing figure respectively in an ongoing nonnegotiated interaction parallel to the negotiation and interfering with it, or in one concern that some parties have been trying to push through the negotiation. But she can also step a little further away, and identify and choose, in the background of the negotiation, one pattern or dimension that is attractive to her discipline or research approach, and that will become the figure organizing her work. For instance, she may reexamine the overall geopolitical situation, or the whole economic system of which the negotiation studied is but one interaction, or the overall multilateral system of international relations of which this particular negotiation is one episode.

The legitimacy, both analytical and practical, of such moves, is obvious at first sight, and most analyses of negotiation situations contain numerous openings to such wider and recognized patterns in the background. The questions raised here are: What are the limits of such moves? Under what conditions can they be expected to be fruitful in the analysis of NANs? These questions derive directly from consideration of the complexity of international negotiation and of its importance for the analysis of NANs. Complexity of a situation means that the negotiator and the analyst can find innumerable patterns in the background that may be connected with the negotiation situation. The difficulty is not so much one of finding patterns, but of limiting oneself in the number to be used, and choosing the one — or the very few — that will organize one given analysis to make it significant and useful. This is, again, the added value criterion we introduced earlier, associated with the fact that the analyst who operates in a complex situation cannot claim to build an overview, but only to articulate an elaborate, partial analysis for a wider debate that he alone cannot embrace.

In the exercise of screening the background for relevant figures, the analyst can mobilize powerful resources. Is not the driving force of academic life to screen the background — any background! — to find in it (sometimes, to plant in it) one figure (or set of figures) one knows to have potential for serious treatment? In the discussion of NANs, each such reframing of the situation as part of the much wider picture of one dimension of international relations can be seen as one move in a cognitive postdisagreement negotiation that has been triggered by the lack of closure of the initial negotiation. In this context, we suggest the following criterion to assess the added value of a given analytical proposal: what exactly would be its contribution to initiating and supporting a new round of interaction following the absence of agreement of the negotiation? As it redefines the parties involved, the issues to be considered, what light do these redefinitions throw on the negotiation that ended in no agreement? Does it make the lack of agreement appear as an exercise in shared figure/background definition that was incomplete? Does it then help to define lacking elements (issues, parties), useful different framings that can help complete and redefine interaction? Or does it make the negotiation with no agreement appear to be an irrelevant episode, a dead end in the trajectory of the parties and of the issues involved?

This last set of questions alerts us to the fact that many perspectives that approach a negotiation in the much wider framework of one discipline or school of thought are apt to explain the failure to reach agreement in a way that displaces the frame of analysis so far away from the studied negotiation — and often from negotiation in general — that negotiation becomes quite peripheral in the analysis. This per se is not necessarily a problem: the complexity of human systems involves many crucial processes that are at least as crucial as negotiation! It is a problem, however, in the context of negotiation research. Here, the guiding principle is that there is wisdom, both practical and theoretical, to gain from serious analysis centering on negotiation processes and outcomes. For analysts of NANs who are endeavoring to interpret the negotiation and the absence of agreement with analysis based on the very general frames provided by their disciplines or theories, this principle can help in two ways. It can help each analyst judge to what extent one explanation for the absence of agreement reflects the specific features of the negotiation situation and process he is studying, as opposed to the general limits the perspective he has adopted entails on negotiation in general as a means of transforming international situations. For the analysts of a NAN taken as a group, it can help them collectively manage the plurality of perspectives that is necessary to forcefully reframe the failed negotiation by providing guiding questions that do not measure the value of the various contributions on the way they reflect the intrinsic force of each discipline or school of thought, but on their contribution in making sense of the no agreement situation. What is really of interest to negotiation research is interpretations that help us understand how this NAN situation came about, and what prospects it may hold for further, for other negotiations.

At this point in the discussion, we would like to note that the study of NANs can raise more generally the issue of the relevance of negotiation research as an academic field, as compared to the many fields of research that may also focus on international relations, or the treatment of international problems. In NLAs, analysts versed in the study of negotiation are in phase with the practical, negotiated ordering of the situation. In NANs, on the contrary, with negotiated ordering having failed in practice, many avenues of analysis may rebound toward perspectives that radically question the significance of negotiation, its capacity to have a specific impact on the issues at stake and on international relations, or its relevance and specificity as a topic for academic study. This is one more reason for trying, as we have done in this paper, to identify clearly the type of avenues that can help the analyst reorient the analysis of a NAN in a way that is useful to the understanding of negotiations in general.

CONCLUSION

Complexity is a major dimension of most if not all international negotiations. In itself, it can hardly be seen as a cause for negotiation failure. But the complexity of international negotiations has many consequences that the theories of complexity can help us identify. Here, we have underlined the fact that it deeply transforms the respective positions of the analyst and the practitioner. In his opening to a milestone workshop called "The Science and Praxis of Complexity" in Montpellier, Soedjatmoko, rector of the United Nations University in Tokyo, sees this transformation as amounting to "the disappearance of the traditional distinction between the observer and the observed" (Aida et al., 1984). He states that "to understand and attempt to manage systems that are marked by uncertainty, instability, unpredictability and vulnerability," in a context where, moreover, the roots of social science have extended beyond one particular culture, "the role of the social scientist has [shifted] from observer to participant — and then from participant to activist." Here, we have been somewhat less provocative and simply taken as our starting point that the analysts of a given negotiation and the negotiators themselves are participants in the same practical and cognitive situation. This situation is quite different when the negotiation has led to agreement, and when it has stopped without agreement.

In NLAS, the form embodied in the agreement reorganizes the situation, both practically and cognitively. It gives salience to some aspects of the situation and links them in a given structure. It pushes various other aspects out of the scene, into backgrounds, ready for oblivion. The analyst is then placed in a favored situation. In crafting his interpretations, he can take advantage at will of the efforts by the negotiators themselves to bring order into complexity, while at the same time being free to add in his own simplifications of complications. Moreover, since the agreement provides a broad framework ready to be shared by parties and by many observers, he can leverage his analysis on this shared reference. We have tried to show that a major contribution of the analyst should then be, in a variety of ways, to re-root the (comparatively) simple figure of the negotiated agreement into the complex backgrounds which underpin its meanings: the background from which it was elaborated by the negotiators, and that into which it will have to push its developments if it is going to be implemented and make a difference. Even if the analyst endorses the role of activist, or takes an aggressively critical stance,[3] his intervention will still occur in a situation structured and polarized to a large extent by the existing agreement.

In NANs, the analyst's situation is dramatically different: from the start, hers is but one voice among dissenting voices. In her effort to make sense of dissensus, she is in danger not of being locked in (or out of) the self-explanatory circle of consensus, but of being dissolved or carried away in the complexities of a situation that the negotiators have not managed to bound successfully. As one groping (cognitive) negotiator among groping (cognitive and practical) negotiators, she has to take a stance that will (hopefully) provide her with an Ariadne's thread in this labyrinth. In this chapter, we have considered four options that she can choose from. The first is to cling to the idea that agreement was almost there, and base the analysis on this "quasi-agreement." This approach can be very deceptive. In most cases, it is at best a preliminary step, before turning to one of the three next, more serious, options. Each of them proposes to replace, in a specific way, the NAN in a wider frame. Option 2 is to identify, if there is one, another modality of interaction at work between the parties (confrontation, avoidance, etc.) that imposes its own overarching structure on the situation. Option 3 is to reconsider the whole situation from the perspective of one of the interests, concerns, issues, or parties, in the negotiation. Option 4 is to view the negotiation as just one part, or one moment, of the more general system one is academically inclined to study (international relations, economic equilibrium, etc.), and see how this can contribute to understanding the situation that has been negotiated and the absence of agreement.

In the last three options, the ones we think are of greatest interest, the role of the analyst can be summarized in one phrase: to reroute attention toward backgrounds and interactions that may help parties understand why a particular negotiation does not seem to succeed in translating a given complex situation into agreeable language. When there has been no agreement, the major task the analyst and the negotiators are confronted with is to reorient cognitive and practical efforts on alternative tracks that may yield better results. This is an exercise in reframing: finding what frame(s) may usefully initiate, and then guide, new avenues of action for parties, or interaction between parties.

In this chapter we have presented this exercise mostly from the standpoint of the analyst. How useful can it be for the practitioner — that is, the negotiator? Well, the "disappearance of the traditional distinction between the observer and the observed" we quoted in the introduction to the paper does not affect only the observer (the analyst): it also concerns the observed (the negotiator). Complexity is not a finite problem to be solved "out there." It is a condition in which the negotiator is placed; his practice is an effort of "decomplexification"; his effort is one of promoting a given interpretation of a complex situation. Accepting the complexity of international negotiation means, for the negotiator, accepting the lot of the "reflexive practitioner" — dangerously close to that of the analysts![4] If the negotiation has reached no agreement, his problem of rerouting will be essentially the same as the analyst's, as we endeavored to outline it here. He will have to take it up with his own resources. In many respects, they are stronger than those of the analysts. In others, the analyst may provide complementary information, insights, or recommendations. Negotiators and analysts are more and more in the same "business." If a successful negotiation is associated, as Peter Haas (1990) shows, with an "epistemic community" of analysts and negotiators sharing issues within a similar worldview, a negotiation without agreement maroons both negotiators and analysts in an epistemic broken circle, an unfinished gestalt which they must choose to insist on completing (option 1), to put aside so as to take care of another, competing, circle of understanding and interaction (option 2), to transform by starting anew from their aspirations (option 3), or to replace (at least temporarily) by wider, established, readings of a much larger and definitely complex world (option 4).

NOTES

1. Aida et al. (1984) give a particularly good overview of this movement of thought in its diversity and coherence.

2. For the sake of the specific discussion in this paper, we consider mostly the ability of negotiations to order and simplify complex situations. One should also note the opposite ability of negotiators and negotiation processes to enrich the discouraging

simplicity of stalemate into a set of questions and issues complex enough to offer maneuvering space for negotiations.

3. And this can be vitally useful, as we advocate elsewhere: see Mermet, 2006.

4. Maybe this is why, in informal discussions with experienced negotiators, we have found that they amicably tend to view analysts of negotiation as badly informed and less competent negotiators, packing cumbersome academic impedimenta.

PART SEVEN

Conclusions

Failures

Lessons for Theory

In principle, a party engages in a negotiation because he thinks he can obtain something he would not otherwise. This difference is the added value of negotiating. Ultimately a party signs an agreement because this agreement brings an added value sufficient to justify his signature. It is obvious that an agreement must include the implementation so that it is not just a piece of paper. Thus, the Munich Accords of 1938 fall into the vast category of unfinished business, for they were not respected. The negotiations aiming to end World War I in 1916 belong to the same category. The parties did not reach any conclusion, and deaths went on and numbered in the millions.

However, a poor agreement is not always preferable to no agreement. There is a whole set of negotiations that should in principle reach an outcome and that did not end with an agreement. This means that for at least one of the parties, the status quo is considered still more desirable than the acceptable terms by the other party. This is the type of negotiation that we are dealing with. They do not come to an agreement while they should have or could have.

In fact, incomplete negotiation does not mean failure, as one does not sign an agreement at any cost. In addition, the process itself may be useful in many ways: developing a channel for discussion, testing the other, knowing more about the other party and the overall situation, or getting recognized by the other as a legitimate counterpart. Thus, success may be defined the way

Churchill put it, as simply "going from failure to failure without losing enthusiasm." Agreements often do not meet expectations. Their integrative potential may be far from being maximized. Sometimes, parties just agree to meet
again, which may mean that they agree to disagree.

To better understand and control negotiation processes, research has been
most focused on negotiations that led to an agreement and that have usually
been considered "successful." The concept of a "successful negotiator" is difficult to construct, for it is a subjective, polymorphous, and value-laden concept.
Success is no more final than failure is fatal. Some analysts have, for instance,
considered the Israeli-Palestinian negotiations as having gone through what
they labeled as a "breakthrough" in 1993 with the Oslo Accords (Watkins and
Rosengrant, 2001). We usually judge a tree from its fruits. What is important
is not so much a signed piece of paper but what happens in reality. Here, the
consequence has been an escalation in suicide bombings and rockets launched
on one side, and on the other side a wall to separate both populations and full-
scale war.

However, there is much to learn from negotiations that did not reach any
agreement because failure, even temporary, besides being a most effective
school for thinking, has a second virtue. Actors are not inclined to naively
reproduce the model as they would do in the case of a negotiation considered
as successful or at least completed.

"History is the science of the misfortune of men," wrote French writer
Raymond Queneau (1966). One could add in particular the history of their
failures. So, in order to not endlessly repeat the same mistakes, it is essential
to understand their causes. This is the purpose served by this book. The analytical method applied in this research isolates causes. However, failures are
often multicausal, and what may happen is that either one cause dominates
over others, or parties come close to breakaway and one cause, that may not
be of importance per se, triggers the rupture of the process. This secondary
cause operates like a drop of water that makes the water run over the vase.
Another classical process is when two or more causes combine at the same
time and produce a multiplication effect that will lead to an ultimate failure.
From the cases presented in the first part of the book, thirty-nine explanatory
factors of nonachievement of negotiations have been identified and grouped
into broader categories along the classical analytical structure used by PIN with
actors, structure, strategies, process, and outcome.

ACTORS

The negotiators introduce in the process not only their personal dimension and their subjectivity but also their culture, their motivations, and their memories of past experiences. So far as soft diplomacy is concerned, the value issue is the most important stumbling block. The motto "might makes right" is challenged more and more, and values have to be put to the front. As a consequence, they may conflict with each other. In some cases, the negotiation process may, thus, refer to *incompatible values*, which mean nonnegotiable issues, because a quantity can be split but not a value. A value is met or not met as Shakespeare put it in the mouth of Hamlet, "to be or not to be, that is the question." Thus, for instance, the Taba conference held in 2001 after the failure of Camp David 2 with the same parties and purpose, revealed in the eyes of one party (the Palestinians) a dramatically missing shared sense of justice. Yet, this type of problem is among those that require a great amount of time to be solved, a resource made unavailable by the U.S. style of mediation and the domestic constraints they had to face as President Clinton was leaving office.

Recent debates have led a number of Asian politicians and academics to state that Western concepts of democracy and human rights are not entirely compatible with Asian culture. Conflicts such as those in Eritrea or Kosovo have been deeply rooted in incompatible values about nation-state authority and respect for and autonomy of minorities. In other places, negotiations fail because of a conflict between justice and peace and the practical consequences of prioritizing one over the other. Negotiators and mediators often face this dramatic dilemma: on the one hand, to achieve peace one has to first establish justice, but on the other hand, prioritizing peace will ultimately bring justice. Devastating conflicts in Africa such as in Darfur (Sudan) and in the Democratic Republic of Congo (DRC) have not been resolved for the reasons given above. In each case, the mediators have been forced to confront the challenges in pursuing peace and justice simultaneously. Peace implies to find some kind of agreement with parties or leaders that could be considered as war criminals by Western standards and subsequently punished. Sometimes making a deal with criminals is unavoidable and necessary to prevent further conflict and suffering. As these criminals are unlikely to want a prison cell as a reward for their hard-won peace agreement, mediators frequently resort to amnesties as an incentive, which goes against the idea of justice.

The *lack of preparation* of the negotiation team may not just lead to some faux pas during the process but explain some of the failures. Improper or deficient preparation means essentially just responding to the other, reacting to various tactics instead of handling the process rationale. If there is no real strategy, the overall conduct will dramatically lack coherence and subsequently effectiveness. Neither experience nor bargaining skills can compensate for such a shortcoming. On many occasions, negotiators do not sufficiently prepare their negotiation. They just set their goals and their bottom line and get to the negotiation table with the idea of seeing what will happen. Heads of delegations often work from a huge amount of more or less useful notes written by their staff members that does not really help to conceive a strategy.

Then, technical preparation is far from being enough. It is certainly essential to know the subject, but one has to go far beyond those basic requirements and, for instance, analyze the power relation, to learn about the culture of the counterpart. What is, for example, the meaning of a silence? Culture determines the way people perceive and approach the negotiating process. Parties to the negotiation have specific perspectives on authority, honesty, time, risk, and the importance of the relationship.

During the first round of the Korea-U.S. Free Trade Agreement talks, held in Washington in June 2006, the Korean official who was part of the labor section negotiation team stated that they were learning new things while they were negotiating with the American representatives. The U.S. was demanding the introduction of a so-called public communication system, which was a term that they had never heard of before.

Knowledge, experience, training, and preparation are necessary requirements to achieve a productive outcome. They were clearly lacking — in the Munich case during the hostage taking of Israeli athletes. The absence of know-how or practice, the urgent character of the situation, the effect of surprise, and the unawareness about the counterparts resulted into a most dramatic outcome with the slaughter of all the hostages.

The *absence of chemistry* may also play a role, because people at the negotiation table or negotiation teams wherever they are, as human beings, have their personalities, their tempers, their pasts, their emotions, their fears, and their hopes. The very poor chemistry between Ehud Barak and Yasser Arafat explains, at least partly, the difficulties that Israelis and Palestinians had to face during the 2000 Camp David summit. In this so important negotiation, they hardly met face to face. Conversely, the chemistry between Kissinger and Zhou

Enlai had greatly contributed to improving relations between the United States and China. Even if a personality-driven foreign policy approach cannot do the job without dealing with the substance of the issues that are in the national interests, personal chemistry between leaders or their representatives is often considered an important ingredient of diplomacy. In the Waco case, one can even hardly speak about chemistry, as there was no proper interaction between the two sides, just two parallel monologues matched by an absence of listening of the other.

Face concerns may in some circumstances and with some cultures play a crucial role. Face refers to someone's public self-image, the social perception of a person's prestige. In the Middle East and Asia as a whole, people place an extremely high value on their own reputation, that of the family, or that of the group. Face is typically a social construct that has to be enhanced and protected, therefore, playing a critical role in many interactions. During the Camp David summit, for instance, the Palestinian representatives deeply resented the negotiation, for they experienced it as a succession of denials of dignity from their Israeli counterparts. The representative function does not do less than reinforce the problem, because what can in a pinch be tolerated for a person becomes totally unacceptable if it is a whole population that is humiliated.

Fear, animosity generated by a highly competitive attitude, or even hostile behavior from the other party may trigger a *demonization* process. Demonization is the characterization of people as evil for purposes such as denying any possibility of entering into discussions or continuing negotiation with them. Sometimes it is even used to justify an attack. Demonizing an individual generally involves a suspension of the normal considerations of human behavior and respect. Any means of "self-defense" may be considered to be legitimate in relation to the magnitude of the threat. For instance, demonizing Saddam Hussein or Slobodan Milosevic creates conditions for taking military action to destroy them instead of striving for an agreement that would keep them at the head of their country.

The demonization process may result in an escalation of the image of the counterpart (Zartman and Faure, 2005a). This is a complex process that addresses first the psychological dimension, by building up anxiety, and then the strategic dimension, by disqualifying the other party in order to allow any type of action against him. Images have their own lives, their own rationales, and their own ways to escalate when confronting each other. They tend to maintain consistency with the emotions and beliefs, therefore, fueling and strengthening the conflict. When emotions tend to dominate over objective realities, escalation in negative representations of the other hampers any continuation of the negotiation. In the Cyprus case, as in the case of the Camp David 2 summit, a process of demonizing the counterpart has led to considering failure unavoidable, a fatality that is impossible to escape from.

STRUCTURE

Negotiations may make no headway for structural reasons, such as having not included in the process some important stakeholders, the absence of a Zone of Potential Agreement (ZOPA), excessive linkages, and overly imbalanced power relations. To modify the structure of the game is an essential part of a negotiation; however, a prerequisite is to have such a possibility and that possibility be effectively seized.

Parties who face the risk of a political marginalization in case of peace, or *actors who are kept away from the negotiation process* and have no way to have their interests taken into account will struggle to freeze the process. In the Somalia crisis, the risk of political marginalization was the basic assumption for a number of warlords. Among other groups kept away from negotiation processes nowadays is the Palestinian Hamas.

Negotiation is not just about moving the "bottom line" or security point of the other, but first of all about building a ZOPA. The *absence of* ZOPA usually leads the parties to insurmountable deadlocks. Both sides may feel, through the current damages they have to suffer, the pressing necessity to come to an agreement. However, the demands may reveal that there is no ZOPA, as is the case with the Armenian-Azerbaijan dispute over the Nagorno-Karabakh.

In the Cyprus case, analysis shows that a real ZOPA has never been clearly identified. The Camp David 2 summit of 2000 showed such a dominant zero-sum game rationale because of the major importance of territorial issues that it did not lead to an agreement. Discussions were also made fruitless because of the too-small number of possible options on each one of the four issues on the table. In the case of the discussion between Iran and the European Union, the demands and supposed objectives of each party do not lead to the creation of a ZOPA, which ultimately drives the negotiators to pointless discussion while consuming a considerable amount of time and energy.

When the parties involved turn out to be unable to get out of the structure of a zero-sum game, there is little chance of reaching a positive outcome in the *absence of a resolving formula.* This is the case for the Cyprus discussions, in which parties were endlessly referring to the Swiss model without much of any concrete creative option put forth. The Waco case offers another example of a zero-sum situation that left no room for an acceptable solution.

Often the absence of a ZOPA or a too-narrow bargaining range is simply the product of a flawed analysis based on faulty assumptions. Furthermore, it is followed by a process characterized by a lack of creativity and the inability of the stakeholders to build a formula for agreement.

One of the major difficulties for negotiators is the *inability to modify — the structure of the game.* The context evolves; for instance, elections are due to happen soon for one of the parties, or the media interest has shifted. If negotiation does not anticipate such a phenomenon, the negotiation will end up as a sum of missed opportunities. Iranian elections have led to a verbal outdoing and a hardening of positions, making any accord most unlikely. Similarly, the Convention on Biological Weapons has not reached any agreement, particularly because of the U.S. elections that brought a considerable change in the U.S. government administration. Factors such as a *swing in the media interest,* the "CNN effect," drive the media to focus on other topics than the ongoing but motionless negotiation, thus reducing the pressures on the parties themselves. This was the case for Somalia, which ended in the late 1980s by an international indifference as a low-priority region in the post–Cold War era, resulting in inaction and worsening of the situation on the ground. When there is no visible crisis, it does not mean that international community should not act. However, in many cases the apparent reduction of the crisis is considered the measure against which policies are evaluated. Wishful thinking becomes a policy instrument.

One important cause of deadlocks and ultimate negotiation failure concerns the *semantics.* The same wording refers to totally different meanings. The syndrome of the UN Security Council resolution 242 on the "withdrawal of Israel armed forces from territories occupied" in the aftermath of the Six Day War is still operational. Should it be understood as "from some" or "from all territories"? Some diplomats viewed it as "constructive ambiguity" facilitating the agreement, while others as rather "destructive ambiguity," as it has sown the seeds for more wars in the future. Tehran's interpretation of the agreements with the IAEA concerning Iran's nuclear program made this country considerably reduce the amount of information that it delivers. Thus, it increases the fear that Tehran has much to hide about its nuclear ambitions and may be building a clandestine enrichment facility. Here the same text leads to very different interpretations of the obligations of both sides. In the case of the Conference on the Biological Weapons Convention, the term "verification" is similarly understood in radically different ways. Some parties like to speak about compliance enhancement, others about verification. In the same wake, there is an ambiguity about the purpose: peaceful cooperation or nonproliferation.

In some cases, *third parties try (and succeed) to use the conflict to their own benefit.* The great powers in the case of Belgium gained the upper hand and finally decided to impose their views. Concerning Cyprus, the European Union looks for secondary gains, and for Iran, the United States wants to bring the conflict to the UN Security Council. This is not an unusual strategy. For instance, Israel has used the PLO/Hamas conflict over the control of Gaza (2006) to get better leverage on the coming negotiations with the Palestinian Authority.

Many ethnically diverse societies have experienced, at one time or another, interethnic conflict. While the violent forms of conflict such as wars are frequent, the potential for violent interethnic conflict is even greater, threatening to involve neighboring nations. Almost every multi-ethnic society is a potential source for such type of conflict. Then, there might be a temptation to trigger a *war by proxy.* Typically, a war by proxy is when two countries use third parties as substitutes for fighting each other directly. The purpose is to strike an adversary without running the risk of a full-scale war. During the Cold War, on more or less ideological grounds, the two superpowers profusely resorted to wars by proxy, as in Korea, Vietnam, Congo, Angola, Mozambique, and Afghanistan, to name a few.

Extremely imbalanced power relations may lead the weakest party not to accept the mere idea of an agreement either, because the weak party can still keep going without an agreement or because she considers the power relation may be modified throughout time, reducing her disadvantage. This was the case with the Palestinians during the Camp David 2 summit. They considered that if the actual outcome of the negotiation was strictly reflecting the balance of power, they would get so little that they would prefer to avoid talking. The war between the United States and North Vietnam could have led to much earlier negotiations, but the North Vietnamese strategists believed that time was on their side and that if the American army did not win quickly, it would appear to be a quasi defeat and put them in a much better bargaining position.

An extremely imbalanced power relation between the different republics making up former Yugoslavia made it impossible to find a fair outcome through negotiations.

The counterpart may also consider that the *disorganization of the other party*, here the Palestinian side during the Camp David 2 negotiation, greatly hampers the credibility of reaching an agreement and its chances of implementation. As a general rule, multiparty coalitions, either strong or weak, are often paralyzed by their own structure and little able to develop any real policy. A recent example was the U.S.-Turkish negotiation to allow American troops to use Turkish territory to conduct military operations on Iraq. The Turkish Grand National Assembly finally rejected the motion because of the disorganization of the Adalet ve Kalkınma Partisi, the ruling party, whose leader may have been unaware that it did not have enough votes to win. Archetypal disorganized counterparts that make any negotiation hopeless and useless are so-called governments of countries such as Congo or Somalia. Even if an attempt results in a signed agreement, there is very little chance that they will reach a position enabling them to implement it.

The existence of a Mutually Hurting Stalemate (MHS) is a dynamic condition for the acceptance of the principle of negotiating, but it is also a strong incentive for reaching a positive outcome. The *absence of* MHS, at least in terms of perception, or an insufficiently hurting stalemate, becomes an incentive not to strike a deal. The added value of a possible agreement can be perceived as unsatisfactory to justify the ultimate efforts to reach it. In the Cyprus case, the status quo has already been perpetuated over the course of thirty-four years and, if not really satisfactory, is felt as bearable.

Camp David 2, in spite of the strong tensions and the litany of human dramas that mark out the Israeli-Palestinian conflict, has not been boosted by an MHS strong enough to lead both parties to make the last step and become convinced that the solution cannot be unilateral. The Belgian case also illustrates the absence of a sufficient degree of pain to stop it voluntarily and find an arrangement. The pain can be just a habit and may be not as much felt after some time. Prestige, pride, and reputation may also play their part inciting the parties to stand a suffering that they normally should not accept. Thus, in the summer of 1944 Germany should have capitulated in World War II but did not, beyond all reason. The same should have been done by Japan in 1945 after the battle of Okinawa if the Japanese government had been rational.

There are situations for which there exists a focal point, a salient solution that can greatly help to reach an agreement. When *no* focal point is in view, negotiations are either reduced to stillness or to redundancy, following the example of the discussions between the EU and Iran. Among principles that reduce the size of the bargaining space and couple various parties' contributions, equal cuts represent a *focal point* in the sense of Schelling (1960). It is equilibrium more likely to be chosen by the negotiators because it seems special, natural, and somehow obvious. Equal-measure treaties are widespread because they have some inner quality that can greatly facilitate the reaching of an agreement. A focal point is defined by parties' perceptions, not by objective reality; it does not need to have any particular scientific quality. However, because it stands out in negotiators' perceptions, an incremental departure from it, as would be obtained by slightly shading a negotiated deal to one party's advantage, looks like a big change. Subsequently, focal-point solutions are characterized by a strong stability that stems from the convergence of negotiators' expectations.

Negotiation can be described as a system of approaching issues and problems offering ways to solve them. Linkages are indispensable tools for parties to avoid getting into zero-sum diplomacy. Nevertheless, on occasion this method can be totally counterproductive. The structure of the game can be made extremely complicated by *adding nonessential linkages* that may lead to snarls impossible to disentangle. It is the case with Cyprus for which, for instance, the Kurdish minority in Turkey itself has been introduced as an issue. It has been also the case with the Paris Agreement (2005) between the EU and Iran, which called for cooperation between Iran and the EU against international terrorism while clearly establishing a direct linkage between the nuclear issue and any future progress on Iran-EU trade talks and issues such as EU support for Iran's bid to join the WTO. This agreement was conceived as a comprehensive, multilevel approach following the prescriptions of linkage diplomacy whereby the future of long-standing negotiations between Iran and the EU on the "Trade and Cooperation Agreement" were yoked to the net result of the nuclear talks. Ultimately the overall negotiation failed to achieve its major objectives.

International decision-making processes sometimes reduce to nothing any potential convergence, when taking into account the *difference in timing*. For instance, Camp David 2, where a top-down process can be observed on the Arab side, whereas on the Israeli side it is a strictly reverse process, bottom up, that operates, making any parallel progress unlikely. To take another example, the EU dramatically lacks effective decision-making mechanisms to deal with crisis diplomacy. Resorting to a cost–benefit analysis for each of the twenty-seven state members only leads to general paralysis. As underlined by Schelling (1966), collective decisions depend on internal politics and government bureaucracy, on the chain of command, on the lines of communication, on parties' structures, on pressure groups, as well as on individual values and careers. In crisis diplomacy it can be essential to be able to get inside the decision-making system of the other side to influence or delay, or even paralyze the internal process.

According to the object of the negotiation, consequences of no agreement can be felt in the short term or in the long term. In some negotiations, failure or postponement of agreement can have immediate dramatic consequences. For instance, hostage situations, open conflicts, and wars involve human lives to be spared. This was the case with the Munich hostage situation or the Waco siege (see Goodwin, "Two Hostage Negotiations," in this book). If there is death instead of an agreement at the end of the discussion, the negotiators will be considered as bearing some responsibility in what happened. That can entail various types of consequences such as a sense of guilt, remorse, apprehension about being kept in the current position, anxiety about being reelected or promoted, or punishment.

Other negotiations may not have spectacular results but only long-term effects, such as those addressing environmental issues (Faure and Rubin, 1993). Results may only be felt by the next generation or only felt by nonhuman species. Thus, important negotiations may be postponed or protracted almost indefinitely because they carry *no sense of urgency*. Especially in negotiation conferences, events where responsibility is shared among many parties and finally much diluted, the joint communiqué at the end can be hardly more than just telling that all parties agreed to meet again some time. Unless some external parties such as media, public opinion, NGOs, or interest groups get into the game and apply enough pressure, nothing substantial may come out of these negotiations.

A classic saying summarizing the spirit that the search for an agreement is supposed to follow is "no pain, no gain." Here it would be "no pain, no agreement." As long as there is no MHS and the pain is not shared and felt, or is felt only by one party, there is not enough incentive to reach an accord. And if there are no shared benefits, at least shared pain can help to do the job.

One can also find negotiations that, having been extremely protracted, having given rise to so many attempts in so many directions, have so disorganized the negotiation system that it becomes extremely difficult to bring enough coherence to the discussion. Thus, *the Humpty Dumpty problem* becomes a cause for failure. The very high number of parties involved, as it is the case in the UN or at the WTO, only operates as an aggravating factor for jamming the whole system.

A number of experts contend that, like Humpty Dumpty in the story, U.S. public diplomacy has had a great fall. There have been some thirty-three separate studies, reports, and findings about America's public diplomacy issued by governmental and nongovernmental boards, commissions, associations, and ad hoc groups that converged on this conclusion. America's diplomatic failures have come not from a lack of expertise nor because of flawed technique, but because of systemic failures. The whole system has fallen to pieces, lost its rationality and much of its synergy. Realigning boxes on an organization chart and drawing lines of authority and relationships have been strongly emphasized as a most difficult challenge but an urgent necessity by analysts (Kiehl, 2003). As the nursery rhyme tells, "All the king's horses and all the king's men could not put Humpty Dumpty together again."

STRATEGIES

Strategies organizing the overall action of the negotiators may be incompatible, even counterproductive to such an extent that the parties themselves are brought to give up any hope of reaching an agreement. When parties do not have a *common problem definition*, one may feel that the negotiator is aiming to solve a nonproblem or to not really address the problem he is facing. In the Camp David 2 negotiations, the absence of shared vision of the problem at hand led to having the two least compatible strategies, which can only deadlock the whole process. As to the Waco case, both parties seem to have not been facing the same situation, thus they were trying to impose contradictory solutions, setting up a lose–lose situation. The classical opposition between warriors and shopkeepers illustrates this difficulty. Warriors as hard bargainers will tend to resort to competitive strategies and borrow from a wide array of tough tactics, whereas the shopkeepers will tend to use soft strategies. Such a disharmonious concert cannot last long, as no one meets the expectations of the other, as the shopkeeper is usually not suicidal. The latter may switch to tougher means, and the final outcome will be escalation (Zartman and Faure, 2005b:303).

Parties resorting to *strategies that are too basic*, too poor in terms of sophistication and innovation, such as the carrot and stick routine, finally lead to a deadlock or a failure because they are unacceptable by the counterpart as not properly addressing the complexities of the real situation. In the case of the Biological Weapons Convention, even countries on the same side, such as the United States and the EU, split at a certain stage, because of the American strategy of "take it or leave it," making any agreement from the others, even close allies, most unlikely.

The use of hard bargaining strategies with the other party may also elicit unexpected and nonsought consequences, such as the strengthening her power position in her own country by generating a nationalistic reaction. This was the case with Milosevic in Serbia, making any agreement most improbable. In the case of hard bargaining strategies, resorting to tactics that appear unclear or with little credibility, such as inflated threats, may contribute to freezing the process instead of accelerating it. This happened for the first intervention against Iraq, in 1991, when the message issued by the U.S. representative to Saddam Hussein was not properly understood by her Iraqi counterpart. In the same way, during the second Iraqi war, Saddam Hussein's threat to drown half of Israel in its own blood did not appear very serious and thus did not do the job, which was to maintain the status quo and prevent Americans from attacking.

Strategies are conceived in order to reach defined goals. *Unrealistic goals* make any conceivable strategy ineffective. Thus, in the Belgian case, the stubbornness of the Dutch downgraded the king's strategy to nothing more than wishful thinking, which is a quite insufficient argument to reach an advantageous outcome.

Sometimes goals are so excessive that they do not authorize any real concession. When there is no room to maneuver, when the security point has been reached, the negotiation reaches a standstill. The inability of the parties to evaluate the cost of inaction comes as an aggravating factor. It is much easier to provide an estimation of what one gives or receives than to evaluate the costs of uncertain consequences of a situation often unclear or somewhat complex. For instance, following the drawing up of the text of a Comprehensive Test Ban Treaty in 1994–96, the Conference on Disarmament in Geneva dealt with the negotiation of a fissile materials treaty (fissban). Some parties' demands were no less than the elimination of all military fissile materials and thus had been judged by many observers as most unrealistic.

A *drastic change of strategy* during the negotiation may just contribute to freezing the process and leading to failure. Either such a shift disorientates the other party, who, losing his certainties and reference marks, does not dare to make another move, or this change is understood as a tactical decoy and only generates increased distrust. In the Camp David summit, the Palestinian side comes to consider that, as the negotiation in terms of substance does not move on in a favorable way for them, they can still play deadlock as time is on their side. It is most difficult to have a radical strategic shift successful. As told by Dietrich Bonhoeffer, a German theologian executed by the Nazis, "If you board the wrong train, it is no use running along the corridor in the opposite direction."

A cooperative strategy is shouldered by an essential negotiation variable: trust. One must be in a position to believe the words of the other, take his commitments as reliable, to be sure that the other has the ability to carry out its promises, to believe that the agreement will be implemented in conformity with the joint decision taken. In fact, the *absence of trust*, the nonimplementation of CBMs (Confidence Building Measures) leads to adopting a low risk-taking behavior and not making much of any more move in an unknown or uncharted area. The Camp David summit ended up with such a deficiency. As has been the case concerning the various steps along the road to peace, for which none of the parties fulfilled their obligations, there was no clear guarantee of proper implementation of any agreement. The trust issue also played a role during the Cyprus mediation, as the Greek Cypriots were strongly suspected of acting in bad faith.

If the initiation of CBMs does not require trust as a prerequisite, building trust requires reliability. On these grounds negotiations with counterparts such as North Korea or Iran have failed. In the dispute over Iran's nuclear program, a deep lack of trust prevailed between the United States and Iran. Recurring deceptions and misbehaviors strongly eroded the little trust Americans had in Iranian intentions. Iran's diplomats were simply perceived as pathological liars and, if diplomacy is the name of the game, the opportunity to engage in comprehensive, high-level talks was totally jeopardized because of this complete lack of trust on both sides. Concerning North Korea, Washington has always maintained its time-honored hostile policy, which is strongly based on absolute mistrust during the six-party talks. Any American proposal is treated by Pyongyang as little more than "old wine in a new bottle" and in addition as a proposal by the real "empire of evil." Conversely, American viewpoints tend to present North Korean politics as "organized crime," and the North Korean government as promoting "drug dealing as state policy." This country is most often described as a failing Stalinist dictatorship held together by the ruthless repression of a mad ruler in his Communist straitjacket who dreams of firing nuclear weapons at Los Angeles. In such a tense and unfavorable context, trust has no room to blossom.

Suspicion of hidden agendas flourishes in negotiations, like conspiracy theories in the political world. Thus, the United States was suspected by a number of UN member states as having a hidden agenda regarding Iraq after September 11, which was to invade Iraq, whatever the attitude of Saddam Hussein would be and for reasons that did not have much to do with creating a democracy. In Camp David 2, each party strongly suspected the other side of trying to carry out a hidden agenda as the lies and distortions of Middle Eastern politicians do not inspire a belief that what is said is the same thing as what is meant. Going comfortably through the labyrinthine minds of negotiators involved in the Byzantine politics of the Middle East is extremely unusual. Suspicion about hidden agendas leads to "procès d'intention" and, as a direct consequence, the failure of the negotiation.

In the Iranian case, the EU always suspected their counterparts of having hidden intentions and just keeping negotiating to gain time with delaying tactics. In the Belgian case, the great powers and the Dutch were extremely distrustful of one another. Even the great powers among themselves were not able to build any trust. The French and the Brits always assumed that the conservative central and eastern European empires did not seriously care about the situation but worried more about their own interests and future consequences.

PROCESSES AND OUTCOME

Within an overall situation, the process is the core of a negotiation, its engine, and its driving force. Throughout the process, strategies are developed and tactics implemented. By definition, an outcome is the result of the process, and so can be a failure. Negotiating activity can be described as a sequence of stages, either organized in well-articulated patterns or overlapping and developing over time in a haphazard or even confused way (Dupont and Faure, 2002). Grasping the rationale for the process, conducting it in an effective way, and, in other words, combining conflicting positions into a common position is in many cases a challenge. Several major obstacles may crop up and render the task vain, adding to the list of reasons why negotiations remained unfinished business.

All the cases presented in his book have in common the *absence of a Mutually Enticing Opportunity*. For instance, in the Iranian case, there is no resolving formula devised, no focal point put forth, no salient solution brought to the fore, no turning point. What negotiation dramatically misses in these cases is creativity, the ability to go beyond usual mechanisms and beyond their own uncertainties. In a process, parties should look for "branching points" that would really make a difference and not turn the negotiation into a recurrent process of missed opportunities. Salient moves meeting history could do the job, such as Egyptian president Sadat's visit to Israel (1977), the French-German reconciliation after World War II, or the Sharon policy of disengagement and the Palestinians' subsequent withdrawal from Gaza and the dismantling of settlements, only interrupted by his own death (2006). In some circumstances, one has to make the decision to cross the Rubicon.

Insufficient gathering of information has led to dramatic events such as the outbreak of the Second World War. Hitler got enough certainty about the weak effectiveness of Allied intelligence about his military preparation and thus became convinced that there would be no preventive action against him. In that case, the negotiation reached an outcome with the Munich Pact in 1938, but the failure was in the implementation, which has to be considered part of the negotiation. Precisely, a number of negotiation failures are due to the poor gathering of strategic information by the authorities before or during the process. In the Israeli hostage case in Munich, the police, deprived of specialized technical assistance, resorted to assault while even ignoring the real number of terrorists involved. Whether their choice had been to undertake the "tactical solution" or to carry out the negotiation until an agreement was reached, much more data should have been collected before taking any strategic option.

In some cases, *escalation* was not avoided by setting any agreement aside. The escalation process of the conflict could be triggered by negative reciprocity, such as vengeance, protection, or deterring another from keeping the same strategy, or because parties consider that they have not yet made enough use of their resources to harm the other. The Munich hostage case displays several levels of escalation on the hostage-takers' side, from issuing threats, then throwing a dead body out of the front door of the building in which they were barricaded, and finally slaughtering all the remaining hostages.

Escalation as a mutually coercive mechanism does not just result in simple intensification but in a change of nature (Zartman and Faure, 2005a). Thus, de-escalation for the purpose of adopting a more cooperative stance is most difficult to enact, as it is far more than just reducing quantitatively the means allocated to put pressure on the other side. Escalation tends to take on a life of its own. It works as a lethal mechanism leading parties to a situation where they never imagined they could be and in any case they never wanted to be. World War I was a tragic example of that competitive irrationality, starting with one assassination and ending with millions dead, thirty-nine countries involved, and the collapse of four empires. Warning systems may play a role not just in preventing crisis but also in preventing escalation. There are signals that if properly picked out and interpreted may reveal that an escalation process is under way. The point is to build an information system with reliable indicators so that the negotiation can be kept on track and not get out of control. Looking, for instance, at the nuclear program of Iran, a military attack on its nuclear facilities would probably mark the beginning of a regional, and possibly global, military, and terrorist escalation.

Ineffective risk management is another cause of failures. Parties can be caught in the "Alphonse et Gaston" paradox. No one wants to move first because she fears that the other may get the benefits. Then, neither found a way to make their move at the same time. They did not find (or did not think of looking for) a mediator who could help them to achieve this stage. Risk can relate to not reaching an agreement, or getting caught in the process dynamics by making too-costly concessions, but also to exposing oneself by releasing information that could normally help reach a satisfying outcome. Handling risk can be done by resorting to the available techniques in the risk assessment paradigm, such as cost-benefit analysis, modeling, scenario analysis, computer simulations, and uncertainty analysis. However, in most of the situations, negotiators employ much less sophisticated approaches when not simply relying on intuition. The precautionary principle dominates many negotiations and prevents countries from adopting a common attitude toward such global issues as climate change, biological diversity, and trans-boundary air pollution. Such a twist perverts the normal course of a negotiation process by nullifying the commitment of some parties to the purpose of the negotiation task.

Fear may also act not to pressure someone to make some move but as a paralyzing factor. Fear of losing too much, fear of escalation, fear of the unknown future, fear of losing one's reputation all tend to freeze the whole process. Fear of being trapped with no satisfactory exit strategy may also incite parties not to carry on with the negotiation process, the possible commitments to make and to accept a reduction of maneuvering room. Entrapment has been dramatically illustrated for Americans by the Vietnam War, in which over fifty-eight thousand U.S. soldiers and several million Vietnamese died, and by the ten-year Soviet-Afghanistan war during which one million Afghans died, along with thirteen thousand Soviet soldiers.

Now fear of being trapped may stay in the mind of negotiators when getting involved in an interactive process that they may not be able to fully control and whose end remains most uncertain. If fear comes to dominate, parties cannot disclose enough information to build an agreement formula or work effectively on the transformation of the problem. Parties may also tend, as a safety measure, to give the same high level of importance to too many issues, thus making it impossible to build a package deal. The Camp David 2 case illustrates this difficulty.

An *improper management of stages* in negotiation may also freeze the process. Building no trust and as a consequence struggling over details without having built a formula leads nowhere except to more fights. For example, again the Camp David 2 negotiation reflects that type of shortcoming and strategic error. When creativity is the most needed, parties indulge in distributive bargaining, sterilizing the integrative potential of the situation. The U.S. carrot and stick diplomacy to promote democracy in Africa is another typical example as it tends to erase all classic stages of international negotiation, thus not enabling negotiators to make a proper use of technical resources stemming from the process management.

A lack of continuity in the course of action may affect the whole negotiation. Inconsistencies may just destroy the initial strategy or reveal that there is *no clear strategy*, but just a series of tactics implemented. Negotiators do not properly conduct a coherent strategy, but react to moves initiated by the other side. For instance, in the Munich case, the German side shifted from one type of action to another, giving the impression it was floating along with circumstances. The negotiation started with German political authorities and the Munich chief of the police, to whom were added later on two Egyptian advisers to the Arab League, then a group of German border police, poorly trained, ill prepared, and with no specific operational plans in place for the rescue. Five snipers were chosen to ambush the kidnappers on the grounds that they were sharpshooters during their leisure time. Two Israeli advisers were present, but their advice was never sought. During the Waco siege, no fewer than forty negotiators, from the Bureau of Alcohol, Tobacco and Firearms, the local police, the FBI, the National Guard, and scholars specializing in apocalypticism intervened in the discussions with the Davidians, making any coherent action highly unlikely. Another consequence of the disorganization on the authorities' side was a loss of credibility and the instillation of a serious doubt on the offers made by them.

Typical examples of unclear strategy when negotiating are the UN peace operations in Somalia, Congo (DRC), Sierra Leone, Afghanistan, and Darfur. Another example of strategic confusion is the EU negotiating a peace settlement on the many war episodes during the collapse of Yugoslavia. Camp David 2 was viewed by some observers as the last negotiation, or in other words, the way to end the Middle East peace process. Its failure was sometimes explained by an unclear strategy from the U.S. mediator who left Palestinian and Israeli negotiators puzzled about what they could really expect as an outcome.

There is a ripe moment to get to the negotiation table. Once negotiating, there is also a ripe moment to close the deal. It could be framed as a Rubicon problem, because jumping to the final offer is crossing a threshold. There is a *sense of timing* involved. Offering to close too early would mean not having taken enough care to explore all the possibilities for an effective formula. Letting too much time pass could be like staying on the platform when the train leaves. A missed opportunity may not come again soon as external circumstances may be changing.

If the overall situation is degrading, the more a person waits to act, the more there will be to do and the higher will be the costs. Preventing World War I would have saved so many human lives and so much cost. On the Iraq issue, public pressure played an important role and accelerated the deadline for closing an agreement. In the Munich hostage case, external pressures, especially from the Israeli government, led the German authorities to act too hastily. In the opposite direction, the biological convention lasted so long that main parties became tired and skeptical about the effectiveness of the whole process.

In the Taba Summit, Israeli and the U.S. mediator had run out of political time. Prime Minister Barak was due to face an election soon, and President

Clinton was leaving office. The whole negotiation process between Israel and Palestine had only been substantially revived in December, and the new U.S. presidency was to start in January, which did not allow enough time to come up with an agreement on such thorny issues as territorial limits, Jerusalem, and the Temple Mount ("Haram esh-Sharif," the "Noble Sanctuary," for the Arabs), plus the right of return for refugees.

On occasion, *mediators* bear an important responsibility in negotiation failures. They may provide insufficient efforts or efforts too late to be effective and pave the way for enough cooperation. One of the most important qualities that a mediator must have is persistence.

In some cases spoilers have enough influence to make reaching an agreement impossible. The job of a powerful mediator is to keep these spoilers away or limit their grip on the negotiation process. In the Belgium case, the great powers, instead of mediating, went the other way and finally arbitrated making the decision themselves instead of the parties.

In a general way, if one considers the situation in which mediation takes place, the personality and the effective role played by the mediator can lead to failure. For instance, this may happen because of insufficient effort, as mentioned by Zartman ("Process Reasons for Failure," in this book), in the case of Cyprus and Camp David 2. Mediators lacked persistence, neglected substantive demands, and did not resort enough to incentives and sanctions to keep parties on track. In the never-ending negotiations to end the partition of Cyprus (Saner, "The Cyprus Conflict," in this book), the U.S. mediator did not give much push to really trigger some converging moves.

An insufficient political will is not unusual. In October 1941, a public opinion poll carried out in the United States showed that over 70 percent of the Americans opposed getting involved in the war against Germany. The insularity of the mind can be part of the reasons why the mediator does not consent to give the necessary impetus.

In some cases, spoilers freeze the negotiation process because an agreement would not bring them any benefit. This is clearly the case in the Middle East talks with Iran and Hizbulla. Then, the job of the mediator is to reduce their influence or keep them away from the core negotiation. This raises the issue of the credibility of the mediator who either does not display enough of a commitment to reach an agreement, or appears too biased to be trusted and play the role of an honest broker. When, for instance, major powers leave part of the job of restructuring the whole field to NGOs or private foundations, there is a failure in terms of responsibilities and potential influence. This has been the case with the U.S. mediation with regard to Palestine, and it has also been the case with the UN in Somalia.

The mediator has to find the right balance between the role of inactive observer and that of the actor who finally makes the decision instead of the parties. This last strategy was ultimately adopted by the great powers in the Belgian case, where at last they made all the decisions, leaving some of the parties feeling quite helpless (see Fridl, "The Negotiations on the Status of Belgium," in this volume). It is also the job of an effective mediator to make sure that the negotiation is done in good faith and that parties are really seeking peace. It is not unusual to have parties negotiating for side effects, such as gaining time to build up a better power position on the ground, to get publicity, to increase prestige, or to obtain intelligence.

For negotiators having scheming objectives, using a well-respected mediator is a way to gain legitimacy and also to have someone on which to put the blame if a protracted deadlock occurs. That may have been the case with the Israeli-Palestinian negotiation in the 1990s.

Turning warriors into peace seekers is always a most difficult challenge. If enforcement mechanisms are not part of the agreement, skepticism about the value of the agreement will dominate, and the motivation to reach a deal will remain low.

Often what also happens is a phenomenon of *self-fulfilling prophecy*. The failure of the negotiation is anticipated and parties will behave accordingly, finally making the failure happen (Merton, 1968). They may be the victims of cognitive dissonance and thus strengthened in their pessimistic views until things get totally hopeless. Some observers considered Camp David 2 as doomed to fail from the very start in the mind of the protagonists.

Many current situations are viewed as bearing the risk of triggering such a phenomenon. Considering, for instance, Iran's nuclear program, the military option may ring as a self-fulfilling prophecy. First, there is no guarantee that attempts to destroy Iran's nuclear potential will succeed. Moreover, as a victim of foreign aggression, Iran's nuclear weapons ambitions would be fully legitimized with heavy consequences on nuclear proliferation in the region. The current deadlock may thus, for many countries, lead to extremely negative outcomes. Reflecting on another case, if China and Russia are treated as emerging enemies, such an attitude from the West can generate a self-fulfilling prophecy, as these countries would react accordingly. However, trade with and investment in these countries, the way it was done in Germany after World War II, may just hasten the day of reckoning by contributing to their technological progress, adding thus a strategic dilemma to the initial risk.

Another cause of protracted deadlock lies in the inability of the parties — and of the mediator when there is one — to consider a *forward-looking outcome* addressing both the roots of the conflict and the future relations. In some cases, heads of state must have a sense of history and express it through some significant gesture. In these circumstances negotiation must not follow public opinion and media views but move ahead and show the way. For doing so one has also to avoid analytical-cognitive lacunas stemming from a narrow view of the overall situation and avoid indulging in self-serving analysis.

The integration of the forward-looking outcome dimension in the relations and negotiations led the United States to give up the idea of punishing Japan at the end of World War II and thus to avoid the birth of a resentment from the Japanese population. In the same way, it was based on a historical vision far beyond the immediate interests of France that General De Gaulle began negotiations that resulted in the Accords d'Evian. These agreements put an end to the war in Algeria and led to the independence of this country.

The forward-looking outcome approach may apply to all sorts of situations and does not necessarily implicate dealing with the destiny of a nation. A much smaller community can also be as concerned. It was the case, for instance, with the Waco siege where precisely this forward-looking outcome dimension has been cruelly missing. The failure of the negotiations resulted in a massacre in which seventy-six people, including twenty-one children, lost their lives in an assault that was supposed to save them.

Finally, failures may also be explained by the fact that parties have only been able to provide *incomplete (or ill-adapted) answers to complex problems*, such as in the Israeli-Palestinian case or the Somalia crisis. Doing so, they often offer short-term solutions to long-term issues and do not address the roots of the problem, an easy path that has a price in the long run. In other situations, they also may provide partial solutions closer to a cease-fire than to a resolution of the crisis. In reality, the negotiation ends with at best a signed piece of paper that does not solve the pending problems, and this paper may finally be nothing more than a clever formula to indicate that both parties agree to acknowledge their disagreement.

Complex problems have mostly been dealt with as complicated problems, which means negotiations addressing a number of heterogeneous issues that are related in such a way that the situation exceeds the capacity of the parties to foresee the consequences of a given move. Thus, if simplified they cannot generate solutions that deal with the complexities of the problem. Complex problems should be, as pointed out in this book by Mermet ("Managing Complexity"), first considered as having other characteristics such as ambiguity, incomplete knowledge, instability, or behavioral unpredictability. Then, dealing with them implies thinking in complex ways and resorting to systemic approaches, which is something negotiators are not trained to do.

Consider, for instance, the Taba talks, another Israeli-Palestinian American-mediated failure. They had been structured around four committees, each one handling a different theme: refugees, security, borders, and Jerusalem. These issues involve a number of dimensions, among them the human, moral, economic, strategic, religious, historical, cultural, symbolic, and psychological dimensions. There is no common yardstick that can help to measure consequences of moves on one or another dimension. The final failure shows how difficult it can be to prioritize among crucial issues — considering the values and the deep-rooted stakes behind — and finally to conceive the problem in a systemic way.

A mediator unable to properly capture the complexity of a situation and, as a consequence, to deal with the whole reality of the problem adds to the difficulty. For instance, in the case of the Camp David summit, the collapse of the negotiations over the issue of Jerusalem was partly due to the assumption that the religious dimension of the conflict could be put aside. Jerusalem is, first of all, a religious city, and this fact concerns even more parties than just Israel and Palestine. The whole of Islam considers Al-Quds (the Holy), Jerusalem in Arabic, as one of the most sacred places in the world. It was easier to carry out talks about the control of historical monuments and archaeological sites in the old city than to discuss the link between the religious sanctity and political status of the place. However, it fell short of addressing the whole problem in its full complexity.

CONCLUSION

There are a considerable number of reasons why negotiations do not reach any agreement. They belong to all registers of negotiation, including actors, context, strategies, and process. Their diversity is already a useful outcome of research.

Learning from difficulties is the beginning of wisdom. When asking negotiators, one may often get an explanation for failure such as that "nothing
could be done," "it was hopeless," "no way with them," "too much bad faith,"
"too much bad will on their side," "they are just irrational people; no way to
get them to understand reason," "they do not even realize their own interest," "they deadlocked the whole process intentionally," "their plans from the
very beginning were to make the negotiation fail." In fact, there is no historical determinism orchestrating negotiations. Achieving an outcome has simply
to do with human volition within a set of constraints. One major challenge
to any negotiation is to select the right paradigm in order to play construc-
tively. This selection requires putting the emphasis first on the analysis of the
situation.

Among the thirty-nine factors causing failures in negotiations, six of them
appear quite prominent and would deserve a special attention for future research. They have to be considered as polar causes, around which other causes
may aggregate, producing a multiplicative effect. They all belong to different
analytical categories of the negotiation.

On the side of the actors, although often not recognized as such, *demonization* is a well-spread process that nullifies all efforts to interact in a positive
way. To have the counterpart's status shifting to that of a devil entails its dele-
gitimization as an acceptable party to the negotiation and subsequently of the
negotiation itself. The responsibility of the negotiation's failure is transferred to
the other as a demon. Thus, one will keep to the status quo. If the logic of the
new attribution is pushed further, demonization provides a reason to switch
to other types of action than discussion, such as resorting to force or armed
action.

The *inability to adapt the negotiation process to the external changes* that
may occur during protracted negotiations within a turbulent environment is
another major cause of failure. Analyzing the situation adequately, selecting
the right negotiation paradigm, and being able to shift if the context changes,
are always challenging tasks. However, it is a quite essential undertaking as it
relates structure and strategies within the negotiation framework. When the
negotiation is prolonged over a considerable period of time, the context may
change, new coalitions may be formed, new technologies may appear, and new
imperatives may be imposed on the parties. The negotiation mode may also
evolve and take into account these changes as well as the advances made in
negotiation techniques in conflict resolution.

Improper mediation is another important cause of failure. The mediating party does not have enough means of influence or not enough will, not enough commitment, or not enough interest to facilitate an agreement. The mediator may not be able to properly manage the timing or seize the right moment — when to give a push, when to suggest reciprocal concessions, when to reward, and when to deliver warnings or even threats. Mediating is playing within the process, but after having modified the structure of the game. This new situation provides to the mediator wider room for maneuvering than when parties were discussing face to face. The triangular structure allows, for instance, initiatives on the side of the mediator, proposals that would have no credibility if coming from one or the other party. When parties do not meet physically, the mediator may manipulate the information he conveys back and forth.

What happens in a number of situations is that there is simply *no ZOPA* and none of the parties realizes it, as they do not know the security point of the counterpart. Thus, they can strive for a long time to reach a deal to finally attribute the responsibility of the standstill to the other's bad will when, in fact, the problem is structural. As a consequence, the first imperative is not to struggle in order to obtain maximum gains in a system for which there is no possibility of agreement but to build a structure for the game that afterward will enable both sides to strike an agreement.

Trust is a most difficult condition to build, especially in a negotiation bringing together foes who may be inclined to see the bargaining table as another arena for war. However, if there is not at least a minimum trust, how can one believe anything coming from the other side, or take seriously their promises and commitments? The final point in a negotiation is not to obtain a piece of paper with the signatures of both parties but to have the agreement implemented. To satisfy this condition, some kind of confidence has to be established. Taking into account the nature of the relation between both parties, it is a most necessary but challenging task to achieve.

However, there are examples of successful negotiations with no shared trust, such as the Congress of Vienna of 1814–15, where Talleyrand, the French negotiator, was not even trusted by his own constituents and even less by the king he was representing. However, in that case, he had outstanding technical skills and could show enough credibility in the arguments he used to sign at the end of the process a secret alliance with England and the Austro-Hungarian Empire against Prussia and Russia.

Ultimately, one must have a *sense of timing* to know when to offer to close the deal. Again, it is something essential but extremely difficult to analyze and control, as it is as much intuitive as rational. When is a situation ripe for closure? This sense of timing is mainly psychological as it is based on assumptions about the state of mind of the counterparts. It is also strongly dependent on the level of expectation of the negotiator. Nevertheless, it also depends on the evolution of the substance of the discussions. This is typically when negotiation is no more a science but becomes an art.

Besides these six topics that deserve a special attention in future research, the very nature of the negotiation may also play a preponderant role. It is far easier, for instance, to design a win–win solution in a purely economic negotiation than in a political discussion where border delimitation issues or security questions are dealt with.

Lessons for Practice

FRANZ CEDE

For those involved by profession in international negotiations, the explanation for the collapse of a negotiation in which they have participated normally lies on the other side of the table. It seems to be part of human nature that participants in negotiations are biased when it comes to identifying the root causes of failure. Usually they take a defensive line by offering their own version of the case. When engaging in a negotiation the actor is obviously convinced that his own arguments are the right ones. Quite understandably he identifies himself with the position he is supposed to present. He defends his case and hopes that his arguments will ultimately prevail. If eventually the negotiation collapses he is probably the worst analyst one can possibly find to explain the negative outcome. A confession to the effect that the negotiator will admit he was responsible "for the mess" is not something heard often. Therefore, researchers are well advised to give little weight to the utterances of negotiators telling their story of how and why a particular negotiation went down the drain.

The actor on one side of the table will be inclined to give a positive assessment of her role, asserting that she was responsible for a breakthrough, while the counterpart on the other side of the situation explains the collapse of the negotiation. A second observation of this author, as a practitioner of international negotiations, may come as a surprise to those who live outside the arcane world of diplomacy. In real life, negotiators are rarely endowed with the kind of special knowledge that negotiation theorists propagate in their teachings. The real persons sitting at the negotiation table are seldom experts in negotiation theory. In spite of the fact that many universities now include negotiation theory in their curricula, it would be wrong to conclude that this has significantly altered the general picture, which shows little or no impact of negotiation theory on the persons who conduct the business of international negotiations. A personality such as Henry Kissinger, who combines the highest academic qualifications with the experience of a seasoned negotiator, can be considered as a rare exception. Negotiators come from very diverse backgrounds. They may have climbed the career ladder in the political arena or made their names as experts in a field that happens to be in demand for a particular type of negotiations. In many cases negotiators acquire their skills on the spot. "Learning by doing" appears to be the normal initiation to the negotiation game. Stressing this point should not be seen as a digression from our subject matter, since one often hears the argument that negotiations foundered because of insufficient training of negotiators in negotiation theory.

The best expert in negotiation theory does not automatically become the best negotiator in practice. Of course, excellent training in negotiation techniques does not harm and will always be useful. However, experience shows that in many cases persons who have no theoretical background whatsoever may turn out to be very efficient and successful negotiators. In their long practice they may have acquired an excellent ability to communicate, psychological awareness, and empathy, as well as the capacity to make the right decision at the right moment. The theorist may be perfectly able to analyze the negotiation process in hindsight and describe the mistakes of others better than the negotiator but may be lacking all the abilities of a successful actor in the real game. To draw a parallel to the world of politics: the best president of the United States may not necessarily be the best political scientist boasting academic degrees from the most prestigious universities. A successful president may even have been a movie star, a peanut farmer, or a haberdasher in his previous life. In fact, the characteristics of his personality may just be right for the office of the president. Something similar can be said about a good negotiator. The point is that lack of education in negotiation theory must not necessarily become a recipe for disaster in the real world.

PURPOSE OF THE PRESENT CHAPTER

In the conclusions from the preceding chapters an attempt is made to identify the possible causes of the breakdown of negotiations with a view toward developing strategies for successful negotiations, bearing in mind the lessons from past failures.

Eight major reasons are given to explain failures, many of which have been described in the preceding chapters. Each of these reasons leads to a corresponding recommendation. While the reasons given are meant to explain failure of past negotiations, the recommendations seek to offer useful suggestions for the future. The focus of the concluding observations is put on the structural elements, whereas the case studies serve to illustrate the causes of unsuccessful negotiations.

REASON I. THE SINGLE-CAUSE TRAP

In analyzing the reasons for incomplete negotiations there is a temptation to put the finger on one single cause. It must be said, however, that monocausal explanations often miss the point. The complexity of a case generally cannot be reduced to a single-cause explanation (see Fridl, "The Negotiations on the Status of Belgium"). An approach, for instance, that ignores the history of a particular situation or dispute is bound to go astray. The same holds true for an explanation that does not do justice to the arguments of both sides. On the other hand, despite the complexity of a given situation or the realities that make up the negotiation environment, some dominant factors usually emerge that explain why a particular negotiation did not succeed (see, e.g., Saner, "The Cyprus Conflict," and Marschik, "The UN Security Council and Iraq"). Such dominant factors may be quite diverse and even contradictory. The challenge is to weigh them properly in order to arrive at a balanced assessment.

Let us assume there are five factors that have a negative impact on the outcome of a negotiation: mutual dislike of the chief negotiators, ensuing lack of trust between the actors, false information provided by one or the other party, a wrong institutional framework, or misconceptions about strategy (see Wanis-St. John, "Nuclear Negotiations"). If one of the five reasons given in this situation is identified as the only stumbling block (e.g., bad personal chemistry between the actors), leaving out the other factors, or underestimating their relevance, the negotiators run the risk of making wrong decisions. If they misinterpret the hurdles standing in the way of progress they will be unable to extricate themselves from the predicament they may find themselves in. In a single-cause explanation for failure that put the blame only on the incompatibility of the actors involved, changing the negotiators would be the obvious recipe for rescuing the negotiation. However, it might soon turn out that a change of the negotiators alone would not do the trick, since the substantial problems besetting the negotiation would not disappear.

RECOMMENDATION I. MAKE SURE TO GRASP
THE COMPLEXITY OF THE PROCESS

Drawing from the mistake that identifies only one cause or blames the wrong factor for the lack of agreement, every effort should be made to examine all elements of the negotiation in a comprehensive way. The complexity of any negotiation requires a holistic approach encompassing all elements of the process. The stakes involved, the framing of the issues (see Hopmann, "Issue Content and Incomplete Negotiation"), the history of the case, the legal framework, the international environment, the domestic situation, and the psychological factors are but a few indicators that need to be studied carefully before it is advisable to engage in a negotiation experience. A rational analysis of the chances for success should be made well before the beginning of the negotiation. It is not wise to rush into a negotiation without having properly studied the various aspects of the situation. The negotiators need to have a clear understanding about all elements that are likely to derail the negotiating process. They must put these elements in the right context and then make a strategic decision on how they will deal with them.

In assessing all relevant factors, due regard should also be given to the expectations of all parties involved. Considerable time and energy should be devoted to preparing the negotiation. Thorough preparation of the talks, a good knowledge of the issues at stake, correct assumptions about the positions, and no illusions about the determination of the opposite party are useful tools for successful negotiations.

REASON II. IGNORANCE OF THE EXTRANEOUS FACTORS

Every negotiation is characterized by its own dynamic and intrinsic logic. The process can be viewed as a system determined by both constant elements and variables. The actors, their negotiating positions, and the institutional framework belong to this system. An analysis of the negative outcome of negotiations often misses the "extraneous factors," that is, those that at first sight are discarded since they are considered as not forming part of the negotiating framework. To illustrate this point, the example of the most recent negotiations leading to a cease-fire between Israel and Hamas may be cited. These negotiations evidently took account of the change of the U.S. presidential administration. Even the exact date of the setting into force of the cease-fire was made dependent on events in Washington. No sensible analyst would classify political developments in the United States as irrelevant for the Middle East peace process, although in a formal sense one might argue that the change of government in a country is to be considered an extraneous factor with regard to an ongoing negotiation between two other parties. Another example was cited in the chapter on structural approaches (Wanis-St. John and Dupont, "Structural Dimensions of Failure in Negotiation"). The authors set out the linkage between internal (domestic) and external (international) negotiations. Especially in the framework of recent WTO negotiations, this linkage constituted a significant obstacle to agreement. Analysts who disconnect the domestic level as extraneous from the international plane will fail to understand the interrelationship between the two. By ignoring the impact of domestic policy they will obviously overlook one of the important causes of incomplete negotiations.

More broadly, the general context shapes the possibilities of an agreement, to the point where a particular envisaged outcome that could provide a resolution to the conflict at one time would be a failure in a different context. Potential solutions that are salient at one time have not yet gained or have lost their acceptability at another. Examples are myriad: among the cases discussed in this volume, the bicommunal bizonal federation for Cyprus could have been a winner before the Nicosia government's admission to the European Union on behalf of the entire island; the proposed resolution in the UN Security Council on Iraq supposedly would have gained unanimity, according to the claims of some members, if Iraq had just been given one more chance (the nineteenth chance) to show its good faith; the final agreement on Belgium waited a decade to be accepted.

RECOMMENDATION II. CONSIDER ALL EXTERNAL FACTORS SURROUNDING THE NEGOTIATIONS PROPER

Some authors were right in stressing the impact of "extraneous factors." They attest to the truth that negotiation processes cannot be viewed as closed shops but are embedded in an environment that must be equally taken into appropriate account. Therefore, negotiators should integrate them properly in their evaluations and not limit their judgment by taking a narrow view of the negotiation framework. One should look beyond this framework in order to see all factors that might have a bearing on the process. In a second step, negotiators should assess the relevance and weight of the extraneous elements with regard to their own position and those of the negotiating partner. Such a comprehensive assessment is crucial to making the right choices and prevents the matter from ending up on a dead-end street at the closure of the negotiations. If, in fact, some factors such as domestic policy, public opinion, and so forth have an impact on the negotiations in a tangible manner, they must be included in the structure of the relevant negotiation. Whether they are in a strict sense external to the formal negotiating framework does not matter.

REASON III. LACK OF TRUST: A RECIPE FOR FAILURE

Stating the obvious does not by itself mean that the obvious must be wrong. It is evident that the principle of good faith (bona fides) underlies all serious relationships, be they between individuals or between entities such as states or other actors on the international plane. In international law the bona fides principle plays a crucial role. It is enshrined in a number of legal instruments (e.g., Charter of the United Nations, Vienna Convention on the Law of Treaties, to name just two of them). The emphasis put on the principle of good faith proceeds from the recognition of the simple truth that without a minimum of honesty the entire international system would fall apart. What is meant by trust in the context of international negotiations? In simple terms one may describe trust by the fundamental expectation that each party conducts its business with a measure of decency and credibility. If these ingredients are missing, negotiations have little chance of success (see Fridl, "The Negotiations on the Status of Belgium"). There may be different approaches to the very concept of decency in the value system of the negotiators. Irrespective of such differences there is no denying that without a minimum platform of shared expectations with regard to the credibility and authority, negotiations cannot be brought to a mutually satisfactory outcome. One can apply the good faith principle without reservation to all negotiations. Unfortunately, an analysis of a great number of incomplete negotiations reveals a lack of trust on both sides. Recent negotiations conducted within the framework of the UN Security Council (see Marschik, "The UN Security Council and Iraq") illustrate this argument. In all fairness, it has to be stated that lack of trust does not always mean that the negotiators cheat deliberately. It may well be that the cultural differences and the mutual animosity of the actors are such that they cannot find a common basis for their interaction. A third complication often stems from the fact that the concepts of a particular negotiation are viewed by each side in a fundamentally different way. Whereas one party may play for time and may not be interested in an outcome that would change the status quo, the opposite party may earnestly strive for tangible progress to be reached within a reasonable time span. Measured against these two conflicting strategies the termination of the negotiation without any result will be judged as a success by the first party and as a failure by the latter. These contradictory visions are to a great measure due to a lack of understanding of the basic positions and of the strategies. If these conflicting views of the purpose of the whole negotiation exercise are irreconcilable there is a likelihood that at some point a crisis will erupt, resulting in mutual accusations of "negotiating in bad faith" (see the section "Negotiations Intended to Fail," in Hopmann, "Issue Content and Incomplete Negotiation"). Another occurrence of bad faith may reside in the deliberate misrepresentation of facts. The dictum that the truth is the first casualty of war unfortunately applies to many negotiations as well. Exerting undue pressure on the other side belongs in the category of indecent behavior by negotiators. Many case studies show how the "bad faith factor" has wrecked negotiations (see Marschik). It is to be considered one of the major causes of failure.

RECOMMENDATION III. CREATE A CLIMATE OF TRUST AND HONESTY

Although it certainly would be naïve to believe that in this world of harsh realities "love and brotherhood" permeate all human activities, the old-fashioned advice to attach greater importance to the "trust factor" should not be ruled out altogether when considering how the chances of completing negotiations could be enhanced. What should be done?

In the first place, "confidence-building measures" should be taken in order to dispel any illusions about purported bad motivations of the other side (see the concept of Mutually Enticing Opportunity [MEO] in Zartman, "Process Reasons for Failure"). Building trust between the players should start by informing the other party about the main goals and objectives pursued. Each party should give at least an indication of what it really considers "nonnegotiable." Of course, the underlying tactics will not always allow going all the way down in revealing what one has in mind. However, it is to be expected that each party explains at the outset what it conceives as the goal of the particular negotiation or what it views as the bottom line of a compromise. Such an exchange about the respective expectations should be conducted in an informal and confidential manner. The word "confidential" itself indicates how important it is to have a common platform of understanding of the process before the talks actually start. There are many methods available to create a climate of trust. Negotiators will find no difficulty in taking the confidence measures of their own choice. Creativity in building an atmosphere of trust knows no limits.

REASON IV. WRONG FACTS AND FALSE INFORMATION

Deliberately using wrong facts or information belongs to the category of bad faith. Although such deceptive behavior is actually not as infrequent as one would think, the problem often encountered is of a different nature. It consists in the controversy both about the relevant facts and their correct interpretation in the context of a particular negotiation (see Kydd, "A Failure to Communicate"). Both parties may have the best possible intentions about the facts, but they frequently diverge over their interpretation. In addition to a controversial reading of the facts, public opinion in the two camps may also exert a damaging influence on the course of negotiations. In the modern information society, public opinion as projected by the media plays an important role in determining the international agenda. As a consequence the negotiators are under constant pressure by their respective public opinions. The views expressed by the media may contribute to the escalation of a conflict and harden the positions of the negotiators seeking to meet the growing expectations raised by the media. It goes without saying that the impact of the media factor combined with a lack a common understanding about the facts has the potential to wreck an ongoing negotiation.

RECOMMENDATION IV. AGREE ON THE FACTS
AND ASSESS THEM PROPERLY

Do not let the battle over the facts endanger the negotiations. In spite of serious differences about the facts and data that are relevant for the negotiations, no effort should be spared to reach a common platform of understanding on the factual parameters of the issue. There are several ways this can be done. One is to share relevant information. The transparency of the negotiations will be greatly furthered by such information sharing or, if this appears unfeasible, by jointly ascertaining the data and facts. The establishment of a joint fact-finding body might be considered. If this appears impractical, an agreement should be reached to the effect that the facts are not an issue.

Negotiators also have the possibility of framing the issues of their talks in a way that is conducive to a positive result. They must find a common understanding on the parameters of the talks. If they fail to do so they will go in different directions from the beginning.

Brushing aside differences over the facts or the framing of the negotiations at the beginning of the negotiations means proceeding from different assumptions that will have, at a later juncture, a disruptive effect on the negotiations. An additional complication may come from the distorted image the media create about the facts. In this regard it is more difficult to offer good advice. The simple recipe is to keep cool and not be drawn into the spiral of the passing whispers of the media. One can only appeal to the sense of responsibility of the actors to place a positive outcome of the negotiations higher than the short-lived applause of public opinion.

The last piece of advice with regard to the issue of information concerns the need to put all data and facts in the right perspective. The overall aim — namely, the goal of reaching a sustainable agreement with the other party — necessitates a value judgment on what one considers most important when the chips are down. On balance, sticking to a position on a detail may turn out not worth the energy when evaluating the overriding interest of finding a reasonable settlement. In this perspective negotiators should decide on what concessions they are ultimately willing to make for the sake of reaching an agreement. In other words, they need to have a clear view of what represents the bottom line for them and of what they are prepared to forsake in the overriding interest of reaching an agreement.

REASON V. LACK OF SENSITIVITY TO THE PSYCHOLOGICAL FACTOR

Closely linked to the matter of trust is the psychological factor. It may happen that the personal chemistry between the key actors does not work. Obviously, negotiations are conducted by human beings with their own sympathies and antipathies. They also have their idiosyncrasies. Underestimating the human element has caused more than one negotiation to founder. Ignoring the cultural values and traditions of the other party may also be put under the rubric of lack of psychological sensitivity that puts the success of the negotiation at risk (for a detailed discussion of the psychological causes, see Jönsson, "Psychological Causes of Incomplete Negotiations"). The incompatibility of characters frequently leads to situations in which the presentation of the respective positions is done without any consideration of the psychological or cultural factors. Negotiators showing no sensitivity to the "psycho factor" have an inclination to bully their counterparts into accepting their position at any cost. It is to be expected that the reaction will be negative. Ignorance of the personal background of the partner combined with a lack of interest in his character is often responsible for misunderstandings in the course of the negotiations. The "insensitive negotiator" is inclined to put forward his arguments in an uncompromising way that creates in itself an atmosphere of tension and stress for the other negotiator. Someone put under pressure will not be likely to go the extra mile required for achieving a positive outcome at the end of the day. Of course, it is hard to measure exactly to what extent the subjective elements come into play. But that they do exist has been sorely learned by many negotiators who have failed because they had brushed aside the psychological aspects. Of course, these factors are subjective in that they belong to the psyche and the mind-set of the other party. However, this admission in no way decreases their actual importance. When trust and understanding for the human being sitting on the other side are missing, the chances for a successful outcome are indeed bad.

RECOMMENDATION V. BE SENSITIVE TO THE "PSYCHO FACTOR" AT ALL TIMES

It is highly recommended that one study the personal background of the partner. In this perspective, learning about her cultural, educational, and intellectual characteristics is mandatory. It may be the precondition for dealing with her successfully. Understanding does not necessarily mean sharing the same values and traditions. However, a good knowledge of the character of the person one has to deal with will facilitate the creation of an atmosphere of mutual trust and respect. In addition to the study of the character of the opposite number, the establishment of a personal relationship with her is advisable before starting the talks. Networking is the name of the game. Diplomats are well aware of the personal relations aspect in the international environment. It makes perfect sense to know the people one has to deal with (see Jönsson, "Psychological Causes of Incomplete Negotiations"). The argument that a cozy relationship with the opposite number runs the risk of damaging the interests to be defended in the negotiations should not be taken too seriously. Professional negotiators know perfectly well what they are paid for. They will not distract themselves from their instructions just because they went on a golf course with their opposite number. As a classic example of how a personal relationship led to a breakthrough in a complex negotiation process, the famous "walk in the woods" may be cited. In 1982, Paul Nitze, then the U.S. chief negotiator in the talks with the Soviets on the issue of intermediate range nuclear missiles, took a walk with his Soviet counterpart in the woods surrounding Geneva and worked out with him there, in a confidential conversation, a formula for severe restrictions on the deployment of both U.S. and Soviet nuclear missiles in Europe.

REASON VI. THE ABSENCE OF A STRATEGIC CONCEPT

As outlined above (under point I) negotiation processes are complex matters that call for a comprehensive approach. Before beginning with the negotiations all aspects and factors possibly bearing on the process must be carefully studied. Ignorance of the key elements that come into play is a recipe for disaster. A similar problem arises if the negotiators do not have a clear strategic concept, that is, a general plan that takes account of all the elements that are relevant for the particular talks. Regrettably, in many negotiations a clear strategy is missing (see Cristal, "Camp David, 2000"). The decision to engage in negotiations is often made hastily, driven by events or short-term tactical reasons rather than determined by a well-designed master plan. Of course, international developments do not always allow for a long-term strategy. If a political crisis erupts, there is a pressing need to deal with it without any delay. In emergency situations, there is little room left for an elaborate scheme. On the other hand, long-term issues calling for sustainable solutions such as the relationship between the European Union and the Russian Federation, or the peace process in the Middle East definitely call for strategic approaches.

RECOMMENDATION VI. DEFINE THE STRATEGY
BEFORE ENTERING NEGOTIATIONS

The settlement of political conflicts by means of negotiation requires a long-term strategy that encompasses the main elements of the process (see Marschik, "The UN Security Council and Iraq"). The perception of the negotiation as a "nego-system" not only requires a comprehensive knowledge of all essential elements of the process but necessitates a clear vision of the objectives to be pursued and a strategy for conducting the negotiations in order to achieve them. With regard to strategy, a whole array of instruments are at the disposal of the experienced negotiator (see Zartman, "Process Reasons for Failure"). The use of carrots and sticks may be considered among other tools. Furthermore, the time factor will come into play, as negotiators must decide whether the situation is ripe for an agreement. In implementing a strategic concept the experienced negotiator will attempt to "frame" the issues and the negotiating process in such a way that they correspond to his interests and objectives (see Albin, "Explaining Failed Negotiations"). In analyzing the relevant nego-system, the seasoned negotiator will look beyond the narrow confines of the agenda in order to reach a sustainable result.

REASON VII. INSTITUTIONAL DEFICITS
ENDANGERING SUCCESS

In both bilateral and multilateral contexts, negotiations may end in a deadlock if the institutional framework is ill-suited for the particular process. Institutional deficits have the capacity to wreck a particular negotiation or may destroy the agreement after it is concluded. The first category is often found in multilateral negotiations. A classic example in this context is the UN Security Council (SC), with its legal features that grant a veto right to the five permanent members. If the positions of the permanent members on an issue are wide apart, chances are that one or another permanent member of the SC will invoke its veto right in order to block a decision. This used to be the rule during the period of the Cold War when the SC was literally paralyzed. Under the present political circumstances the institutional deficits of the SC have resurfaced and frequently prevent negotiations from being successful. A second type of institutional deficit consists in the absence of mechanisms ensuring the implementation of an agreement. The success of a negotiation will be short lived if after the conclusion of an agreement the parties start quarrelling over the interpretation or application of its provisions and no procedure exists to settle such disputes peacefully. A comprehensive survey of institutional causes for incomplete negotiations is given in Boyer, "Institutions as a Cause for Incomplete Negotiations."

RECOMMENDATION VII. MAKE SURE TO CHOOSE THE APPROPRIATE INSTITUTIONAL FRAMEWORK

Choosing suitable institutions or finding an adequate setup is crucial for negotiations to be successful. The example of the UN-SC may be used again: if the actors come to the conclusion that they will not reach an agreement within this institution because of a possible veto by some members, it might work better to circumvent this body altogether and seek another framework that is better suited for a successful negotiation. The second type of institutional deficit (lack of mechanisms ensuring the peaceful settlement of disputes following the agreement) can be remedied if the negotiators take appropriate care about this aspect in good time by including provisions to that effect in the agreement. In addition to clauses providing for the peaceful settlement of disputes over the interpretation and implementation of a treaty, other instruments can be devised, such as the establishment of a monitoring mechanism to which the parties agree. In sum it is suggested that at the outset of negotiations all available options for the institutional framework are examined. In this connection the negotiator ought to look for suitable alternatives. To be sure, in many cases there are some at hand that do in fact merit closer consideration. In order to illustrate this point one may refer to the choice between a bilateral, a regional, and a global negotiating framework. Before they start negotiations, the actors should seriously evaluate the pros and cons of each of the different institutions available. They should also evaluate which mechanisms are best suited for ensuring the sustainability of the agreement envisaged.

REASON VIII. THE LACK OF POSTCONFLICT INCENTIVES

The founding fathers of the United Nations were already aware of the fact that a durable peace requires more than just the absence of war. On the basis of this belief they included in the UN Charter a whole set of provisions that were designed to strengthen the "proactive" elements of international peace and security: the promotion of international cooperation, human rights, the codification of international law, and its progressive development. In a similar vein the leading experts in peace research are unanimous in stressing the importance of creating sustainable conditions for consolidating a post-conflict situation by putting as much emphasis on the civilian side of peace building as on the military aspects. Unfortunately, in many cases the negotiators have failed to offer postconflict incentives to convince the parties that compliance with the terms of the agreement will be beneficial to them in the long term. Zartman, in "Process Reasons for Failure," uses the term "resolving formula" to describe the elements that may induce the parties to conclude an agreement that will bring advantages to both sides in the long term. The reason for not pursuing the path of looking for the resolving formula may consist in a lack of understanding but also in the unwillingness to bank on the future by investing energy and resources in the long-term management of a postconflict situation. Recent history is full of stories in which the reasons for the failure of a durable solution lie in the fact that insufficient efforts were made to offer both sides convincing incentives to comply with the agreement.

To give an example for this state of affairs, attention can be drawn to the insufficient economic efforts accompanying the political settlements with economic incentives. It is obvious that a viable arrangement for the Gaza Strip requires more than just an agreement on a cease-fire. A durable solution to this thorny issue appears to be unthinkable unless a whole range of political and economic incentives will offer a more positive outlook than the negative spiral of escalating violence.

RECOMMENDATION VIII. PROVIDE POST-AGREEMENT INCENTIVES TO ENSURE COMPLIANCE

The need for a resolving formula becomes evident after studying the lessons from aborted negotiations or from those that did not achieve a sustainable outcome. The identification of the mutual benefits of a lasting settlement should be enhanced by incentives designed to strengthen the achievements of the agreement. Such incentives may consist in a combination of political and economic benefits. What matters most is the perception of the negotiators that they have more to lose by a repeated outbreak of the conflict than by committing themselves to the building of a solid and durable peace. It should be understood that investing in a durable solution (resolving formula) is something that generally implies political sacrifices and considerable financial means. The question must be addressed: what am I willing to invest — or to sacrifice — in order to arrive to a negotiated settlement, and, equally important, what am I willing to offer to ensure the compliance with the terms of the agreement once it has been concluded?

REFERENCES

Adair, Wendi A., and Jeanne M. Brett. 2005. "The Negotiation Dance: Time, Culture, and Behavioral Sequences in Negotiations." *Organization Science* 16 (1): 33–51.

Adair, Wendi A., Jeanne M. Brett, Alain Lempereur, Tetsushi Okumura, Peter Shikhirev, Catherine Tinsley, and Anne Lytle. 2004. "Culture and Negotiation Strategy." *Negotiation Journal* 20 (1): 87–112.

Adair, Wendi A., Tetsushi Okumura, and Jeanne M. Brett. 2001. "Negotiation Behavior When Cultures Collide: The U.S. and Japan." *Journal of Applied Psychology* 86 (3): 371–85.

Adair, Wendi L., Masako S. Taylor, and Catherine H. Tinsley. 2008. "Starting Out on the Right Foot: Negotiation Schemas When Cultures Collide." *Negotiation and Conflict Management Research* 2 (2): 138–63.

Adler, Emmanuel. 1997. "The Emergence of Cooperation: National Epistemic Communities and the International Evolution of the Idea of Nuclear Arms Control." In *Knowledge, Power, and International Policy Coordination*, edited by P. M. Haas, 101–46. Columbia: University of South Carolina Press.

Adler, Emmanuel, and Peter M. Haas. 1992. "Conclusion: Epistemic Communities, World Order and the Creation of a Reflective Research Program." *International Organization* 46 (1): 367–90.

Adler, Nancy J. 1991. *International Dimensions of Organizational Behavior*. 2nd ed. Boston: Kent.

Adler, Nancy J., R. Braham, and John L. Graham. 1992. "Strategy Implementations: A Comparison of Face-to-Face Negotiations in the People's Republic of China and the U.S." *Strategic Management Journal* 13 (6): 449–66.

Aggestam, Karin. 2004. "Two-Track Diplomacy: Negotiations between Israel and the PLO through Open and Secret Channels." In *Diplomacy*, vol. 3, *Problems and Issues in Contemporary Diplomacy*, edited by Christer Jönsson and Richard Langhorne, 203–27. London: Sage Publications.

———. 2006. "Internal and External Dynamics of Spoiling: A Negotiation Approach." In Newman and Richmond, *Challenges to Peacebuilding*, 23–39.

Aida, Shuhei, et al., eds. 1984. *The Science and Praxis of Complexity*. Montpellier Symposium. Tokyo: United Nations University Press.

Albertini, Luigi. 1952. *The Origins of the War of 1914*. Translated by I. M. Massey. Oxford: Oxford University Press.

Albin, Cecilia. 1991. "Negotiating Indivisible Goods: The Case of Jerusalem." *Jerusalem Journal of International Relations* 13 (1): 45–76.

———. 1999. "Justice, Fairness and Negotiation: Theory and Reality." In *International Negotiation: Actors, Structure/Process, Values*, edited by Peter Berton, Hiroshi Kimura, and I. William Zartman, 257–90. New York: St Martin's Press.

———. 2001. *Justice and Fairness in International Negotiation*. Cambridge: Cambridge University Press.

———. 2003. "Negotiating International Cooperation: Global Public Goods and Fairness." *Review of International Studies* 29 (3): 365–85.

———. 2005. "Explaining Conflict Transformation." *Cambridge Review of International Affairs* 18 (3): 339–55.

Ali, Tasier, and Robert Matthews. 1999. "Civil War and Failed Peace Efforts in Sudan." In *Civil War in Africa*, edited by Taisier Ali and Robert O. Mathews, 193–220. Montreal: McGill-Queens University Press.

Arnson, Cynthia, and I. William Zartman, eds. 2005. *Rethinking the Economics of War: The Intersection of Need, Creed and Greed*. Washington, D.C.: Woodrow Wilson Center.

Arrow, Kenneth, Robert Mnookin, Lee Ross, Amos Tversky, and Robert Wilson. 1995. *Barriers to Conflict Resolution*. New York: Norton.

Assefa, Hizkias. 1987. *Mediation of Civil Wars*. Boulder, Colo.: Westview.

Atlan, Henri. 1979. *Entre le cristal et la fumée*. Paris: Seuil.

Avenhaus, Rudolf. 2002. "Game Theory." In Kremenyuk, *International Negotiation*, 202–28.

Axelrod, Robert. 1970. *Conflict of Interest*. Chicago: Markham.

———. 1984. *The Evolution of Cooperation*. New York: Basic Books.

Ballentine, Karen, and Jake Sherman. 2003. *Beyond Greed and Grievance: The Political Economy of Armed Conflict*. Boulder, Colo.: Lynne Rienner.

Bamford, James A. 1982. *Puzzle Palace: A Report on America's Most Secret Agency*. Boston: Houghton Mifflin.

———. 2001. *Body of Secrets: Anatomy of the Ultra-Secret National Security Agency*. New York: Doubleday.

———. 2006. "Iran: The Next War." *Rolling Stone*, July 24.

Bar-Siman-Tov, Yaacov, Ephraim Lavie, Kobi Michael, and Daniel Bar-Tal. 2005. *The Israeli-Palestinian Violent Confrontation 2000-2004: From Conflict Resolution to Conflict Management*. Jerusalem: Jerusalem Institute for Israel Studies.

Bartoli, Andrea. 1999. "Mediating Peace in Mozambique: The Role of the Community of Sant'Egidio." In *Herding Cats: Multiparty Mediation in a Complex World*, edited by Chester A. Crocker, Fen Osler Hampson, and Pamela Aall, 245–73. Washington, D.C.: United States Institute of Peace Press.

Bateson, Gregory. 2000. *Steps to an Ecology of Mind.* Chicago: University of Chicago Press.

Bazerman, Max. 1983. "Negotiator Judgment: A Critical Look at the Rationality Assumption." *American Behavioral Scientist* 27 (2): 211–28.

———. 1998. *Judgment in Managerial Decision Making.* 4th ed. New York: Wiley.

Bazerman, Max, and R. J. Lewicki, eds. 1983. *Negotiating in Organizations.* Beverly Hills, Calif.: Sage.

Bazerman, Max, and M. A. Neale. 1983. "Heuristics in Negotiation: Limitations to Effective Dispute Resolution." In *Negotiating in Organizations,* edited by M. H. Bazerman and R. J. Lewicki. Beverly Hills, Calif.: Sage.

———. 1992. *Negotiating Rationally.* New York: Free Press.

BBC. 2003a. "Europe Push to End Iran Row." October 20. http://news.bbc.co.uk/2/hi /middle_east/3206994.stm.

———. 2003b. "Iran Media Spotlight Iran-UK Spat." June 30. http://news.bbc.co.uk/2 /hi/uk_news/3032066.stm.

———. 2004. "Round-up of Iranian Press Reactions Immediately after the Signing of the Paris Agreement." November 16. http://news.bbc.co.uk/2/hi/middle _east/4015525.stm.

———. 2006a. "Iran Deal May Allow Enrichment." June 7. http://news.bbc.co.uk/2/hi /middle_east/5055496.stm.

———. 2006b. "Iran Rejects Talk Preconditions." July 24. http://news.bbc.co.uk/2/hi /middle_east/5210594.stm.

Beaumont, Hardin. 1831. *Adventures of Two Americans in the Siege of Brussels, September 1830.* London: Cornhill.

Beehner, L. 2005. "Iran: Nuclear Negotiations." Council on Foreign Relations website. May 16. http://www.cfr.org/publication.html?id=7730.

Ben Ami, Shlomo. 2004. *A Front without a Rearguard.* Tel Aviv: Miskal Yedioth Ahronoth Books and Chemed Books.

Bercovitch, J. 1996. *Resolving International Conflicts: The Theory and Practice of Mediation.* Boulder, Colo.: Lynne Rienner.

Berdal, Mats, and David Malone. 2000. *Greed and Grievance: Economic Agendas in Civil War.* Boulder, Colo.: Lynne Rienner.

Berdal, Mats, and Achim Wennmann, eds. 2010. *Ending Wars, Consolidating Peace: Economic Dimensions.* London: Routledge.

Berman, Frank. 2004. "The Authorization Model: Resolution 678 and Its Effects." In Malone, *The UN Security Council,* 153–65.

Björkbom, L. 2001. Personal interview. Typescript. December 3.

Bjurulf, Bo, and Ole Elgström. 2004. "Negotiating Transparency: The Role of Institutions." *Journal of Common Market Studies* 42 (2): 249–69.

Blainey, Geoffrey. 1988. *The Causes of War.* 3rd ed. New York: Free Press.

Blix, Hans. 2004. *Disarming Iraq.* New York: Pantheon.

Bloom, J. C. H., and E. Lamberts. 1999. *History of the Low Countries.* New York: Berghahn Books.

Boltz, Frank, Jr., Kenneth J. Dudonis, and David P. Schulz. 2002. *The Counter-Terrorism Handbook: Tactics, Procedures, and Techniques.* Boca Raton, Fla.: CRC Press.

Bonham, G. M., C. Jönsson, S. Persson, and M. J. Shapiro. 1987. "Cognition and International Negotiation: The Historical Recovery of Discursive Space." *Cooperation and Conflict* 22 (1): 1–19.

Boris, Jan-Albert. 1945. *Belgium.* Los Angeles: University of California Press.

Borrie, John, and Vanessa Martin Randin. 2005. *Alternative Approaches in Multilateral Decision Making: Disarmament as Humanitarian Action.* Geneva: United Nations Institute for Disarmament Research (UNIDIR).

Bourquin, Maurice. 1954. *Histoire de la Sainte-Alliance.* Geneva: Librairie Georg.

Boyer, Brook. 1996. "Coalition Structures, Nonstate Actors and Bargaining Orientations in Multilateral Environmental Negotiations." PhD diss., The Graduate Institute of International Studies.

——. 1999. "Implementing Policies of Sustainable Development: Turning Constraints into Opportunities." *International Negotiation* 4 (2): 283–93.

Boyer, Brook, Jerry Velasquez, and Uli Piest. 2002. *Inter-linkages: Synergies and Coordination among Multilateral Environmental Agreements: National and Regional Approaches in Asia and the Pacific.* Tokyo: United Nations University Press.

Brett, J. M., W. Adair, A. Lempereur, O. Tetsushi, P. Shikhirev, C. Tinsley, A. and Lytle. 1998. "Culture and Joint Gains in Negotiation." *Negotiation Journal* 14 (1): 61–85.

Bueno de Mesquita, Bruce, and D. Lalman. 1992. *War and Reason.* New Haven, Conn.: Yale University Press.

Bunn, G. 1992. *Arms Control by Committee: Managing Negotiations with the Russians.* Stanford, Calif.: Stanford University Press.

Busby, J., and A. Ochs. 2004. "From Mars and Venus Down to Earth: Understanding the Transatlantic Climate Divide." In *Climate Policy for the 21st Century: Meeting the Long-Term Challenge of Global Warming,* edited by David Michel, 35–76. Baltimore: Johns Hopkins University Press.

Buttery, E. A., and T. K. P. Leung. "The Difference between Chinese and Western Negotiations." *European Journal of Marketing* 32 (3): 374–89.

Buzan, Barry. 1981. "Negotiating by Consensus: Developments in Technique at the United Nations Conference on the Law of the Sea." *American Journal of International Law* 75 (2): 324–48.

Byers, Michael. 2004. "Agreeing to Disagree: Security Council Resolution 1441 and Intentional Ambiguity." *Global Governance* 10 (2): 165–87.

Call, Charles T. 1999. "From Soldiers to Cops: 'War Transitions' and the Demilitarization of Public Security in Latin America and the Caribbean." Ph.D. diss., Stanford University.

———. 2002. "Assessing El Salvador's Transition from War to Peace." In Stedman, Rothchild, and Cousens, *Ending Civil Wars*, 383–420.

Call, John A. 1999. "The Hostage Triad: Takers, Victims and Negotiators." In *Lethal Violence: A Sourcebook on Fatal Domestic, Acquaintance, and Stranger Violence*, edited by Harold V. Hall, 561–88. Boca Raton, Fla.: CRC Press.

Cammaerts, Emile. 1939. *The Keystone of Europe: History of the Belgian Dynasty 1830–1939*. London: Peter Davies.

Carter, A. 1989. *Success and Failure in Arms Control Negotiations*. Oxford: Oxford University Press.

Carter, Jimmy. 1982. *Keeping Faith*. New York: Bantam Books.

Cede, Franz. 2002. "The Legal Perspective on International Negotiations." In Kremenyuk, *International Negotiation*, 145–58.

Center for Nonproliferation Studies. 2006. *Chronology of Key Events Related to the Implementation of IAEA Safeguards in Iran*. Accessed June 16. http://www.cns.miis.edu/pubs/week/060120.htm.

Chasek, Pamela. 1994. "The Negotiating System of Environment and Development." In Spector, Sjöstedt, and Zartman, *Negotiating International Regimes*, 21–41.

Checkland, P. 1989. "Soft Systems Methodology." In *Rational Analysis for a Problematic World: Problem Structuring Methods for Complexity, Uncertainty and Conflict*, edited by J. Rosenhead. Chichester: Wiley.

Chen, D. 1999. "Three-Dimensional Chinese Rationales in Negotiation." In *Negotiation Eclectics*, edited by D. Kolb, 50–66. Cambridge, Mass.: PON Books.

Chevrier, Marie Isabelle. 1990. "Verifying the Unverifiable: Lessons from the Biological Convention." *Politics and the Life Sciences* 9 (1): 93–105.

———. 2006. "The Politics of Biological Disarmament." In *Deadly Cultures: Biological Weapons since 1945*, edited by Mark Wheelis, Lajos Rózsa, and Malcolm Dando, 304–28. Cambridge, Mass.: Harvard University Press.

Cialdini, R. B. 1984. *Influence: How and Why People Agree to Things*. New York: William Morrow.

———. 1993. *Influence: The Psychology of Influence and Persuasion*. New York: Quill.

Cohen, Raymond. 1991. *Negotiating across Cultures: Communication Obstacles in International Diplomacy*. Washington, D.C.: United States Institute of Peace Press.

Collier, Paul, et al. 2003. *Breaking the Conflict Trap: Civil War and Development Policy*. Washington, D.C.: World Bank.

Cooper, Helene, and Steven R. Weisman. 2007. "West Tries a New Tack to Block Iran's Nuclear Agenda." *New York Times*, January 2. http://www.nytimes.com/2007/01/02 /world/middleeast/02sanctions.html?scp=5&sq=Iran+nuclear&st=nyt.

Corti, Egon Caesar. 1923. *Leopold I of Belgium: Secret Pages of European History*. New York: Brentano's.

Craig, Gordon. 1960. "The System of Alliances and the Balance of Power." In *The New Cambridge Modern History*, vol. 10, *The Zenith of European Power 1830-70*, edited by J. P. T. Bury, 246–73. Cambridge: Cambridge University Press.

Crocker, Chester, Fen Osler Hampson, and Pamela Aall, eds. 1999. *Herding Cats: Multiparty Mediation in a Complex World*. Washington, D.C.: United States Institute of Peace Press.

———. 2004. *Taming Intractable Conflicts: Mediation in the Hardest Cases*. Washington, D.C.: United States Institute of Peace Press.

———. 2005. *Grasping the Nettle: Analyzing Cases of Intractable Conflict*. Washington, D.C.: United States Institute of Peace Press.

Croft, S. 1996. *Strategies of Arms Control: A History and Typology*. New York: Manchester University Press.

Daalder, Ivo. 2000. *Getting to Dayton*. Washington, D.C.: Brookings Institution Press.

Daalder, Ivo, and M. E. O'Hanlon. 2000. *Winning Ugly: NATO's War to Save Kosovo*. Washington, D.C.: Brookings Institution Press.

Dahl, Robert. 1957. "A Postscript to Professor Dahl's 'Preface': A Rejoinder." *American Political Science Review* 51 (4): 1053–56.

Dajani, Omar M. 2005. "Surviving Opportunities: Palestinian Negotiating Patterns in Peace Talks with Israel." In *How Israelis and Palestinians Negotiate: A Cross-Cultural Analysis of the Oslo Peace Process*, edited by Tamara Cofman Wittes, 39–80. Washington, D.C.: United States Institute of Peace Press.

Daley, P. 2006. "Challenges to Peace: Conflict Resolution in the Great Lakes Region of Africa." *Third World Quarterly* 27 (2): 303–19.

Dando, M. R. 2002. *Preventing Biological Warfare: The Failure of American Leadership*. Basingstoke: Palgrave.

Darby, John. 2001. *The Effects of Violence on Peace Processes*. Washington, D.C.: United States Institute of Peace Press.

De la Marre, Victor. 1832. *La Belgique et la Hollande: Lettre à Lord Aberdeen*. Brussels: Berthot.

De Lichteruelde, Comte Louis. 1930. *Leopold First: The Founder of Modern Belgium*. New York: Century.

De Meeus, Adrien. 1962. *History of the Belgians*. New York: Frederick A. Praeger.

De Soto, Alvaro. 2005. *The Case of Cyprus*. Working Group on Collective Representation and Identity, Third International Conference on Federalism, Brussels, March 4.

Deutsch, Morton. 1949. "A Theory of Co-operation and Competition." *Human Relations* 2 (2): 129–52.

Dhanapala, Jaynatha. 1998. Personal communication. June 29.

Diamond, L., and R. Fisher. 1995. "Integrating Conflict Resolution Training and Consultation: A Cyprus Example." *Negotiation Journal* 11 (3): 287–301.

Docherty, Jayne Seminare. 2001. *Learning Lessons from Waco: When the Parties Bring Their Gods to the Negotiation Table.* Syracuse, N.Y.: Syracuse University Press.

Dodd, C. H. 1998. *The Cyprus Imbroglio.* Huntington: Eothen Press.

Downie, B. M. 1991. "When Negotiations Fail: Causes of Breakdown and Tactics for Breaking the Stalemate." *Negotiation Journal* 7 (2): 175–86.

Druckman, Daniel. 2004. "Departures in Negotiation." *Negotiation Journal* 20 (2): 185–204.

Druckman, D., A. A. Benton, F. Ali, J. S. Bagur. 1976. "Cultural Differences in Bargaining Behavior: India, Argentina, and the U.S." *Journal of Conflict Resolution* 20 (3): 413–52.

Druckman, D., J. L. Husbands, and K. Johnston. 1991. "Turning Points in the INF Negotiations." *Negotiation Journal* 7 (1): 56–67.

Duncan, Annabelle, and Robert J. Matthews. 1996. "Development of a Verification Protocol for the Biological and Toxin Weapons Convention." In *Verification*, edited by J. B Poole and Robert Guthrie, 151–70. Boulder, Colo.: Westview.

Dupont Christophe, and Guy Olivier Faure. 2002. "The Negotiation Process." In Kremenyuk, *International Negotiation*, 39–63.

Easton, David. 1965. *A Systems Analysis of Political Life.* New York: Wiley.

——— . 1994. *International Multilateral Negotiation: Approaches to the Management of Complexity.* San Francisco: Jossey-Bass.

Edgeworth, Francis Y. 1932. *Mathematical Physics: An Essay on the Application of Mathematics to the Moral Sciences.* London: London School of Economics and Political Science.

Edmundson, George. 1902. "The Low Countries." In *The Cambridge Modern History.* Vol. 10, 517–44. New York: Macmillan.

Eichengreen, Barry, and Marc Uzan. 1993. "The 1933 World Economic Conference as an Instance of Failed International Cooperation." In *Double-Edged Diplomacy: International Bargaining and Domestic Politics*, edited by Peter Evans, Harold K. Jacobson, and Robert D. Putnam, 171–206. Berkeley: University of California Press.

Elgström, Ole. 1992. *Foreign Aid Negotiation: The Swedish-Tanzanian Aid Dialogue.* Aldershot: Avebury.

——— . 2000. "Norm Negotiations: The Construction of New Norms Regarding Gender and Development in EU Foreign Aid Policy." *Journal of European Public Policy* 7 (3): 457–76.

Enderlin, Charles. 2003. *The Failure of the Peace Process in the Middle East, 1995–2002.* Translated by Susan Fairfield. New York: Other Press.

Eppstein, John. 1944. *Belgium.* Cambridge: Cambridge University Press.

Ertel, D. 1999. "Turning Negotiation into a Corporate Capability." *Harvard Business Review* 77 (3): 55–70.

EU (European Union). 2001. "European Parliament Resolution on the Communication from the Commission to the European Parliament and the Council on EU Relations with the Islamic Republic of Iran (Com [2001] 71-C5-0338/2001 — 2001/2138[Cos]), European Union, December 13." http://www.iranwatch.org/international/EU /eu-parlaimentresolution-121301.htm.

————. 2005. "Framework for a Long-Term Agreement between the Islamic Republic of Iran and France, Germany and the United Kingdom, with the Support of the High Representative of the European Union." http://www.pircenter.org/data /resources/IranFramework050805.pdf.

EUP and EC (European Union Presidency and European Commission). 2002. "Joint Press Release on the Opening of Negotiations with Iran." December 12. http://www .iranwatch.org/international/EU/eu-tradenegotiations-121202.pdf.

Evans, Peter B., Harold K. Jacobson, and Robert D. Putnam, eds. 1993. *Double-Edged Diplomacy: International Bargaining and Domestic Politics.* Berkeley: University of California Press.

Evriviades, E. 2005. "Cyprus in the EU: Prospects for Reunification, Peace with Turkey, and Regional Stability." *Mediterranean Quarterly* 16 (3): 1–16.

Evrivriades, M., and D. Bourantonis. 1994. "Peacekeeping and Peacemaking: Some Lessons from Cyprus." *International Peacekeeping* 1 (4): 394–412.

Farnham, Barbara, ed. 1994. *Avoiding Losses / Taking Risks: Prospect Theory and International Conflict.* Ann Arbor: University of Michigan Press.

Farrell, Joseph, and Matthew Rabin. 1996. "Cheap Talk." *Journal of Economic Perspectives* 10 (3): 103–18.

Faure, Guy Olivier. 2002. "International Negotiation: The Cultural Dimension." In Kremenyuk, *International Negotiation,* 392–415.

————. 2003. *How People Negotiate: Resolving Disputes in Different Cultures.* Norwell, Mass.: Kluwer Academic.

————. 2009. "Negotiation and Escalation of Images." In *Diplomacy in Theory and Practice: Essays in Honor of Christer Jönsson,* edited by Karin Aggestam and Christer Jönsson, 87–103. Malmö: Liber.

Faure, Guy Olivier, and Jeffrey Rubin, eds. 1993. *Culture and Negotiation: The Resolution of Water Disputes.* Thousand Oaks, Calif.: Sage.

Faure, Guy Olivier, and I. William Zartman, eds. 2010. *Negotiating among Terrorists.* London: Routledge.

Feakes, D., and J. Littlewood. 2002. "Hope and Ambition Turn to Dismay and Neglect: The Biological and Toxin Weapons Convention in 2001." *Medicine, Conflict and Survival* 18 (2): 161–74.

Fearon, James D. 1994. "Domestic Political Audiences and the Escalation of International Disputes." *American Political Science Review* 88 (3): 577–92.

———. 1995. "Rationalist Explanations for War." *International Organization* 49 (3): 379–414.

Finel, Bernard I., and Kristin M. Lord, eds. 2002. *Power and Conflict in the Age of Transparency*. New York: Palgrave MacMillan.

Fischer, Fritz. 1975. *War of Illusions*. New York: W. W. Norton.

Fisher, Roger D. 1981. "Playing the Wrong Game?" In *Dynamics of Third Party Intervention: Kissinger in the Middle East*, edited by Jeffrey Z. Rubin, 95–121. New York: Praeger.

———. 1996. "Facilitated Joint Brainstorming: A Powerful Method for Dealing with Conflict." Unpublished manuscript. Cambridge, Mass.: Harvard Negotiation Project.

Fisher, Roger D., Elizabeth Borgwardt, and Andrea Kupfer Schneider. 1994. *Beyond Machiavelli: Tools for Coping with Conflict*. Cambridge, Mass.: Harvard University Press.

Fisher, Roger D., and William Ury. 1982. 1st ed. *Getting to Yes: Negotiating Agreement without Giving In*. Boston: Houghton Mifflin.

Fisher, Roger D., William Ury, and Bruce Patton. 1992. *Getting to Yes: Negotiating Agreement without Giving In*. 3rd ed. New York: Penguin Books.

Fisher, Ronald. J. 2001. "Cyprus: The Failure of Mediation and the Escalation of an Identity-Based Conflict to an Adversarial Impasse." *Journal of Peace Research* 38 (3): 307–26.

Fishman, J. S. 1988. *Diplomacy and Revolution: The London Conference of 1830 and the Belgian Revolt*. Amsterdam: Chev.

Fiske, S. T., and S. E. Taylor. 1991. *Social Cognition*. New York: McGraw-Hill.

Fitzmaurice, John. 1966. *The Politics of Belgium: A Unique Federalism*. London: Hurst.

Follett, Mary P. 1941. *Dynamic Administration: The Collected Papers of Mary Parker Follett*. London: Pitman.

Fortna, Virginia Page. 2004. "Scraps of Paper? Agreements and the Durability of Peace." *International Organization* 57 (2): 337–72.

Fox, C., and A. Tversky. 1995. "Ambiguity Aversion and Comparative Ignorance." *The Quarterly Journal of Economics* 110 (3): 585–603.

Francis, J. N. P. 1991. "When in Rome: The Effects of Cultural Adaptation on Intercultural Business Negotiations." *Journal of International Business Studies* 22 (3): 403–28.

Fraser, Malcolm. 2005. "Sovereignty, International Law and Global Cooperation."

In *Globalisation and the Rule of Law*, edited by Spencer Zifcak, 165–83. London: Routledge.

Fuehr, Alexander. 1915. *The Neutrality of Belgium: A Study of the Belgian Case under Its Aspects in Political History and International Law*. New York: Funk and Wagnalls.

Gallagher, N. W. 1999. *The Politics of Verification*. Baltimore: Johns Hopkins University Press.

Gartner, Scott, and Molly Melin. 2009. "Assessing Outcomes: Conflict Management and the Durability of Peace." In *The Sage Handbook of Conflict Resolution*, edited by Jacob Bercovitch, Victor Kremenyuk, and I. William Zartman, 564–79. London: Sage.

Geary, Barbara A. 1990. "The Failure of Negotiation by Design: Releasing the Hostages at Revolutionary Airstrip." *Negotiation Journal* 6 (4): 337–51.

Geissler, E., and J. P. Woodall, eds. 1994. *Control of Dual Threat Agents: Vaccines for Peace Programme*, vol. 15 of SIPRI *Chemical and Biological Warfare Studies*. Oxford: Oxford University Press.

Gelfand, M. J., and J. M. Brett, eds. 2004. *The Handbook of Negotiation and Culture*. Stanford, Calif.: Stanford Business Books.

Gelfand, M. J., and C. McCusker. 2002. "Metaphor and the Cultural Construction of Negotiation: A Paradigm for Research and Practice." In *The Blackwell Handbook of Cross-Cultural Management*, edited by M. J. Gannon and K. L. Newman, 292–313. New York: Blackwell.

Gelfand, M. J., L. H. Nishii, K. M. Holcombe, N. Dyer, K. I. Ohbuchi, and M. Fukuno. 2001. "Cultural Influences on Cognitive Representations of Conflict: Interpretations of Conflict Episodes in the U.S. and Japan." *Journal of Applied Psychology* 86 (6): 1059–74.

George, A. L. 1980. *Presidential Decision-making in Foreign Policy: The Effective Use of Information and Advice*. Boulder, Colo.: Westview.

Gibson, Hugh. 1939. *Belgium*. New York: Doubleday.

Glennon, Michael J. 2003. "Why the Security Council Failed." *Foreign Affairs* 82 (3): 16–35.

Goblet, D'Alviella. 1864. *Mémoires Historiques: Dix-huit mois de politique et de négociations se rattachant à la première atteinte portée aux traités de 1815*. Paris: Librarie Internationale et Cie.

Goemans, Henk Erich. 2000. *War and Punishment: The Causes of War Termination and the First World War*. Princeton, N.J.: Princeton University Press.

Goldstein, Erik. 2003. "The British Official Mind and the Lausanne Conference, 1922–23." *Diplomacy and Statecraft* 14 (2): 185–206.

Goodwin, D. 2005. *The Military and Negotiation*. London: Routledge.

Goosh, D. Brison. 1963. *Belgium and the French Revolution*. The Hague: Martinus Nijhoff.

Government of France. 2006. "Elements of a Revised Proposal Made to Iran by the E3+3". Communicated to Iran by Javier Solana, Ministère des Affaires Étrangères, June 6. http://www.diplomatie.gouv.fr/en/article-imprim.php3id_article=5314.

Government of Iran. 2002. Statement by H. E. Reza Aghazadeh, Vice-President of the Islamic Republic of Iran and President of the Atomic Energy Organization of Iran at the 46th General Conference of the International Atomic Energy Agency, Vienna, September 16. http://www.iaea.org/About/Policy/GC/GC47/Statements/iran.pdf.

———. 2003. Statement of the Government of Iran at the IAEA Board of Governors' Meeting of June 6. http://www.iaea.org/ NewsCenter/PressReleases/2003 /06JUNEstatementIRAN.pdf.

———. 2005a. General Framework for Objective Guarantees, Firm Guarantees, and Firm Commitments (negotiation proposal to the E3/EU). Undated document. Approximately March 23. http://abcnews.go.com/images/International/iran_eu _objectives.pdf.

———. 2005b. Iranian Nuclear Policy & Activities, Complementary Information To the Report of the IAEA Director General (GOV/2005/67), submitted to the IAEA September 12, distributed as INFCIRC 657. http://www.iaea.org/Publications /Documents/Infcircs/2005/infcirc657.pdf.

———. 2005c. Permanent Mission of Islamic Republic Iran to the United Nations, Note Verbale No.: 350–1–17/928, August 1, distributed by the IAEA as INFCIRC 648. http:// www.iaea.org/Publications/Documents/Infcircs/2005/infcirc648.pdf.

———. 2005d. Response of the Islamic Republic of Iran to the Framework Agreement Proposed by the EU3/EU. Undated document. http://www.basicint.org/coun- tries/iran/IranResponse.pdf (summary available at http://www.acronym.org.uk /docs/0508/doc03.htm#iran).

———. 2006a. Islamic Republic of Iran's Response to the Package Presented on June 6, dated August 22. http://www.isis-online.org/publications/iran/iranresponse.pdf.

———. 2006b. Letter from President Mahmood Ahmedi-Najad to President George Bush, May 8. http://news.bbc.co.uk/2/shared/bsp/hi /pdfs/09_05_06ahmadinejadletter.pdf.

———. 2006c. Message of H. E. Dr. Ali Larijani, Secretary of Supreme Security Council of the Islamic Republic of Iran to the Director General of the IAEA, February 2. Circulated by IAEA as INFCIRC 666. http://www.iaea.org/Publications/Documents /Infcircs/2006/infcirc666.pdf.

———. 2006d. Statement at the IAEA Board of Governors, by Ambassador A. A. Soltanieh, Resident Representative of Islamic Republic of Iran, February 2. Vienna. http://iaea.org/newscenter/focus/iaeairan/bog020206_statement-iran.pdf.

Government of the UK. 2005. Statement by the United Kingdom on behalf of the European Union at the IAEA Board of Governors, August 9. http://www.iaea.org /NewsCenter/Focus/IaeaIran/bog092005_statement-eu.pdf.

Government of the U.S. 2003. Statement by U.S. Ambassador Kenneth C. Brill, IAEA Board of Governors Meeting, Vienna, Austria, September 8.

——. 2006a. Secretary of State Condoleeza Rice, Department of State, Press Conference, April 13. Transcript available at http://www.iranwatch.org/government /US/DOS/us-dos-rice-interview-hearst-041306.htm.

——. 2006b. Secretary of State Condoleeza Rice, Department of State, Press Conference on Iran, May 31. Transcript available at http://2001-2009.state.gov /secretary/rm/2006/67103.htm.

Governments of UK and France. 2006. Draft Security Council Resolution of May 3. Accessed at http://lcnp.org/disarmament/iran/draftresUNSC03may.pdf.

Graham, J. 1993. "The Japanese Negotiation Style: Characteristics of a Distinct Approach." *Negotiation Journal* 9 (2): 123–40.

Graham, J. L., and Y. Sano. 1989. *Smart Bargaining: Doing Business with the Japanese.* Los Angeles: Sano.

Grattan, Thomas Colley. 1955. *The History of the Netherlands.* New York: Bradley.

Gray, Colin S. 1992. *House of Cards.* Ithaca, N.Y.: Cornell University Press.

Guillaume, P. 1937. *La Psychologie de la forme.* Paris: Flammarion.

Haas, Ernst B. 1952. *Belgium and the Balance of Power.* Ann Arbor: University Microfilm.

Haas, Peter. 1990. *Saving the Mediterranean: The Politics of International Environmental Cooperation.* New York: Columbia University Press.

——. 1997a. "Banning Chlorofluorocarbons: Epistemic Community Efforts to Protect Stratospheric Ozone." In *Knowledge, Power, and International Policy Coordination,* edited by Peter Haas, 187–224. Columbia: University of South Carolina Press.

——, ed. 1997b. *Knowledge, Power and International Policy Coordination.* Columbia: University of South Carolina Press.

Haas, Richard, and Martin Indyk. 2008. *Restoring the Balance: A Middle East Strategy for the Next President.* Washington, D.C.: Brookings.

Habeeb, William Mark. 1988. *Power and Tactics in International Negotiation: How Weak Nations Bargain with Strong Nations.* Baltimore: Johns Hopkins University Press.

Hall, E. T., and M. R. Hall. 1990. *Understanding Cultural Differences: Germans, French and Americans.* Yarmouth, Maine: Intercultural Press.

Hamilton, D. L., S. J. Sherman, and C. M. Ruvolo. 1990. "Stereotype-Based Expectancies: Effects on Information Processing and Social Behavior." *Journal of Social Issues* 46 (2): 35–60.

Hampson, Fen Osler. 1996. *Nurturing Peace: Why Peace Settlements Succeed or Fail.* Washington, D.C.: United States Institute of Peace Press.

Hampson, Fen Osler, and Michael Hart. 1995. *Multilateral Negotiations.* Baltimore: Johns Hopkins University Press.

Hanieh, Akram. 2001. "Camp David Papers." *Journal of Palestine Studies* 30, (2): 75–97.

Hart, Paul 't, Eric K. Stern, and Bengt Sundelius, eds. 1997. *Beyond Groupthink: Political Group Dynamics and Foreign Policy-Making*. Ann Arbor: University of Michigan Press.

Helmreich, Jonathan E. 1976. *Belgium and Europe: A Study in Small Power Diplomacy*. The Hague: Mouton.

Heradstveit, D., and G. M. Bonham. 1986. "Decision-Making in the Face of Uncertainty: Attributions of Norwegian and American Officials." *Journal of Peace Research* 23 (4): 339–56.

Hernandez, Cristina. 2003. "Cancun 5th WTO Ministerial: A Discussion Paper." Centre for Applied Studies in International Negotiation, Geneva.

Hersh, Seymour. 2006. "The Iran Plans: Would President Bush Go to War to Stop Tehran from Getting the Bomb?" *New Yorker*, April 17, http://www.newyorker.com /archive/2006/04/17/060417fa_fact.

Hirsch, John. 2001. *Sierra Leone*. Boulder, Colo.: Lynne Rienner.

Hobbes, Thomas. 1968. *Leviathan*. New York: Penguin.

Hoffman, Aaron M. 2002. "A Conceptualization of Trust in International Relations" *European Journal of International Relations* 8 (3): 375–401.

Hoffmeister, Frank. 2006. *Legal Aspects of the Cyprus Problem: Annan Plan and EU Accession*. Leiden: Martinus Nijhoff.

Hofstede, G. 1980. *Culture's Consequences: International Differences in Work-Related Values*. Newbury Park, Calif.: Sage.

Höglund, Kristine. 2004. "Violence in the Midst of Peace Negotiations." Report No. 69. Uppsala University.

Holbrooke, Richard C. 1998. *To End a War*. New York: Random House.

Holsti, Kalevi. 1992. Governance without Government: Polyarchy in Nineteenth-Century European International Politics. In *Governance without Government: Order and Change in World Politics*, edited by James N. Rosenau and Ernst-Otto Czempiel. Cambridge: Cambridge University Press.

Holsti, Ole R. 1968. "Cognitive Dynamics and Images of the Enemy." In *Image and Reality in World Politics*, edited by John C. Farrell and Asa P. Smith. New York: Columbia University Press.

Hopmann, P. Terrence. 1991. "The Changing International Environment and the Resolution of International Conflicts: Negotiations on Security and Arms Control in Europe." In *Timing the De-escalation of International Conflicts*, edited by Louis Kriesberg and Stuart J. Thorson, 31–57. Syracuse, N.Y.: Syracuse University Press.

———. 1995. "Two Paradigms of Negotiation: Bargaining and Problem Solving." In *Flexibility in International Negotiation and Mediation*, edited by Daniel Druckman and Christopher Mitchell. London: The Annals, Sage Periodicals Press.

———. 1996. *The Negotiation Process and the Resolution of International Conflict.* Columbia: University of South Carolina Press.

———. 1999. *Building Security in Post-Cold War Eurasia: The OSCE and U.S. Foreign Policy.* Peaceworks #31. Washington, D.C.: United States Institute of Peace.

———. 2001. "The OSCE Role in Ukraine and Moldova." *Studien und Berichte zur Zicherheitspolitik* 1:25–61.

———. 2009. "Constituting a Reunified Cyprus: A View from the USA." *Journal of Balkan and Near Eastern Studies* 11, no. 4:413–26.

Horgan, J., and M. Taylor, eds. 2000. *The Future of Terrorism.* London: Frank Cass.

Huntington, Samuel P. 1999. "The Lonely Superpower." *Foreign Affairs* 78 (2): 35–49.

Hutchison, Walter, ed. 2003. *Belgium the Glorious: Her Country and Her People.* London: Hutchinson.

IAEA. 1974. The Text of the Agreement between Iran and the Agency for the Application of Safeguards in Connection with the Treaty on the Non-Proliferation of Nuclear Weapons. INFCIRC 214, December 13. http://www.iaea.org/Publications/Documents /Infcircs/Others/infcirc214.pdf.

———. 2003a. Report by the Director General of the IAEA to the Board of Governors, June 6. "Implementation of the NPT Safeguards Agreement in the Islamic Republic of Iran." IAEA document GOV/2003/40. http://www.iaea.org/NewsCenter/Focus /IaeaIran/index.shtml.

———. 2003b. Report by the Director General of the IAEA to the Board of Governors, August 26. "Implementation of the NPT Safeguards Agreement in the Islamic Republic of Iran." IAEA document GOV/2003/63, accessed at http://www.iaea.org /Publications/Documents/Board/2003/gov2003-63.pdf.

———. 2003c. Report by the Director General of the IAEA to the Board of Governors, November 26. "Implementation of the NPT Safeguards Agreement in the Islamic Republic of Iran." IAEA document GOV/2003/75. http://www.iaea.org/NewsCenter /Focus/IaeaIran/index.shtml.

———. 2003d. Resolution adopted by the Board of Governors on September 12. Implementation of the NPT Safeguards Agreement in the Islamic Republic of Iran. GOV/2003/69. http://www.iaea.org/Publications/Documents/Board/2003/gov2003 -69.pdf.

———. 2003e. Tehran Declaration, "Statement by the Iranian Government and visiting EU Foreign Ministers," October 21. http://www.iaea.org/NewsCenter/Focus /IaeaIran/statement_iran21102003.shtml.

———. 2004a. E3/EU-Iran Agreement (The "Paris Agreement"), November 15. Submitted to and distributed by the IAEA as INFCIRC 637, released November 26. http://www.iaea.org/NewsCenter/Focus/IaeaIran/index.shtml.

———. 2004b. Report by Director General of the IAEA to the Board of Governors.

"Implementation of the NPT Safeguards Agreement in the Islamic Republic of Iran." Sixth IAEA Report on Safeguards Implementation, September 1. IAEA document GOV/2004/60. http://www.iaea.org/NewsCenter/Focus/IaeaIran/index.shtml.

———. 2004c. Report by the Director General of the IAEA to the Board of Governors in Preparation for the March Board of Governors Meeting, February 24. "Implementation of the NPT Safeguards Agreement in the Islamic Republic of Iran." IAEA document GOV/2004/11. http://www.iaea.org/NewsCenter/Focus/IaeaIran /index.shtml.

———. 2005a. Communication dated August 1 received from the Permanent Mission of the Islamic Republic of Iran to the Agency, Note Verbale No.: 350-1-17/928, IAEA INFCIRC 648, released August 1.

———. 2005b. Introductory Statement to the Board of Governors by IAEA Director General Dr. Mohamed El-Baradei. September 19. http://www.iaea.org/NewsCenter /Statements/2005/ebsp2005n009.html#iran.

———. 2006a. Report by Director General of the IAEA to the Board of Governors, February 27. "Implementation of the NPT Safeguards Agreement in the Islamic Republic of Iran." IAEA document GOV/2006/15. http://www.iaea.org/Publications /Documents/Board/2006/gov2006–15.pdf.

———. 2006b. Resolution adopted by the Board of Governors on February 4. Implementation of the NPT Safeguards Agreement in the Islamic Republic of Iran. GOV/2006/14. http://www.iaea.org/Publications/Documents/Board/2006/gov2006 –14.pdf.

———. 2007a. Communication dated August 27, from the Permanent Mission of the Islamic Republic of Iran to the Agency concerning the text of the "Understandings of the Islamic Republic of Iran and the IAEA on the Modalities of Resolution of the Outstanding Issues," INFCIRC/711. http://www.iaea.org/Publications/Documents /Infcircs/2007/infcirc711.pdf.

———. 2007b. "Dr. el-Baradei Calls for "Timeout" on Iran Nuclear Issue." IAEA News Centre, News Update on IAEA and Iran, January 30. http://www.iaea.org /NewsCenter/Focus/IaeaIran/iran_timeline4.shtml#january07.

———. 2007c. Report by the Director General of the IAEA to the Board of Governors. "Implementation of the NPT Safeguards Agreement and the Relevant Provisions of Security Council Resolutions 1737 (2006 and 1747 (2007) in the Republic of Iran." November 15, IAEA document GOV/2007/58. Accessed at http://www.iaea.org /Publications/Documents/Board/2007/gov2007-58.pdf.

———. 2008a. "Islamic Republic of Iran's Proposed Package for Constructive Negotiation." Communicated to the IAEA for circulation, June 18. INFCIRC/729. http://www.iaea.org/Publications/Documents/Infcircs/2008/infcirc729.pdf.

———. 2008b. "Letter and Offer of June 12, 2008, from Javier Solana to Manuchehr

Mottaki." INFCIRC/730, July 1. http://www.iaea.org/Publications/Documents
/Infcircs/2008/infcirc730.pdf.

———. 2008c. "Q&A with Director General on Iran." Videotaped interview with Dir.
Gen. el-Baradei. February 28. http://www.iaea.org/NewsCenter/Multimedia/Videos
/DG/QandA220208/index.html.

———. 2010a. Report by the Director General of the IAEA to the Board of Governors.
"Implementation of the NPT Safeguards Agreement and relevant provisions of
Security Council resolutions 1737 (2006), 1747 (2007), 1803 (2008) and 1835 (2008)
in the Islamic Republic of Iran." February 18. Gov/2010/10. http://www.iaea.org
/Publications/Documents/Board/2010/gov2010-10.pdf.

———. 2010b. "The Root Cause of Iran's Confidence Deficit vis-à-vis Some Western
Countries on Assurances of Nuclear Fuel Supply." Iran's March 1 request for IAEA
Adjudication in letter to Director General Yukiya Amano. March 2. INFCIRC/785.
http://www.iaea.org/Publications/Documents/Infcircs/2010/infcirc785.pdf.

Iida, Keisuke. 1993. "Analytic Uncertainty and International Cooperation: Theory and
Application to International Economic Policy Coordination." International Studies
Quarterly 37 (4): 431–57.

Iklé, Fred C. 1964. How Nations Negotiate. New York: Praeger.

Independent International Commission on Kosovo. 2000. The Kosovo Report: Conflict,
International Response, Lessons Learned. Oxford: Oxford University Press.

Indyk, Martin. 2005. "Lessons of Arab-Israeli Negotiating: Four Negotiators Look Back
and Ahead." Middle East Institute. Transcript.

Ipsen, K. 1991. "Explicit Methods of Arms Control Treaty Evolution" In The
International Law of Arms Control and Disarmament: Proceedings of the Symposium,
Geneva, 28 February–2 March 1991, edited by Julie Dahlitz and Detlev Dicke. New
York: United Nations.

Israel, Jonathan I. 1982. The Dutch Republic and the Hispanic World, 1606–1661. Oxford:
Clarendon Press.

———. 1990. Empires and Entrepots: The Dutch, the Spanish Monarchy and the Jews,
1585–1713. London: Hambledon Press.

———. 1995. The Dutch Republic: Its Rise, Greatness and Fall, 1477–1806. Oxford:
Clarendon Press.

Janis, Irving. L. 1972. Victims of Groupthink: A Psychological Study of Foreign Policy
Decisions and Fiascoes. Boston: Houghton Mifflin.

———. 1982. Groupthink: Psychological Studies of Policy Decisions and Fiascoes. 2nd ed.
Boston: Houghton Mifflin.

Jarque, Xavier, Clara Ponsatí, and Jozsef Sákovics. 2003. "Mediation: Incomplete
Information Bargaining with Filtered Communication." Journal of Mathematical
Economics 39 (7): 803–30.

Jervis, Robert. 1976. *Perception and Misperception in International Politics*. Princeton, N.J.: Princeton University Press.

Jonas, Eva, Stefan Schulz-Hardt, Dieter Frey, and Norman Thelen. 2001. "Confirmation Bias in Sequential Information Search after Preliminary Decisions: An Expansion of Dissonance Theoretical Research on Selective Exposure to Information." *Journal of Personality and Social Psychology* 80 (4): 557–71.

Jones, Edward E., and Kenneth E. Davis. 1965. "From Acts to Dispositions: The Attribution Process in Person Perception." In *Advances in Experimental Social Psychology*, edited by Leonard Berkowitz, 220–66. New York: Academic Press.

Jones, Edward E., and Richard E. Nisbett. 1971. "The Actor and the Observer: Divergent Perceptions of the Causes of Behavior." In *Attribution: Perceiving the Causes of Behavior*, edited by Edward E. Jones, David E. Kanouse, Harold H. Kelley, Richard E. Nisbett, Stuart Valins, and Bernard Weiner. Morristown, N.J.: General Learning Press.

Jönsson, Christer. 1975. "The Soviet Union and the Test Ban: A Study in Soviet Negotiating Behavior." PhD diss., Lund University.

———. 1990. *Communication in International Bargaining*. London: Pinter.

———. 1991. "The Suez War of 1956: Communication in Crisis Management." In *Avoiding War: Problems of Crisis Management*, edited by Alexander L. George, 160–90. Boulder, Colo.: Westview.

Joyner, Christopher C. 2003. "United Nations Sanctions after Iraq: Looking Back to See Ahead." *Chicago Journal of International Law* 4 (2): 229–353.

Judah, Tim. 2002. *Kosovo: War and Revenge*. New Haven, Conn.: Yale University Press.

Juste, Theodore. 1850. *Histoire du Congrès National de Belgique de la Fondation de la Monarchie*. Vol. 1. Brussels.

Kahneman, D., and A. Tversky. 1979. "Prospect Theory: An Analysis of Decision under Risk." *Econometrica* 47 (2): 263–92.

Kaldor, Mary. 2006. *New and Old Wars*. 2nd ed. London: Polity Press.

Kelley, H. H. 1971. "Attribution in Social Interaction." In *Attribution: Perceiving the Causes of Behavior*, edited by Edward E. Jones, David E. Kanouse, Harold H. Kelley, Richard E. Nisbett, Stuart Valins, and Bernard Weiner. Morristown, N.J.: General Learning Press.

Kelley, H. H., and J. L. Michela. 1980. "Attribution Theory and Research." *Annual Review of Psychology* 31:457–501.

Kelly, D. 2002. "The Trilateral Process: Lessons for Biological Weapons Verification." In *Verification Yearbook 2002*, edited by Trevor Findlay and Oliver Meier, 93–109. Nottingham: Russell Press.

Kelly, G. B., and F. Burton Nelson, eds. 1995. *A Testament to Freedom: The Essential Writings of Dietrich Bonhoeffer*. 2nd ed. San Francisco, Harper.

Kervers, O. 2002. "Strengthening Compliance with the Biological Weapons Convention: The Protocol Negotiations." *Journal of Conflict and Security Law* 7 (2): 275–92.

———. 2003. "Strengthening Compliance with the Biological Weapons Convention: The Draft Protocol." *Journal of Conflict and Security Law* 8 (1): 161–200.

Kesner, Idalene F., and Debra L. Shapiro. 1991. "Did a 'Failed' Negotiation Really Fail?" *Negotiation Journal* 7 (4): 369–76.

Kiehl, W. P. 2003. "Can Humpty Dumpty Be Saved?" *American Diplomacy*, November 13, http://www.unc.edu/depts/diplomat/archives_roll/2003_10-12/kiehl_humpty /kiehl_humpty.html.

Kimball, Lee A. 1999. "Institutional Linkages among Multilateral Environmental Agreements: A Structured Approach Based on Scale and Function." Paper prepared for Inter-linkages: International Conference on Synergies and Coordination between Multilateral Environmental Agreements. Tokyo.

King, Charles. 1997. *Ending Civil Wars*. Oxford: Oxford University Press.

Kirilov, Viktor. 1995. "The Conflict in the Trans-Dniestr Region: History and Current Situation." In *Crisis Management in the CIS: Whither Russia?* ed. Hans-Georg Ehrhart, Anna Kreikemeyer, and Andrei V. Zagorski, 55–65. Baden-Baden: Nomos Verlagsgesellschaft.

Kirkbride, P. S., S. F. Tang, and R. I. Westwood. 1991. "Chinese Conflict Preferences and Negotiating Behaviour: Cultural and Psychological Influences." *Organization Studies* 12 (3): 365–86.

Kissinger, Henry A. 1982. *Years of Upheaval*. Boston: Little, Brown.

Koh, Tommy. 1986. "Negotiating a New World Order for the Sea." In *Negotiating World Order: The Artisanship and Architecture of Global Diplomacy*, edited by A. Henrikson, 33–45. Wilmington, Del.: Scholarly Resources.

———. 1990. "The Paris Conference on Cambodia: A Multilateral Negotiation that 'Failed.'" *Negotiation Journal* 6 (1): 81–87.

Koh, Tommy, and S. Jayakumar. 1985. "The Negotiating Process of the Third United Nations Conference on the Law of the Sea." In *United Nations Convention on the Law of the Sea, 1982: A Commentary*, vol. 1, edited by Myron H. Nordquist, 29–134. The Hague: Martinus Nijhoff.

Koll, Johannes. 2003. *Die Belgische Nation: Patriotismus und Nationalbewusstsein in den Suedlichen Niederlanden im spaeten 18. Jahrhundert*. New York: Waxmann Muenster.

Koremenos, Barbara. 2001. "Loosening the Ties that Bind: A Learning Model of Agreement Flexibility." *International Organization* 55 (2): 289–325.

———. 2002. "Open Covenants, Clandestinely Arrived At." Manuscript. University of Michigan.

Korobkin, Russel, and Jonathan Zasloff. 2005. "Roadblocks to the Road Map: a

Negotiation Theory Perspective on the Israeli-Palestinian Conflict after Yasser Arafat." *Yale Journal of International Law* 30 (1): 1–80.

Kossmann, E. H. 1978. *The Low Countries, 1780–1940*. Oxford: Oxford University Press.

Krasner, Steven, ed. 1983. *International Regimes*. Ithaca, N.Y.: Cornell University Press.

Kremenyuk, Victor, ed. 2002. *International Negotiation: Analysis, Approaches, Issues.* 2nd ed. San Francisco: Jossey-Bass.

Kumar, R. 1997. "The Role of Affect in Negotiations: An Integrative Overview." *Journal of Applied Behavioral Science* 33 (1): 84–100.

Kumin, A. J. 2003. "Negotiations on the Comprehensive Nuclear Test Ban Treaty." In *Professional Cultures in International Negotiation: Bridge or Rift?*, edited by Gunnar Sjöstedt, 101–29. Lanham, Md.: Lexington Books.

Kydd, Andrew. 2003. "Which Side Are You On? Bias, Credibility and Mediation." *American Journal of Political Science* 47 (4): 597–611.

———. 2005. *Trust and Mistrust in International Relations*. Princeton, N.J.: Princeton University Press.

———. 2006. "When Can Mediators Build Trust?" *American Political Science Review* 100 (3): 449–62.

Kydd, Andrew, and Barbara Walter. 2002. "Sabotaging the Peace: The Politics of Extremist Violence." *International Organization* 56 (2): 263–96.

Lakoff, George. 1987. *Women, Fire, and Dangerous Things: What Categories Reveal about the Mind*. Chicago: University of Chicago Press.

Lall, A. 1966. *Modern International Negotiation: Principles and Practice*. New York: Columbia University Press.

Lamy, Pascal. 1999. Speech at World Trade Organization Ministerial Conference in Seattle Appraisals and Prospects. European Parliament Plenary Session, Strasbourg, December 13.

———. 2006. "WTO Director General Pascal Lamy's Speech to the Group of Eight Summit at St. Petersburg." July 17. http://www.wto.org/english/news_e/sppl_e/sppl32_e.html.

Lang, W. 1993. "A Professional's View." In *Culture and Negotiation: The Resolution of Water Disputes*, edited by Guy Olivier Faure and Jeffrey Z. Rubin, 38–46. Thousand Oaks, Calif.: Sage.

Larson, D. W. 1988. "The Psychology of Reciprocity in International Relations." *Negotiation Journal* 4 (3): 281–301.

Lax, David, and James Sebenius. 1986. *The Manager as Negotiator*. New York: Free Press.

———. 1991. "Thinking Coalitionally: Party Arithmetic, Process Opportunism, and Strategic Sequencing." In *Negotiation Analysis*, edited by H. Peyton Young, 153–93. Ann Arbor: University of Michigan Press.

Lebow, Richard. 1981. *Between War and Peace: The Nature of International Crisis.* Baltimore: Johns Hopkins University Press.

Lehman, R. F. 1991. Statement of Ronald F. Lehman, Head of the United States Delegation, Biological and Toxin Weapons Convention, Third Review Conference, September 10.

Leitenberg, Milton. 1996. "Biological Weapons Arms Control." *Contemporary Security Policy* 17 (1): 1–79.

Le Moigne, J. L. 1984. *The Intelligence of Complexity: The Science and Praxis of Complexity.* Montpellier: United Nations University.

———. 1990. *La théorie du système général.* Paris: PUF.

Leung, K. 1997. "Negotiation and Reward Associations across Cultures." In *New Perspectives on International Industrial/Organizational Psychology,* edited by P.C. Earley and M. Erez, 640–75. San Francisco: Jossey-Bass.

Levy, Jack S. 1996. "Loss Aversion, Framing, and Bargaining: The Implications of Prospect Theory for International Conflict." *International Political Science Review* 17 (2): 179–95.

Lewicki, Roy, Barbara Gray, and Michael Elliott, eds. 2002. *Making Sense of Intractable Environmental Conflicts: Concepts and Cases.* Washington, D.C.: Island Press.

Linden, H. Vander. 1920. *Belgium: The Making of a Nation.* Translated by Jane Sybil. Oxford: Clarendon Press.

Littlewood, Jez. 2005. *The Biological Weapons Convention: A Failed Revolution.* Aldershot: Ashgate.

Luck, Edward. "Bush, Iraq, and the U.N.: Whose Idea Was This Anyway?" In *Wars on Terrorism and Iraq: Human Rights, Unilateralism, and U.S. Foreign Policy,* edited by Thomas G. Weiss, Margaret E. Crahan, and John Goering, 135–54. New York: Routledge, 2004.

Mac Ginty, Robert. 2006a. "Northern Ireland: A Peace Process Thwarted by Accidental Spoiling." In Newman and Richmond, *Challenges to Peacebuilding,* 153–72.

———. 2006b. *No War, No Peace: The Rejuvenation of Stalled Peace Processes and Peace Accords.* Basingstoke: Palgrave Macmillan.

Mahley, D. A. 2001. Statement by Ambassador Donald A. Mahley, United States Special Negotiator for Chemical and Biological Arms Control Issues, Geneva, July 25.

Mahbubani, Kishore. 2004. "The Permanent and Elected Council Members." In Malone, *The UN Security Council,* 253–66.

Malley, Robert, and Hussein Agha. 2001. "Camp David: The Tragedy of Errors." *New York Review of Books,* August 9, http://www.nybooks.com/articles/archives/2001 /aug/09/camp-david-the-tragedy-of-errors/.

Malone, David, ed. *The UN Security Council: From the Cold War to the 21st Century.* Boulder, Colo.: Lynne Rienner.

March, J. G., and H. A. Simon. 1958. *Organizations*. New York: Wiley.

Markus, Hazel Rose, Shinobu Kitayama, and Rachel J. Heiman. 1997. "Culture and 'Basic' Psychological Principles." In *Social Psychology: Handbook of Basic Principles*, edited by E. Tory Higgins and Arie W. Kruglanski, 857–913. New York: Guilford.

Marschik, Axel. 2005. "Legislative Powers of the Security Council." In *Towards World Constitutionalism: Issues in the Legal Ordering of the World Community*, edited by Ronald St. John Macdonald and Douglas M. Johnston, 457–92. Leiden: Martinus Nijhoff.

Martin, Lisa L. 2000. *Democratic Commitments: Legislatures and International Cooperation*. Princeton, N.J.: Princeton University Press.

Mason, T. D., J. P. Weingarten, and P. J. Fett. 1999. "Win, Lose or Draw: Predicting the Outcome of Civil Wars." *Political Research Quarterly* 52 (2): 239–68.

Masterson, J. T., S. A. Beebe, and N. H. Watson. 1989. *Invitation to Effective Speech Communication*. Glenview, Ill.: Scott, Foresman.

Matthews, R. J. 2000. "Approaching the End-Game in the Negotiation of the BWC Protocol: Lessons from the Chemical Weapons Convention." *The CBW Conventions Bulletin* 47:1–4.

Mautner-Markhof, Frances, ed. 1989. *Processes of International Negotiations*. Boulder, Colo.: Westview.

McCarthy, Patrick. 2005. "Deconstructing Disarmament: The Challenges of Making the Disarmament and Arms Control Machinery Responsive to the Humanitarian Imperative." In *Alternative Approaches in Multilateral Decision Making: Disarmament as Humanitarian Action*, edited by John Borrie and Vanessa Randin Martin, 51–66. Geneva: United Nations Institute for Disarmament Research.

McDermott, Rose. 2004. *Political Psychology in International Relations*. Ann Arbor: University of Michigan Press.

McDuff, I. 2006. "Your Pace or Mine? Culture, Time, and Negotiation." *Negotiation Journal* 22 (1): 31–45.

McMains, Michael J., and Wayman C. Mullins. 2001. *Crisis Negotiations: Managing Critical Incidents and Hostage Situations in Law Enforcement and Corrections*. Cincinnati: Anderson.

McWhinney, Edward. 2004. *The September 11 Terrorist Attacks and the Invasion of Iraq in Contemporary International Law: Opinions on the Emerging New World Order System*. Leiden: Martinus Nijhoff.

Mearsheimer, John J. 2001. *The Tragedy of Great Power Politics*. New York: Norton.

Meerts, Paul, and Franz Cede, eds. 2004. *Negotiating European Union*. New York: Palgrave.

Meeus, Adrian de. 1962. *History of the Belgians*. London: Praeger.

Mermet, Laurent. 2006. "Ouvrir de nouveaux espaces critiques: Clarifier, renouveler, pluraliser les ancrages normatifs des recherches." In *Concertation, décision et environnement: Regards croisés*, vol. 4, edited by Ministère de l'écologie et du développement durable, 75–92. Paris: La Documentation Française.

Merton, Robert K. 1968. *Social Theory and Social Structure*. New York: Free Press.

Metcalfe, L., and D. Metcalfe. 2002. "Tools for Good Governance." *International Review of Political Science* 68 (2): 267–86.

Metternich, Clemens Wenzel Lothar, Fürst von. 1880–82. *Memoirs of Prince Metternich*. Vol. 5. New York: C. Scribner's Sons.

Migdalovitz, Carol Cyprus. 2005. Status of UN Negotiations. CRS Issue Brief for Congress.

Miller, Aaron. 2005. "Lessons of Arab-Israeli Negotiating: Four Negotiators Look Back and Ahead." Middle East Institute. Transcript.

Miller, Abraham H. 1980. *Terrorism and Hostage Negotiations*. Boulder, Colo.: Westview.

Miller, Steven E. 2002 "The End of Unilateralism or Unilateralism Redux?" *Washington Quarterly* 25 (1): 15–29.

Mitchell, Christopher. 1995. "Cutting Losses." Working Paper 9. Institute for Conflict Analysis and Resolution, George Mason University.

Moncrieff, A. R. Hope. 1920. *Belgium Past and Present: The Cockpit of Europe*. London: A. and C. Black.

Moravcsik, Andrew. 1999. "Theory and Method in the Study of International Negotiation." *International Organization* 53 (4): 811–14.

Morin, Edgar. 2005. *Introduction à la pensée complexe*. Reprint. Paris: Seuil.

Morris, Benny, and Ehud Barak. 2002. "Camp David and After: Continued." Response to Hussein Agha and Robert Malley, "Camp David and After: An Exchange: 2. A reply to Ehud Barak." *New York Review of Books*, June 27.

Morris, Stephen. 2001. "Political Correctness." *Journal of Political Economy* 109 (2): 231–65.

Morrow, James D. 1994. "Modeling the Forms of International Cooperation: Distribution vs. Information." *International Organization* 48 (3): 387–423.

Msabaha, Ibrahim. 1995. "Negotiating an End to Mozambique's Murderous Rebellion." In *Elusive Peace: Negotiating an End to Civil Wars*, edited by I. William Zartman, 204–30. Washington, D.C.: Brookings Institution Press.

Muir, Jim. 2003. "Analysis: U.S.-Iran Rift Widens," BBC News website. May 25, 2003. http://news.bbc.co.uk/2/hi/middle_east/2936016.stm.

Mutwol, Julius. 2009. *Peace Agreements and Civil Wars in Africa*. Amherst, N.Y.: Cambria.

Myerson, Roger B. 1991. "Analysis of Incentives in Bargaining and Mediation." In *Negotiation Analysis*, edited by H. Peyton Young, 67–86. Ann Arbor: University of Michigan Press.

Myrdal, A. 1976. *The Game of Disarmament*. New York: Pantheon Books.

Narlikar, Amrita. 2010. *Deadlocks in Multilateral Negotiations: Causes and Solutions*. Cambridge: Cambridge University Press.

Narlikar, Amrita, and Diana Tussie. 2004. "The G20 at the Cancun Ministerial: Developing Countries and Their Evolving Coalitions in the WTO." *The World Economy* 27 (7): 947–66.

Nash, John. 1950. "The Bargaining Problem." *Econometrica* 18 (2): 155–62.

Natlandsmyr, J. H., and J. Rognes. 1995. "Culture, Behavior, and Negotiation Outcomes: A Comparative and Cross-Cultural Study of Mexican and Norwegian Negotiators." *The International Journal of Conflict Management* 6 (1): 5–29.

Neale, M. A., and M. H. Bazerman. 1991. *Cognition and Rationality in Negotiation*. New York: Free Press.

Nelken, M. 2001. *Understanding Negotiation*. Cincinnati: Anderson.

Neumann, J. von, and O. Morgenstern. 1947. *Theory of Games and Economic Behavior*. 2nd ed. Princeton, N.J.: Princeton University Press.

Newman, Edward, and Oliver Richmond, eds. 2006. *Challenges to Peacebuilding: Managing Spoilers during Conflict Resolution*. Tokyo: United Nations University Press.

NIC (National Intelligence Council). 2007. *National Intelligence Estimate. Iran: Nuclear Intentions and Capabilities*. Office of the Director of National Intelligence, Washington, D.C.

Nisbett, R., and L. Ross. 1980. *Human Inference: Strategies and Shortcomings of Social Judgment*. Englewood Cliffs, N.J.: Prentice-Hall.

Noesner, G. W. 1999. "Negotiation Concepts for Commanders." *FBI Law Enforcement Bulletin* 68 (1): 6–14.

Nolan, Janne E. 1993. "The INF Treaty: Eliminating Intermediate-Range Nuclear Missiles, 1987 to the Present." In *Encyclopedia of Arms Control and Disarmament*, vol. 2, edited by Richard Dean Burns. New York: Scribner's.

O'Brien, James C. 2005. "The Dayton Agreement in Bosnia: Durable Cease-Fire, Permanent Negotiation." In *Peace Versus Justice: Negotiating Forward- and Backward-Looking Outcomes*, edited by I. William Zartman and Victor Kremenyuk, 89–112. New York: Rowman and Littlefield.

Odell, John. 2000. *Negotiating the World Economy*. Ithaca, N.Y.: Cornell University Press.

———. 2005. "Chairing a WTO Negotiation." *Journal of International Economic Law* 8 (2): 425–48.

Ogilvie-White, Tanya. 1996. "Is There a Theory of Nuclear Proliferation? An Analysis of the Contemporary Debate." *The Nonproliferation Review*, Fall: 43–60.

Ohlson, Thomas. 1998. "Power Politics and Peace Policies." PhD diss., Uppsala University.

Ould-Abdallah, Ahmenou. 2000. *Burundi on the Brink, 1993–1995.* Washington, D.C.: United States Institute of Peace Press.

Ozkok, Hilmi. 2006. "Defending Our Interests in Cyprus Constitutes the Cornerstone of Our Security in Eastern Mediterranean." Cyprus PIO: Turkish Press and Other Media. January 2. HRNet: Hellenic Resources Network. http://www.hri.org/news /cyprus/tcpr/2006/06-01-02.tcpr.html#01.

Palley, Claire. 2005. *An International Relations Debacle: The UN Secretary-General's Mission of Good Offices in Cyprus, 1999–2004.* Oxford: Hart.

Pareto, Vilfredo. 1971. *Manual of Political Economy.* Edited by Ann S. Schwier and Alfred N. Page. 1906. Reprint. New York: A. M. Kelley.

Pearson, G. S. 2000. "Strengthening the Biological and Toxin Weapons Convention." *The CBW Conventions Bulletin* 49:15–23.

Perls, F. S. 1977. *Gestalt Therapy Verbatim.* New York: Bantam Books.

———. 1981. *In and Out of the Garbage Pail.* New York: Bantam Books.

Petric, E. 2006. Ambassador of Slovenia to IAEA. Telephone interview. February 23, 2006.

Pfetsch, Frank. 1999. "Institutions Matter: Negotiating the European Union." In *International Negotiation: Actors, Structure/Process, Values,* edited by Peter Berton, Hiroshi Kimura, and I. William Zartman, 191–221. New York: St. Martin's Press.

Pillar, Paul R. 1983. *Negotiating Peace: War Termination as a Bargaining Process.* Princeton, N.J.: Princeton University Press.

Pinkley, R. L., T. L. Griffith, and G. B. Northcraft. 1995. "'Fixed Pie' à la Mode: Information Availability, Information Processing, and the Negotiation of Suboptimal Agreements." *Organizational Behavior and Human Decision Processes* 62 (1): 101–13.

Powell, Robert. 2002. "Bargaining Theory and International Conflict." *Annual Review of Political Science* 5 (6): 1–30.

Prigogine, I. 1984. *New Perspectives on Complexity. The Science and Praxis of Complexity.* Montpellier: United Nations University.

Pronin, E., T. Gilovich, and L. Ross. 2004. "Objectivity in the Eye of the Beholder: Divergent Perceptions of Bias in Self Versus Others." *Psychological Review* 111 (3): 781–99.

Pruitt, Dean G. 1981. *Negotiation Behavior.* New York: Academic Press.

———. 1983. "Achieving Integrative Agreements." In *Negotiating in Organizations,* edited by Max H. Bazerman and Roy J. Lewicki, 35–50. Beverly Hills, Calif.: Sage.

———. 1991. *Strategy in Negotiation.* San Francisco: Jossey-Bass Publishers.

———, ed. 1997a. "Lessons Learned from the Middle East Peace Process: Introduction." *International Negotiation* 2 (2): 175–76.

———. 1997b. "Ripeness Theory and the Oslo Talks." *International Negotiation* 2 (3): 237–50.

———. 2002. "Mediator Behavior and Success in Negotiation." In *Studies in International Mediation*, edited by J. Bercovitch, 41–54. 2nd ed. New York: Palgrave Macmillan.

Pruitt, Dean G., and P. J. Carnevale. 1993. *Negotiation in Social Conflict*. Pacific Grove, Calif.: Brooks-Cole.

Pruitt, Dean G., and Sung Hee Kim. 2004. *Social Conflict: Escalation, Stalemate and Settlement*. 3rd ed. New York: Random House.

Pruitt, Dean G., and S. A. Lewis. 1975. "Development of Integrative Solutions in Bilateral Negotiation." *Journal of Personality and Social Psychology* 31 (4): 621–33.

Pruitt, Dean G., and Paul Olczak. 1995. "Beyond Hope: Approaches of Resolving Seemingly Intractable Conflict." In *Conflict, Cooperation, and Justice: Essays Inspired by the Work of Morton Deutsch*, edited by Barbara Bunker and Jeffrey Rubin, 59–92. San Francisco: Jossey-Bass.

Pruitt, Dean G., and J. Z. Rubin. 1986. *Social Conflict: Escalation, Stalemate and Settlement*. New York: Random House.

Putnam, R. D. 1988. "Diplomacy and Domestic Politics: The Logic of Two-Level Games." *International Organization* 42 (3): 427–60.

Quandt, W. 1993. *Peace Process: American Diplomacy and the Arab-Israeli Conflict since 1967*. Washington, D.C.: Brookings Institution Press.

Queneau, Raymond. 1966. *Une histoire modèle*. Paris: Gallimard.

Rabinovitch, Itamar. 2004. *Waging Peace: Israel and the Arabs, 1948–2003*. Princeton, N.J.: Princeton University Press.

Raiffa, Howard. 1982. *The Art and Science of Negotiation*. Cambridge, Mass.: Harvard University Press.

Raiffa, Howard, J. Richardson, and D. Metcalfe. 2002. *Negotiation Analysis*. Cambridge, Mass.: Belknap Press of Harvard University.

Rapoport, Anatol. 1960. *Fights, Games, and Debates*. Ann Arbor: University of Michigan.

Renier, G. J. 1930. *Great Britain, and the Establishment of the Kingdom of the Netherlands 1813–1815*. London: George Allen and Unwin.

Richmond, Oliver. 1998. "Devious Objectives and the Disputants' View of International Mediation." *Journal of Peace Research* 35 (6): 707–22.

———. 2006a. "The Linkage between Devious Objectives and Spoiling Behaviour in Peace Processes." In Newman and Richmond, *Challenges to Peacebuilding*, 59–77.

———. 2006b. "Shared Sovereignty and the Politics of Peace: Evaluating the EU's Catalytic Framework in the Eastern Mediterranean." *International Affairs* 82 (1): 149–66.

Riley, John G. 2001. "Silver Signals: Twenty-Five Years of Screening and Signaling." *Journal of Economic Literature* 39 (2): 432–78.

Rissanen, Jenni. 2002. "Left in Limbo: Review Conference Suspended on Edge of Collapse." *Disarmament Diplomacy* 62 (January–February): 18–45.

Roberts, G. B. 2003. "Arms Control without Arms Control: The Failure of the Biological Weapons Convention Protocol and a New Paradigm for Fighting the Threat of Biological Weapons." Occasional Paper Number 49. The United States Air Force Institute for National Security Studies.

Robinson, J. P. P., T. Stock, and R. G. Sutherland. 1994. "The Chemical Weapons Convention: The Success of Chemical Disarmament Negotiation." In *SIPRI Yearbook 1993: World Armaments and Disarmament*, 705–34. Oxford: Oxford University Press.

Rooney, John W. 1982. *Revolt in the Netherlands: Brussels, 1830*. Lawrence, Kans.: Coronado Press.

Rosenau, James. 1969. *Linkage Politics: Essays on the Convergence of National and International Systems*. New York: Free Press.

Rosenberg, B. H. 2001. "Allergic Reaction: Washington's Response to the BWC Protocol." *Arms Control Today* 31:6.

Ross, Dennis. 2005. "The Missing Peace: The Inside Story of the Fight for Middle East Peace." Middle East Institute. Transcript.

Ross, Lee. 1977. "The Intuitive Psychologist and His Shortcomings: Distortions in the Attribution Process." In *Advances in Experimental Social Psychology*, vol. 10, edited by L. Berkowitz, 174–221. New York: Academic Press.

Ross, Lee, and Constance Stillinger. 1991. "Barriers to Conflict Resolution." *Negotiation Journal* 7 (4): 389–404.

Ross, Lee, and Andrew Ward. 1995. "Psychological Barriers to Dispute Resolution." In *Advances in Experimental Social Psychology*, vol. 27, edited by Mark P. Zanna, 255–304. San Diego: Academic Press.

Rothchild, Donald, and Carolyn Hartzell. 1995. "Interstate and Intrastate Negotiations in Angola." In *Elusive Peace: Negotiating an End to Civil Wars*, edited by I. William Zartman, 175–203. Washington, D.C.: Brookings Institution Press.

Rothman, Jay. 1997. *Resolving Identity-Based Conflict in Nations, Organizations, and Communities*. San Francisco: Jossey-Bass.

Rubin, Jeffrey Z., and B. R. Brown. 1975. *The Social Psychology of Bargaining and Negotiation*. New York: Academic Press.

Rubin, Jeffrey Z., Dean G. Pruitt, and Sung Hee Kim. 1994. *Social Conflict: Escalation, Stalemate, and Settlement*. 2nd ed. New York: McGraw Hill.

Rubinstein, Danny. 2003. "Camp-David 2000, What Really Happened There." [in Hebrew]. *Yediot-Ahronot*.

Sabatier, P. A., and H. C. Jenkins-Smith, eds. 1993. *Policy Change and Learning: An Advocacy Coalition Approach*. Boulder, Colo.: Westview.

Salacuse, Jeswald W. 1999. "Intercultural Negotiation in International Business." *Group Decision and Negotiation* 9 (3): 217–36.

——. 2000. "Lessons for Practice." In *Power and Negotiation*, edited by I. William Zartman and Jeffrey Z. Rubin, 255–70. Ann Arbor: University of Michigan Press.

Samore, G. 2004. "Meeting Iran's Nuclear Challenge." The Weapons of Mass Destruction Commission No. 21. http://www.blixassociates.com/wp-content/uploads/2011/03/No21.pdf.

Saner, Raymond. 2005. *The Expert Negotiator*. 2nd ed. The Hague: Martinus Nijhoff.

Saner, Raymond, and L. Yiu. 2002. "External Stakeholder Impacts on Official and Non-Official Third-Party Interventions to Resolve Malignant Conflicts: The Case of a Failed Intervention in Cyprus." *International Negotiation* 6 (3): 387–416.

Sanford, Rosemary. 1992. "Secretariats in International Environmental Negotiations: Two New Models." In *International Environmental Treaty Making*, edited by Lawrence E. Susskind, Eric Jay Dolin, and J. William Breslin, 27–51. Cambridge, Mass.: PON Books.

Sartori, Ann E. 2002. "The Might of the Pen: A Reputational Theory of Communication in International Disputes." *International Organization* 56 (1): 121–49.

Saunders, Harold. 1991. *The Other Walls*. Princeton, N.J.: Princeton University Press.

——. 1996. "Prenegotiation and Circum-negotiation. Arenas of the Peace Process." In *Managing Global Chaos: Sources of and Responses to International Conflict*, edited by Chester A. Crocker, Fen Osler Hampson, and Pamela Aall, 419–32. Washington, D.C.: United States Institute of Peace Press.

Saunders, Harold, and Cecilia Albin. 1993. *Sinai II: The Politics of International Mediation, 1974–1975*. Washington, D.C.: Johns Hopkins Foreign Policy Institute.

Schelling, Thomas C. 1960. *The Strategy of Conflict*. New York: Oxford University Press.

——. 1966. *Arms and Influence*. New Haven, Conn.: Yale University Press.

Schultz, Kenneth A. 1998. "Domestic Opposition and Signaling in International Relations." *American Political Science Review* 92 (4): 829–44.

Schwartz, S. H. 1992. "Universals in the Content and Structures of Values: Theoretical Advances and Empirical Tests in 20 Countries." In *Advances in Experimental Social Psychology*, edited by M. P. Zanna, 1–65. San Diego: Academic Press.

Schwartz, S. H., and L. Sagiv. 1995. "Identifying Culture-Specifics in the Content and Structure of Values." *Journal of Cross-Cultural Psychology* 26 (1): 92–116.

Sebenius, James K. 1992. "Challenging Conventional Explanations of International Cooperation: Negotiation Analysis and the Case of Epistemic Communities." *International Organization* 46 (1): 323–65.

——. 2002. "International Negotiation Analysis." In Kremenyuk, *International Negotiation*, 229–55.

Sharkansky, I. 1970. "Environment, Policy, Output, and Impact: Problems of Theory and Method in the Analysis of Public Policy." In *Policy Analysis in Political Science*, edited by I. Sharkansky, 61–80. Chicago: Markham.

Sher, Gilead. 2001. *"Just Beyond Reach": The Israel-Palestinian Peace Negotiations 1991–2001: A Testimony.* Tel Aviv: Miskal.

Sillars, A. L. 1981. "Attributions and Interpersonal Conflict Resolution." In *New Directions in Attribution Research*, vol. 3, edited by J. H. Harvey, W. Ickes and R. F. Kidd, 281–306. Hillsdale, N.J.: Lawrence Erlbaum.

Simon, Herbert. 1952. "Comments on the Theory of Organization." *American Political Science Review* 46 (4): 1130–39.

———. 1969. *The Sciences of the Artificial.* Cambridge, Mass.: MIT Press.

Sims, Nicholas A. 1969. *The Sciences of the Artificial.* Cambridge, Mass.: MIT Press.

———. 1986. "Biological and Toxin Weapons: Issues in the 1986 Review." Faraday Discussion Paper No. 7. The Council for Arms Control, London.

———. 1988. *The Diplomacy of Biological Disarmament: Vicissitudes of a Treaty in Force, 1975–1985.* New York: St. Martin's Press.

———. 1990. "The Second Review Conference on the Biological Weapons Convention." In *Preventing a Biological Arms Race*, edited by Susan Wright, 267–88. Cambridge, Mass.: MIT Press.

———. 2002. "Route-Maps to OPBW: Using the Resumed Fifth Review Conference." *The CBW Conventions Bulletin* 56:1–5.

———. 2003. "Biological Disarmament Diplomacy in the Doldrums: Reflections after the BWC Fifth Review Conference." *Disarmament Diplomacy* 70: http://www.acronym.org.uk/dd/dd70/70op2.htm.

Singer, J. David. 1979. *Correlates of War.* New York: Free Press.

Sisk, Timothy. 2001. "Profile: South Africa." In *The Effects of Violence on Peace Processes*, edited by John Darby, 101–14. Washington, D.C.: United States Institute of Peace Press.

Sjöstedt, Gunnar, ed. 1993. *International Environmental Negotiations.* Newbury Park, Calif.: Sage.

———. 2003. "Norms and Principles as Support to Postnegotiation and Rule Implementation." In Spector and Zartman, *Getting It Done*, 89–111.

Sjöstedt, Gunnar, Bertram I. Spector, and I. William Zartman. 1994. "Looking Ahead." In Spector, Sjöstedt, and Zartman, *Negotiating International Regimes*, 233–50.

Sked, Alan. 1979. *Europe's Balance of Power, 1815–1848.* London: Macmillan.

Smith, Adam. 1789. *An Inquiry into the Nature and Causes of the Wealth of Nations.* Philadelpia: Thomas Dobson.

Snyder, Glenn H., and Paul Diesing. 1977. *Conflict among Nations.* Princeton, N.J.: Princeton University Press.

Sollom, R., and D. Kew. 1996. "Humanitarian Assistance and Conflict Prevention in Burundi." In *Vigilance and Vengeance: NGOs Preventing Ethnic Conflict in Divided Societies*, edited by Robert I. Rotberg, 235–62. Washington, D.C.: Brookings Institution Press.

Spector, Bertram I. 1996. "Metaphors of International Negotiation." *International Negotiation: A Journal of Theory and Practice* 1 (1): 1–9.

———. 1998. "Deciding to Negotiate with Villains." *Negotiation Journal* 14 (1): 43–59.

———. 2003. "Deconstructing the Negotiations of Regime Dynamics." In Spector and Zartman, *Getting It Done*, 51–88.

Spector, Bertram I., Gunnar Sjöstedt, and I. William Zartman, eds. 1994. *Negotiating International Regimes: Lessons Learned from the United Nations Conference on Environment and Development (UNCED)*. London: Graham and Trotman.

Spector, Bertram I., and I. William Zartman. 2003. *Getting It Done: Postagreement Negotiations and International Regimes*. Washington, D.C.: United States Institute of Peace Press.

Statens Offentliga Utredningar. 2003. *Ett diplomatiskt misslyckande: Fallet Raoul Wallenberg och den svenska utrikesledningen*. (A Diplomatic Failure: The Case of Raoul Wallenberg and the Swedish Foreign Ministry.) Stockholm: Fritzes.

Stedman, Stephen J. 1991. *Peacemaking in Civil War: International Mediation in Zimbabwe, 1974–1980*. Boulder, Colo.: Lynne Rienner.

———. 1996. "Negotiation and Mediation in Internal Conflict." In *The International Dimensions of Internal Conflict*, edited by Michael E. Brown, 341–75. Cambridge, Mass.: MIT Press.

———. 1997. "Spoiler Problems in Peace Processes." *International Security* 22 (2): 5–53.

———. 2000. "Spoiler Problems in Peace Processes." In *International Conflict Resolution after the Cold War*, edited by Paul Stern and Daniel Druckman, 178–218. Washington, D.C.: National Academies Press.

———. 2003. "Peace Processes and the Challenges of Violence." In *Contemporary Peacemaking: Conflict, Violence and Peace Processes*, edited by John Darby and Roger Mac Ginty, 103–13. New York: Palgrave.

Stedman, Stephen J., Donald Rothchild, and Elizabeth Cousens, eds. 2002. *Ending Civil Wars: The Implementation of Peace Agreements*. Boulder, Colo.: Lynne Rienner.

Stein, Janice G. 1989. "International Negotiation: A Multidisciplinary Perspective." *Negotiation Journal* 4 (3): 221–31.

———. 1993. "International Cooperation and Loss Avoidance: Framing the Problem." In *Choosing to Cooperate: How States Avoid Loss*, edited by J. G. Stein and L. W. Pauly. Baltimore: Johns Hopkins University Press.

Stengers, Jean, and Eliane Gubin. 2002. *Le Grand Siècle de la Nationalité Belge: De 1830 a 1918*. Brussels: Editions Racine.

Stern, Alfred. 1905. *Geschichte Europas seit den Vertragen von 1815 bis zum Frankfurter Frieden von 1871*. Vol. 3. Berlin: W. Hertz.

Stern, Paul C., and Daniel Druckman, eds. 2000. *International Conflict Resolution: After the Cold War*. Washington, D.C.: National Academy Press.

Strange, S. 1992. "States, Firms and Diplomacy." *International Affairs* 68 (1): 1–15.

Strikwerda, Carl. 1997. *A House Divided: Catholics, Socialists, and Flemish Nationalists in Nineteenth-Century Belgium.* Oxford: Rowman and Littlefield.

"Summary of the Fifth Session of the United Nations Forum on Forests." 2005. *Earth Negotiations Bulletin* 13:16–27.

Susskind, Lawrence E. 1994. "What Will It Take to Ensure Effective Global Environmental Management? A Reassessment of Regime-Building Accomplishments." In Spector, Sjöstedt, and Zartman, *Negotiating International Regimes,* 221–32.

Susskind, Lawrence E., and J. Cruikshank. 1987. *Breaking the Impasse: Consensual Approaches to Resolving Public Disputes.* New York: Basic Books.

Swisher, C. E. 2004. *The Truth about Camp David: The Untold Story about the Collapse of the Middle East Peace Process.* New York: Nation Books.

Talbott, Strobe. 1985. *Deadly Gambits.* New York: Vintage.

Tallberg, Jonas. 2002. "The Power of the Chair in International Bargaining." Paper prepared for presentation at the 2002 ISA Annual Convention, New Orleans.

Tawney, R. H. 1952. *Equality.* Sydney: Allen and Unwin.

Teixeira da Silva, Pascal. 2004. "Weapons of Mass Destruction: The Iraqi Case." In Malone, *The UN Security Council,* 205–18.

Thibaut, John W., and Harold H. Kelley. 1959. *The Social Psychology of Groups.* New York: Wiley.

Thomas, H. Daniel. 1959. *The Guarantee of Belgian Independence and Neutrality in European Diplomacy, 1830's–1930's.* Kingston, R.I.: D. H. Thomas.

Thomas, K. 1976. "Conflict and Conflict Management." In *Handbook of Industrial and Organizational Psychology,* edited by M. D. Dunnette. Skokie, Ill.: Rand McNally.

Thompson, L. 1998. *The Mind and Heart of the Negotiator.* Englewood Cliffs, N.J.: Prentice-Hall.

Thompson, L., and G. F. Lowenstein. 1991. "Egocentric Interpretations of Fairness and Interpersonal Conflict." Working Paper. Dispute Resolution Research Center, Northwestern University.

Thuderoz, Christian. 2003. *Négociations: Essai de sociologie du lien social.* Paris: PUF.

Tinsley, Catherine H. 1998. "Models of Conflict Resolution in Japanese, German, and American Cultures." *Journal of Applied Psychology* 83 (2): 316–23.

———. 2001. "How Negotiators Get to Yes: Predicting the Constellation of Strategies Used across Cultures to Negotiate Conflict." *Journal of Applied Psychology* 86 (3): 583–93.

Tinsley, Catherine H., K. M. O'Connor, and B. A. Sullivan. 2002. "Tough Guys Finish Last: The Perils of a Distributive Reputation." *Organizational Behavior and Human Decision Processes* 88 (2): 621–42.

Tinsley, Catherine H., and M. M. Pillutla. 1998. "Negotiating in the United States and Hong Kong." *Journal of International Business Studies* 29 (4): 711–27.

Tobin, Harold J. 1934. "The Role of the Great Powers in Treaty Revision." *American Journal of International Law* 28 (3): 487–505.

Toft, Monika. 2010. *Securing the Peace*. Princeton, N.J.: Princeton University Press.

Tóth, T. 1997. "A Window of Opportunity for the BWC Ad Hoc Group." *The CBW Conventions Bulletin* 37:1–5.

———. 1999. "Time to Wrap Up." *The CBW Conventions Bulletin* 46:1–3.

Tóth, T., E. Geissler, and T. Stock. 1994. "Verification of the BWC." In *Control of Dual-Threat Agents: The Vaccines for Peace Programme*, edited by Erhard Geissler and John P. Woodall, 67–76. Oxford: Oxford University Press.

Touval, Saadia. 1991. "Multilateral Negotiation: An Analytical Approach." In *Negotiation Theory and Practice*, edited by W. Breslin and J. Z. Rubin, 351–66. Cambridge, Mass.: Program on Negotiation at Harvard Law School.

———. 1996. "Coercive Mediation on the Road to Dayton." *International Negotiation* 1 (3): 540–70.

———. 2002. *Mediation in the Yugoslav Wars: The Critical Years, 1990–1995*. New York: Palgrave Macmillan.

Touval, Saadia., and I. William Zartman, eds. 1985. *International Mediation in Theory and Practice*. Boulder, Colo.: Westview Press.

Tversky, A., and D. Kahneman. 1974. "Judgement under Uncertainty: Heuristics and Biases." *Science* 185:1124–31.

Underdal, Arild. 1983. "Causes of Negotiation 'Failure.'" *European Journal of Political Research* 11 (2): 183–95.

———. 2002. "The Outcomes of Negotiation." In Kremenyuk, *International Negotiation*, 110–25.

United Nations. 1993. Ad Hoc Group of Governmental Experts to Identify and Examine Potential Verification Measures from a Scientific and Technological Standpoint, BWC/CONF.III/VEREX/9, pp. 1–2.

———. 1994. Special Conference of the Parties to the Convention on the Prohibition of the Development, Production and Stockpiling of Bacteriological (Biological) and Toxin Weapons and on Their Destruction. Geneva, BWC/SPCONF/1 Part IV.

———. 2004. Statement of the Secretary-General at the 4970th meeting of the Security Council on May 17. UN Doc. S/PV.4970.

UNSC (United Nations Security Council). 2006a. Presidential Statement S/PRST/2006/15, March 29. http://daccessdds.un.org/doc/UNDOC/GEN/N06/290/88/PDF/N0629088.pdf?Open Element.

———. 2006b. S/Res 1696 (2006), Adopted by the Security Council at its 5,500th meeting, July 31. http://www.un.org/News/Press/docs//2006/sc8792.doc.htm.

————. 2006c. S/Res 1737 (2006), Adopted by the Security Council at its 5,612th meeting, December 27. "Ad Hoc Group of the States Parties to the Convention on the Prohibition of the Development, Production and Stockpiling of Bacteriological (Biological) and Toxin Weapons and on Their Destruction." Working Paper submitted by China, Cuba, Islamic Republic of Iran, Indonesia, Libyan Arab Jamahiriya, Pakistan, and Sri Lanka. Joint Statement on the Process of the BTWC Ad Hoc Group Negotiations. Geneva, BWC/AD HOC GROUP/WP.451 (May 4).

————. 2007. S/Res 1747 (2007), Adopted by the Security Council at its 5,647th meeting, March 24. http://daccess-dds-ny.un.org/doc/UNDOC/GEN/N07/281/40/PDF/N0728140.pdf?OpenElement.

————. 2008. S/Res 1803 (2008), Adopted by the Security Council at its 5,848th meeting, March 3. http://www.iaea.org/NewsCenter/Focus/IaeaIran/unsc_res1803-2008.pdf.

Ury, William. 1993. *Getting Past No: Negotiating with Difficult People.* New York: Bantam.

U.S. Congress. 1993. Technologies Underlying Weapons of Mass Destruction Office of Technology Assessment OTA-BP-ISC-115 Washington, D.C.: Government Printing Office. http://www.iaea.org/NewsCenter/Focus/IaeaIran/unsc_res1737-2006.pdf.

U.S. Department of State. 2005. Statement by Secretary of State Condoleezza Rice, "U.S. Support for the EU-3." Office of the Spokesman, March 11. http://islamabad.usembassy.gov/pakistan/h05031401.html.

USIP (United States Institute of Peace). 2002. *Special Report U.S. Negotiating Behavior,* Special Report 94.

Van de Weyer, Sylvain. 1873. "Histoire des Relations extérieures de la Belgique depuis 1830." In *Patria Belgica.* Brussels.

Van Evera, Stephen. 1984. "The Cult of the Offensive and the Origins of the First World War." *International Security* 9 (1): 58–107.

Voeten, Erik. 2001. "Outside Options and the Logic of Security Council Action." *American Political Science Review* 95:845–58.

Volkan, V. D. 1979. *Cyprus — War and Adaptation: A Psychoanalytic History of Two Ethnic Groups in Conflict.* Charlottesville: University Press of Virginia.

Wagner, Lynn. 1999. "Negotiations in the UN Commission on Sustainable Development." *International Negotiation* 4 (1): 107–31.

————. 2008. *Problem-Solving and Bargaining in International Negotiations.* Leiden: Martinus Nijhoff.

Wallensteen, Peter, and Margareta Sollenberg. 2000. "Armed Conflict, 1989–99." *Journal of Peace Research* 37 (5): 635–49.

Walter, Barbara. 2002. *Committing to Peace: The Successful Settlement of Civil Wars.* Princeton, N.J.: Princeton University Press.

Walton, Richard, and Robert McKersie. 1965. *A Behavioral Theory of Labor Negotiations.* New York: McGraw-Hill.

Wanis-St. John, Anthony. 2006. "Back-Channel Negotiations: International Bargaining in the Shadows." *Negotiation Journal* 22 (2): 119–44.

———. 2008. "Peace Processes, Secret Negotiations and Civil Society: Dynamics of Inclusion and Exclusion." *International Negotiation* 13:1–9.

———. 2011. *Back Channel Negotiations: Secrecy in the Middle East Peace Process.* Syracuse, N.Y.: Syracuse University Press.

Ward, A., and G. P. Goosch, eds. 1922–23. *Cambridge History of British Foreign Policy, 1783–1919.* Vol. 2. New York: Cambridge University Press.

Ward, K. D. 2004. "The BWC Protocol: Mandate for Failure." *The Nonproliferation Review* 11 (2): 1–17.

Watkins, Michael. 2003. "Strategic Simplification: Toward a Theory of Modular Design in Negotiations." *International Negotiation* 8 (1): 149–67.

Watkins, M. and S. Rosegrant. 2001. "Building Coalitions." In *Breakthrough International Negotiation: How Great Negotiators Transformed the World's Toughest Post-Cold War Conflicts,* 211–27. San Francisco: Jossey-Bass.

Watzlawick, P. 1994. *The Language of Change: Elements of Therapeutic Communication.* New York: W. W. Norton.

Weiss, Stephen E. 1994. "Negotiating with 'Romans' — Part 1." *Sloan Management Review,* January 15, 51–99.

Weller, M. 1999. "The Rambouillet Conference on Kosovo." *International Affairs* 75 (2): 211–51.

Wennmann, Achim. 2005. "Resourcing the Recurrence of Intra-State Conflict: Parallel Economies and Their Implications for Peace Building." *Security Dialogue* 36 (4): 486–87.

Werner, Suzanne. 1999. "The Precarious Nature of Peace: Resolving the Issues, Enforcing Settlement, and Renegotiating." *American Journal of Political Science* 43 (3): 912–34.

Weston Markides, Diana. 2001. *Cyprus 1957–1963: From Colonial Conflict to Constitutional Crisis: The Key Role of the Muanicipal Issue.* Minneapolis: University of Minnesota.

White, Ralph K. 1970. *Nobody Wanted War.* New York: Doubleday.

White House. 2009. Videotaped Remarks by the President in Celebration of Nowruz. March 20. http://www.whitehouse.gov/Nowruz/. P.154.

Wickman, Stephen B. 1984. *Belgium: A Country Study.* Washington, D.C.: U.S. Government Printing Office.

Wicksteed, Philip H. 1950. *The Common Sense of Political Economy.* 1910. Reprint. New York: A. M. Kelley.

Wilder, D. A., and W. E. Cooper. 1981. "Categorization into Groups: Consequences for Social Perception and Attribution." In *New Directions in Attribution Research*, vol. 3, edited by J. H. Harvey, W. Ickes and R. F. Kidd, 247–77. Hillsdale, N.J.: Lawrence Erlbaum.

Winham, Gilbert R. 1977. "Negotiation as a Management Process." *World Politics* 30 (1): 87–114.

Winter, A. de. 1919. *La Belgique, Champ de Bataille de L'Europe*. Brussels: Van Oest and Cie.

Witte, Els, Jan Craeybeckx, and Alain Meynen. 2000. *Political History of Belgium: From 1830 Onwards*. Brussels: Standaard Viegeverij/VUB University Press.

Woodward, G. C., and R. E. Denton Jr. 1996. *Persuasion and Influence in American Life*. Prospect Heights, Ill.: Waveland Press.

World Summit Outcome. 2005. Outcome Document. A/60/L.1. September 20.

Yamin, Farhana, and Joanna Depledge. 2005. *The International Climate Change Regime: A Guide to Rules, Institutions and Procedures*. Cambridge: Cambridge University Press.

Yesilada, Birol A., and Ahmet Sozen. 2002. "Negotiating a Resolution to the Cyprus Problem: Is Potential European Union Membership a Blessing or a Curse?" *International Negotiation* 7 (2): 261–85.

Young, Oran. 1989. *International Cooperation: Building Regimes for Natural Resources and the Environment*. Ithaca, N.Y.: Cornell University Press.

———. 1992. "The Effectiveness of International Institutions: Hard Cases and Critical Variables." In *Governance without Government: Order and Change in World Politics*, edited by James N. Rosenau and Ernst-Otto Czempiel, 160–94. Cambridge: Cambridge University Press.

———. 1993. "Perspectives on International Organizations." In *International Environmental Negotiation*, edited by Gunnar Sjöstedt, 244–61. New York: Sage.

Zahar, Marie Joëlle. 2003. "Reframing the Spoiler Debate in Peace Processes." In *Contemporary Peacemaking: Conflict, Violence and Peace Processes*, edited by John Darby and Roger Mac Ginty, 114–24. New York: Palgrave.

———. 2006. "Understanding the Violence of Insiders: Loyalty, Custodians of Peace, and the Sustainability of Conflict Settlement." In Newman and Richmond, *Challenges to Peacebuilding*, 40–58.

Zartman, I. William. 1974. "The Political Analysis of Negotiation: How Who Gets What and When." *World Politics* 26 (3): 385–99.

———. 1976. *The 50% solution: How to Bargain Successfully with Hijackers, Strikers, Bosses, Oil Magnates, Arabs, Russians, and Other Worthy Opponents in This Modern World*. Garden City, N.Y.: Anchor Press.

———, ed. 1978. *The Negotiation Process*. London: Sage.

———. 1989. *Ripe for Resolution.* New York: Oxford University Press.

———. 1992. "International Environmental Negotiation: Challenges for Analysis and Practice." *Negotiation Journal,* April, 113–23.

———. 1994a. "The Elephant and the Holograph: Toward a Theoretical Synthesis and a Paradigm." In *International Multilateral Negotiations: Approaches to the Management of Complexity,* edited by I. William Zartman. San Francisco: Jossey-Bass.

———, ed. 1994b. *International Multilateral Negotiations: Approaches to the Management of Complexity.* San Francisco: Jossey-Bass.

———. 1994c. "Introduction: Two's Company and More's a Crowd." In *International Multilateral Negotiations: Approaches to the Management of Complexity,* edited by I. William Zartman, 1–10. San Francisco: Jossey-Bass.

———. 1995a. "Dynamics and Constraints in Negotiations in Internal Conflicts." In *Elusive Peace: Negotiating an End to Civil War,* edited by I. William Zartman, 3–27. Washington, D.C.: Brookings Institution Press.

———, ed. 1995b. *Elusive Peace: Negotiating an End to Civil Wars.* Washington, D.C.: Brookings Institution Press.

———. 1998. "Putting Humpty-Dumpty Together Again." In *International Spread of Ethnic Conflict: Fear, Diffusion, and Escalation,* edited by David Lake and Donald Rothchild, 317–36. Princeton, N.J.: Princeton University Press.

———. 2000. "Ripeness: The Hurting Stalemate and Beyond." In *International Conflict Resolution after the Cold War,* edited by Paul C. Stern and Daniel Druckman, 225–50. Washington, D.C.: National Academy Press.

———. 2002. "The Structure of Negotiation." In Kremenyuk, *International Negotiation,* 71–84.

———. 2003a. "Conclusion: Managing Complexity." *International Negotiation* 8(1): 179–86.

———. 2003b. "Negotiating the Rapids: The Dynamics of Regime Formation." In Spector and Zartman, *Getting It Done,* 13–50.

———, ed. 2003c. "Negotiating with Terrorists." *International Negotiation* 8 (3): 443–50.

———. 2004. *Options: The Processes of International Negotiations,* Summer.

———. 2005a. *Cowardly Lion: Missed Opportunities for Preventing State Collapse and Deadly Conflict.* Boulder, Colo.: Lynne Rienner.

———. 2005b. "Negotiating with Terrorists." *PIN Points* 25:3.

———. 2006. "Ripeness Revisited: The Push and Pull of Conflict Management." In *Deeskalation von Gewaltkonflikten seit 1945,* edited by Corinna Hauswedell, 173–88. Essen: Klartext.

———. 2008. "Ripeness Revisited: The Push and Pull of Conflict Management." In *Negotiation and Conflict Management: Essays on Theory and Practice,* 232–44. London: Routledge.

Zartman, I. William, and Maureen Berman. 1982. *The Practical Negotiator*. New Haven, Conn.: Yale University Press.

Zartman, I. William, Daniel Druckman, Lloyd Jensen, Dean G. Pruitt. 1996. "Negotiation as a Search for Justice." *International Negotiation* 1 (1): 79–98.

Zartman, I. William, and Guy Olivier Faure. 2005a. "The Dynamics of Escalation and Negotiation." In *Escalation and Negotiation in International Conflicts*, edited by I. William Zartman and Guy Olivier Faure, 3–20. Cambridge: Cambridge University Press.

———. 2005b. *Escalation and Negotiation in International Conflicts*. Cambridge: Cambridge University Press.

Zartman, I. William, and Victor Kremenyuk, eds. 1995. *Cooperative Security: Reducing Third World Wars*. Syracuse, N.Y.: Syracuse University Press.

———, eds. 2005. *Peace Versus Justice: Negotiating Backward- and Forward-Looking Outcomes*. Lanham, Md.: Rowman and Littlefield.

Zartman, I. William, and Jeffrey Z. Rubin. 2000. *Power and Negotiations*. Ann Arbor: University of Michigan Press.

Zittrain, Laura Eisenberg, and Neil Caplan. 1998. *Negotiating Arab-Israeli Peace: Patterns, Problems, Possibilities*. Bloomington: Indiana University Press.

CONTRIBUTORS

WENDY ADAIR is associate professor of organizational psychology at the University of Waterloo in Ontario, Canada. Her research and teaching focus on cross-cultural communication, negotiation, conflict, and multicultural teams.

KARIN AGGESTAM is associate professor and director of Peace and Conflict Studies at the Department of Political Science, Lund University. She has published on conflict resolution, negotiation, diplomacy, and the Israeli-Palestinian conflict. Her most recent books are *The Study of Just Peace, Diplomacy in Theory and Practice*, and *War and Peace in Transition*.

CECILIA ALBIN is professor of peace and conflict research at Uppsala University in Sweden. Her main research interests are international negotiation and conflict resolution in different topic areas including civil war, arms control, trade, and the environment. She has published widely on the role of justice in negotiation and durable peace, among other subjects.

BROOK BOYER leads the Monitoring and Evaluation Section of the United Nations Institute for Training and Research. Prior to this appointment in 2009, he was affiliated with the institute's Multilateral Diplomacy Training Programme. He holds a doctorate in international relations from the Graduate Institute of International and Development Studies in Geneva, Switzerland.

FRANZ CEDE, ambassador, ret., is a docent at the Andrassy University in Budapest and a senior adviser to the Austria Institute for Europe and Security Policy.

MOTY CRISTAL is CEO and founder of NEST Consulting, a global firm specializing in managing complex negotiation systems. A Harvard Kennedy School of Government graduate with extensive international experience in the Israeli-Arab negotiations, he is a professor of practical negotiations at the Skolkovo School of Management and an adjunct faculty member at Tel Aviv University and the Interdisciplinary Center in Herzlia.

CHRISTOPHE DUPONT was born March 25, 1922, and passed away April 18, 2010, after a long and distinguished career. He directed the Laboratory for Applied Studies and Research on Negotiation at the ESC Lille Business School. He also was an active participant in the Processes of International Negotiation international negotiators network. He was a special adviser for research at the Institute for Research and Education on Negotiation in Europe and the author of numerous books on negotiation.

GUY OLIVIER FAURE, at the Sorbonne University, Paris, has introduced and developed international negotiation, conflict resolution, and strategic thinking and action. He is a member of the editorial board of the three major international journals dealing with negotiation and conflict resolution and is a director at the Processes of International Negotiation Program. Among his most recent publications are *How People Negotiate, Escalation and Negotiation, Negotiating with Terrorists*, these three books with William Zartman, and *Engaging Extremists*.

DANIELLA FRIDL is director of training and education at the Center for International Development and Conflict Management at the University of Maryland. She directs the ICONS Project and the minor in international development and conflict management. Her recent work has focused on the mediation process and techniques in international negotiations over issues of state formation. She holds a PhD specializing in conflict management and international law from SAIS, Johns Hopkins University.

DEBORAH GOODWIN, Royal Military Academy, Sandhurst, focuses her research on military negotiation, crisis negotiation, and peacekeeping skills and issues. She has published *The Military and Negotiation* (Routledge, 2005).

P. TERRENCE HOPMANN is professor of international relations and director of the Conflict Management Program in the Johns Hopkins University School of Advanced International Studies in Washington, D.C. He served as the director of the Global Security Program at the Thomas J. Watson Jr. Institute of International Studies. He is the author of *The Negotiation Process and the Resolution of International Conflicts* and of numerous articles and book chapters on negotiations, conflict management, arms control and disarmament, and regional security institutions.

CHRISTER JÖNSSON, professor emeritus of political science at Lund University, Sweden, is a member of the Royal Swedish Academy of Sciences. In 2009–12 he is serving as chairman of the board of directors of the Academic Council on the United Nations System. His research interests include diplomacy, international negotiation, transnational networks, and international organization. He is the author of *Communication in International Bargaining* (1990), coauthor of *Essence of Diplomacy* (2005), and coeditor of *Transnational Actors in Global Governance* (2010).

ANDREW KYDD is associate professor of political science at the University of Wisconsin. He studies a variety of topics related to international security, including conflict resolution, mediation, reassurance, and terrorism.

JEZ LITTLEWOOD is an assistant professor at the Norman Paterson School of International Affairs at Carleton University, Ottawa, Canada. He previously served under secondment to the Counter-Proliferation Department of the UK Foreign & Commonwealth Office (FCO) (2005–2007) and as associate officer to the Department of Disarmament Affairs of the United Nations Office in Geneva (1999–2001) and at the University of Southampton (2002–2006).

Ambassador ALEXANDER (AXEL) MARSCHIK, doctor of law, University of Vienna, Austria, is permanent representative of Austria to the European Union's Political and Security Committee.

LAURENT MERMET is a professor at the Ecole Nationale du Génie Rural, des Eaux et des Forêts. His interests focus on environmental negotiations, strategic analysis, and prospective approaches.

RAYMOND SANER is the cofounder of CSEND, a Geneva-based nongovernmental research and development organization established in 1993. His research and consulting focuses on conflict studies and international negotiations at bilateral, plurilateral, and multilateral levels in the fields of trade (WTO); employment and poverty reduction (ILO, PRSP); trade and development (WTO, UNCTAD, EIF); human and social capital development in the educational sector (GATS/ES/WTO, OECD); and trade, investment, and climate change (UNCTAD).

MASAKO TAYLOR is a professor in the Department of Business Administration at Osaka Gakuin University in Japan, as well as a visiting instructor at the Bond University MBA program in Australia, where she teaches organizational behavior, strategic human resources management, and international management. Her research interests include intercultural management, work motivation, and global human resources management.

CATHERINE H. TINSLEY is a professor of management at the McDonough School of Business at Georgetown University. She is also the executive director of the Georgetown University Women's Leadership Initiative. She studies how factors such as culture, reputation, and gender influence negotiation and conflict resolution. She also studies how people make decisions under risk.

ANTHONY WANIS-ST. JOHN is assistant professor of international peace and conflict resolution at the School of International Service, American University, and an adviser to the United States Institute of Peace. He is the author of *Back Channel Negotiation: Secrecy in the Middle East Peace Process* (Syracuse University Press, 2011).

I. WILLIAM ZARTMAN is Jacob Blaustein Professor Emeritus of International Organization and Conflict Resolution at the School of Advanced International Studies of the Johns Hopkins University. His latest book, with Fen Osler Hampson, is *The Global Power of Talk: Negotiating America's Interests*, and he is editor, with Mark Anstey and Paul Meerts, of *The Slippery Slope to Genocide: Reducing Identity Conflicts and Preventing Mass Murder* for the PIN Program.

INDEX

CPSIA information can be obtained at www.ICGtesting.com
Printed in the USA
BVOW010023080812

297313BV00001B/3/P